SEPTEN.

ORIENS

OCCIDENT

MERID.

4

24

Sorthmym

Poittra

Durhams

Dancershill CHACE

Kiekesend

Hadley

Bernet

A

Enfeylde

Ludgraues

Grensteti

Durante

Ponders ende

OF WAL

Mersditch

Sea River

Chigwell

East Bernet

Winchmorhill

Edm-strete

Bury strete

Chingford

Whetstone

Edmondton

Wyerhall

Pymes

PARTE OF

Woodford

Fryarn Barnet

Friarn

Mamer

Brunsfyld

Strete

Macklins

Dars Soy sors

Ric Martins

ESSEX

Northend

Cony hatche

Brumsfwel

East Ende

Mussell hill

Tottenham

Hollicke

Ducats

Walthamstow

Lodgehill

Harnesey

Cruch end

Tottenham highe. cr.

7

Wansted

Chyldes hill

Highgat

Newington

Layton

Hamsted

Habways

Belsyse

Chalcote

Kentish

towne

Canbury

Illington

Pane-

ras

Newington grene

Shacklewell

Clapton

Hackeney

Paddington

ston grene

Marebone

Totten

Courte

Kinsland

Hockesdon

Olde-

forde

Estbourne

Hyde parke

S. Gyles

Clerkenwell

Shoradch

Mers strete

Bush: holl

Strat fordo

forde

9

Kensington

Knight

bridge

Brompton

Chelsey

LONDON

Stepney

Blackwall

Hamersmyth

Pursem

grene

Fulham

Southworke

Limehowse

Isle of

doges ferm

Charleton

Lambeth

Battersey

Newington

Derford

Grenewich

Clapham

Wansworth

Putney

10

Part of Kente

Kingston

RREY

Caracters distinguishing the difference of places

Market townes

Parishes

Hamletes or villages

Howses & Palaces of Quen. Eli

Howses of Nobilitie

Howses of Knightes, Gent. &c.

Castles & fortes

Monasteries or religions howses

Bushops Seas

Hospitales

Places where battells have bene

Decayde places

Lodges in forestes chases &c.

Mylles.

Ioannes Norden Angl. descripsit 1593.

14   16   18   20   22   24

A DAUGHTER'S LOVE

Also by John Guy

Tudor England
The Reign of Elizabeth I: Court and Culture in the Last Decade
My Heart is My Own: The Life of Mary Queen of Scots

A DAUGHTER'S LOVE:
THOMAS & MARGARET MORE

JOHN GUY

FOURTH ESTATE • London

First published in Great Britain in 2008 by
Fourth Estate
An imprint of HarperCollins*Publishers*
77–85 Fulham Palace Road
London W6 8JB
www.4thestate.co.uk

Visit our authors' blog: www.fifthestate.co.uk

Endpapers: Map of Middlesex from John Norden, *Speculum Britanniae.
The first parte* (London, 1593). Bb*.10.46(E). Reproduced with the
permission of the Cambridge University Library.

A catalogue record for this book is available from the British Library

ISBN 978-0-00-719231-1

Typeset in Minion by
Newgen Imaging Systems (P) Ltd, Chennai, India

Printed in Great Britain by Clays Ltd, St Ives plc

Mixed Sources
Product group from well-managed
forests and other controlled sources
www.fsc.org Cert no. SW-COC-1806
© 1996 Forest Stewardship Council
FSC

FSC is a non-profit international organisation established to promote the
responsible management of the world's forests. Products carrying the FSC
label are independently certified to assure consumers that they come
from forests that are managed to meet the social, economic and
ecological needs of present and future generations.

Find out more about HarperCollins and the environment at
www.harpercollins.co.uk/green

For Julia

Birth, marriage, death – ploughing, seedtime and harvest – all move in tune and the cosmic relationships are mirrored in the human relationships.

GEOFFREY WAGNER on Lewis Grassic Gibbon,
Essays in Criticism, 1952

CONTENTS

ILLUSTRATION CREDITS

The Bridgeman Art Library

Self Portrait by Hans Holbein the Younger, Galleria degli Uffizi, Florence.

Portrait of a woman, possibly Catherine of Aragon (oil on panel) by Michiel Sittow, Kunsthistorisches Museum, Vienna.

Portrait of Nicholas Kratzer (oil on panel) by Hans Holbein the Younger, Louvre, Paris, *Giraudon/The Bridgeman Art Library*.

King Henry VIII (oil on oak panel) by Hans Holbein the Younger, Thyssen-Bornemisza Collection, Madrid.

Portrait of Erasmus (oil and egg tempera on panel) by Hans Holbein the Younger, Private Collection.

Sloane MS 2596 fo.52, 'Map of London, the River Thames and London Bridge', 1588, British Library, London © *British Library Board. All Rights Reserved.*

Anne Boleyn (oil on panel), English School (sixteenth century), Hever Castle, Kent.

Peter Gilles (oil on panel) by Quentin Massys or Metsys, Koninklijk Museum voor Schone Kunsten, Antwerp, *Giraudon/The Bridgeman Art Library*.

Cambridge University Library

'The King of the Apes', from S. Brant, *Esopi appologi siue mythologi cum quibusdam carminum et fabularum additionibus* (*Aesop's Fables*), 1501 edn, Sel.3.111 (unpaginated).

'Burning of Thomas Hitton', from J. Foxe, *Actes and monuments of matters most speciall and memorable, happenying in the Church . . . Newly revised*, 1583 edn, vol. 2, Young.200, p.998.

'Death of Richard Hunne', from J. Foxe, *Actes and monuments of these latter and perillous days, touching matters of the Church*, 1563 edn, vol. 1, Sel.2.15a, p.390.

Map of Middlesex 1593, by John Norden, from *Speculum Britanniae. The first parte*, Bb*.10.46(E), no.6, between pp.8 and 9.

Title page from *The workes of Sir Thomas More Knyght*, 1557 edn, Young.242.

Reproduced with the permission of the Cambridge University Library.

Frick Collection

Sir Thomas More (oil on panel) by Hans Holbein the Younger. *Copyright The Frick Collection, New York.*

Thomas Cromwell (oil on panel) by Hans Holbein the Younger. *Copyright The Frick Collection, New York.*

Kunstmuseum Basel

Preparatory sketch of *The Family of Thomas More* by Hans Holbein the Younger, Kupferstichkabinett. Inv. 1662.31, photo credit Kunstmuseum Basel, Martin Bühler.

Metropolitan Museum of Art, New York

Miniatures of William Roper and Margaret More, wife of William Roper (vellum laid on card), by Hans Holbein the Younger, Rogers Fund, 50.69.1, 50.69.2. *Photograph © 1979 The Metropolitan Museum of Art.*

National Trust

Sir Thomas More and His Family, by Rowland Lockey after Hans Holbein the Younger, from the Lower Hall at Nostell Priory. *By kind permission of Lord St Oswald & The National Trust © NTPL/John Hammond.*

Royal Library, Windsor

Drawings by Hans Holbein the Younger of Thomas More (2 images), Judge John More, John More the Younger, Anne Cresacre, Elizabeth Daunce, Cecily Heron, Margaret Giggs, Bishop John Fisher (R.L. 12270, 12228, 12229, 12269, 12226, 12224, 12225, 12268, 12202): *The Royal Collection © 2008, Her Majesty Queen Elizabeth II.*

Wroclaw University Library

Letter of Margaret Roper to Erasmus (2 pages), Letter of Thomas More to Erasmus (2 pages), from MS R.254, fos.309, 310, 354, 356. *By kind permission of the University Library in Wroclaw.*

Yale University, Beinecke Rare Book and Manuscript Library

Map of the island of Utopia, from the first edition of Thomas More's *Utopia*, 1516 edn.

Annotated folio (fo.xlvii) of Sir Thomas More's Psalter.

Title page of Margaret Roper's *A deuoute treatise vpon the Pater noster*, *c.*1525 edn.

Engraving illustrating the executions of Thomas More and John Fisher, from Richard Verstegan, *Theatrvm crudelitatum haereticorum nostri temporis*, 1592 edn.

ACKNOWLEDGEMENTS

Although the More family's archives have long been lost or destroyed, most of their major life transactions and those of their in-laws, even before the proliferation of parish registers, can be reconstructed from unpublished deeds, marriage settlements, land conveyances, court pleadings, witness depositions, wills and so on. All but thirty or so of Thomas's surviving letters and memos and all of Margaret's extant letters are collected in the invaluable *The Correspondence of Sir Thomas More* (Princeton University Press) and *St Thomas More: Selected Letters* (Yale University Press), both edited by Elizabeth Frances Rogers. Yale University Press has published in fifteen indispensable volumes *The Complete Works of St Thomas More*, and I thank the publisher for permission to cite extracts from copyright material. The letters of Erasmus are published in *The Complete Works of Erasmus: the Correspondence of Erasmus* in (to date) twelve volumes by the University of Toronto Press, whom I also thank for granting permission for quotations.

I am deeply grateful to the staff of the Large Documents Room at the National Archives at Kew for producing over three hundred legal cases and over a thousand deeds and other documents, and for granting me access to the original volumes of the State Papers in preference to the microfilms. I have tried, whenever possible, to read the original documents instead of the briefer, more elliptical abstracts in the Victorian printed calendars, which are so often taken to pass for the originals despite omitting large chunks of the material. The availability of new electronic searching aids has given me an advantage over earlier biographers, although many of the most interesting and important enrolled deeds and lawsuits still have to be tracked down using the sixteenth-century Latin repertories and docket rolls, since no modern finding aids exist.

I gladly acknowledge the kindness of archivists and curators at the British Library, the Bodleian Library, Cambridge University Library, Wroclaw University Library, Guildhall Library, the House of Lords Record Office, King's College Cambridge Archives Centre, the National Portrait Gallery, Westminster Abbey Muniments, the Folger Shakespeare Library, the Bibliothèque Nationale de France, the Frick Collection, and the Metropolitan Museum of Art, New York. The genealogical tables and map were drawn and digitized by Richard Guy of Orang-utan Productions from my rough drafts. For helping me with picture research and clearing reproduction rights, I am most grateful to Emma Brown.

I've nothing but thanks and admiration for Peter Robinson and Emma Parry, my agents in London and New York, for their constant encouragement and for giving helpful advice on the manuscript. I owe an immense debt to Mitzi Angel, my editor at Fourth Estate, for her patience when the manuscript was a year late, and her insightful comments on my first draft when it finally arrived, pitched exactly right. I express heartfelt gratitude to my former students at the Universities of Bristol, St Andrews and Cambridge for their contributions to Special Subjects, seminars and supervisions involving Thomas and Margaret. I am in debt to my former student, Dr Jessica Sharkey of Clare College, for discussing Wolsey and Thomas More's relationship with me on innumerable occasions and for supplying me with a transcript of a document from the Vatican. Frances and David Waters offered constant encouragement, once more uncannily predicting the date on which I'd deliver the final revised manuscript, and making sure we had tickets for Handel's *Teseo* for the very next night.

Julia has lived through the last four years with Margaret and Thomas as if their struggle with Henry VIII was happening in our bedroom, reading innumerable rough drafts, discussing them over mugs of tea at two and three o'clock in the morning, and taking time out of her own biography of Jane Boleyn to help with research problems. I can never adequately thank her or repay her love. Susie, Gemma and Tippy did what cats always do, but alas their eager contributions in the shape of jaunts across my keyboard did not make the final cut.

London
8 November 2007

THE COLT AND ELRYNGTON FAMILIES

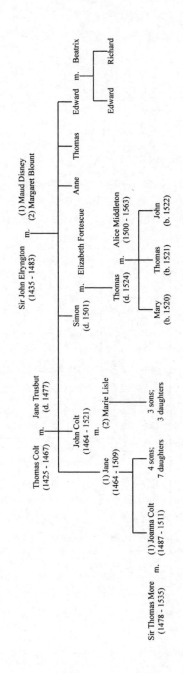

THE MORE FAMILY

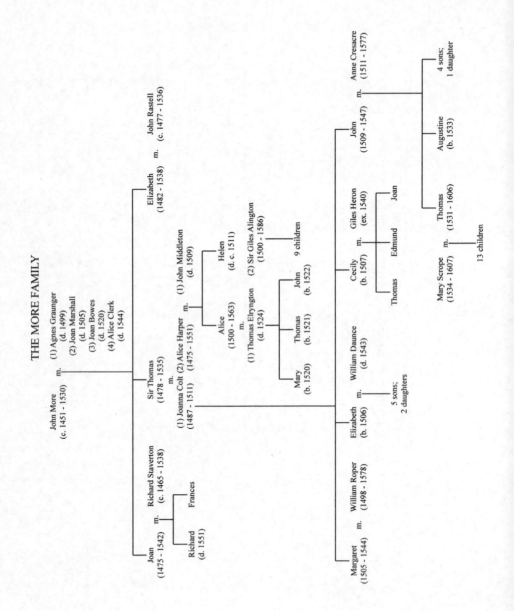

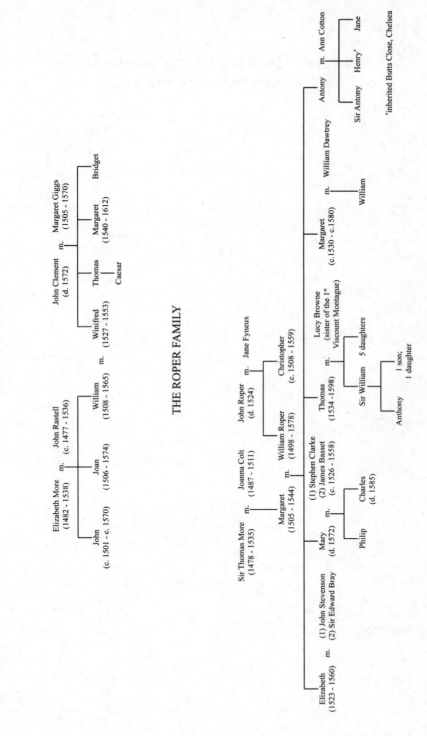

THE RASTELL FAMILY

THE ROPER FAMILY

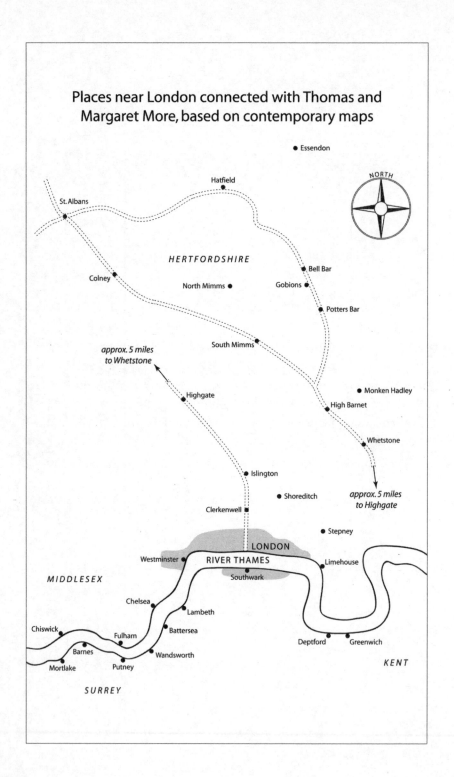

Places near London connected with Thomas and Margaret More, based on contemporary maps

NOTE ON UNITS OF CURRENCY

In citing units of currency, the old sterling denominations of pounds, shillings and pence have been retained. There are 12 old pence in a shilling (modern 5p. or US 10c.), twenty shillings in a pound (£1 or US $2), and so on. Equivalents for Tudor gold and silver coins are: noble (modern 45p. or US 90c.), angel (33p. or US 66c.), royal or rose noble (50p. or US $1), sovereign (100p. or US $2), groat (1.6p. or US 3c.). A mark is 13s. 4d. (66p. or US $1.25). One hundred marks is £66 (US $135). Rough estimates of modern values for sixteenth-century units of currency can be obtained by multiplying all the numbers by a thousand. Equivalents for European denominations are worked out from 'Money and Coinage of the Age of Erasmus', in *CWE* 1, pp.311–47, and P. Spufford (ed.), *Handbook of Medieval Exchange* (London, 1986).

PROLOGUE

ARLY ONE MORNING in August 1535, during the wettest year that anyone could remember, a twenty-nine-year-old gentlewoman and her maid boarded a wherry from a wharf outside their riverside home at Butts Close, Chelsea, and were rowed three miles along the River Thames to London Bridge. It was the most convenient, if expensive, way to travel: the fare was two shillings, three if the oarsmen had to row against the tide, the equivalent of a week's wages for a bricklayer or the price of six whole salmon or a dozen hens. This summer, it took courage to leave the sweet fresh air of the countryside for the foul smells and contagion of the city, since flooding and overflowing drains had triggered recurrent outbreaks of plague. Hundreds of Londoners were to die, encouraging the wealthier citizens to shut up their houses and evacuate their families to the countryside until the epidemic abated. Henry VIII, now forty-four, beginning to put on weight and ever fearful of death and disease, had already left with his queen, Anne Boleyn, for a summer of hawking and hunting in the Severn Valley in Gloucestershire. His chief minister, Thomas Cromwell, accompanied them with his greyhound, but had no time for sport. His priority was paperwork, not pleasure.

London Bridge was one of the city's major landmarks. Spanning twenty stone piers, each sixty feet high and thirty feet thick, it stood on the site of an ancient timber river-crossing first established during the Roman occupation of Britain and rebuilt by the Anglo-Saxons, when it was supported by piles and broad enough for two wagons to pass each other. The later stone bridge, begun in 1176, had taken thirty-three years to complete. Continuous structural repairs were needed because of storms and fires and the excessive weight of more than a hundred shops and houses crowding in over the carriageway. In 1481 a house toppled over the side, drowning five men. Since the bridge doubled as a fortress protecting the city from rebels or invaders, it boasted a tower on each side of its disused central drawbridge with a portcullis and fortified gatehouse at its more vulnerable southern end.

When the wherry reached its destination, the women paid the oarsmen and climbed the thirty or so wooden steps up from the river towards the fish market. They attracted no attention; so hazardous was it for boats to pass under the arches of the bridge given the rapid currents and the narrowness of the gaps between the piers, passengers routinely disembarked here, if necessary continuing their journey from the other side.

The gentlewoman was dressed in a black gown more suitable for winter than summer. She had large brown eyes, a haunting sorrow and looked ten years older than she really was. Everyone would have guessed she was in mourning. Her wedding ring, clearly visible, was set with a ruby, and she may have worn her favourite pectoral or medallion, in which case passers-by would have made out the image of St Michael, the keeper of paradise, fighting with Lucifer in the shape of a dragon. The maid carried her mistress's purse and a basket, not surprisingly since they seemed to be about to purchase fish.

Except that the women turned onto the bridge and kept walking until they reached the north tower before the drawbridge. Looking up, they would have noticed four stones with 'Jhesus' carved on them in large antique lettering. However, their gaze was fixed to the dozen or more skulls on poles protruding from a ledge of the parapet, parboiled and coated with tar to protect them from scavenging by the circling, screaming gulls.*

This wasn't the gentlewoman's first visit; she'd been here perhaps as many as a dozen times recently. When she'd first come, she'd recognized several of the skulls. One belonged to John Houghton, Prior of the London Carthusians, another to Bishop John Fisher of Rochester. Both had been executed for treason after refusing to swear an oath to the legitimacy of Anne Boleyn's marriage to Henry and after denying the king's revolutionary new claim to be the Supreme Head of the Church in England. For his loyalty to Rome, Pope Paul III had created Fisher

---

* Traitors' heads were displayed from the north tower until 1577, after which they were moved to the tower above the gatehouse at the Southwark end.

a cardinal a month before his trial. His red hat had arrived at Calais, awaiting delivery across the Channel. Henry, spiteful, vengeful, indignant at the news, placed an embargo on the hat. Then, laughing uproariously, he promised Anne Boleyn that he'd teach Fisher a lesson once and for all. 'Let the Pope send him a hat when he will,' he exclaimed, 'but I will so provide that whensoever it commeth, he shall wear it on his shoulders; for head shall he have none to set it on.'

The maid knocked at the bridge-master's door, which opened to admit the women. After a brief conversation, the maid unclasped the purse and handed over some coins. In return, she received a skull, gently wrapping it in a linen cloth before placing it in the basket. The women immediately left and returned to Chelsea.

The gentlewoman was Margaret Roper, her maid Dorothy Colley, and the head they had surreptitiously recovered that of Sir Thomas More, Margaret's father, executed just over four weeks earlier. More, famous for his wit and charm, had won a European reputation as the author of *Utopia*. Henry had invited him to Court to serve as his secretary and intimate adviser before turning vindictively against him. Like Houghton and Fisher, he'd been interrogated by Cromwell and tried and convicted of high treason by a special court commissioned by Henry to destroy men he'd come to regard as enemies of the state. The difference was that, whereas Houghton and Fisher had contradicted the royal supremacy and Fisher had campaigned openly against Henry's divorce from his first wife, Katherine of Aragon, Thomas More had kept silent. He'd neither defended the papal supremacy nor denied the king's. He'd even offered to acknowledge Anne Boleyn as the lawful queen (but not Henry's lawful wife) and her children as heirs to the throne. He'd been a conscientious objector, holding fast to his opinions, but as far as the official record went, always keeping them to himself, staunchly professing his loyalty to the king as head of state. The closest he came to the abyss before his trial was to say: 'in my conscience this was one of the cases in which I was bounden that I should not obey my Prince, sith [i.e. since] that whatsoever other folk thought in the matter . . . yet in my conscience the truth seemed on the other side.'

After More's execution, his head too had been boiled and tarred and set up on London Bridge. The custom was that it would remain there for between a fortnight and six weeks, when it would be taken down to make room for other heads. The bridge-master, as for everything else he did, had a system. As new heads arrived, he moved the old ones along the row until, when they reached the end of the line, he threw them into the river. Margaret had been carefully watching their progression. She tracked her father's skull along the row, identifying it by a missing tooth. As she stared up at these heart-rendingly gruesome relics of people she had known, she couldn't but have realized the bitter irony of the lines in the Latin grammar book she'd been reading with her children. The book by Robert Whittinton, a friend of one of her father's early mentors, set the following translation exercise:

> More is a man of an angel's wit and singular learning. He is a man of many excellent virtues . . . I know not his fellow. For where is the man . . . of that gentleness, lowliness and affability. And as time requireth, a man of marvellous mirth and pastimes, and sometime of sad gravity, as who say 'A Man for All Seasons'.

And yet, just two pages later, the students were asked to translate:

> Upon London Bridge I saw three or four men's heads stand upon poles . . . it is a strange sight to see the hair of the heads disappear away, and the gristle of the nose consumed away.

When Margaret arrived back in Chelsea, she lovingly unwrapped the skull and packed it with spices to preserve it, intending to take it with her to the grave.

Cromwell returned to London in October. Hearing of her visit to the bridge-master, he summoned Margaret before the Privy Council, where she was accused of attempting to propagate a cult and of concealing her father's papers. She ably defended herself, replying: 'I have saved my father's head from being devoured by the fishes with the intention of burying it, and I have hardly any books and papers, except a very few personal letters, which I humbly beseech you to allow me to keep.' She was permitted to leave unharmed.

Her husband William Roper had been frantically writing to his younger brother, Christopher, a lawyer and building-surveyor in Cromwell's household. Not content with letters, William sent a messenger every other day to see if his brother could be traced. He couldn't understand why Christopher wouldn't use his influence to mitigate the forfeiture of the More family's estates, for William wasn't of the stuff that martyrs are made, swearing Henry's oath and sitting on the jury for the trial of two Middlesex priests accused alongside Prior Houghton, a fact he strove for ever afterwards to conceal.

Margaret Roper never cared much for possessions. Always her father's favourite child whom he educated to become one of Europe's leading women intellectuals, she dedicated her life and talents after his arrest to helping him conquer his physical and mental fears and emerge morally victorious over a tyrant. But along the way there would be casualties. Henry's marriage to Anne Boleyn would result in cataclysmic political changes splitting families asunder, and the Mores would be no exception. For as long as she could remember, Margaret's aunt and uncle, Elizabeth and John Rastell, had been as close as anyone to her father other than his own wife and children, and ever since they'd known each other her father and uncle had yearned to reshape society and their world. Both had utopian visions of the future, but their friendship was to collapse in tatters when Rastell introduced draft legislation into Parliament seeking to overthrow some of his brother-in-law's most cherished beliefs. And even the internationally renowned Erasmus of Rotterdam, the most illustrious and charismatic of her father's friends whom Margaret had known since he'd stayed at her home when she was four, would all but abandon him, lacking his inner steel. 'Mine,' said Erasmus in a rare bout of candour, 'was never the spirit to risk my life for the truth. Not everyone has the strength needed for martyrdom.'

Deserted by his sons-in-law, and especially by William Roper, and visited in the Tower only once in fifteen months by his wife Lady Alice, Thomas More was too gregarious, too emotionally dependent on those dearest to him, to face Henry's wrath alone, because, for all his outward assurance, he was prone to fear and doubt. Margaret, at first tentatively and unconsciously, and then with increasing confidence and ingenuity, would step into the breach. And when at last her father became a victim of Henry's tyranny, she came again to his rescue. One of the main underlying themes of this book will be her role in achieving her father's fame. Without her, a dossier of letters compiled while he was a prisoner in the Tower could not have been created and preserved. Without it, we could never have heard his own voice not just whispering across a prison courtyard to his 'dearly beloved Meg', but speaking openly to us across the centuries, telling us why he felt he had to die in a moral cause and why he felt so strongly and passionately about it.

While her father's place in history is secure, Margaret's has generally been less so. Although a character in Robert Bolt's feature-film version of *A Man for All Seasons*, she was largely confined to the domestic scenes at Chelsea and omitted from the public ones, for she had long before been airbrushed out of the political events by her father's official Catholic biographer Nicholas Harpsfield, for whom a woman's independent role was anathema. A truly heroic figure did not need a woman's support. A martyr was supposed to go to his death confidently, not reluctantly. He wasn't meant to have had his own inner demons as Thomas More did, and even if doubts were expressed, they were not meant to be shared with a woman.

Bolt saw Thomas as a man with an adamantine sense of his own self. He knew where he began and where he left off, what area of himself he could safely yield to his enemies, and which to his friends and those he loved. While this is partly true, it is not wholly so, for in the Tower he almost collapsed under the weight of his fears and without Margaret talking and praying with him as often as she could in that cold, bleak cell, it is far from certain that he would have been able to do what he did. 'You alone,' he said as they kissed and embraced for the very last time, 'have long known the secrets of my heart.'

Margaret lived in a patriarchal society, where gender stereotypes required women to be 'chaste, silent and obedient'. Besides shockingly contravening that stereotype shortly after marrying William by writing and publishing a book, a step by itself as dramatic and inflammatory in its own day as anything said by her father in *Utopia*, her later interventions in her father's cause were rightly seen as a threat by men like Cromwell, fully aware of the danger to Henry if she were ever allowed to tell the whole truth. In spite of prudently dissembling, saying that she had hardly any of her father's books and papers, her enduring achievement would be to make sure that these very same materials, and a great deal more, would one day be published, so that everyone could know the story of the man who'd kept silent. Without hearing his and her voices so vividly, so distinctly, so authentically as we do in his wonderful letters to 'Meg' and her own soul-rending letter to her stepsister Alice Alington, which even more than *Utopia* would be Thomas More's political testament, the story would have been impoverished and her father become just another footnote in history.

PART I

MARGARET'S WORLD

1

A CHILD IS BORN

MARGARET, THE ELDEST CHILD born to Thomas More and his wife Joanna,* would always remember her first home, the Barge at Bucklersbury. A sought-after location, Bucklersbury lay off the east end of Cheapside, one of London's grandest, broadest thoroughfares and most popular processional routes. Some 500 yards north of the Thames, it was noisier and less exclusive than the area around Guildhall, where the Court of Hustings met and the Mayor and Aldermen sat in Common Council, but closer to the main food markets. What had always struck her father most about this district was its sheer bustle and excitement: the din, the quarrels, the thousand enticements, the feigned love and honeyed poisons of smooth flatterers trying to sell their wares. 'Wherever you turn your eyes,' he once exclaimed, 'what else will you see but confectioners, fishmongers, butchers, cooks, poulterers, fishermen, fowlers, who supply the materials for gluttony and the world!'

Just round the corner, a stone's throw away, was the Stocks Market, where meat, poultry and fish were sold and the waste products thrown into the adjacent Walbrook stream. So often had this stream become blocked (with consequent noxious smells) that a civic ordinance banned the owners of the neighbouring houses from connecting private latrines to it, forcing them to install cesspits in their gardens. A particular irritant was the keeping of poultry and pigs which often roamed the streets. Ducks and hens caused little inconvenience besides noise, but pigs were a recurring nuisance. And when one enterprising resident built his pigsty directly over the stream so that the excrement could be swept straight

* She is often called Jane by modern writers, but in handwritten family documents her name is either 'Joanna' or occasionally 'Joan'.

into it, the Common Council stepped in and ordered these pigs to be removed.

Opposite the east end of Bucklersbury, where it intersected with a street called Walbrook and on the far side of the junction, stood the parish church of St Stephen Walbrook, built in limestone with a fine timber roof covered in lead, its nave 100 feet long. A majority of the parishioners were grocers or sold pepper and spices; the rest were medical practitioners or apothecaries. In fact, the character of the district changed discernibly during Margaret's lifetime. Once mainly populated by grocers, the parish came to be dominated by apothecaries, whose stocks of fresh and dried herbs may have gone some way to counteract any residual smells from the stream.

The Barge was a 'great mansion', built of stone and timber, set back from the road behind a gatehouse. Until 1495 or thereabouts, it had been a commercial property: a public weigh-house, operated on behalf of the civic authorities by the Grocers' Company, containing the 'great beam' or balance used by wholesalers for weighing the heaviest bales of spices and other dry foodstuffs. Larger than the average single dwelling, it was the last house on the south-east corner of Bucklersbury, overlooking St Stephen's. At the rear were stables and a delightful south-facing garden which, until the stream had been partly covered with paving, was accessible by barge, hence the house's name. The freehold was owned by the Hospital of St Thomas of Acre in Cheapside, meaning to all intents and purposes the Mercers' Company, which elected the Master and managed the hospital's affairs. On recovering vacant possession from the grocers, the mercers had divided up the Barge into tenements, converting them for residential occupation. When the Mores first moved in, they had a lease for a part of the property only, and it took Margaret's father eight years and some trouble and expense to obtain a forty-year lease of the whole site.

We can go some way towards reconstructing the architectural and physical setting at the Barge. A decade or so after Margaret's death, two witnesses in a lawsuit gave evidence including full inventories of the rooms and their contents, explaining that all the bulkier, heavier items of furniture and many of the interior decorations had hardly been touched since the Mores had departed. So much so that in the list of items remaining in the study, we find 'a table' (meaning a panel portrait) 'of Sir Thomas More's face' still hanging where someone had left it.

The main access for visitors after they walked past the gatehouse was through the great hall, where dinner was normally served. Here 'a great map of all the world' and four gilded escutcheons or armorial shields took pride of place on the walls. A buffet or 'great cupboard of wainscot' stood on the dais near to the fireplace, displaying 'five Venice glasses' – more likely bowls or vases than wine glasses. A window, maybe a bay or oriel window providing a convenient recess for private conversation, would have offered guests a view into a courtyard. In winter it was hung with a curtain of yellow buckram, lined with canvas, to keep out draughts.

A staircase beyond the lower end of the hall enabled the family and servants to reach a first-floor gallery where a mechanical clock of gilt-metal with a chain and weights hung from the wall. A number of doors led off the gallery: one was to a bedroom containing a bed and a great chest or coffer of cypress wood which, on lifting the lid, was seen to contain a set of smaller boxes or inner compartments. In a closet or alcove was 'an image of Christ's head', maybe a panel painting of Christ wearing the Crown of Thorns. Suspended from a hook was a large bassoon-like instrument with a deep bass tone known as a serpent: made of wood, covered with leather and formed with three U-shaped turns, it lay conveniently at hand for use at the family's Christmas or Twelfth Night revels, when itinerant minstrels or 'waits' would entertain everyone in the great hall, singing and playing from the gallery above.

Next along from here was a maid's room where napkins, sheets and other household items were stored. Still at first-floor level, a narrow corridor led to Thomas More's study, his inner sanctum that his children were rarely allowed to penetrate. Anyone entering would have gazed in wonder at the extraordinary number of bookcases, reaching from floor to ceiling, the shelves carefully spaced to accommodate volumes of different sizes from the smallest octavos to the largest folios. One of the family traditions is that Thomas rose at two or three o'clock in the morning to write. It almost seems as if, to obtain inner peace and a sense of personal fulfilment, to justify his very existence, he had to write something every day. He'd begun with impromptu speeches for family revels, once casually mentioning to an old schoolmaster the 'additions' he'd made to a comedy about King Solomon. About the time Margaret was born, he wrote (and went on later to publish) a slapstick poem entitled *A Merry Jest how a Serjeant would learn to play the Friar*. Writing came naturally to him;

it was a vital outlet for his creative energies. He once described himself as swept along by a spontaneous urge to write: everything came pouring out of his head onto the page.

Strikingly, he kept a four-poster bed with a tester or canopy in his study, suggesting that he often spent the night here, working late and rising early, surrounded by his precious books and papers, taking pleasure otherwise only in a few portraits of his friends and family, a set of a dozen or so stained or painted glass roundels of a type specially favoured by Renaissance artists, and a prized collection of Roman coins and antique gems.

Further along the passage was a 'closet' or antechamber with a section partitioned off, known as 'the counting house'. In most Tudor households, we should expect to find a locked iron chest here containing ledgers and ready cash for such items as food purchases, the servants' wages and other daily running expenses, but not in this one, where the counting house was crammed with overflow piles of books.

Immediately off the closet was a private chapel, one of the main focal points of the family's daily life, with two brass candlesticks, 'a great Crucifix' and a set of portable images of the saints on the altar. Otherwise sparsely furnished, the chapel was small, although not wholly austere. Members of the family sat on low stools when listening to Bible readings and knelt on cushions while they prayed, also resting their books on cushions placed on their reading desks.

Still on the first floor but closest to the upper end of the hall was the grandest, most formal room, the great chamber. It could also be reached via a spiral stone staircase built into the wall behind the dais at the upper end of the great hall, the route that guests were expected to take after dinner. Doorways at both ends of this room had elaborately carved portals to signify that it was the principal reception area. Inside, apart from the usual collection of chairs and stools, stood a buffet with open shelves for exhibiting silver or pewter, two desks to display rare books, a great wainscot chest and a fireplace with an oversized grate. Adorning the walls while the Mores still lived here, but removed to various ground-floor storerooms by the time the inventories were compiled, were several large wall-hangings on painted cloth. Such tapestry substitutes, intended for families who were comparatively affluent, but still couldn't afford the real thing, generally depicted classical or biblical scenes painted on canvas or linen. Leading off the great chamber was a smaller, more intimate parlour or withdrawing room, reached through a door in the panelling, maybe used for conversation or entertaining relatives and close family friends.

After visitors had returned downstairs and back through the screens at the lower end of the great hall towards the main entrance, they would have noticed along the passage a flight of stairs down to a cellar containing firewood, coal and cooking oil. At ground-floor level, this passage led on round a corner to the service quarters: the pantry, larder and finally the kitchen. A side door for the use of the servants led to the stables and garden. Next to the larder window around the side of the house was a chicken coop, guaranteeing a ready supply of the fresh eggs that Margaret's father is known to have particularly enjoyed.

Elsewhere on the ground floor was a spacious summer parlour with garden access for the family's use, the equivalent of a modern conservatory. Not far from the pantry and the larder stood the laundry with its tubs and scrubbing boards, with living quarters for half a dozen indoor servants scattered in between a run of storage rooms. According to the inventories, the storage rooms were stuffed full of broken furniture, old planks and decaying building materials left over from when the Grocers' Company had leased the property. 'A great tackle' or hoist took up part of the space in the front courtyard, the remnant of the time when the Barge had been a public weigh-house.

The site's crowning glory, perhaps the reason the family chose to extend their lease to include the whole of the property, was the garden, one of the largest in London still in private hands, occupying some 4,000 square yards. Here, despite living at the very heart of the restless, over-crowded city, the family was able to enjoy the seclusion of no fewer than three shady arbours with fruit trees, flowers and shrubs. Most likely Thomas and Joanna had planned and built them, for Thomas liked nothing better than to sit there relaxing on a hot summer's evening, eating his supper in his doublet and hose without a ruff or collar. The most remarkable garden feature was a vast pergola containing an aviary or 'great cage' made of wood and wire-netting, housing the family's collection of exotic birds. A street map of London drawn between 1561 and 1570 shows the garden with its pergola still standing, by which time the aviary and east wing of the house had disappeared. The inventories do not record when the Mores built their aviary, what species of birds they chose, and where they came from, but the relative importance to the family of their outdoor space is proved by the valuation of the arbours and aviary, together amounting to £20 and around an eighth of the value of the freehold of the site.

Margaret was born at home, some time between late August and the beginning of October 1505. Her mother, whom an uncle's evidence in a newly discovered lawsuit shows to have been just eighteen, endured a painful, protracted labour, proved by the fact that she made a special thank-offering to God at St Stephen's shortly afterwards, and by her choice of the baby's name, usually significant if it didn't already run in the family. Names were linked to patron saints and St Margaret was the patron saint of childbirth. In Latin, *margarita* means a pearl which is shining white, small and powerful, after Margaret of Antioch, one of Christianity's earliest women saints, disowned by her father and cruelly tortured by the Roman prefect. The climax of her legend is a prison confrontation with the devil in the shape of a hideous dragon. He assails her and would have devoured her in a single gulp, but she makes the sign of the cross, causing him to vanish. The prefect then tries to burn her alive in a furnace, then to drown her, all to no avail. Finally, he orders her decapitation, but after appealing for a brief respite, she is allowed to pray for her tormentors, adding a prayer that any woman who invokes her aid when suffering a difficult labour will give birth to a healthy child.

Before Margaret was eight days old, she was carried by the midwife across the street to church to be baptized. Rarely, if ever, did a mother attend her own child's baptism, since canon law forbade newly delivered women from entering a church until they had been ritually purified. About three weeks afterwards, Joanna would have stood at the church door wearing a veil and holding a candle in order to be sprinkled with holy water by the priest and readmitted into church.

At the christening itself, Margaret's godparents would have promised to protect her 'from fire and water and other perils' until she was seven, and teach her the Lord's Prayer, the 'Ave Maria' (or 'Hail Mary') and the Creed. Taking her gently in his hands, the priest would have immersed her three times in the font, once for the Father, once for the Son and a third time for the Holy Spirit, then dipped his thumb in holy oil, making the sign of the cross on her forehead, shoulders and breast, before wrapping her in a white linen christening robe as a symbol of purity and, more practically, to prevent the holy oil from being rubbed off. According to the Church's teaching, baptism exorcized the guilt of original sin but did not remove its stirrings. If Margaret subsequently committed a sin other than a venial one which might be expiated by repeating the Lord's Prayer or saying the rosary (150 'Hail Marys'), she would forfeit the goodness conveyed by baptism until she confessed and was absolved.

After the ceremony everyone would have gathered in the great hall at the Barge, where wine and sweetmeats would have been served. Even at comparatively frugal christening parties, two gallons of claret and several quarts of sweet white wine would be consumed. Family members and godparents would bring presents, often money or a silver christening cup. The guests would then have trooped upstairs to see Joanna, either in her bedroom or in the great chamber, where she would have greeted and embraced them. They would then have withdrawn downstairs again to the hall, laying out their gifts on the open shelves of the 'great cupboard of wainscot' on the dais beside the fireplace for others to admire.

The party over, the midwife handed Margaret to a wet-nurse, almost certainly the wife of Thomas Giggs, a man featuring in legal testimony as occupying a small dwelling adjacent to the Barge. 'Mistress Giggs' had lately given birth to a daughter herself, another Margaret. Joanna, as was then the norm for mothers wishing to conceive again quickly, would have breast-fed her child until the day of the baptism, but afterwards paid someone else to feed her, perhaps for a year or more. And who better than a neighbour?

Although Margaret couldn't have remembered much about the time she spent next door, her young namesake was soon destined to become her foster-sister and dearest, lifelong friend. When 'Mistress Giggs' sadly died not long after returning her young charge, the Mores decided to adopt her own bereaved daughter, a step considered to be perfectly normal at the time, much to the relief of her worried father, the indoor servant of a mercer, often sent on errands abroad to help with cloth exports and unable to cope with bringing up a child on his own.

No toys are mentioned in the inventories of the Barge, but we can catch a glimpse of how Margaret's father would have amused her and Margaret Giggs when they were toddlers in the late winter afternoons or in the garden in the heat of the summer. He always remembered with love and affection his own childhood nurse, 'Mother Maud', telling him animal stories from Aesop's *Fables*, and would have wanted to do the same for his own children. In later life Margaret still knew by heart all these stories, which were full of wonderful talking lions, apes, asses, foxes, wolves, cats, dogs, birds, rats and weasels. When she and Margaret Giggs were in the nursery, they would have sat spellbound on her father's lap as he picked his (and their) favourites, improvising all the appropriate gestures and intonations to hoots and screams of delight. Her father's own favourite stories were those of the fox and the grapes, the ass in a lion's skin, the dog and his shadow, the goose that laid the golden egg (except that for Thomas More it was always a hen, because he would insist on telling the story from a Latin edition of the *Fables* rather than using Caxton's popular translation), the sheep and the wolves, and the snail and her shell. All of Aesop's *Fables* have a moral point to ponder when the laughter fades, which is why Thomas More thought them ideal for children and adults alike. 'There is almost no tale so foolish,' he goes out of his way to say, 'but that yet in one matter or other, to some purpose it may hap to serve.'

Most parents began with such simpler, shorter tales as those of the nightingale, and the fox and the wolf. Finding a sparrow-hawk, a bird of prey, devouring her chicks, a nightingale at length obtains relief from a hunter who catches the sparrow-hawk in a net, carrying him off. 'He that oppresseth the innocents shall have an evil death,' is Aesop's moral, which listeners likened to the biblical tale of Cain and Abel. As to the fox, his malice and envy cause his downfall, for when he approaches a wolf's lair ostensibly on a friendly visit, his secret intent is to steal. Thwarted in his nefarious plan, the fox calls on a nearby shepherd to inform him of the wolf's whereabouts, only to be torn apart himself by dogs.

Of all Aesop's *Fables*, it was the tougher, political tales that stuck in Margaret's memory. A quarter of a century later, when her father was a prisoner in the Tower of London, one of those she remembered was about a flatterer and an honest man who decide to visit a distant country ruled by apes. The King of the Apes has them brought before him. Sitting like an emperor on his throne beneath his cloth of estate with all his apes about him, he demands of them who he is.

'Thou art emperor and king, the fairest creature that is on earth,' says the flatterer, stepping forward.

'And who be these about me?' asks the King of the Apes.

'Sir, they be your knights and your subjects for to keep your person and your realm.'

'Thou art a good man,' answers the king. 'I will that thou be my great steward of my household and that every one bear to thee honour and reverence.'

When the honest man hears this, he naively supposes that if only he tells the unvarnished truth, he will be even more highly rewarded. So when the king turns to him, he answers: 'Thou art an ape and a beast right abominable. And all they which be about thee are like and semblable to thee.'

The furious king orders the apes to tear the honest man into tiny pieces with their teeth and claws. 'And therefore,' concludes Aesop, 'it happeneth often that the liars and flatterers be enhanced and the men of truth be set low and put back. For often times (for to say) truthful men lose their lives, the which thing is against justice and equity.'

When Margaret first heard this story from her father, she could scarcely have imagined that, one day in a bleak stone cell in the Tower, they would pace up and down, repeating to one another this and other fables, adapted to suit the case of Henry VIII and his councillors. In her childhood innocence, she simply revelled in the tales, made all the more compelling by the fact that her father brought home a monkey as a pet. A friend of her father's, staying with the family at the Barge, describes it. After accidentally injuring himself, the monkey was permitted to run loose around the garden to hasten his convalescence. And by then, there was a rabbit pen fixed to a wall at the bottom of the garden, besides the chicken coop. A weasel came to attack the pen, steadily gnawing away at it from the rear in the hope of prising it from the wall. The monkey, watching nonchalantly until the weasel at last toppled the pen, leapt forward in a flash, replacing it so expertly that a human couldn't have done it better. The rabbits were saved, but in their ignorance happily kissed the weasel through the fence.

The story may be apocryphal, and yet through it we catch a flavour of the precious laughter, love and tenderness that enveloped Margaret in her childhood years, and which is unobtainable from the grittier archival sources, however visceral and intriguing they may otherwise turn out to be.

2

FAMILY MATTERS

THREE MONTHS AFTER MARGARET was baptized, her grandfather, John More, summoned as many of the family as he could muster to his second wife's funeral. His house lay at the north end of Milk Street off Cheapside, less than half a mile from Bucklersbury and to the north-east of St Paul's Cathedral, close to Guildhall. The street took its name from the milk wholesalers who once lived there, before a disastrous fire cleared the way for property speculators to move in. Buildings little more than sheds or shops, with living quarters above, were lavishly renovated and extended outwards and upwards, three, four or five storeys high, creating some of the 'fairest' houses in the city, complete with cheekily carved corbels and eaves nudging each other mischievously across the narrow street almost blocking out the sun.

Marrying a wealthy widow, Joan Marshall, six years before at the age of forty-eight, and within six months of the death of his first wife, had dramatically transformed John More's fortunes. Up until then, he'd been modestly successful, but hardly prominent. A lawyer practising at Lincoln's Inn, he was something of a Jekyll and Hyde figure. He could be bluff, genial and witty, full of disarming candour and merry jests; at other times opinionated and dictatorial. A sturdy, prudent, practical man with sharp, penetrating eyes and a ruddy complexion, he condoned actions for the forfeiture of lands and the recovery of rents or debts in his legal practice that were little short of predatory. This may have been unavoidable in a professional capacity, where his list of clients included Edward Stafford, Duke of Buckingham, the greatest and richest nobleman in the country. Despite this, an acquisitive impulse coloured his private transactions, one that cannot be disguised, and which he couldn't have suppressed even if he'd tried.

Thomas More later described his father as 'a civil man, pleasant, harmless gentle, pitiful, just, and uncorrupted'. 'Pitiful' meant compassionate; when amplified by 'just' and 'uncorrupted', it extols John More's qualities as a judge at the end of his career. 'Harmless gentle' more accurately describes his carefully rehearsed domesticity; the phrase is respectful, while still being consistent with his character. He'd seen his second marriage as an opportunity to secure his status in the social hierarchy, choosing the widow of a rich mercer and fellow parishioner, John Marshall, who'd died leaving shops and houses in London, with manors and lands in several southern and Midlands counties. His widow was to enjoy a life interest in the profits of half of these estates; the rest were given to charities. Her children would inherit her share after her death, but were to have nothing while she was alive. John More therefore became the immediate beneficiary of the will by right of his second wife, even if his new stepson didn't care for the idea. We know that, in fact, he didn't care for it at all. To prevent his son from contesting the will, John Marshall had inserted a special clause threatening to disinherit him for ever.

John More's second marriage wasn't made in heaven. Handwritten testimony from Margaret's uncle, John Rastell, who'd married Elizabeth, Thomas More's younger sister and Margaret's favourite aunt, enables us to dig down deeply into the family's affairs. Joan Marshall was 'choleric and fumous', a woman 'of such nature' that she 'could neither patiently suffer her husband's sayings nor words', nor would she let anyone else get a word in edgeways. John More lived 'in fear' of her. He 'durst not' contradict her; in particular, he daren't pay out money she hadn't authorized. John More had married for money, so now he must suffer patiently his domineering wife's stings and taunts.

Throughout his life, Margaret's grandfather loved to joke about wives and women. 'Every man,' he used to say, 'is at the choice of his wife.' Picking wives is like a man dipping his hand 'into a blind bag full of snakes and eels together, seven snakes for one eel. Ye would, I ween, reckon it a perilous choice to take up one at adventure, though ye had made your special prayer to speed well.' If he happened to overhear husbands chiding their wives or calling them 'shrews', he'd say: 'they defame them falsely. For he sayeth plainly that there is but one shrewd wife in the world, but he sayeth indeed that every man weeneth he hath her.' This wasn't at all a compliment: the pun had few, if any, of the more positive connotations it has today. 'Shrews' were scolds: malicious, vexatious, evil women who railed incessantly at their husbands. Their 'shrewdness' was the 'craft' or 'cunning' of the serpent in the story of Adam and Eve.

John More was in something of a bind. Although the conventions of his time required him to be master in his own house, his worldly ambition had to be funded by his cool-headed speculations on the marriage market. Margaret's father gives us our best insight, telling us his family came to be held in 'honest esteem', even if it wasn't 'famous', and explaining what this meant. 'Let us now consider,' he writes, 'good name, honest estimation, and honourable fame . . . a good name may a man have be he never so poor.' Anyone could be judged to be a person of good character, and the ownership of property didn't come into it, whereas 'honest estimation, in the common taking of the people, belongeth not unto any man but him that is taken for one of some countenance and havour [sic], and among his neighbours had in some reputation.'

It was this 'havour' and 'reputation' that John More coveted. The word 'havour' is from the French *avoir*, denoting material substance or wealth. Those who have it acquire social status and recognition; this relates particularly to the landowning middle class. In fact, the bigger the land-holding, the greater the 'reputation' of its owner. Thomas went on to distinguish 'honest estimation' from 'honourable fame', deriving from 'the renown of great estates, much and far spoken of'.

The status hierarchy was rooted in the ownership of land. Birth or titular rank were meaningless without it; wealth earned by trade or in the professions lacked comparable prestige. Lawyers like John More, who rented chambers in the Inns of Court and earned their livings in the royal courts at Westminster Hall, were titular gentry, but unless also land-owners, their place in the social hierarchy would be inconsequential. His own father had been a baker; his first wife's was a tallow-chandler, boiling the carcasses and intestines of animals in huge smelly vats to make candles and soap. John More knew his position in society would always be inferior if he didn't conform to the stereotype. Like every London-based lawyer, he yearned to possess a substantial manor or manors within a day or so's riding distance that he and his extended family could enjoy during the hot summer months, and which he could pass on to his son, and then his grandchildren. He'd inherited a small plot called Gobions at North

Mimms in Hertfordshire, seventeen miles north of London. The land
had been acquired by his grandfather, and after his second marriage John
More began purchasing the neighbouring fields, using his legal skills to
get the best deals and doubling the size of his estate. He sent in builders
to improve the manor house, which he redesigned and surrounded with
a deer park, erecting a fence, or palisade, around the four acres nearest the
living quarters, creating a vista from his house onto the park, which he
stocked with twenty deer 'for his pleasure'.

The solemn dirge and requiem to which, in the throes of an unusually
cold winter, John More summoned his family were held at the parish
church of St Lawrence Jewry, beside the gateway to Guildhall just round
the corner from the north end of Milk Street. Built in the late twelfth
century, St Lawrence's was a local landmark, its tall square tower with
pinnacles at each corner clearly visible against the skyline. The windows
were glazed, and in the last thirty years the spacious interior had been
transformed by the generosity of Sir Geoffrey Boleyn, a Norfolk
merchant who'd come to London to make his fortune, rising to be Lord
Mayor and leaving generous bequests to pay for an exquisitely carved
rood-loft and screen dividing the nave from the chancel and two side
chapels in the choir. On top of the rood-loft stood a great crucifix flanked
by images of the Virgin Mary and St John, illuminated by lights burning
continually, the oil lamps and candles replenished daily by silent figures
who climbed hidden stairs. Painted on the lower panels and on the
central doors of the screen were rows of brilliantly coloured saints, their
azure and vermilion mantles trimmed with gold leaf, their haloes with
miniature pearls, iridescent in the light.

Hanging from a stone pillar by an iron chain towards the back of the
nave, two objects as spiritually haunting, if incongruously macabre,
caused generations of parishioners to gape. One was the tooth of 'some
monstrous fish', maybe from a whale stranded at low tide on the shore of
the Thames; the other a gigantic shin-bone, doubtfully said to be a man's,
maybe an elephant's from the royal menagerie at the Tower. Symbols of
the cadaver and skull, of death and mortality, Thomas More knew them
well for this was the church in which he'd worshipped with his family as
a boy. Such 'grisly apparitions', he said, evoke the 'very fantasy and deep
imagination' of our own deaths, for it was only 'by the feeling of that
imagination in our hearts' that we would humble ourselves before God.

Lit by wax torches and candles and with everyone dressed in black from head to toe, John More's second wife was buried alongside her first husband in the stone and alabaster tomb he'd built for them both in the Lady Chapel. But scarcely had the tomb been sealed before tongues would have been wagging throughout the parish, because everyone had to return again to church for John More's third wedding. With his characteristic alacrity where money and status were at stake, he proposed to a second wealthy widow, another Joan, also lately married to a mercer, Thomas Bowes, who was buried in the church of St Mary Aldermanbury, less than five minutes' walk from Milk Street.

Although Thomas Bowes had owned little in the way of land, he'd left a vast stock of merchandise, and cash and jewellery hoards. A third of everything came to his widow outright, a third went to charity, and a third was put into trust for his teenage children, who were to receive equal shares at twenty-one, or when they married if that was earlier. These children, unlike Joan Marshall's, caused no ripples, and for his part, John More did not pause. Continuing to spend heavily on improvements at Gobions, he took possession of his new wife's assets, suing her debtors and maximizing her assets, while putting the finishing touches to his new house and deer park, which he could afford to complete in exactly the way he'd envisaged.

Not everything, however, went so smoothly. Conspicuously absent were Margaret's aunt and uncle, Elizabeth and John Rastell. Seven years earlier, Elizabeth had married Rastell, a versatile law student of twenty-one, predicting a bright future for himself as an entrepreneur, his head teeming with exciting, original ideas. But Rastell was soon quarrelling with his father-in-law. John More, despite giving his blessing for the wedding, had insisted that Rastell live at Milk Street with his wife and in-laws for five years. Beneath his mask of affability lay a thrifty, sparing, miserly instinct that told him he could exploit their youth and inexperience to save money. In fact, he charged the Rastells the arbitrarily high rate of £10 a year for their board and lodging, to be deducted in advance from Elizabeth's dowry of £100, so reducing his cash outlay by half. He readily had his way, because both Rastell's parents were dead. Elizabeth's dowry was to be paid directly to Rastell, who agreed to provide his wife with jointure lands worth £10 a year. This was the income she and any young children she might have were expected to live on if Rastell unexpectedly died.

The Rastells had tolerated the arrangement until tempers flared after Joan Marshall's arrival. Elizabeth's marriage settlement, signed at the time of her betrothal, had included a clause allowing the Rastells to recover the full proceeds of the dowry in cash if John More remarried, but when Joan Marshall refused to honour it, Rastell and his wife's stepmother came close to blows. As soon as Rastell had qualified at the Middle Temple and was able to earn an independent living as a barrister, he and Elizabeth decided to cut their losses and move out, taking their two servants and a few small items of furniture and setting up house at Coventry in Warwickshire. Thus it was that they had declined to make the three-day journey south for their old adversary's funeral, or return for John More's third wedding.

Happily the focus had shifted by the spring of 1506, when Margaret's mother knew she was expecting her second child. Her pregnancy was going smoothly, so Thomas decided to visit Coventry and see his sister and brother-in-law. Perhaps he hoped to reconcile his father to them, but more likely went to act as a godparent to their latest child. His sister was to have three surviving children: John, her eldest, born in or about 1501, Joan in 1506, and William in 1508. Thomas would have been an obvious choice as godfather to his niece, for he and his sister were always particularly close.

During the next two years, Margaret's younger sisters, Elizabeth and Cecily, were born. Elizabeth was named after her aunt, Rastell's wife; Cecily after St Cecilia, the patron saint of music, for by now the family at Bucklersbury owned a variety of musical instruments and Joanna More was learning to sing while accompanying herself on the lute. According to his descendants, Thomas himself sang (if badly) in the church choir.

When Cecily was a year old, Thomas decided to visit the universities of Paris and Louvain, near Brussels. Describing his trip, lasting for no more than six to eight weeks, he confessed laconically that he'd done his best to discover what each university taught and in what ways: 'I have so far discovered no reason, either in what I heard while I was there or in what I learnt since I left, why . . . I ought to prefer either one of them to Oxford or Cambridge for the education of my own children, for whom I want strictly the best.' He must, of course, have been thinking exclusively about the principles of education, as he could hardly have overlooked the fact that women would be denied entry to every university in Europe for centuries to come. But plainly, his mind was on the topic of education, because Margaret, now three, had already started learning to read. One can imagine her holding up, to her father's delight, one of the easier English translations of Aesop's *Fables* with their graphic woodcut illustrations, 'sounding and saying' the individual vowels and letters to build simple words and phrases, and pointing to the pictures in the way children were taught then.

But his biggest surprise on returning home from the Continent was learning of the imminent return of the Rastells to London. They'd already leased a tenement near Fleet Bridge, a wooden crossing over the Fleet ditch (really an open sewer) opposite land just north of the river belonging to the Hospitallers of Clerkenwell, an area ripe for redevelopment where prices were affordable. Not that Rastell was poor any longer, as a rich aunt living in Coventry had died. After a small bequest to her goddaughter, the bulk of her estate came to Rastell, enabling him to plan a future for himself as a printer as well as a part-time barrister. For he intended to unleash his imagination and put his novel ideas into practice; to use the new printing technology developed by Caxton and his successors to make English law, hitherto the sole preserve of arcane specialists who worked mainly from crabby notebooks, accessible to everyone. Always the budding entrepreneur, he even had a business plan. He would begin by selling reference works and student cribs for which a secure market existed, and when he had sufficient turnover, move on to more ambitious translations, compilations and abridgements, and much more besides.

Rastell would have taken a year, perhaps two or three, to establish his press. A shorter timescale wouldn't have been feasible, because printing in London was a cut-throat business. Its practitioners were notoriously protective of their craft, passing on their founts of type and other tools of the trade from father to son, or selling them at a hefty premium to reflect their scarcity value. Rastell had to make a journey to France to secure an adequate stock of type, finally purchasing it from a printer of books of hours in Rouen.

After Thomas had returned from the Continent, his priority was to earn some money. He began taking on the cases of litigants in the civic courts of London, quickly building up a list of regular clients. His descendants claimed many years later that he built up a legal practice worth £400 a year, but even for the ablest, most experienced lawyers this was rare. Many advocates were earning under £150 after twenty or more years in the profession, and John Rastell, admittedly part-time, reckoned on no more than £26 a year.

Margaret, even as an adult, never liked to ask her father how the family managed for money. She always had new clothes as a child, as her father, teasing her when a teenager, would one day remind her, saying that 'even when a tiny child you could never endure to be decked out in another's finery.' But whenever anyone dared to shift a conversation towards money, he would be disconcertingly vague. Up until now, despite following in his own father's footsteps and qualifying as a lawyer at Lincoln's Inn, he hadn't really put his mind to earning a living. Instead, he'd drawn on the money from his wife's dowry to purchase the lease on the Barge and furnish the property, and maybe meet the costs of landscaping the garden and erecting the 'great cage' for the birds too. We don't know how much his father-in-law, John Colt of Netherhall, a country squire living about a mile and a half south of Roydon in Essex, had offered as his daughter's marriage portion, but a sound basis of comparison is the £150–200 paid by others in his position. Although dowries were meant to provide an annuity for a woman and her children if she was widowed, the investment, by mutual consent, might be delayed, so releasing capital to meet the costs of establishing the household at the outset. Thomas's strategy had been to settle his family in their home, then gradually earn enough to secure their long-term future, an arrangement the bride's father would have been expected to condone, since he retained a degree of moral influence over how the dowry was spent.

When Margaret was rising four, her parents passed another significant milestone. At last they could celebrate the birth of their only son John, their fourth and last child, and with the Rastells back in London, the christening could become the occasion for a great family party. As with Margaret and her sisters, the baby, wrapped in a shawl, would have been carried across the street to St Stephen's Church by the midwife.

With his wife, four children and an adopted daughter, Margaret Giggs, to provide for, Margaret's father now settled down in earnest to make his living. Soon he began to be noticed as a brilliant advocate and public speaker, one with impeccable family connections, as within a few months of young John's christening, Thomas's father would be promoted by King Henry VII to the position of serjeant-at-law, one of the élite cadre of barristers who would advance to the judiciary as vacancies arose, and be retained as legal counsel by the City of London and Westminster Abbey, besides being admitted to the Mercers' Company as one of their honorary members.

On 21 March 1509 the Mercers' Company also chose Margaret's father as an honorary member. He'd become a lawyer of choice among the members of this, the wealthiest and most ancient of the livery companies, and was elected a freeman of London, a privilege separately conferred on him at Guildhall by the Mayor and Aldermen. Everyone must have been delighted, and after the induction ceremonies there would have been a private celebration in the great hall at the Barge attended by all the family, the older children playing together and everyone agreeing that the future looked bright indeed.

3

RITES OF PASSAGE

WHEN NEARLY FOUR, an excited Margaret would have stood with her mother in the crowds in Cheapside on the eve of Midsummer Day, watching her father make one of several speeches during Henry VIII's coronation procession. A month after Thomas More had been elected an honorary mercer and freeman of London, King Henry VII died, to be succeeded – after an interval of two days while his councillors plotted, Kremlin-style, how to keep their jobs – by his younger son Henry. Almost eighteen, and armed with the necessary dispensation from Pope Julius II, Henry promptly married the Spanish princess Katherine of Aragon, his deceased elder brother's widow, declaring himself to be deeply in love and sweeping aside the objection that she was six years older than he was. Henry, who began his reign with a flurry of grand gestures, planned a double coronation for Katherine and himself, ushering in a new golden age. 'Our king's heart is set not upon gold or jewels or mines of ore,' a fawning courtier waxed lyrical, 'but upon virtue, reputation and eternal fame.' This was to prove as unfounded as it was untrue, but for the More family the coronation was memorable since Margaret's father had his own small part to play.

Henry and Katherine had lodged overnight at the Tower ready for the spectacle beginning at four o'clock in the afternoon, the citizens and their families cheering, the fronts of the houses ablaze with colour: those by the Stocks Market closest to Margaret's home draped with velvet and silks; those along Cheapside with rich tapestries and cloth of gold. People craned their necks out of their windows to catch sight of Henry and his twenty-three-year-old wife as they passed by. And along the route, at strategic points, stood the serried ranks of the livery companies, showing off their finest, gaudiest gowns: the goldsmiths, grocers, skinners, drapers, fishmongers, vintners, ironmongers and mercers, waiting for their turn to offer homage and congratulations to their king.

The Knights of the Bath in their long blue gowns with hoods and white tassels led the way. The Duke of Buckingham, the hereditary Constable of England and Margaret's grandfather's richest client in his law practice, was next. Astride his white charger, he was resplendent in a robe of shimmering gold and silver thread speckled with hundreds of tiny diamonds, clasping his silver staff of office in his right hand; around his neck a fine gold chain. The heralds followed, their coats emblazoned with badges and escutcheons, carrying their hats in their hands. Then Henry himself appeared, borne in a chariot drawn by she-mules, seated on his throne beneath an embroidered silk canopy fixed to golden poles held aloft by lords walking beside. He looked magnificent, every inch a king: clad in a mantle of crimson velvet trimmed with ermine, with a matching cap covering his short red hair, his collar of solid gold studded with rubies, the front panel of his cloth of gold surcoat fringed with sable fur and glittering with diamonds, emeralds and pearls. Six feet two inches tall, and as lean as he was fit before gluttony caused him to bulge, he dazzled and delighted his subjects. His one obvious flaw was his inability, like his father before him, to look people straight in the eye.

Approaching the Great Conduit, a public water fountain beside Mercers' Hall, Henry's chariot halted and, at a signal from the duke, the mercers stepped forward in their violet gowns and hoods. Thomas More then spoke on their behalf in florid Latin, directly addressing the man who later claimed to be his friend, but ended up as his nemesis. Speaking unfalteringly for a quarter of an hour, he praised his sovereign's looks, intellect, physical prowess and respect for justice and the rule of law. In a calculated risk, he said the new king had 'banished fear and oppression' – a remark tantamount to an open rebuke of Henry VII's methods in his final years, but exactly what the young king (who could understand most of what was said) wanted to hear. But Henry, married for less than a fortnight and in the first flush of love for Katherine, was gratified most of all when Thomas acclaimed her as the future 'mother of kings'. 'Fecund in male offspring,' he declared, 'will she render your dynasty stable and enduring for all time.'

The oratory over, the mercers bowed low as the king's chariot resumed its journey, but even as Thomas had been speaking, the sky turned pitch black and it poured on Henry's parade. Katherine, slim and elegant and following at a dignified interval, was soaked to the skin when the ornate canopy above her collapsed under the weight of water, ruining her ermine mantle and white satin dress, and turning her loosely flowing hair into a tangle. Hastily taking shelter under the awning of a nearby draper's stall, she waited for the storm to end before continuing along Cheapside so as not to disappoint the waiting crowds.

Margaret and her mother would have been drenched too, but would also have remembered the day for different reasons, since, to prepare such an important speech, her father would have disappeared into his study at the Barge days beforehand, asking to be left undisturbed, and even when the event itself was over, more had to be done, for the mercers asked him to commission a deluxe bound copy of his eulogy as their coronation gift to Henry, complete with brilliantly coloured illustrations by one of the finest miniaturists of Ghent or Bruges. When it was ready, Margaret's father once again retreated to his study to compose a new verse making fun of the rainstorm together with a surprisingly droll preface seeking to distance himself from any imputation of sycophancy. Never at ease with the flattery and false blandishments that were the staple diet of conversation at princely courts, he was already wriggling with embarrassment, so decided to tell Henry somewhat back-handedly that 'to give my clownish verses a better claim to your favour, I hit on applying some colour to them, like a girl who piles the cosmetics on thick, mistrusting her natural looks.' Alas we have no inkling as to whether Henry read this, or even opened the book before placing it on the shelves of the royal library.

Even if Margaret, herself just beginning to read, couldn't yet have gained a sense of how far her father, practising as a legal advocate, had carved out a reputation for style and oratory, she at least would have glimpsed something unusual when, within weeks of the coronation, a man always honoured by her father as his dearest, lifelong friend, and a towering presence in her own life for over twenty years, came to stay with the family. Erasmus of Rotterdam, a roving, maverick, hypochondriac genius, ten years older than her father, had first met him in 1499, when they'd been introduced by a young nobleman, William Blount, Lord Mountjoy.

Although Blount's London mansion lay in Silver Street, surrounded by the shops and houses of the silversmiths and a short walk from Milk Street, he'd got to know the Mores after marrying the daughter of their next-door neighbour in Hertfordshire, Sir William Say of Essendon. Like Margaret's aunt, Elizabeth Rastell, Sir William's daughter had been considered too young to leave home at first, so Blount made as many visits to see her as he could fit in between travelling to Paris for his studies. Essendon lay on the opposite side to Gobions of a muddy, often flooded and impassable track running between Potters Bar and Bell Bar on the way to Hatfield Park. Both Sir William and Margaret's grandfather were county magistrates, travelling to St Albans and Hertford Castle together every few months to empty the gaols, empanel juries and indict or acquit the prisoners.

A priest's illegitimate son, Erasmus had begun life in a monastery but obtained leave to study theology in Paris, eking out a living as a part-time tutor. Gaunt and tall with darting eyes, thin lips, hollow cheeks and a pointed nose, he combined grit and ambition with charm and charisma, rarely losing an opportunity to promote the latest, most exciting theories, or position himself as their instigator if he could get away with it. His ideas were sparkling, his intellect incisive, his style angelic, his wit coruscating. In his earliest letter to Thomas More, he'd revelled in what he called his 'Spartan' preference for truth over politeness. Always short of cash, he'd taken Blount as a pupil, then returned with him to Essendon. And thanks to Blount's stepfather, Erasmus, Thomas and a fellow law student had been invited to visit the royal schoolroom at Eltham Palace, the first time they'd set eyes on Henry VII's children. That had been Thomas's very first encounter with the future Henry VIII, then eight years old. He'd presented the prince with some verses he'd composed, but hadn't forewarned Erasmus, who, at dinner afterwards, received 'a little note . . . to challenge something from my pen'. Within days he'd rushed off a Latin ode of 150 lines, entitled 'A Description of Britain, King Henry VII and the King's Children', craftily prefaced by a dedication comparing Prince Henry to a second Alexander the Great, except that it failed to attract a reward, leaving Erasmus crestfallen.

Returning to England just over six years later, Erasmus had been a guest at Bucklersbury for six weeks. Although next door with her wet-nurse then, Margaret would later in life be able to read a graphic account of that visit in an edition of Erasmus's letters. Providing us with his earliest character sketch of her father, Erasmus had described him as:

> so full of eloquence that he could not fail to carry any argument, even with an enemy, and whom I regard with such affection that even if he ordered me to join the rope-circle and dance, I should obey him without hesitation . . . I believe (unless I am deluded by the intensity of the love I bear him) that nature never created a livelier mind, or one quicker, more discerning, or clearer . . . Moreover, he has an exceptionally charming disposition and a great deal of wit; yet the wit is good-natured; so you could not find him lacking in a single one of the qualities needed by the perfect barrister.

Thomas, it appears, was persuasive enough 'to make camels dance'. As Erasmus hated dancing, resolutely refusing to join in the family's celebrations in the great hall, his remark is the more telling.

Margaret's own first meeting with her father's great friend was when he returned from Italy as soon as the news of Henry's coronation broke, staying with the family for over a year before moving on to Cambridge and elsewhere. However little else she might have noticed, she would have been aware that he spent many long hours closeted with her father in his study, and that even when, at mealtimes, they finally emerged, they spoke nothing but Latin, for her father knew neither Dutch nor German, and Erasmus knew no English, refusing even to consider learning it, which made table talk almost impossible for the children and their mother. Margaret would, admittedly, have seen all too much of Erasmus on Monday and Tuesday mornings, when her father went to Guildhall to represent his clients in the Court of Hustings, and on Thursday and Friday mornings, when he went to the Sheriffs' Courts at Bread Street or the Poultry. Erasmus, left on his own, was awkward, restless and unsociable, trying the patience of Margaret's mother by complaining endlessly about an attack of the kidney-stone and of unexplained delays in the arrival of his trunk and books from Italy. He grumbled that 'with nothing to do, I began to amuse myself with a eulogy of folly. I had no idea of publication but [wrote it] simply as a distraction from the pain of my complaint. Once started, I let some close friends have a look at what I'd done, so as to add to my amusement by sharing the joke.'

Erasmus refers, of course, to one of his most famous works, the *Praise of Folly* (in Latin *Moriae encomium*, a pun, as Margaret soon gathered, on the family's name), written almost entirely at Bucklersbury while her father went out to work.

'If anything I've said seems rather impudent,' says Erasmus, 'you must remember it's "Folly" and a woman who's been speaking.' The book, scabrously funny and full of lacerating observations about all that was wrong in the Church and the monasteries, calling in thinly veiled terms for root and branch reform, caused a literary sensation when it was published two years later, casting shafts of reflected glory onto Thomas More, to whom the book was dedicated in extravagant homage for his friendship. So nimble, so trenchantly ironic, so dangerously irreverent and close to the bone was this jewel of a *jeu d'esprit*, it would run through thirty-six editions in its author's lifetime alone. Not everyone saw the joke, but Margaret's father revelled in it, unable or unwilling to see how lethal and inflammatory the satire could be; how vulnerable to accusations of blasphemy; just how much embarrassment it would cause him when Erasmus's enemies came in for the kill.

But for the moment, the main effect on Margaret of Erasmus's stay with her family was to make her realize that her father led what was tantamount to a double life: he had his everyday career as lawyer in the civic courts, and (as it seemed) a quite different sort of life as an intellectual in the giddy world of letters, although from her vantage-point the effects of each were exactly the same: her father was disappointingly apart from her, and for increasingly longer periods than had been the case when they'd first happily turned the pages of Aesop's *Fables* together.

For Margaret, that trend would only continue after her father was chosen by the Mercers' Company to represent them. The English cloth merchants had been quarrelling for several years with the City of Antwerp over their trading privileges. Margaret of Savoy, the regent of the Low Countries, was keen to settle the disputes, arranging for the 'pensionary', or city clerk of Antwerp, to visit England. When, in September 1509, the envoy made his first grand entry into Mercers' Hall, he found Thomas already there, 'sitting upon the high bench's end next to the window', ready to greet him in elegant, fluent Latin. Further discussions and adjournments ensued, and after four days' haggling, More came up with the basis of a compromise acceptable to all.

Word must have travelled, because soon afterwards the Mayor of London sent a messenger to fetch Margaret's father to settle a complex boundary dispute between the city and St Bartholomew's Hospital. After that, he was appointed as a commercial arbitrator in the Court of Chancery by the Lord Chancellor and Archbishop of Canterbury, William Warham. He didn't go out of his way to seek advancement, but found himself sought out by others. Thus, when Henry summoned Parliament in 1510, he didn't stand for election, but when one of the chosen representatives for London withdrew at the last moment, he stood in, taking a cautious line in the House of Commons, and saying little.

The event creating feverish excitement at Bucklersbury came after Parliament was adjourned, when Margaret was to discover her father had been elected one of the two undersheriffs of London. For as long as anyone could remember, two sheriffs, usually merchants who weren't legally qualified, were chosen annually to oversee the administration of justice, empanel juries and account for feudal taxes. Each was assigned a qualified lawyer as a deputy, and as time went by the undersheriffs took over most of the work, sitting alone as judges in the civic courts. Civil and criminal pleas were heard, and each court had a prison attached to it run by a porter.

At his ceremonial induction at Guildhall, Thomas swore: 'Well and truly will I serve my master who is elected sheriff, and that I will not fail, for gift or favour, or for promises or for hate, to deal equal law and right unto all manner of persons, as well poor as rich . . . so help me God and all the saints.' He was instantly popular with Londoners for keeping his promises, for always sitting in person and not delegating their cases to lowly subordinates, and for checking that all petitions filed in his court were correctly entered and legally sufficient before a writ was issued, so avoiding fruitless delays and expense. His own courtroom was at the Poultry, just along from the Stocks Market near the family home, his income, with all the many perks of the job, around £250 a year, enough to maintain his family in some style.

The perks, however, caused a family tiff. Margaret's older uncle, Richard Staverton, a 'scrivener' or professional copyist of legal documents married to her Aunt Joan, John More's elder daughter, was a favourite of her grandfather's. In Henry VII's reign, he had paid for Staverton's admission to Lincoln's Inn as a law student, although to little effect as he was never called to the bar. Then, as one of the Duke of Buckingham's lawyers, John More used his influence to beg a favour of Cardinal John Morton, one of the old king's most trusted and senior councillors, who'd then written to the Mayor and Aldermen, asking that Staverton be granted a post of attorney in the civic courts. The city had always resented lobbying, but had no choice other than to yield to this request. So before long, Staverton was filing legal documents for his clients besides copying them, paying their court fees, securing their release on bail from prison, and obtaining writs on their behalf. Attorneys were, however, forbidden from speaking in court or entering legal pleas, tasks restricted to qualified advocates.

Now Margaret's grandfather wanted Thomas to find a more comfortable sinecure for Staverton in the civic bureaucracy, and there were plenty of opportunities. An undersheriff needed a secondary (or deputy), a clerk of the papers and four or five under-clerks. He also vetted applicants for the junior posts of attorney, already occupied by Staverton. Someone less honest than Thomas would have used his civic appointment to obtain jobs and perks for his friends and relations, irrespective of merit. He was, in fact, willing to play the patronage game sometimes, putting in a good word here and there, and even helping a friend to obtain a Church living for one of his chaplains. But in spite of such opportunities, Margaret's grandfather found that his pleas on Staverton's behalf fell on deaf ears. The most Thomas would do was to recommend his brother-in-law to the churchwardens of his own parish church, who put him on a small retainer, otherwise leaving the scrivener to continue in his low-grade job.

Such coolness contrasts to the warmth he showed towards Margaret's favourite uncle and aunt, John and Elizabeth Rastell. The Mores and Rastells were exceptionally close-knit, and in the autumn of 1510 Thomas came to his sister's house to ask a favour. A neighbour's daughter, Joyce Lee, a remarkably devout young woman, had lately entered a nunnery. Her family had always lived locally; her grandfather had been a warden of the Grocers' Company and three times Mayor of London. The chief benefactors of St Stephen's Church, the family was so pious that when Joyce's father died, he asked to be buried on the spot where he'd knelt in daily prayer since a boy. Joyce's brother,

Edward, had been Thomas More's childhood friend, and so as a gift for Joyce, Thomas had adapted and translated a biography of a pious citizen of Florence, Pico della Mirandola, together with extracts from his writings. Now he came to ask John Rastell if he would print his manuscript ready for New Year, the season (rather than Christmas then) for the exchange of gifts between cherished family and friends, also making a special presentation copy for Joyce. The biography was a highly moral work, since, setting out to unlock the secrets of the universe, Pico had fallen foul of the Church for his pride and presumption before, at last, redeeming himself by burning his 'wanton' books, giving away all his wealth to the poor, and flagellating himself.

Christmas 1510 should have been a wonderfully joyous season, for Margaret and her adopted sister, Margaret Giggs, were both five and taking a lively interest in everything. Elizabeth and Cecily were four and three respectively, and baby John had been returned to his mother by his wet-nurse. Money was no longer a problem; the children had their presents and their father had never seemed happier. And yet, instead of enjoying dinner with his family and playing with his children over the Twelve Days of Christmas, his chair stood empty. And he was nowhere to be seen when the London 'waits' called, as they did at the houses of all civic dignitaries, singing carols and entertaining the household, playing their oboes and cornets and taking down the serpent from its hook on the wall, before drinking from a wassail cup filled with hot milk curdled with wine and spices. Instead, he was at Lincoln's Inn, where he'd been elected to preside over the Christmas and New Year revels, playing the fool as 'Lord of Misrule' (or king of hoaxing) and making merry. He was an obvious choice for, as Erasmus had noted in his dedication of the *Praise of Folly*, he had a natural, laughing, bantering, rapier wit that he found it hard to suppress even on the most serious of occasions: Erasmus likened him to a second Democritus or 'laughing philosopher'. He would have been in his element at his Inn of Court, where the Christmas revels marked the climax of the lawyers' social calendar, except that it was an honour that kept him away from home.

Still, the family did their best to enjoy themselves in his absence. Erasmus had been asked back for the festive season, and Margaret's mother, Joanna, still no more than twenty-four, had graciously allowed him to invite his own guests, even Andrea Ammonio, an opinionated Italian said to have the manners of a prizefighter and the appetite of a horse, whom she expected would stay until Twelfth Night.

Six months later, Ammonio was still there, refusing to depart. As he wrote to Erasmus, then away in Paris arranging for the *Praise of Folly* to be printed, More's 'most agreeable wife [is] extremely well' and 'never mentions you without blessing your name'. Then tragedy struck. Ammonio's letter is the last time Joanna is recorded as alive. By September 1511 she would be dead, struck down by a fatal disease. Overnight the family's happiness would turn cruelly to sorrow.

4

ENTER ALICE

IN LATE AUGUST or early September 1511 a crisis engulfed Margaret's family, observed by Ammonio from start to finish. Since he lived through it, it's a shame he was such a mean, selfish, uninformative witness, preening his feathers after landing a plum position as Henry VIII's Latin secretary. He did, however, send snippets of news to Erasmus, living by now in Cambridge as a lecturer, along with hogsheads of wine. Although himself convalescent, recovering from a debilitating viral infection, Erasmus replied, thanking Ammonio for the hogsheads and bitterly complaining about Cambridge, which he found to be a miserable place, always wet and cold, the academics boring and unfriendly and the wine sour.

To thwart the courier's prying eyes, Ammonio had written in Greek. When Erasmus replied, he said it would be wrong of him not to excuse Thomas More (not specifying what it was he'd said or done), distracted as he'd been by such appallingly grave concerns. Erasmus confessed himself amazed that Ammonio had lingered so long at the Barge, rather than fleeing from danger, as if he were a stork glued to its nest. The implication is that disease had struck, maybe the sweating sickness, more likely influenza, typhus or dysentery, or conceivably plague, which had revisited London that summer.

The 'sweat' or sweating sickness can be discounted. A viral pulmonary disease, variously known as the 'hot ills', the 'hot sickness', 'stopgallant' (because it stopped young gallants in their tracks), and the 'posting sweat', it had first reached London in 1485, when it claimed many thousands of lives. The symptoms were myalgia and headache, leading to abdominal pain, vomiting, increased headache and delirium, followed by cardiac palpitation, paralysis and death, all in less than twenty-four hours. Erasmus, ever the hypochondriac, genuinely believed he'd caught it, which is improbable: fatal in a fraction of the time he'd been ill, most acute in the cases of middle-aged men; if he'd really had it, his chances of survival were slim.

Moreover, although it had returned in 1506 and 1507, it disappeared again for a decade. Erasmus had probably suffered from a virulent strain of influenza; and as epidemic diseases spread most rapidly in urban settings, it is the probable cause of Joanna's death too. Typhus or dysentery cannot be discounted, but they most commonly attacked the poor, relying as they did on inadequate food and untreated water from street fountains and, still more dangerously, on rows of public latrines on the banks of the Thames or beside the city ditches. It isn't likely that Joanna had caught plague, since if 'buboes' or other cutaneous signs appeared in a sick person they had to be reported to the authorities, leading to the imposition of quarantine and to the household being shut up. Ammonio wouldn't have lingered for a moment if that had happened.

Joanna's funeral was at St Stephen's where she'd regularly attended mass and her children had been baptized, not at Roydon where she'd been born and her grandfather was buried. It must have been a bleak, harrowing occasion. The Church took death in its stride; Margaret and her siblings wouldn't have been excluded from the solemn dirge and requiem. When their mother's corpse lay cold on the bier, covered by a purple pall before the high altar, and afterwards when it was interred in its white linen shroud beneath the flagstones of the nave or chancel – their father hadn't even had sufficient warning to commission a makeshift tomb – the children would have watched, holding hands and weeping inconsolably as a deacon ritually purified it with incense, beginning each time with the head. And after the Creed in the requiem mass, when it was time for the offertory, Margaret, the eldest child, had to step forward and recite a prayer for her mother's everlasting joy and salvation.

Further emotional turmoil was to come. For their father, following in his own father's footsteps, remarried a wealthy widow within a month. His new wife was Alice, widow of John Middleton, a wool exporter and mercer born in Beverley in Yorkshire but living and working in Fenchurch Street in London, whom the Mores and several of their Hertfordshire friends knew as the daughter of an old mutual acquaintance.

John Middleton had fallen ill in October 1509, dying a few weeks later. He left his goods in London and Calais, his lands and rents in Hertfordshire and London, to Alice. His will shows that he desperately wanted a son, and that Alice was pregnant when he died. Despite careful provision for this unborn child, sadly Alice miscarried. This left two daughters: young Alice, nine when she lost her father, and her younger sister Helen, already sick when her father made his will. Money was placed in trust for their future dowries, and when Helen died, her share reverted to her sister. John Middleton assumed that his London property would be sold after his death, and that his widow would retire to Hertfordshire or remarry. At thirty-six, it was biologically possible that she might conceive again.

Our source for the wedding is unimpeachable: John Bouge was deputizing at St Stephen's, because a new rector, John Kite, was regularly absent from his post, moonlighting as a royal chaplain. Later a Carthusian monk, Bouge set down a vignette of Thomas More before he died:

> He was my parishioner at London. I christened him two goodly children [i.e. Cecily and her brother John]. I buried his first wife, and within a month after, he came to me on a Sunday at night late, and there he brought me a dispensation to be married the next Monday without any banns asking . . . This 'Master More' was my ghostly child; in his confession to be so pure, so clean, with great study, deliberation and devotion, I never heard many such; a gentleman of great learning, both in law, art and divinity . . . Item, a gentleman of great soberness and gravity . . . of little refection and marvellous diet. He was devout in his divine service, and what more, keep you this privily to yourself, he wore a great hair next his skin . . . it tamed his flesh till the blood was seen in his clothes.

Thomas talked Alice into agreeing to marry him as quickly as possible, then obtained a special licence to avoid the wedding banns being read in church for three consecutive Sundays. Bouge's opinion of his parishioner's asceticism isn't surprising, but this is the first time we learn that he wore a hair-shirt next to his skin. According to Bouge, he kept this from Alice for almost a year, and so successfully, she 'marvelled where his shirts were washed'. Finally learning the truth, she asked Bouge 'to counsel him to put off that hard and rough shirt of hair'.

While Joanna had been alive, Thomas hadn't worn a hair-shirt. Possibly he chose to mortify his flesh now, believing that Alice, three years older than he was, had already passed the menopause. The Church held that the main justification for sexual intercourse was the procreation of

children, but exceptions had always been allowed for older people on
grounds of mutual love and affection. A hair-shirt wasn't considered to
be a scourge to celibacy specifically, but a constantly chafing reminder of
the temptations of the devil in general, and of the inestimable sufferings
of Christ to save the souls of the faithful. Although unusual, Thomas
wasn't alone among pious laymen in scourging himself. 'Since,' he wrote
afterwards as Henry VIII's prisoner in the Tower, 'Our Master endured so
many kinds of painful shame, very proud beasts may we well think
ourselves if we disdain to do as Our Master did.'

Quite what Alice made of it all and of the family into which she'd
married is hard to fathom. The best way forward is to meet her.

Alice Middleton came from a distinguished lawyer family, granddaughter
on her mother's side of Sir Peter Ardern, a former Chief Baron of the
Exchequer and Justice of the Court of King's Bench, who owned Markhall
manor in Essex. Her mother, Elizabeth, a feisty character known for her
quick wits and sharp tongue, married Sir Richard Harper as the second
of her three husbands. He hailed from Epping, close to where Alice herself was born, but purchased the manor of Latton, adjacent to Markhall,
as his main home when she was ten. She loved this gently undulating
Essex countryside so much, she could hardly bear to leave it. That time
came all too soon since, when she was sixteen, her father arranged for
her to marry John Middleton.

She moved to London, where her own children were born. Her grandfather's estates were split up and sold, and when her father died, he
bequeathed Latton to his eldest son. In 1501 Sir John Shaa, a London
citizen and goldsmith, bought the Markhall estate and part of Latton,
dying two years later, when his son Edmund, still a minor, became the heir.

Alice's ambition in life was to recover her ancestral home. Since
Markhall was held by feudal tenure, Edmund's wardship* was auctioned
by Henry VII to the highest bidder. If John Middleton joined in the
auction, he was outbid. Consequently, Alice spent the next twenty years
tracking the fortunes of the estate. One of her ideas was to marry her
daughter, young Alice, to Edmund Shaa when he was twenty-one and

---

* Should a landowner by feudal tenure die while his heir was a minor, feudal law decreed
that the heir became a legal ward of the king. The wardship, highly profitable, would
generally be given to a courtier or else sold.

legally allowed to claim his inheritance. Edmund wasn't much older than young Alice, herself a good marriage prospect.

After marrying Thomas More, Alice Middleton hoped to draw him into her plans to recover Markhall, maybe calculating from the outset that she was acquiring a clever lawyer as well as a husband. And the traffic was two-way, because she taught him over the ensuing years that diffidence and otherworldliness didn't pay dividends in the marriage market, and that securing advantageous alliances for his own children would require an investment of time and effort similar to hers.

Alice wasn't just sassy and redoubtable, she was at ease with herself and the world, taking charge at Bucklersbury from the moment she arrived; her resourcefulness ran in the blood. If More's 'counting house' was to be used for his overflow piles of books, then the household ledgers and iron chest containing ready cash would be moved to her bedroom. She began as she meant to go on, evicting Ammonio and giving him a piece of her mind. Thomas, embarrassed by her candour, found him lodgings in Cheapside, receiving little thanks in return, for no sooner had he unpacked his belongings there than he was complaining biliously about the food, the dirt and the size of his room.

Erasmus, back in London from Cambridge on a visit, avoided Bucklersbury. He depicted Alice as loud, bossy and ignorant, more fishwife than lawyer's wife, calling her 'capable and vigilant' in Latin words that weren't meant to be complimentary. Ammonio called her 'aged, blunt and rude', and yet More 'full entirely loved her'. Lampooning her nose as 'the harpy's crooked beak', Ammonio conjures up a woman who talked incessantly and wasn't easily crossed. For her part, Alice thought Erasmus and his friends no better than scroungers and time-wasters. Unlike the long-suffering Joanna, she refused point-blank even to try to speak to them in Latin.

Thomas More, under Erasmus's spell, occasionally allowed himself to connive in his dearest friend's sport, quipping that in marrying Alice he'd chosen 'neither a pearl nor a girl'. This was less feline than it sounds, for the wit lay in the wordplay. He'd adapted a well-known quotation from St Augustine, unlike Erasmus, whose teasing of Alice could be vulpine, mocking her as a creature 'to be tamed before she could be trained'. Few husbands, continued Erasmus, could 'secure as much obedience from their wives by severity and giving them orders' as More did by his kindness and good humour. Thomas, 'by his wit and persuasion', could make her 'do anything'. Stupid as she was, he managed to teach her to play the lute, the virginals and the recorder. He assigned her 'a set piece of work every day'.

One can palpably detect Erasmus's pique at the fact that he and Ammonio were no longer allowed unlimited free food and wine at More's table. His image of Alice is his revenge.

Of course, Alice was entirely different to the younger, self-effacing, amiable, accommodating Joanna, and yet her worldly wisdom, forthright speech and practical efficiency were exactly what Thomas needed, for once his appointment to civic office had given him sufficient income, he'd begun to settle down all too comfortably. Alice gave him new challenges. Spirited, courageous and unsentimental, she had the will for him to succeed. A woman with Joan Marshall's head for business without the mean streak, she could be sensible and frugal, while still being generous and warm-hearted. According to one of his great-grandchildren, Thomas had once said of her, 'she was often penny-wise and pound-foolish, saving a candle's end and spoiling a velvet gown.' And he candidly confesses how she berated him early on in their marriage for failing to focus sufficiently on his career.

'What will you do,' she would ask him, 'that you list not to put forth yourself as other folk do? Will you sit still by the fire and make goslings in the ashes with a stick as children do? Would God I were a man, and look what I would do.'

'Why wife,' said Thomas, 'what would you do?'

'By God,' she said, 'go forward with the best of them, for, as my mother was wont to say . . . it is ever more better to rule than to be ruled.'

To which he couldn't resist replying, 'By my troth, wife, in this I dare you say truth, for I never found you willing to be ruled yet.'

Alice, it appears, gave as good as she got. Her ability to hold her own became legendary; Thomas liked to call her 'a stout master woman'. Despite her impatience with some of his friends, she squared the circle of his world. He had four children of his own, plus Margaret Giggs, to care for, and young Alice had joined the family as a stepdaughter. What Margaret and her siblings thought about their new stepmother, or the speed of her arrival, can scarcely be imagined, although she must have treated them gently and lovingly, since within a relatively brief space of time, according to the stories told afterwards by their own children, they were laughing and teasing her as if she were their natural mother.

Thomas found Alice's money especially useful. Joanna's dowry was spent, and Alice had inherited goods and cash from her late husband, supplemented by rents from property in Hitchin in Hertfordshire. It wasn't as much as John More had earned by remarrying, but it did provide Thomas with more than enough capital to renew and extend his lease at Bucklersbury.

When Margaret had still been with her wet-nurse and Erasmus had first come to stay, he and her father had amused one another by translating the work of Lucian of Samosata, a second-century Greek writer whose witty irony and biting satire were the closest thing the two friends could find to their own ideal of humour. Lucian wasn't simply funny, he was trenchant, pithy, caustic: the master of derision, the scourge of arrogance, folly and superstition. Like Aesop in his fables, he was fundamentally a moral author, puncturing pride and pretension as if pricking balloons; painting charlatans and impostors in their true colours; showing that the worst of the pretenders were priests and politicians. His *leitmotif* was that ordinary citizens were much better at spotting fraud and corruption in high places than the intelligentsia or ruling class, an idea appealing greatly to Thomas More, who always liked to think he retained the common touch and knew what people were thinking.

What most brought Thomas and Alice together was their shared love of comedy. Never could Margaret's father tell a tragic or a heroic story without making it appear faintly absurd. He could conjure up repartee and darts of irony in seconds, rarely suffering fools gladly, often wittiest when least amused, oblivious to the resentment his humour stirred in lesser men. As one of these, a Gray's Inn lawyer and chronicler, Edward Hall, complained:

> his wit was fine, and full of imaginations, by reason whereof he was too much given to mocking, which was to his gravity a great blemish . . . I cannot tell whether I should call him a foolish wise man, or a wise foolish man, for undoubtedly he, beside his learning, had a great wit, but it was so mingled with taunting and mocking, that it seemed to them that best knew him, that he thought nothing to be well spoken except he had ministered some mock in the communication.

Thomas treated laughter as a gift of God ideally suited for cutting sinners (including himself) down to size, revelling in wordplay and the joys of carnival, clowning and telling 'merry tales' as spontaneously as Chaucer did in the *Canterbury Tales*. He'd jest at every opportunity, dramatizing real-life or imaginary scenes and, when inventing his own characters, giving them lines to speak in the first person as in a play. 'A merry tale commeth never amiss to me,' he would gleefully say when relaxing with friends or family.

One of his favourites is about a poor man accused of slandering a priest. The man, he says, 'had found a priest over-familiar with his wife', and because he'd told everyone about the scandal, but couldn't prove it, the priest sued him in the bishop's court for defamation. The poor man's punishment was to stand up in church on Sunday morning during high mass and say before the congregation, 'Mouth, thou liest.' And so, when the moment came, 'he set his hands on his mouth and said, "Mouth, mouth, thou liest."' Except that, immediately afterwards, 'he set his hand upon both his eyes and said, "But eyes, eyes, by the mass ye lie not a whit!"'

Alice, it emerged, enjoyed repartee and banter as much as her husband, and could be just as lethal when turning the events of everyday life into a comedy. We have a record of several such scenes. On one occasion the pair had been invited to dinner by Antonio Bonvisi, a merchant banker from Lucca and one of Thomas's most intimate friends. He dealt in fine Florentine cloths and luxury goods, also importing jewels and tapestries for Henry VIII and his leading courtiers. He acted as a government banker, transmitting money in the form of letters of credit to English ambassadors abroad. A scholar and art connoisseur, he'd first entertained Thomas More around the time that Joan Marshall quarrelled with the Rastells and was famous for his wry, dry wit. Inviting an insufferably pretentious theologian, puffed up with pride, to his table, he proceeded to invent obscure biblical quotations, citing non-existent chapter and verse, to gull his guest into explaining them and so appear a fool. As a prisoner in the Tower, Thomas More would describe Bonvisi as 'of all friends most trusty and to me most dearly beloved . . . the apple of mine eye'. He'd so often dine or sup with him, he'd regularly fail to turn up for meals at home.

When, then, Alice one day accompanied her husband to Bonvisi's, she had barely sat down at the dinner-table before making her point. She roundly upbraided their host for detaining her husband at mealtimes.

'Forsooth Mistress,' replied Bonvisi, 'in my company nothing keepeth him but one. Serve you him with the same, and he will never be from you.'

Alice asked what this extraordinary dish might be.

'Forsooth Mistress,' Bonvisi explained, 'your husband loveth well to talk, and when he sitteth with me, I let him have all the words.'

'All the words?' she replied. 'Marry, that I am content he shall have all the words with good will as he hath ever had, but I speak them all myself!'

At moments like this, Thomas and Alice's relationship turned into a real-life equivalent of the Lucianic burlesque in which he was to revel until the moment that he faced the executioner's axe. When in full flight, Alice sounds just like one of the speakers debunking pride, cant and hypocrisy in Erasmus's *Praise of Folly*. She is the epitome of straightforward common sense.

Thomas himself told stories thinly based on her. One, clearly tongue-in-cheek, describes a husband's efforts to teach his wife the rudimentary principles of science. Ptolemy had argued in the second century that the spherical earth is at the centre of the universe and, lacking a scientific theory of gravity, that the lowest point is the centre of the earth towards which all objects appear to fall. As this was still the prevailing belief, the husband tries to explain how, if a hole is bored through the earth and a millstone thrown into it, the millstone will fall towards the centre of the earth and then stop. But his wife refuses to accept the argument, saying it defies logic. After bombarding him with interruptions, she asks her maid to go and fetch her spinning-wheel with its spindle and whorl,* demanding a practical experiment. She demonstrates how, if an enlarged version of the whorl is the world, and its central hole is the one into which the stone is thrown, the stone won't stop in the middle, but will emerge at the far side and will give any man standing there a blow on the head that will make him shriek for pain. We can safely assume that Thomas declined to cooperate by standing beneath the whorl to test her theory, and that Alice left the room in triumph.

Another story raises the vexed question of the couple's sleeping arrangements. Reflecting back on the events of his life from his cell in the Tower, Thomas remarks that many monks and nuns have been content to live out their lives in solitude. To have a door shut on us is no real punishment. The fear is entirely in the mind, 'enhanced of our own fantasy'. To clinch his point, he tells a tale of a woman who comes to visit a poor prisoner. She finds him living in a chamber that is 'meetly fair'. What shocks her is that the gaoler bolts the door of his cell at night. 'For

---

* I.e., a fly-wheel fixed on the spindle of a spinning-wheel to maintain or regulate the speed.

by my troth,' she says, 'if the door should be shut upon me, I would ween [think] it would stop up my breath.' On hearing her words, the prisoner laughs, because he knows very well that 'she used on the inside to shut every night full surely her own chamber to her, both door and windows too'. Hence 'what difference then as to the stopping of the breath, whether they were shut up within or without?'

Is there something significant here? If the woman is Alice (as several biographers have claimed), she speaks of 'her own chamber' rather than 'their' chamber. So does that mean that Thomas avoided sleeping with his second wife? It seems decidedly tenuous, not least because it was the norm then for married couples at the higher social level not to share a bedroom. They had separate rooms with a connecting door or passage, enabling access to each other without disturbing their privacy. Almost twenty years after marrying Alice, Thomas told a friend: 'I remember that you once wrote to me that the most pleasant sleep is in a bed without a wife.' Then he quipped: 'These are the words of husbands on the first nights after their wives have been sent away, for on the remaining nights desire comes creeping back and, unless the wife has left a "proxy" [i.e. a stand-in], it makes sleep unpleasant.' Elsewhere, he joked of wives and women that 'it isn't possible to live with even the best of them without any inconvenience at all'. He was paraphrasing a proverb, adding as an afterthought: 'This is what every man says, but still he marries. Yes, when his sixth wife dies, he marries a seventh.'

Such banter finds its comedy in ancient stereotypes and cannot be taken literally or used to draw too many conclusions. Margaret's father, we must conclude, loved her stepmother in his own way and she him. Within a year or two of his first wife's death, he'd decided to build a proper tomb for her with a memorial inscription he'd written himself. Except, by then, his plan was for Alice and Joanna to share a tomb with him when the time came, and the inscription, he decided, would honour all three. Alice must have been consulted, since she had to choose whether she would prefer to be buried beside him rather than beside John Middleton, whose tomb in the chancel of St Katherine Coleman's Church already had a space reserved for her. She chose to stay with Thomas, who was delighted. 'How happily we could have lived all three together if fate and religion permitted,' he exclaimed. 'Thus death will give us what life could not!'

Even when contemplating death, it seems, he couldn't resist a joke.

5

A GO-BETWEEN

A FTER THOMAS MORE MARRIED Alice, his career took off as never before and Margaret found him away from home for longer periods. She was six when the Mayor and Aldermen chose him as their preferred go-between to the royal Court after the declaration of war with France. Two years into his reign, the young Henry VIII began to overrule the older, duller statesmen among his councillors, openly proclaiming his ambition to win the throne of France, projecting himself as a warrior like Edward the Black Prince or Henry V, capturing vast spoils and performing knightly feats. Pope Julius II led the alliance or 'Holy League' that Henry joined alongside his father-in-law, King Ferdinand of Aragon, and the Holy Roman Emperor and titular ruler of Germany, Maximilian I. The pope's aim was to expel a French army of occupation from Italy. When the French had been forced to retreat, Henry and Ferdinand would be expected to invade France.

Thomas More's first task was to oversee the provision by the London bakers of the huge quantities of dry biscuit needed for Henry's navy. When war finally began, he was responsible for checking that the nightly watches were properly conducted in each of the wards or administrative districts of the city, tracking the movements of suspect foreigners, especially Frenchmen.

In 1512 Henry was abandoned, ignominiously, by his feckless father-in-law, who slipped off to annex Navarre. The following year, he decided to do things differently, personally leading a massive invasion of northern France. Brushing all objections aside, he picked his own supremo for military and diplomatic affairs: Thomas Wolsey, a butcher's son from Ipswich, an administrative wizard aged forty, who after a brilliant career at Oxford had used Church patronage to leap into power.

Ebullient, energetic and supremely ambitious, Wolsey was an instinctive, indefatigable politician who could master thousands of small details and retain them in his head. A workaholic, he always stayed cool and urbane. At the height of a crisis, as a gentleman-usher reported, he could work for twelve hours at a sitting, during which time he 'never rose once to piss, ne yet to eat any meat but continually wrote his letters with his own hands, having all that time his nightcap and kerchief on his head'.

With thousands of barrels of dry biscuit on board, Henry's fleet transported the English army to Calais – the last remnant of Henry V's continental possessions and still in English hands – where Henry and Wolsey landed on 30 June 1513. A month later, their main force besieged the nearby citadels of Thérouanne and Tournai. The French played cat and mouse until a skirmish with one of their cavalry units, accidentally intercepted at a distance, enabled Henry to claim a famous victory. He entered the towns in triumph with grand processions and choirs singing *Te Deum*, ignoring the otherwise unpalatable facts that Thérouanne had been flattened by artillery and Tournai had little strategic value. Given its astronomical expense, the war was pointless.

Margaret's father knew the truth, because his brother-in-law, John Rastell, had been at Tournai and would give the family the inside story. He'd joined a unit commanded by Sir Edward Belknap, Master of the Ordnance, was assigned to the artillery and, on returning home, supervised the unloading of the largest and most valuable cannon from eighteen ships at Tower Wharf, transferring them to store in the royal armoury.

More wrote a celebratory ode in praise of Henry's campaign, but on closer examination the piece is thoroughly ambiguous:

> Warlike Caesar vanquished you, seemingly invincible Tournai,
> Not without disaster to both sides.
> Henry, a mightier and better prince than Caesar, took you bloodlessly.
> He felt he'd gained honour by conquering you.
> You felt yourself it was just as useful to be captured.

The ode was entitled 'On the surrender of Tournai to Henry VIII, King of England'. The sting lay in the fact that in 57 BC the town, then called Nervia and occupied by the Nervii, the largest of the Belgic tribes of northern Gaul, had been conquered in a notoriously wasteful and bloody battle by Julius Caesar, leaving tens of thousands dead.

Henry followed war by diplomacy. After Pope Julius died, his successor, Leo X, saw himself as a peacemaker. Pope Leo sent a special nuncio to France and England, and Wolsey cooperated, realizing that the cost of another season's campaigning would force the crown seriously into debt and that a peace treaty, if suitably engineered to maximize Henry's honour, could be just as glorious, less risky and infinitely cheaper.

The papal 'orator', as the nuncio was styled, spent six months in France and the Low Countries before meeting Wolsey in March 1514. He was a Neapolitan: Gianpietro Carafa,* Bishop of Chieti, a remarkable man of thirty-seven. Single-minded, austere, with a hatred of heresy and unremittingly dedicated to the task of purging the Church of its abuses, he was a vocal and consistent upholder of the papal supremacy.

On 7 August a peace with France was agreed. Louis XII, a gouty dotard of fifty-three, was to marry Henry's eighteen-year-old younger sister, Mary, who accepted her fate with surprising composure after extracting a promise that she would be free to choose her next husband for herself. Wolsey, taking the credit for the treaty even though Carafa did most of the work, secured the archbishopric of York as his reward. He also gained the bishopric of Tournai, afterwards lobbying Leo for an appointment as a cardinal and plenipotentiary papal legate with powers above the Archbishop of Canterbury's. For this blatant bid to become the *de facto* head of the English Church, Wolsey would shortly obtain Henry's full support, but the pope wasn't to be hurried quite so fast.

In London Carafa encountered Erasmus, who, despite their differing emphases on the papal primacy, judged him to be a model bishop, saying that if the Church had been led by more men like this, he wouldn't have found it necessary to write the *Praise of Folly*. It was, however, Thomas More who was to spend more time with the nuncio than anyone save Wolsey himself. In his most sensitive and demanding assignment so far, he was asked by Wolsey to be Carafa's official interpreter and the King's Council's intermediary with the city in a *cause célèbre*.

The case had arisen in the Court of Star Chamber after the Duke of Suffolk, Henry's favourite jousting partner, seized a valuable cargo of

* Later Pope Paul IV.

alum at Southampton. An essential fixer of dyes for wool, silk and linen fabrics, also used by tanners, painters and apothecaries, alum was manufactured from alunite, imported in the Middle Ages from the Near East, but found in vast quantities at Tolfa, near Rome, in the middle of the fifteenth century. By 1500 there were four mines at Tolfa, all run by the papacy. The alum that the duke had confiscated, in excess of 4,000 barrels worth the princely sum of £2,655, belonged to Pope Leo, whose factor, Giovanni Cavalcanti, a Florentine merchant in London, was responsible for marketing it. Cavalcanti worked hand-in-glove with his compatriots, the Bardi and Frescobaldi families, using a company he'd set up with Pierfrancesco Bardi to supply Henry and Wolsey with luxury items.

In theory, there should have been no problem over the cargo: Henry had granted trading concessions to the Florentines in return for armour and munitions for his war effort. Cavalcanti and Bardi had a licence to defer paying customs duties for five years, on top of which Cavalcanti had become a naturalized Englishman. He had clients lined up for the shipment, and all would have gone smoothly but for Suffolk's opportunism.

Leo had demanded restitution and compensation, after which the Mayor and Aldermen had entered the fray. They'd been targeting Bardi and Cavalcanti for non-payment of civic tolls for over a year, and had realized that Cavalcanti intended to sell on the alum, if he recovered it, to the Bardi and to Pietro Corsi, another Florentine merchant. In the city's eyes, such transactions were illegal: the city had long disputed the right of overseas merchants to sell their imports directly to other foreigners, even when trading wholesale.

Cavalcanti had sued Suffolk in the Star Chamber, the most important (and the most political) of all the royal courts at Westminster. Archbishop Warham presided, and Thomas More found himself in the awkward position of interpreting in the morning for Carafa, who spoke no English, then returning to the city in the evening to explain to the Mayor and Aldermen why the case wasn't going their way. He had to walk a tightrope. Henry and Wolsey wanted to satisfy the pope; the duke to keep the alum; the city to vindicate its right to exact tolls and regulate foreign trade.

So challenging and complex was this important case, More hired John Batmanson, a Doctor of Laws of Seville and expert in international and mercantile law, to advise him, enabling him to concentrate on translating for Carafa, except that a fortnight before Christmas he ended up proposing an out-of-court settlement, and one so fair and rational that Warham recommended it on the spot. Thomas then began the delicate task of securing a certificate from the city permitting the resale of the alum, otherwise Pope Leo would be unable to recoup his losses.

On 27 March 1515 the certificate was sealed and the Anglo-papal *entente* restored. Leo was delighted, and so were Henry and Wolsey. So keen had the king and his chief minister been to please the pope, they'd already marked out Thomas as a high-flyer.

So it was that six weeks later, Margaret's father was granted unpaid leave from his undersheriff's post, before kissing his family goodbye and mounting his horse to ride via Canterbury to Dover. It was no ordinary excursion, for he was travelling abroad, for the first time since his visits to Paris and Louvain, on a royal embassy to Bruges. Louis XII had died in January, to be succeeded by Francis I. Three years younger than Henry, the new French king was also six feet tall and, if anything, more flamboyant. First and foremost a man of action, Francis lusted after women and fame; he and Henry would be rivals in conspicuous consumption for the rest of their lives. If Francis built magnificent new palaces, so did Henry. If Francis had the finest musicians, poets or architects at his Court, so must Henry. They fenced over tapestries and artistic patronage, even if Henry could never cap Francis in attracting Leonardo da Vinci to stay or in keeping the *Mona Lisa* in his bathroom. To outflank Henry, Francis set about wooing his most powerful neighbours, driven by an obsession that lasted all his life: he meant to recover the Italian lands from which his predecessor had been expelled, especially the Duchy of Milan. He meant to recover Tournai and Thérouanne too; the peace was on borrowed time.

Francis first made overtures to Queen Katherine's nephew, Charles of Castile, then no more than fifteen. Charles had inherited the Low Countries, Franche-Comté, Luxembourg and Brabant, and was heir to the thrones of Aragon, Castile and Naples. Skilfully portrayed by his spin doctors as moral and upright, he would grow into a ruler as aggressive and acquisitive as Francis with dreams of a global empire. Francis would soon have to fight him, but for the moment wished only to neutralize him. He therefore began cordially, persuading Charles to put obstacles in the way of English cloth exports, which is why Henry

and Wolsey now sent a delegation, including Thomas More, to talks
at Bruges.

Cuthbert Tunstall, its leader and one of three career diplomats chosen
for the task, was charged with securing a fresh amity with Charles, but the
diplomats needed commercial specialists from London on their team,
and More was appointed in conjunction with John Clifford, the Governor of the Merchant Adventurers. When the negotiations began, Charles's
delegates procrastinated, wrangling over procedure for several months.
The career diplomats were then called separately to Brussels; More and
Clifford were left loitering in Bruges. Since Wolsey had sent insufficient
funds, Thomas was forced to join in an appeal for cash, for 'there be not
[enough] remaining past three or four days'. It seems he was hard-
pressed, for as Tunstall explained, 'Master More, at this time as being at
a low ebb, desires by Your Grace to be set on float again.'

And yet, Thomas was in his element, enjoying himself more than ever
before at work. He was reunited with Erasmus, then sauntering through
the Low Countries on his way from London to Basel in Switzerland, who
gave him letters of introduction to a whole new circle of friends. He was
able to overcome the travel restrictions on English visitors by using his
diplomatic passport, and was invigorated by the places he visited, chiefly
Antwerp.

Like many a diplomat before and since, left alone in his lodgings to
amuse himself in whatever way he chose and with time on his hands,
Thomas More decided to turn his mind to something new and exciting.
The result would be a work of singular imagination and disruptive
energy, his literary masterpiece, *Utopia*.

Written in Latin and so addressed to the ruling élite, but with its heady
cocktail of ideas for the redress of economic ills and the transformation
of society on principles of justice and equality for all,* the book started
life as a series of conversations in Antwerp with Peter Gillis, the city's
chief clerk of the court of justice, who performed duties similar to More's
as undersheriff. Just eight years younger, Gillis was a fluent linguist,
had already translated Aesop's *Fables* and would edit the works of Lucian
and the letters of Erasmus. As a memento of that lazy summer, Gillis
and Erasmus would afterwards commission a diptych containing their

* See chapters 10, 13.

portraits from the foremost Antwerp painter, Quentin Massys, sending it to Thomas as a gift. Only when talking and joking with his children would he experience such joy in his life as when chatting away at Gillis's house and exchanging letters about it with Erasmus afterwards. He felt that he'd found a soul-mate second only to Erasmus, and of a type that his wife Alice, for all her strengths, could never be. We can glimpse something of Gillis's character, as he is the author of a series of witty caricatures of worldliness and folly: a mixture of sketches, doodles and aphorisms from classical literature still preserved in the archives in Antwerp. One of these, a quotation from Terence, a Roman comic playwright, exactly captures More's mood as the ideas for *Utopia* flooded into his head: 'With age we rightly attain wisdom enough for everything. Old age brings one vice alone to us, that we're too greedy than we ought to be for property.'

Thomas himself tells the story. After Tunstall and his fellow diplomats had left for Brussels, he made his way to Antwerp, where Gillis proved to be so witty and congenial he decided to stay for a while. One day after mass at the Cathedral of Notre Dame, a short distance from the River Scheldt close to where the English merchants had their warehouses, he emerged into the sunlight to find the market-square buzzing with life, for Antwerp had become a hub of world trade and finance, and the gateway to the Portuguese and Spanish territories in Africa, the East Indies and the New World. The result was a vibrant, cosmopolitan, materialist, racially diverse metropolis, thriving on rumours and travellers' tales about ships and storms and fortunes to be made in strange lands beyond Cathay. Antwerp was teeming with stories, true or imaginary, of the secrets of navigation or geography known only to the Portuguese, fuelling a thirst for information readily satisfied by writers, printers, map-makers and booksellers alike.

More wrote *Utopia* in two stages. The first, lasting perhaps as little as six weeks, was when his and Gillis's conversations gave the pair an idea for a traveller's tale to be told by a fictional Portuguese sailor. They called him 'Raphael Hythloday', an ingenious creation to show he would be taking readers on a voyage of discovery into the world of the mind. Like 'Folly' in Erasmus's *Praise of Folly*, Hythloday will seemingly talk arrant, dangerous 'nonsense': his surname in Greek means 'well-learned in trifles'. His journey is to an island called Utopia that is both 'no-place' (*Outopia*) and 'happy place' (*Eutopia*). Except there's method in his madness: as with Aesop's *Fables*, there's something morally profound to ponder, something that may change our lives for ever, when the laughter fades.

The game began when More claimed to have stumbled into this elderly, sunburnt man in the square as he'd left Notre Dame that day after mass. With his long beard and cloak, it isn't difficult to guess he is a ship's captain. He was talking to Gillis, who introduces him, and as *Utopia*'s principal narrator, he describes the customs and social system of the Utopians, playing the role of an 'ancient mariner' figure whom Thomas uses to draw his readers towards that far-distant republic: the New World of the mind that he now had sufficient leisure to develop and explore.

Hythloday isn't the only character with a speaking part in *Utopia*. As More incorporates his conversations with Gillis into his first draft, they too cease to be real-life people, and turn into actors playing themselves on the stage. We're led into the interior world of the book, because More prompts Gillis to name Hythloday's classical equivalents: 'His sailing hasn't been like that of Palinurus but more that of Ulysses, or really like Plato.' Palinurus, the only professional sailor of the three, had been Aeneas's pilot, overcome by Somnus, the god of sleep, and falling overboard. Ulysses, who in Homer's *Odyssey* had led the Greeks in the Trojan War, was admittedly an experienced traveller, but Gillis includes him as someone who can read other people's minds. Plato, always Thomas More's favourite philosopher, had travelled to Italy and Egypt, but that isn't why he's mentioned. As author of the *Republic* or description of an 'ideal' commonwealth, Plato, like Hythloday, is on a quest for the perfect society.

But More had barely finished his first draft when he was recalled to Bruges, leaving no more time for writing that summer. Back in the world of diplomacy, a fresh round of delays and excuses wore him down, until, finally missing Alice and the children too much and without either Gillis or Erasmus to talk to, he asked Clifford if he would mind continuing the commercial side of the negotiations on his own. He'd been away for almost six months and was badly short of cash again. As he complained (scarcely tongue-in-cheek), 'I have to support two households, one at home and the other abroad . . . I failed completely (although I am, as you know, a kind husband, an indulgent father, and a reasonable master) to persuade my family for my sake to go without eating.' He petitioned Wolsey for an honourable discharge, leaving as soon as it was granted.

On 22 December Henry dismissed Warham as Lord Chancellor in favour of Wolsey, whom Pope Leo had appointed a cardinal. Looking resplendent in his scarlet robes and hat as he walked in procession behind his metropolitan cross or rode his mule, Wolsey had got where he wanted to be. Sworn into office by Henry on Christmas Eve, he promised to 'do right to all manner [of] people, poor and rich, after the laws of this realm'. For this, he won golden accolades, not least from Thomas More, who made known his intention of dedicating *Utopia* to the minister when he'd revised it. On his return, More found himself increasingly needing to visit or report to Wolsey in his capacity as an intermediary between the city and the King's Council, and from what he'd seen so far, he judged Wolsey to be a model statesman and social reformer on a grand scale.

Margaret, delighted to have her father safely back after so long, would have helped her stepmother to nurse him in the spring of 1516 when he suffered a severe bout of sickness. But as soon as he'd recovered sufficiently, he disappeared once more into his study to resume *Utopia*. Now his writing took on a different, more personal, more topical dimension; his career was at a crossroads, because Henry had offered him a Court appointment: 'one,' said Thomas, 'that was very much not to be despised, whether one considers the honour or the profit of it.' Exactly what Henry had proposed isn't made explicit, but from Thomas's own account – his self-effacement is typical of him in such circumstances – it was an invitation to join the King's Council with a salary of £100.

'Hitherto I have refused it,' he reassured a worried Erasmus, 'and it looks to me as though I should maintain my refusal. If I accepted it, I should have either to abandon my present position in London, which I prefer even to something better, or (what is not at all to my liking) to incur some unpopularity among my fellow-citizens.' Gossip from Ammonio, on the other hand, suggests the offer was alluring: '[More] haunts those smoky palace fires in my company. None bids my Lord of York [Wolsey] good morrow earlier than he.' Thomas, it would appear, was becoming seriously attracted to a career in royal service, but needed more time to consider what exactly it would mean for his family.

At the very least, he'd been noticed. And in that he wasn't alone: several of his circle were already moving in the same direction. His fellow undersheriff, Thomas Neville, had been elected Speaker of the House of Commons. Knighted on the spot, he'd promptly resigned his civic office for a place at Court, where his main task was to act as Wolsey's agent for the vetting of grants. Ammonio, in post as Henry's Latin secretary, was in regular contact with Wolsey, although still lodging in Cheapside. William Blount, Lord Mountjoy, who'd first introduced Thomas More to Erasmus, had been given the post of lord chamberlain to Queen Katherine. John Rastell continued to serve Sir Edward Belknap. And last, but far from least, Wolsey had coopted Thomas's father, still awaiting his promotion to the judiciary but now at the front of the queue, onto the King's Council as a legal assessor. In fact, at his very first meeting in May 1516, John More had heard Wolsey briefing Henry and his councillors at length, and in graphic detail, about some of his more ambitious proposals for streamlining the legal system to make it more 'equal' and 'equitable' to litigants whether rich or poor, a Utopian scheme that surely must have struck a resounding chord.

By writing *Utopia*, which he published later in the year, Thomas More showed that he wanted to reshape society and his world. His work as an undersheriff and as a civic intermediary with Wolsey and the King's Council had set him firmly on this path. Now he had the chance to move beyond anything he'd so far imagined. *Utopia* was no longer just a game to be played as he laughed and joked with Gillis in the Antwerp sun, it had become deadly serious. No longer a reflection of his innermost thoughts, it was turning into his ideal job description. As he revised and completed the book after returning from Bruges, he would begin to set out in depth the rudiments of his mature philosophy. He had been marked out for promotion by Henry and Wolsey, already invited to Court. His father and many of his friends had taken a similar route. But on the embassy to Bruges he'd experienced what Henry's diplomats found happened all too often, and he had been forced to kick his heels for months apart from his family. He'd missed Margaret's birthday, and now he found himself pulled in two contradictory directions, towards a career at Court and away from it. And so still he hesitated.

6

AN ABSENT FATHER

IN MARCH 1518, AFTER brooding over Henry's offer for two whole years, Margaret's father finally succumbed, accepting a position as a royal councillor. After kissing Alice and the children goodbye again, he rode twenty-six miles from London to Maidenhead in Berkshire, resting overnight before continuing thirteen more miles to Reading Abbey. Henry and a few close courtiers were lodging there on their way to Abingdon and Woodstock, near Oxford, because the 'sweat' had returned with terrifying fury after a ten-year respite. Thousands had died, among them Ammonio who, despite boasting of his rigorous precautions, went to bed intending to ride out with a friend next day and was carried off eight hours later. To Henry's great fear and consternation, the pages sleeping on pallets outside his bedchamber were struck down. He fled to the countryside, determined to spend the spring and summer as far out of danger as possible. Even Wolsey was forbidden to visit, since he'd caught the deadly virus, although he was among the few who lived to tell the tale. The Mores were happily spared, but for once Margaret's father wasn't joking when he told Erasmus, 'I can assure you: one is safer on the battlefield than in the city.'

Arriving at Reading, Thomas found Richard Pace, an extraordinary linguist who'd learned Hebrew in a month, waiting to escort him to the king. A diplomat specializing in the affairs of Venice and Rome, Pace had been Henry's secretary for two years, dealing with his correspondence, reading out the letters received from an absent Wolsey or foreign ambassadors and heads of state, and writing out the replies to Henry's dictation before submitting them for signature.

Henry gave More his 'charge', which (as Pace reported to Wolsey) chiefly concerned 'forfeitures'. Since Thomas was shortly to be appointed to a special court for 'poor men's causes', this possibly concerned an aspect of court fines. It was as an arbitrator and judge in Wolsey's new 'poor men's' court that Thomas would renew his acquaintance with his old teacher at Lincoln's Inn and a highly successful barrister, John Roper, who also held the post of Chief Clerk of the Court of King's Bench, a sinecure affording its incumbent the second highest income after the Chief Justice. John Roper, who'd gone on to marry Jane Fyneux, the Chief Justice's daughter, had large estates in Kent. His eldest son, William, a young law student, about twenty, was just beginning his own career at Lincoln's Inn.

When, a decade later, Thomas More would nostalgically and vividly reflect on these events, he said that Henry had told him to 'first look unto God and after God unto him', saying this at the very moment when he swore his councillor's oath. Henry was obviously aware of More's doubts about the murky world of politics. Maybe asking him not to take his official responsibilities so seriously as to put them above his prayers was his idea of a joke, for the king loved to banter as long as no one took him too literally.

He needn't have worried, for he and More were soon getting on famously, perhaps a little surprising, for whereas Henry, at twenty-seven, was an extrovert, a sportsman and a hedonist in the prime of youth, Thomas, at forty, was more a thinker and connoisseur. But for all his bravado, Henry knew that a reputation for culture could be used to build up his authority, which is where his newest recruit came in. A keen amateur theologian and mathematician and an ardent astronomer, he and More pored late into the night over the diagrams in an edition of Euclid's *Geometry*. Henry would burst unannounced into More's room in the middle of the night, dragging him onto the roofs of royal palaces to gaze at the stars. Surrounded for the most part by self-serving flatterers all of whom had their price, Henry adored having a genuine intellectual at his command. Their relationship, although unequal, blossomed: apart from Wolsey, More was the only councillor with whom the king routinely linked arms as they strolled together round galleries or gardens. And unlike Wolsey, More never took royal favour for granted.

Thomas joked how, when he couldn't get leave for as little as two consecutive days a month to see his children, he'd pretend to be stupid to induce Henry to part with him for a while. But, for most of the time, he was an absent father. Like Erasmus, he had to learn to write with a 'coal' (or charcoal stick) on horseback, even in the pouring rain. A cache of these documents has miraculously survived: from them we gain snapshots of how Margaret and her siblings were growing up and what they were doing.

Up until entering royal service, Margaret's father, whenever he could, had taught all his children himself. When he was too busy, a page in his household, John Clement, deputized for him. A precocious teenager arriving around 1514 and occupying a prominent place in the family circle for the rest of his life, Clement had been a star pupil of St Paul's School in London. His parentage and age are elusive, but as More's page he'd accompanied him on the embassy to Bruges, where he is mentioned as a silent witness to More's conversations with Peter Gillis and the fictional Hythloday. On returning to London, he'd set himself up as a part-time tutor, teaching from a bound collection of texts including a brief history of England, a set of elementary Greek exercises, and a copy of Utopia. About this time, he'd started giving Greek and Latin lessons to Margaret More and Margaret Giggs, and it's likely they too – for at eleven both were old enough – were dipping into Utopia even if they couldn't manage to read all of it yet.

When Thomas More had left Bucklersbury to join Henry and his entourage in the country, no place could be found for Clement, but Wolsey was willing to employ him, sending him to Oxford as a lecturer. There, amid the dreaming spires, he caught the vogue for the newly printed writings of the second-century Greek physician, Galen of Pergamum, becoming so captivated it wasn't long before he resigned his lectureship to travel to Padua and Siena to train as a physician himself.

Now More decided to employ William Gonnell as a full-time tutor for his children, already aware that Gonnell was an inspirational, experienced teacher whom he could depend on to propagate his vision of learning. Hailing from Landbeach, five miles north-east of Cambridge, he'd been carefully vetted by Erasmus, who'd first encountered him while lecturing at the university, staying with his family at Landbeach during an outbreak of plague and stabling his horse there. In a rare compliment, Erasmus described Gonnell as 'not so much a friend as half of my own soul'.

Gonnell arrived in May 1518, when the two Margarets were twelve, Elizabeth was eleven, Cecily ten, and John eight. Young Alice Middleton, their stepsister, was already eighteen and had left home. She'd been betrothed to Thomas Elryngton, a cousin of Thomas More's first wife, on her sixteenth birthday and was married seven or eight months later, for her mother took a measured, unsentimental approach to match-making. Once she'd enmeshed her fish, she was happy to string out the negotiations. Elryngton was one of the most eligible bachelors in London with three large houses and over 2,000 acres of prime farmland in five counties, yet she manoeuvred him into accepting her terms.

Although More's second wife had hoped to marry her only surviving daughter to Edmund Shaa in order to recover her ancestral home at Markhall in Essex, she'd been frustrated. When Edmund had finally come of age, he'd upset everyone by marrying for love. Undeterred, young Alice's mother kept Edmund on her list, just in case his young wife succumbed to plague or the 'sweat'. One of the candidates she plainly had in mind for him was Margaret More. Among the chattier news that Thomas would receive at Court in letters from his children was a bulletin from Margaret on Shaa's state of health. It seems he'd fallen ill, but then recovered. The intriguing point is that she'd been expected to interest herself in Shaa's affairs in the first place.

Thomas's aspirations for his children clearly emerge from his letters to Gonnell and the family. Exceptionally for his era, he wanted his daughters to be educated as thoroughly as his son. He was chiefly influenced by the ideas of Plato and the Florentine theorist Pico della Mirandola, whose biography he'd already abridged and translated. Plato's contention in the *Republic* is that women ought to be as well educated as men: 'They are quite capable of it, and their natures are closely related to those of the men.' For his part, Pico agrees that men and women have exactly the same talent, and both, potentially, can be full citizens.

Despite his own professional training as a lawyer at Lincoln's Inn, Margaret's father was convinced by the time he began *Utopia* that a liberal arts curriculum involving languages, history and philosophy was better suited to the creation of a good society than a vocational one based on law. He believed it met the needs of girls and boys alike: the main difference between what he asks Gonnell to prescribe for his daughters and for his son is that young John was to study rhetoric (or oratory) in addition to his other subjects, mastering the art of 'competitive audition' or public speaking. Unlike the girls, he was to learn to improvise speeches in front of the assembled family. Boys alone were expected to acquire these skills, ready to take their place as leaders in a patriarchal society.

Whereas eloquence of speech in a man was considered to represent authority, dignity and urbanity, in a woman it was judged a sign of impudence, guile and moral laxity, even of sexual promiscuity.

Besides reading widely beginning with the Bible and the early Fathers of the Christian Church such as St Augustine and St Jerome, Thomas More wanted his children to practise Latin translation daily, try their hand at poetry, and prepare 'themes' or short essays (often in Latin) on subjects set by Gonnell. First translating from Latin into English, they were to retranslate their exercises back into Latin without a crib to improve their fluency. Devotional or scriptural 'themes' were thought most suitable at first for the girls, who were also expected to learn music and embroidery.

Their father insisted that all his children practise writing letters, and many of their 'themes' were, in reality, to be structured in an epistolary form, as that had long been thought the easiest way for young students to learn how to express their own ideas. It scarcely mattered that the children would often sit down with Gonnell around a table writing 'letters' to each other about topics, or events, that they already knew about, such as what each of them had been reading, what they'd heard in church, what pets they had, or what games they'd played indoors when it was raining, for the aim was to learn to write in a clear, fluent, elegant, intimate style about the simplest everyday topics, making the 'letters' interesting to read for their own sake.

How Margaret and her siblings must have longed for their father to return to carry on teaching them himself, but it was not to be. To help compensate, Gonnell was to explain a subtler, deeper dimension to 'letters'. According to the classical theory of 'letter'-writing as rediscovered by Erasmus, itself a project he'd worked on when he'd first stayed at Bucklersbury, a 'letter' is nothing more than 'a mutual conversation between absent friends', one that brings them to life and makes them speak as if present in the room, able to convey their innermost thoughts and feelings. 'Letters' in this genre, he says, 'should be neither unpolished, rough, or artificial, nor confined to a single topic, nor tediously long'. They should 'favour simplicity, frankness, humour and wit'. A unique and cherished way of reuniting friends and family members whom fate has parted, they are the means to convey love and emotion, spoken from the heart. 'Their character', concludes Erasmus, ought to be 'as if you were whispering in a corner with a dear friend, not shouting in the theatre . . . for we commit many things to letters, which it would be shameful to express openly in public'.

Thomas More had set the tone within days of leaving Reading ahead of the royal baggage train for Oxfordshire, writing to Margaret and her sisters:

> I cannot adequately express, my delightful daughters, how greatly pleased I am by your charming letters and no less by the fact, as I notice . . . you yet abandon none of your habit either of dialectic exercises or writing 'themes' or composing verse. This fully convinces me that you love me as you ought, since I observe you feel so much concern in my absence that you practise zealously what you know gives me pleasure when I am with you. When I return I shall make you realize that disposition toward me is as profitable to yourselves as I realize it is pleasurable to me. For believe me truly there is nothing which refreshes me so much in the midst of all this bothersome business as reading what comes from you.

Shortly afterwards, he writes to Margaret alone: 'I was delighted to receive your letter, my dearest Margaret . . . Later letters will be even more delightful if they have told me of the studies you and your brother are engaged in, of your daily reading, your pleasant discussions, your essays, of the swift passage of the days made joyous by literary pursuits.' Alas, while we have copies of a dozen or so of his own letters around this time, the first of Margaret's that has survived would be written ten years later, even though we can guess from her father's to her that she wrote regularly, often every day. 'Now I expect from each of you,' he would instruct all his children, 'a letter almost every day. I will not admit excuses . . . such as want of time, sudden departure of the letter carrier, or want of something to write about. No one hinders you from writing, but, on the contrary, all are urging you to do it.'

Gonnell was then asked to set more complex scriptural and patristic passages for the children to study, followed by extracts from Livy's *History of Rome*, a work considered to be a treasure-trove of good phrase and example. Here the technique was one of imitation: both Thomas More and Erasmus believed that, 'since a great part of art consists of imitation, we must acquire a store of vocabulary, a diversity of rhetorical figures, and skill in the disposition of material from authors worth reading.'

The copy-texts chosen would increase in difficulty as the students improved. Thus for Margaret and Elizabeth, 'who are more mature than John and Cecily', their father recommends Sallust, another Roman historian, but whose focus is less on facts than on style, his work enlivened by invented speeches, letters, digressions and character studies.

The elder children had already learned to write in ink before Gonnell arrived, but he would teach the younger ones how to use a quill and shape their letters. Made from the feathers of geese or ravens cut away at the tip with a penknife to make a nib, quills had to be held gingerly so as not to let them blot or scratch the paper. Beginners would be taught how to grip the pen gently while letting their hands glide easily across the paper, how to keep a straight line, how to size the letters in proportion to each other, and how to space letters and words evenly. Gonnell would show his pupils how to rule almost invisible straight lines on a blank sheet of paper with a sharp, dry point, before writing in an italic script, the style most commonly taught in grammar schools and universities. Smooth, graceful and fluid, it was the simplest handwriting to learn. Three surviving sheets by Margaret show how brilliantly she had mastered it. Her confident literals sweep along perfectly spaced lines: tall, vaulted consonants interspersed with soft, cursive vowels to create the impression of a poised, sophisticated, intelligent young woman who found the complexities of Latin syntax as elementary as her ABC.

Over the next three years, Thomas would identify talents in her that he felt could one day rival his own. She became his favourite child, this in spite of his sincere and strenuous efforts to treat all his children equally. He called her 'Meg' or 'my beloved daughter', waiting ever more eagerly and impatiently for her letters to arrive with the courier. Unable to escape the mountain of legal cases that Wolsey delegated to him, his hopes of corresponding daily with each of his children quickly went by the board and he came to rely on his eldest daughter for most of his information about the family.

'I beg you, Margaret,' he writes, 'tell me about the progress you are all making in your studies. For I assure you that, rather than allow my children to be idle and slothful, I would make a sacrifice of wealth, and bid adieu to other cares and business to attend to my children and my family, amongst whom none is more dear to me than yourself, my beloved daughter.' When once she asked him for money, her doting father couldn't deny her, pouring out his love: 'You are too bashful and timid in your request . . . As it is, I send only what you have asked, but would have added more, except that as I am eager to give, so I like to be asked and coaxed by my daughter, especially by you, whom virtue and learning have made so dear to my heart.'

Not everything always went as smoothly. A brief clash of wills exposes the cultural confusion underlying Thomas More's beliefs about education. A year or so after Gonnell's arrival, Margaret had progressed so remarkably, she or her tutor must have said something to the effect that she might herself eventually hope to publish a book. On informing her father, Gonnell triggered a reply rare for its archness, perilously close to a rebuke. Thomas made himself crystal clear: Margaret (as Gonnell had himself reported) possessed 'a lofty and exalted character of mind'. On no account should it be 'debased' by pandering to 'what is vain and low'. Thomas spelt out firmly what he meant by this. Anyone who truly valued learning, and a woman in particular, should know that 'to lay herself out for renown' in this way 'is the sign of someone who is not only arrogant, but ridiculous and miserable'. Men often succumbed out of human frailty, but women should know better. Their place was to show 'appropriate modesty', not least 'since erudition in women is a new thing and a reproach to the sloth of men'. If a woman strove to become a published author, especially in her own lifetime, it could bring the whole ideal of women's education crashing down.

Margaret, her father concludes, mustn't be permitted to debase her talents, but encouraged to 'rise to virtue and true goods'. He wants the best for all his children: Gonnell must continually warn them 'to avoid (as it were) the precipices of pride and vainglory, and to walk in the pleasant meadows of modesty'. In place of 'gaudy trappings', or 'what they erroneously admire in others', such as literary fame, they must substitute moral virtue. Only by avoiding pride will they 'receive from God the reward of an innocent life, and in the assured expectation of it will view death without dread'. 'These,' More says, 'I consider the real and genuine fruits of learning, and though I admit that all literary men do not possess them, I would maintain that those who give themselves to study with such intent will easily attain their end and become perfect.'

In other words, while it was acceptable under the right conditions for men to seek recognition for their work, women must never do so. 'Though I prefer learning joined with virtue to all the treasure of kings,' he concludes, 'yet renown for learning, if you take away moral probity, brings nothing else but notorious and noteworthy infamy, especially in a woman.'

Although Thomas drew his inspiration from the models of Plato and Pico, doing everything he could to give his children the best possible education, he conformed intransigently to the social convention of his time that it was morally disreputable for a woman to seek recognition as a writer. Astonishing as it is to hear this from the author of *Utopia*, it remains an undeniable fact. As long as Margaret remained one of Gonnell's pupils, we hear no more about her literary ambition, but whether she had been convinced by her father's arguments and whether she would always abide by his opinion remains to be seen.

COMING OF AGE

THE SPRING OF 1521, unusually warm, was marred by an outbreak of bubonic plague lasting until the first winter frost. Two of its victims were Margaret's maternal grandfather and paternal step-grandmother. John More's third wife was carried off first, but scarcely had she been laid to rest when this avuncular paterfamilias, whose florid red cheeks radiated an idea of indestructible health, was proposing to his final spouse, Alice, widow of John Clerk, lately a member of the Grocers' Company. A witty, pleasant woman rather than a wealthy one, Alice instantly took to Margaret and the children. Herself over sixty and marrying for the third time, Alice made Milk Street and Gobions happier places than they'd been for many years. Their father quipped that of all his stepmothers, he'd 'never seen a better'.

Then John Colt of Netherhall, on a visit to London, was struck down. After some discussion of where the funeral should be held, his body was taken back to Roydon on a cart. He left a young widow, Marie, his second wife, who had borne him three sons and three daughters. Although the Mores and Colts had enjoyed less frequent contact over the years, the families had kept in touch. In his will, John Colt still spoke admiringly of his first son-in-law, bequeathing him his finest horse and an annuity to pay for the education of his own youngest son, Thomas, who was to board with Margaret and the other children at Bucklersbury until he was twenty, following the same course of study.

Young Thomas Colt's arrival gives a glimpse of what Margaret's father liked to call his 'school' or 'academy'. Also taking lessons there with Gonnell were her cousins, William Rastell and Frances Staverton. William's elder brother, John, chose not to attend, starting work as an apprentice to a mercer and churchwarden of St Stephen's, perhaps after his uncle had stood surety for his good character.

More's fancy was tickled by the very idea of his 'school'. Busier than ever before in the world of politics and the royal Court, he started sending letters home with the salutation: 'Thomas More to his whole school, greeting!' How convenient, he chortled good-humouredly, 'to save both time and paper, which would otherwise have been wasted in listing the names of each one of you'. Away for months at a time, standing in constantly as Henry's secretary after Wolsey began sending Richard Pace abroad more frequently, Thomas hired another tutor to help Gonnell cope with the extra students.

Hearing that Margaret was fascinated by geography and astronomy, Peter Gillis had recommended a brilliant Bavarian, Nicholas Kratzer, to Erasmus, who sent him to London. A wizard with astrolabes and sundials manufactured to his own designs and perhaps mechanical clocks too, Kratzer rose within two years to become Henry's royal astronomer and 'deviser of horologes'. On first reaching London, he made contact with More, who engaged him initially for a month, but he caused such a flurry of excitement that the children insisted on his return. Their father agreed, and soon the younger children were pestering their stepmother for extensions to their bedtimes so that they could go out into the garden to scour the night sky in search of the new moon, the pole star or dog star, while poring with delight during the day over the astronomical instruments that their resourceful tutor carried in his luggage.

Kratzer taught mathematics too. Some of the puzzles he set for Margaret and Margaret Giggs, her adopted sister, were to reappear in a textbook dedicated to her father by its author Cuthbert Tunstall, his colleague from his mission to Bruges. One, a familiar mathematician's conundrum, concerns four stopcocks or faucets connected to the pipes of a cistern. If, when the largest is opened, the cistern takes six hours to empty, eight hours using the second, nine with the third, and twelve with the fourth, how long does it take if all four are opened at once? The student knows the total volume of water, but has to calculate the differential rates of flow along the pipes. Another exercise is the case of four men building a house. If one man finishes in a year, the second in two, the third in three, and so on, how long will it take if everyone works together? The calculation Margaret perhaps most enjoyed is the one about couriers carrying letters from an absent relative. How long would it take four men travelling by different means of transport to arrive at Bucklersbury? Kratzer's own favourite exercise must have been the one about mechanical clocks. If a clock has an hour hand and a minute hand, when and how often will they overlap? A clock of gilt-metal with a chain and weights hung from the wall of the first-floor gallery at the Barge, although whether it had one or two hands is unknown.

More talked incessantly to anyone who'd listen about his 'school' and eldest daughter, for he was starting to realize just how able Margaret really was. Mildly mocking him for his gush, Erasmus freely admitted he'd been sceptical until More had disabused him, but still he could barely grasp the point, continuing to think education for women, like needlework or playing the lute or virginals, to be just another way of avoiding idle or lewd pastimes, although, it had to be said, a vastly superior one.

Almost sixteen, Margaret's growing maturity and talent had earned a deep respect from her father. As he gently teased her:

> There is no reason, my darling daughter, why you should have put off writing to me for a single day, because in your great self-distrust you feared that your [Latin] letters would be such that I could not read them without distaste . . . My dear Margaret, your letters were so elegant and polished, and gave so little cause for you to dread the indulgent judgement of a parent, that you might have despised the censorship of an angry Momos.

A familiar character in Lucian's satires, Momos is fault-finding personified: a god ridiculing the other gods. When Thomas said this, he knew Margaret could beat any of the men at their own game. Previously insisting that girls should translate scriptural or patristic extracts, or the safer passages from the leading Greek and Roman historians, now he allowed Margaret to read whatever she wanted.

Besides tackling the works of the Greek physician Galen, she was about to begin on Seneca, a Roman rhetorician and philosopher and one of her father's own favourites. To read Seneca was to take on a challenge of a quite different order. 'Seneca,' as Erasmus had advised, 'should be read only by the educated, because although he was a man of exceptional learning, he employed an arid, terse style of writing not suitable for the talents of the young,' whereas 'those who are widely read will easily discover that there are great virtues to be found in him.' Erasmus had edited Seneca's *Collected Works* in 1515, a volume arranged almost as a complete course of study in which the reader begins with the simpler ethical writings and moves gradually towards the rhetorical 'declamations' or model speeches. When the student gets to the speeches, no holds are barred. Set-piece examples condemn, but also defend, tyrannicide, prostitution, incest and rape. Students learn to practise arguing both sides of a case, moulding language like wax to sway their audience, elevating style over sincerity, debating-skills over truth, the reason Erasmus had all along considered rhetoric morally subversive for women. But exceptions had always been allowed. One of Seneca's own students, Quintilian, the prince of orators, had said that women's voices, exceptionally, could be heard in public, citing the example of Hortensia, daughter of Quintus Hortensius, who in 64 BC made a speech in Rome before the triumvirs opposing punitive taxation with such force and eloquence that the tax was substantially reduced.

Despite a growing urge to do otherwise, Margaret's father kept his admiration for her within the bounds of propriety when outside the family circle. When showing off her work, it was under the thinly veiled pretence of accidentally discovering it. After one such encounter with John Vesey, Bishop of Exeter, with whom he sat on a committee, he told her:

> I need not express the extreme pleasure your letter gave me, my darling daughter . . . I happened this evening to be in the company of the Reverend Father, John, Bishop of Exeter . . . Whilst we were talking I took out of my pocket a paper that bore on our business and by accident your letter appeared. He took it into his hand with pleasure and began to examine it. When he saw from the signature that it was the letter of a lady, his surprise led him to read it more eagerly . . . Seeing how delighted he was, I showed him your speech. He read it, as also your poems, with a pleasure so far beyond what he had hoped that although he praised you most effusively, yet his countenance showed that his words were all too poor to express what he felt.

He next chatted away happily to John Clement's best friend, Reginald Pole, who was passing through London from Oxford on his way to join Clement at Padua. Reporting Pole's reactions on being shown an example of his eldest daughter's Latin style, her father praises her in a curiously back-handed way. It will be impossible, he tells her, to prevent others questioning whether it is her own unaided work; thus she may never gain the credit she really deserves:

> I cannot put down on paper, indeed I can hardly express in my own mind, the deep pleasure that I received from your most charming letter, my dearest Margaret. As I read it there was with me a young man [Pole] of the noblest rank and of the widest attainments in literature . . . He thought your letter nothing short of marvellous . . . I could scarce make him believe that you had not been helped by a teacher . . . Meanwhile, something I once said to you in a joke came back to my mind, and I realized how true it was. It was to the effect that you were to be pitied, because the incredulity of men would rob you of the praise you so richly deserved for your laborious vigils, as they would never believe, when they read what you had written, that you had not often availed yourself of another's help: whereas of all the writers you least deserved to be thus suspected.

To preserve decorum, Thomas has to present her achievements as being appropriately unbelievable. When she received this letter, she must have wondered whether her father would always insist on behaving like this, or whether, like Quintilian, he might eventually allow exceptions to be made.

On 8 May 1521 sensational news reached the family at the Barge. The Duke of Buckingham, Margaret's paternal grandfather's most valuable client in his law practice, had been indicted at Guildhall and committed for trial at Westminster Hall on a charge of high treason. Henry had come to mistrust him and wanted him dead. The duke, it was said, was plotting to seize the throne, believing the prophecies of a Carthusian monk that he 'should get the favour of the commons and he should have rule of all'. Since Henry had a healthy four-year-old daughter, Mary, by his wife Queen Katherine, but lacked a male heir, this was dangerous talk. The duke also stood accused of slandering Wolsey, calling him 'the king's bawd', which was untrue. He'd admittedly failed to censure Henry for a long-running affair with the entrancing, vivacious Elizabeth Blount, one of Katherine's maids of honour, who'd given birth to an illegitimate son, Henry Fitzroy, now two years old, but Henry wouldn't have accepted a rebuke of that kind from anyone.

Henry, whose egoism, self-righteousness and capacity to brood may have been the effect of being spoilt as a child, decided to strike. It looked as if Katherine would never be able to provide a son, for her gynaecological history was her greatest source of grief. She had a history of stillbirths and miscarriages, and a young son, Henry, created Prince of Wales, had died at the age of seven weeks. When one of Buckingham's disgruntled servants came forward to claim, on the basis of hearsay, that the duke 'hath at all times grudged against everything that our sovereign lord hath done', and was prepared to rebel, just as his father had done against Richard III, Henry moved in for the kill.

Henry, like his father before him, greatly feared the threat of noble revolts, because the bloody civil wars known as the Wars of the Roses had culminated fifty years before in regicide. Such barbaric events as the murder of Henry VI in the Tower of London and the usurpation of Richard III still cast a dark shadow over every member of the royal family. The most important dynastic revolt before Henry VII's victory at the Battle of Bosworth had been against the usurper Richard, led by Buckingham's father in alliance with Cardinal John Morton, whom little more than seven years later the young Thomas More would be serving as a page.

The duke protested that his trial was rigged, for Henry had interviewed and even coached the witnesses, forcing information out of Buckingham's chaplain and so breaking the seal of the confessional. Who would be bold enough to speak out and say the king was mistaken, or that such methods were a denial of due process of law? Not John More, who despite being one of the duke's legal advisers was chosen by Henry to sit with the rest of the judges at Guildhall to indict the duke. The guilty verdict was delivered in the Court of the Lord High Steward in Westminster Hall. 'Your sentence,' blubbed the presiding judge, the old Duke of Norfolk, barely able to control his tears, 'is that you [shall] be led back to prison, laid on a hurdle, and so drawn to the place of execution; there to be hanged, cut down alive, your members [i.e. genitals] to be cut off and cast into the fire, your entrails burnt before your eyes, your head smitten off, your body quartered and divided at the king's will. And God have mercy on your soul.'

Armed guards led Buckingham out of the hall and down to the river stairs, from where he was rowed downstream, then taken on foot along Thames Street back to the Tower, the blade of an axe pointing towards him to show that he was doomed. Although lined up along the streets where they were meant to mock and hiss the convicted prisoner as he passed by, the Londoners cheered him and waved their hats, for he and his lavish retinue had spent liberally in the city: he was the only man in England willing to pay as much as twenty pence for a haircut.

Henry at the last moment decided to spare the duke the humiliation of hanging from the gallows with common thieves and cutpurses. Instead, Buckingham was sent to the scaffold, to be decapitated by the headsman on Tower Hill just a few yards outside the walls of the ancient fortress. But the executioner blundered: it took three strokes to sever the head completely. Kneeling in agony awaiting the fatal blow with blood spurting from his neck, the duke recited verses from the psalms while a vast crowd watched and grown men wept. For three days afterwards, mourners went to the place to dip their handkerchiefs in what remained of the victim's blood, 'reputing him as a saint and a holy man' and 'saying that he died guiltless'.

To pre-empt a popular uprising, Thomas More was sent by Henry to Guildhall to stop 'the lamenting and sorrowing' for the duke. Traitors like that, he was instructed to say, were not to be indulged. He had to threaten the Londoners, telling them that they'd incurred Henry's 'great suspicion, and he will not forget'. To memorialize the duke or invoke his name would be judged by Henry as 'mutiny and sedition'. Forced to return four days later, Margaret's father had to order the Mayor and Aldermen to put the city's constables and night-watchmen on full alert, and to seize and embargo all armour and weapons stored either at Guildhall or in people's homes until the king decided otherwise. So resented by the citizens was this, and so resonant was it of Richard III's tactics after his usurpation of the throne, it was the most taxing, troubling task that Thomas had so far been called on to undertake as Henry's councillor.

To divert and occupy his mind, he chose this moment to set himself a penitential exercise, beginning a book on the Four Last Things – death, judgement, heaven and hell – imitating a more famous work by Denys the Carthusian. Thomas already knew Denys's work inside out, with its vivid, morbid images of disease, pain, suffering and death. This and many similar devotional works dealt with the right ways to live and die, the seven deadly sins, the temptations of the devil, the agony of death, and the need to avoid the mortal sin of despair as one's final hours approach. He left his draft unfinished, but his intention is clear from what remains.

He planned a four-part treatise, a series of meditations, one for each of the Last Things, with subdivisions in each showing how Christians might seek to avoid all the most deadly sins. He judged 'the cursed sin of pride' to be most dangerous, for it was pride that had laid low Buckingham. The 'high mind of proud fortune, rule and authority', to which everyone could be susceptible and not simply great lords, was such that only 'remembrance of death' could redeem it.

Thomas doesn't either support the fact of the duke's execution or condemn it. He wrote allusively and ambiguously, not daring to mention Buckingham by name. But by giving a graphic, fictionalized description of a 'great Duke' secretly accused of high treason and sentenced to death against the evidence in a show trial, he makes his meaning crystal clear. Our mortal life, he says, for all its baubles and vain trappings, is no more than a prison. 'For the king by whose high sentence we be condemned to die, would not of this death pardon his own son. As for escaping, no man can look for [it]. The prison is large and many prisoners in it, but the gaoler can lose none.'

Not only did Margaret talk to her father during this time of crisis, but for the very first time he also invited her into the inner sanctum of his study, where she imitated him in his latest project, beginning her own book on the Four Last Things, maybe following his pattern for the work, maybe devising a model of her own. The topic had always been judged perfect for a woman seeking to offer comfort and support to close family members at times of grief. A little while before, father and daughter had sat down side by side in friendly competition to compose a model speech in a Lucianic style, just as he and Erasmus had done years before. First sketching out their ideas in their heads, they independently prepared Latin orations 'with such great skill that one would not know which to prefer'.

Margaret, we know from someone who heard it later from the mouth of Margaret Giggs, substantially completed her work on the Last Things. According to this witness, a reader of several of her other manuscripts before they disappeared, her father was jubilant, affirming 'most solemnly that the treatise of his daughter was in no way inferior to his own'. And one of Thomas's great-grandchildren goes further, saying that Margaret 'made also a treatise of the Four Last Things, which her father sincerely protested was better than his, and therefore, it may be, never finished his'.

No one will ever know for sure what happened to Margaret's manuscript: it may have been deliberately destroyed, perhaps by her own hand. According to her father's view of the social code, her voice was never to be heard in public. He would soon write to warn her:

> Although you cannot hope for an adequate reward for your labour, yet nevertheless you continue to unite to your singular love of virtue the pursuit of literature and art. Content with the profit and pleasure of your conscience, in your modesty you do not seek for the praise of the public, nor value it overmuch even if you receive it, but because of the great love you bear us, you regard us – your husband and myself – as a sufficiently large circle of readers for all that you write.

Whatever Margaret's own attitude may have been to publishing her version of the Four Last Things, that option wasn't to be offered to her. Modesty dictated otherwise, however much it ran against the grain. In spite of *Utopia*'s radicalism and his pioneering view of women's equality, her father could be paradoxically, intractably conservative when the effects of that radicalism impinged on his own domestic sphere.

But for the moment, Margaret had other things on her mind. As her father's letter for the first time reveals, she was now sixteen and ready to be married. Duty required that she must prepare herself, putting everything else aside and remembering the Church's teaching that a woman on her wedding day is to think that her husband should be dearer to her than anything else in the world.

PART II

THOMAS'S WORLD

8

SPEAKING IN TONGUES

I T WASN'T UNTIL AFTER his father had married for the second time that Thomas More began to think seriously about what he wanted to do with his life.

The year was 1499, when he was twenty-one, a student at Lincoln's Inn, still living at the family home in Milk Street where he'd been born. His mother, Agnes, had died scarcely six months before, aged no more than forty-five. Now she lay cold beside her brother, Abel Graunger, in a tomb in the recently renovated church of St Michael in Basinghall Ward, sixty or so yards beyond Guildhall. Thomas had himself devised the inscription so deftly carved into the marble slab that marked their shared grave:

> Come hither, traveller, and measure with thine eyes
> How small an urn holds two people here.
> What you are today, this man once was, and so was this woman.
> Now each one of them is part of this frozen earth.

Already unusually devout, even though his mind in so many other ways was always searching for the truth behind ideas and beliefs that others merely took for granted, Thomas accepted the Church's teaching that God had recalled his mother in the hope that she would share in the joys of paradise. Ever since he'd been a pupil at St Anthony's School, a free grammar school for the sons of London citizens attached to a hospital in Threadneedle Street twenty minutes' walk from his home, he'd attended the sermons of the preaching friars at St Paul's and at his own parish church of St Lawrence's. To prepare oneself daily for death, the friars insisted, was both necessary and desirable, for nothing mattered more in life than to learn how to die in the right way. Such piety discouraged heresy and sin, edifying the soul, which couldn't be beatified until separated from the body. Then, when the soul was finally severed from the flesh, Christ would lead the blessed souls into heaven to join the angels, while the damned were dragged down by devils into hell. It was a tremendously powerful belief, visually explicit in the doom (or 'Last Judgement') paintings found high on the wall above the chancel arch in almost every London church. The souls of the dead would be weighed in the balance, the sheep separated from the goats. What mortals had to fear wasn't death: it was damnation.

Thomas knew he had to set his grief for his mother aside. If the Church stressed the spiritual benefits of meditation on the Four Last Things, it discouraged excessive or prolonged mourning for individuals. Requiem and votive masses to relieve the pain of the souls of the departed in purgatory were allowed as necessary acts of charity, since only the saints could hope to go directly to heaven. On the other hand, anything implying that death had unfairly stolen away loved ones was a sinful affront to God's providence and mercy.

For Thomas, his mother's death was still a heart-rending experience, one he could hardly have put out of his mind as he took the brief walk to St Lawrence's for his father's wedding to Joan Marshall, because less than a year before, he and his mother had twice taken the same path for the weddings of his sisters.

Approaching the church porch where his father would take his vows before entering the nave with his bride for the nuptial mass, Thomas's first obligation was to welcome his new stepmother. Canon law took a dispassionate view of hasty second marriages: sentiment didn't have to enter into it, provided neither party was closely related to the other, had a living spouse or had taken a vow of chastity, but Joan Marshall's bitter quarrel with the Rastells was to poison the atmosphere at Milk Street, which Thomas couldn't have failed to notice. Seeking to fill the void left by his mother, he would find himself a group of mostly older friends who weren't merely congenial, they were to influence the way he felt and thought for the rest of his life. Whether he too got the sharp side of Joan Marshall's tongue is a matter on which he stayed tactfully silent, but a hint of his opinion of her may be gleaned from a verse he translated from Greek into Latin. In English translation, it reads: ·

> Putting wreaths of flowers on your stepmother's grave,
> You think that her death has put an end to her shrewish behaviour,

But suddenly the monument topples and crushes you.
Stepson, if you are wise, flee even your stepmother's tomb.

Nothing explicitly links Joan to the poem, despite its uncanny resonance with 'shrews' and 'scolds', but the fact that Thomas selected this, of all topics, for translation cannot be a coincidence.

One of Thomas More's defining characteristics is his refusal, except where religion is concerned, to accept unquestioningly the views of those in authority, an outlook that came from his study of the liberal arts, the same areas of knowledge he would one day want for his own children. Most remarkable is that he was tackling Greek in the first place, an exceptional language for a young lawyer to begin, because it wasn't taught at the Inns of Court or even officially in the universities. Since 1499, he'd thrown all his energy into it, neglecting his legal education, cultivating the interests that he felt had been unfairly curtailed when his father had sent him off to study law.

Of course, his father hadn't short-changed him by the usual measure. On the contrary, Thomas More's formal education had matched that of every other young law student. After attending St Anthony's from the age of five or six until he was twelve, he was sent to join the household of the Lord Chancellor and Archbishop of Canterbury, Cardinal Morton, as a page, living for eighteen months at Lambeth Palace on the south bank of the Thames, once the site of a modest manor house now transformed into an episcopal palace, watching the builders as they completed Morton's fine new red-brick gatehouse with its five-storey towers, and seeing Henry VII and his councillors arrive by barge and mount the stairs before talking and dining with Morton. To obtain such a coveted position, John More most likely asked the Duke of Buckingham, his wealthiest client and Morton's friend, for a favour. Most sons of the nobility and aspiring gentry joined the households of great lords or churchmen to get experience, as a page's duties were to attend his lord day and night, sleeping outside his bedchamber on a pallet, waiting on him at table, and helping his esquires and gentlemen-ushers in their tasks.

At Lambeth Thomas gained a reputation as a clever, quick-witted youth with a retentive memory who'd mastered English and Latin grammar, and had a talent for writing and acting. One of the main forms of revelry at festivals and banquets in noble households and the Inns of Court was masquing and play-acting. After dinner, the tables and benches were cleared away in the great hall, and a stage or 'scaffold' erected for the actors. Morton, a patron of dramatists and minstrels second only to the king, retained his own playwright to devise tragedies, romances and comedies. Often these plays included unscripted interludes: comic turns intended to alternate with the more serious scenes; among those taking part were choristers and pages. Thomas not only took part, he stole the show. It was said of him that he'd 'sometimes step in among the players, and never studying for the matter, make a part of his own there presently among them, which made the lookers-on more sport than all the players besides'. So witty and convincing were his impromptu acts, they earned him Morton's patronage.

Morton advised John More to send his son to Oxford University. Although unable to refuse, John More still shared the prejudice of his age that a university education wasn't necessary and, if a gentleman's son did attend and sample lectures, on no account should he sit for his examinations, since that would be socially demeaning. Thus it was that, at fourteen, Thomas had gone to Oxford, where he met William Grocyn, later his parish priest at St Lawrence's and the man who introduced him to Greek.

Grocyn, whose prized possessions apart from his books were his purple gown with a thick collar of black fur and his academic robes of scarlet and silk, was a striking figure, an inspiring teacher. Thomas would have attended his divinity lectures, famous for using the earliest, most authentic Greek sources to rewrite the early history of Christianity by exposing the errors and misapprehensions in the supposedly authoritative Latin versions of the texts. By way of preparation, Grocyn had learned Greek for three years in Italy, mainly at Florence with another Englishman: Thomas Linacre, ten years younger and also from Oxford, a physician graduating at Padua and needing Greek for his research into Galen's medical writings.

When More was sixteen, his father recalled him to London for his legal training, and for the first few years Thomas wholeheartedly complied. Until, that is, Grocyn arrived at St Lawrence's, taking up his post as vicar. The chronology is blurred because there are no parish records before the 1540s, but whatever the exact date, as soon as Thomas and Grocyn were reacquainted, Thomas eagerly embarked on a study of Greek poetry before switching to history and philosophy.

Linacre, meanwhile, returned from Italy, taking a house within fifty yards of St Paul's. In a flurry of excitement he sought out Grocyn to show him the first ever printed edition of Aristotle's complete writings. He'd helped to publish this landmark three-volume set in Venice; his reward for correcting the proofs had been a handsome presentation copy. While chatting to Grocyn, Linacre first met Thomas More and then John Colet, who'd studied philosophy in Italy and was lecturing at Oxford, but hadn't as yet found the time to embark on Greek. Soon they formed a circle of friends seeking to master the liberal arts in a way rivalled only by the greatest teachers in Italy, imagining themselves to be pioneers on a voyage of the mind equal to anything achieved by Christopher Columbus or Amerigo Vespucci in the New World. They had the zeal and enthusiasm of converts, since they believed that to rediscover ancient, and especially Greek, knowledge would change their society for ever. Not for a moment did they see themselves as antiquarians in an ivory tower, lamenting the world we have lost; they ardently maintained it was only their more rigorously informed approach to the sources of knowledge that could picture the future still to unfold. Their idea of progress depended on demystifying primary texts by restoring them to their original, pristine state. They were like-minded, reform-minded visionaries with a conscious desire to serve and make a difference; to help the living rather than the dead; to go out into the world and preach their good news.

The summer of 1499 was when, through William Blount, Lord Mountjoy, the son-in-law of Sir William Say, a neighbour of the Mores at their country estate in Hertfordshire, Thomas and his older friends had first met Erasmus. And the traffic was two-way, for Erasmus had no doubt whatever as to what he had learned from them.

> When I listen to Colet it seems to me that I am listening to Plato himself. Who could fail to be astonished at the universal scope of Grocyn's accomplishments? Could anything be more clever or profound or sophisticated than Linacre's mind? Did nature ever create anything kinder, sweeter or more harmonious than the character of Thomas More?

'I have turned my entire attention to Greek', he finally exclaimed when, dirty and exhausted, he trudged back home through the gates of Paris. 'The first thing I shall do, as soon as I get some money, is to buy some Greek books.'

Although Erasmus hadn't yet sampled the delights of Italy himself, he would glimpse through his encounters with Grocyn and Linacre some of the breathtaking, shocking, subversive possibilities of the revolution of ideas likely if Grocyn was right about the conclusions to be drawn from identifying the authentic Greek manuscripts of standard texts and collating them with the corrupt Latin translations. With his wider European vision, Erasmus was the first scholar to recognize that such methods could be applied not merely to Church history, but to transforming the text of the New Testament, sweeping away the musty cobwebs, and providing a definitive text along the lines of the 'simple philosophy of Christ' that he'd already come to value more than anything else in the world.

Soon Erasmus had come to realize that if the traditional Vulgate edition of the Gospels, the Latin translation made from the Greek by St Jerome in AD 383 and made the basis of religion by the Church, could be purged of its mistakes, then everything from theology to the institutions of the Church and society could be revitalized, and before long he would be carefully deciphering, collating and editing the manuscripts before translating them into fluent, colloquial, accurate Latin. He intended to publish the Greek text and his translation on facing pages so that anyone could easily compare them. He'd grasped that knowledge was power, and no text more powerful than the sacred scripture.

In 1501 Thomas completed his legal studies and was called to the bar, after which he earned a living by lecturing to first-year students preparing for admission to Lincoln's Inn. This was the same year as he wrote to an old schoolmaster: 'I am living my life just as I desire; so please God, may my desires be good. You ask how I am doing in my studies. Wonderfully, of course; things could not be better. I have shelved my Latin books, to take up the study of Greek; even if, while dropping the one, I have not as yet completely caught up with the other.' And afterwards to Colet he let slip that he'd been 'walking in the law courts the other day, unbusy where everybody else was busy', maybe browsing at the bookstalls. He felt elated, not least when his new friends lighted upon two Greek maxims: 'Between friends all is common' and 'Friendship is equality'. For these, it seemed, captured the essence of the liberal arts and Christianity combined.

The trouble was that John More strongly disapproved of his son's distractions, particularly resenting his friendship, and regular correspondence, with Erasmus, whom he judged to be shallow, fickle and dangerously overeducated. Reflecting on this twenty years later, Erasmus said that Thomas as a young man 'devoted himself to the study of Greek literature and philosophy with so little support from his father . . . that his efforts were deprived of all outside help and he was treated almost as if disinherited because he was thought to be deserting his father's profession'.

But 1501 was also the year in which John and Elizabeth Rastell's quarrel with Joan Marshall reached its climax, leading to their decision to move out of Milk Street and make a new home for themselves at Coventry. Within a few weeks or months, Thomas More made a similar choice. His horizons had been widened for ever, and he left his father's house, maybe a little before qualifying as a barrister, maybe a little afterwards. Whenever precisely it was, he moved not to Holborn to live among the clerks, scribes and other newly accredited lawyers like himself, but to West Smithfield to live among the Carthusian monks, in or about the grounds of the Charterhouse on a site surrounded by gardens, fields and burial pits about twenty minutes' walk from Lincoln's Inn.

And this was only the beginning.

9

SPEAKING OUT

THE LONDON CHARTERHOUSE, WHERE Thomas More stayed for about three years, was founded outside the city walls after the Black Death on the site of an old plague pit called 'No Man's Land'. An ascetic, contemplative order, the Carthusians gained their calm and coherence from their cloistered solitude and vows of poverty, chastity and obedience. A prior and twenty-four monks clustered around the quadrangular Great Cloister, occupying cells all but two identifiable by a letter of the Latin alphabet above the door.* Twenty-one cells stood in groups of seven around the north, east and west arcades; the other four were on the south side beside the chapter house, close to the sacristy and the magnificent church with its central octagon and tall wooden steeple surmounted by a cross.

Bare but far from uncomfortable, the cells had plastered walls and, in many cases, tiled floors; some were arranged on two floors; many had their own latrines. Each cell had been paid for by a different benefactor; those built in the last thirty years had the luxury of running water, cascading into lead pipes from a hexagonal stone water-fountain in the middle of the Great Cloister, supplied by an aqueduct carrying water from higher ground beyond Clerkenwell. Many of the cells were heated by stoves in winter.

When Thomas arrived, the Great Cloister's serenity had been restored after a period of disruption caused by major building works, creating more space in the church for altars for votive masses, new chantry chapels and alabaster memorials for the wealthier lay donors, and a second gallery so that women as well as men might come in off the streets to pray, listen to the services or sit in quiet reflection.

* The Latin alphabet has only twenty-three letters.

Most Londoners stood in awe of the Carthusians; few other clergy or pious citizens could hope to match their extraordinary standard of holiness. This meant that the laity often found the clergy officiating in their own parish churches wanting by comparison. Although not regular preachers like the friars, it seems that before printing came into its own, the monks alone satisfied the hunger of literate Londoners for books that were spiritually edifying. They first acquired, then copied by hand, often in bulk, manuscripts of continental and earlier English devotional works, supplying them to other monasteries or to individuals or their parish priests, and which then passed from hand to hand. Each monk kept the necessary writing implements in his cell.

What marked out the London Carthusians from the rest of their order was that, despite their love of solitude, they were such a visible presence in the wider civic community. Every monk had a key to the door of the Great Cloister and could come and go as he pleased. Beyond this, they devoted themselves to prayer and meditation, mainly alone in their cells, gathering in their church only for the night office, morning mass and afternoon vespers. They were supported in their daily tasks by thirteen lay brothers and fifteen servants living in the Little Cloister to the south-west of the church and in St John's Street nearby.

On Sundays and religious festivals, the monks ate together and listened to readings from the Bible and Church Fathers. Once a week they enjoyed a long walk, talking animatedly among themselves while outdoors, their robes and cowls of undyed wool marking them out among the gaudy silks and fine velvets of the more affluent citizens as they strode through the streets or nearby fields. They wore hair-shirts and kept strictly to a diet of fresh or salted fish, mostly ling and cod, milk and dairy products, bread, oatmeal, honey, spices, apples, pears, figs and raisins. Wine and meat were offered to the visitors and lay brothers except in Lent and on Fridays. Large purchases of malt suggest that beer was brewed on site, although whether the monks drank it or merely provided it for others is unknown. Occasionally the monks drank watered-down wine with their dinner.

The guest rooms were in an upper storey of the Little Cloister. Visitors collected their meals from the buttery beside the kitchen, and took them back to their rooms. Thomas may have lodged there, but more likely shared a house within the grounds, built ten years before for the use of long-term visitors, enabling them to gain experience of the religious life free of any obligation to commit to it. Thomas did, however, test his vocation and, as if on cue, a friend of Cardinal Morton, whom he'd served as a page, assigned to the monks the right to choose the rector of the church of North Mimms, where the Mores worshipped while at Gobions. This might just be a coincidence, or it might suggest that some-one in a high position already believed that a parish should be earmarked for Thomas should he decide in the future to be ordained.

Not that he withdrew completely from the world, for he continued to teach young law students, and also returned to St Lawrence's to deliver a series of well-attended lectures on St Augustine's *City of God*, a sequel to a course in St Paul's on a different theme begun, but prematurely aban-doned, by his friend Grocyn. His notes (if he used any) are lost; our only information is that he approached his text from the standpoint of history and philosophy, and not theology.

St Augustine, More's lifelong favourite among the Church Fathers apart from St Jerome, had set out to refute the charge that Christianity had been responsible for the decline and fall of Rome and to explain why, if there was indeed a living God, the Christians had been treated no better than the heathens at the hands of Alaric and his Visigoths. His argument is that the Roman Empire (and by inference any civil society) was neither good nor evil of itself. It was the pride and avarice of its citizens that caused it to collapse. One of his abiding tenets (and Thomas More's) is that pride or vainglory – the love of reputation, status and possessions for their own sake – is worse than sexual lust.

Thomas's lectures and his Greek studies would easily have converged. The maxim 'Know thyself', inscribed on the temple wall at Delphi and trumpeted as a slogan by Erasmus, was the highest ideal of Greek philoso-phy. According to Plato (and later More in *Utopia*), if a society can't discriminate between true and false wisdom, it can never glimpse the true meaning of justice or equality, and to discover how to do so, it is first necessary to be honest about ourselves. Thomas would also have fitted his view of law into his lectures. Following Plato and St Augustine, he took a philosophical approach, more so than any other professional lawyer at the time, interpreting law as a branch of knowledge concerned with the capacity of human beings to engage with their society and reform it by the power of the imagination.

The best way to recapture Thomas's frame of mind is to see him as a lawyer who loved justice more than he liked lawyers, living at a time of rapid social and economic change when the relationship of law and morality was contested. Most lawyers of his generation took the narrow, insular view that English law, based as it was on a set system of customs and principles dating back to Magna Carta, already served and defined the common welfare and shouldn't be changed; that it was more important to avoid introducing novelties and inconsistencies than it was to right a wrong. Thomas fervently disagreed, believing that equitable exceptions should always be available in the interests of true justice on moral grounds. Equity – the idea that a decision in a lawsuit should be given in accordance with wider ethical principles – had so far mainly been the preserve of Church lawyers. There had often been occasions when the methods and ideas of the secular and Church courts had clashed. Thomas's position was to argue for change within the legal profession itself, not to retreat to the cloister. He would always maintain that the best way to improve society wasn't to avoid difficult challenges, but to confront them.

Thomas was twenty-five when he decided on his future. Family duty is likely to have influenced his choice, since his father held stubbornly to the view that his son should pursue a conventional legal career. That wasn't at all what Thomas had in mind; the path he took – initially a civic career in London and later royal service for the public good – would evolve into something highly unconventional because, unlike the majority of eager young professionals, he saw his spiritual life as underpinning his role as a good citizen. What already marks him out is that he never tries to compartmentalize his religious and career values. Whereas religious piety for a majority of Londoners was expressed chiefly by regular church attendance at mass and on saints' days and through charitable donations to the poor; and whereas to build a private fortune or win the edge in a trade or profession wasn't thought to be a matter for over-scrupulous consciences, Thomas More always knew that honesty mattered most to him. Thus as a lawyer he would never take on, or seek to win, a client's case regardless of its merits, or simply to earn a fee. He would advise his clients not to go to law if they could possibly avoid it, and if they couldn't, to try to reach an out-of-court settlement, or else seek a fairer and cheaper solution through arbitration.

He must have left the Charterhouse shortly before Christmas 1503, when he stood for election to the House of Commons. His father, promoted a serjeant-at-law just a few weeks before with access to the most senior members of the judiciary, may have helped to find him a sponsor. Thomas didn't sit as one of the representatives for London, but lesser borough constituencies were routinely available to clever, well-connected lawyers. Unfortunately, the election returns for this Parliament are lost, and no one knows for which constituency Thomas sat. Our only information is that he sat in Parliament and took his place at the opening ceremony on 25 January 1504.

It all went horribly wrong: Thomas came to Henry VII's attention in Parliament in the worst possible way, clashing with the king and his councillors by speaking out against royal taxation. Henry may have restored stability after the Wars of the Roses, but his methods could be brutal. Always secretive and obsessional after his experiences in exile during Richard III's reign, always fearful of plots and pretenders after his return as king, he would compel leading nobles and London citizens to enter into bonds (or legal contracts) obliging them to stay loyal to the Tudor dynasty or else pay substantial fines. Some amounted to blackmail; others were registered as debts 'simple and absolute . . . for his Grace would have them so made'. Henry's apologists said that his 'inward mind' was never to call them in, but outwardly it looked otherwise. It seemed as he grew older as if the king were turning into a second Midas.

The mood was grim, since a month before Parliament assembled, Henry had milked £5,000 from the Londoners, with a further £2,500 to follow. Then, when the session began, he insisted on legislation forcing all the livery companies, of which the most important was the Mercers' Company, to submit their internal statutes and ordinances to vetting by a panel of scrutiny. Ostensibly the aim was to eliminate insider trading, but the true purpose was to strip the city of its control over the companies.

Henry next laid before Parliament his major demand for a tax of £90,000. He lacked any proper justification such as war or military emergency, making no effort to pretend otherwise and calling instead for two feudal aids to be granted retrospectively: one for the knighting of his eldest son, Arthur, and one for the marriage of his eldest daughter, Margaret. Kings were traditionally entitled to such levies, but Arthur, knighted fifteen years before, had been dead for two years. A more plausible claim could be made on Margaret's behalf. Still alive and well, her marriage to James IV of Scotland had taken place only the previous year, costing £10,000. Henry rallied grudging support for his tax until it emerged that he meant to push his claims too far, linking the levies to a possible wealth tax. Thomas More spoke for the opposition, protesting that the king's proposal was 'doubtful, uncertain, and [the cause of] great unquietness' throughout the realm.

What he hadn't bargained for was a wily courtier taking notes as he was speaking and informing the king. Henry's levies were voted down, replaced by a smaller, less burdensome tax, and although Thomas narrowly escaped a short, sharp spell of imprisonment in the Tower, that wouldn't be the end of the matter as his father would be sent there later in the year. In his capacity as a civic legal adviser, John More would be suspected of coaching the livery companies on how to minimize the effects of the vetting of their statutes, and in his role as a magistrate in Hertfordshire of failing to exert himself sufficiently in assessing the substitute tax, the yield of which bore little relation to the county's true wealth. He was left to kick his heels in a cold, damp cell until, a week or so later, his friends 'compounded' with Henry by offering him £100. For both father and son, their brush with royal power would have been chilling, but at least their shared troubles would have served to reconcile them, healing the breach that had divided them over Thomas's forays into the liberal arts.

John More's receipts from Joan Marshall's lands enabled him to repay the £100, and his duties as a serjeant-at-law extended his social horizons. Soon he would find a circle of new friends of his own among the gentry within a twenty-mile range of Gobions across the county border from Hertfordshire into Essex, among them John Colt of Netherhall. The tangible result was that, in or around November 1504, Thomas was betrothed to Joanna, the eldest of Colt's twelve children.

If Erasmus, writing fifteen years later, is to be believed, Thomas left the Charterhouse to marry and not to enter Parliament. He reduced the issue to a ribald jest, saying that his friend 'could not shake off the desire to get married, and so chose to be a chaste husband rather than a lecherous priest'. He ignored, or more likely was simply ignorant of, the fact that Thomas didn't contemplate marriage for another whole year, and that he hadn't even met Joanna when he sat in Parliament.

But by speaking in the Commons and following a career as a civic lawyer, Thomas stepped much closer to marriage, since in a still patriarchal society no one could fully engage in civic and public life as Thomas had chosen to do as a bachelor. He could do so only as a householder, meaning having a wife and children, employing servants and entertaining guests. No bachelor could play a significant role in Tudor society, since he would be judged to lack the necessary authority deriving from a husband's right (as it was believed then) to govern his own family and manage his own household and property, setting an example to others.

Thomas and Joanna's wedding date can be worked out. The knot wasn't tied when Thomas wrote to his friend, John Colet, in October 1504, but indisputably was by late January 1505, which leaves a fairly narrow margin, since the Church forbade marriages between Advent Sunday (1 December) and the week following Epiphany (13 January) and again between the third Sunday before Lent (19 January) and the week after Easter (30 March).* A fair hypothesis is that Thomas and Joanna were betrothed in early November 1504 and married as soon as the wedding banns had been called by the priest on three consecutive Sundays. Maybe the betrothal was slightly earlier, with a wedding before Advent Sunday; maybe a little later, with a wedding in mid-January.

Since Joanna didn't visit London before her betrothal, the couple may have met fewer than six times. Perhaps like John More when he'd rushed headlong into marriage with Joan Marshall, Thomas deflected such questioning with a joke. His descendants said of him that when he'd first 'resorted' to Netherhall, no fewer than three of John Colt's daughters 'provoke[d] him there specially to set his affection'. He thought the second to be the fairest and best, 'yet when he considered that it would be both great grief and some shame also to the eldest to see her younger sister in marriage preferred before her, he then of a certain pity framed his fancy towards her, and soon after married her'.

The idea of Thomas switching his attentions to the eldest sister out of 'pity' has an evocative biblical resonance, and is likely to be a myth. When in the Book of Genesis, Jacob, the great Hebrew patriarch, falls in love with Rachel beside a well and seeks permission to marry her, he is forced to marry her elder sister Leah first, because 'It is not so done in our country, to give the younger [sister] before the first-born.' After Thomas's death, his followers sought to depict a heroic figure who, like Jacob, had

* Dates calculated according to the calendar in force for 1504–5.

undergone trials and tribulations and was a man of destiny, even if their own fate like that of the chosen people of Israel would be to spend many years in exile.

If the story is true and Thomas had three Colt sisters to choose from, then assuming the youngest was born two years after Joanna – it could hardly be less since none of these young women were twins – she was fifteen, since we know from Joanna's uncle's testimony in a lawsuit that Joanna herself was seventeen. Although a woman was legally able to give her consent to marriage at twelve, most parents considered fifteen to be a year too young.

Erasmus couldn't curb his prurience as to why his friend, at twenty-six, should want to marry a teenager. He was blind to the fact that the Mores were climbing the social ladder, taking a definite upward step since John Colt's father had married a rich heiress, bringing him Netherhall and all its estates, and enough money to rebuild the manor house in the latest, most fashionable style: the brickwork decorated with a blue-glazed diaper pattern, complete with a great hall, a sumptuous first-floor lodging, an imposing gatehouse, a curtain wall and a surrounding moat.

As to why the Colts found it profitable to ally with the Mores, the speck on their horizon was a dispute between John Colt and the Duke of Buckingham over which of them rightfully owned the manor of Little Parndon, east of Roydon. The Colts had it for now, but the quarrel would simmer for a decade before boiling over in a series of damaging and costly lawsuits. Until then, John Colt would keep the powerful duke at bay by putting his Essex lands into a trust controlled by John and Thomas More and his own and Joanna's relations. A direct and fruitful consequence of Joanna's marriage, the new trust had the effect of pitting Buckingham against his very own legal adviser, John More, making it unlikely that he would sue for Little Parndon while the Mores were co-trustees. And sure enough, the duke waited until 1514, when John Colt changed his trustees on the marriage of George, his eldest son, at which point he pounced.

Thus, while Thomas and Joanna's marriage suited everyone, John Colt had as much or more to gain. Although once a student at the Middle Temple, Colt doesn't seem to have completed his course or practised law. He was a typical country squire who saw an alliance with an upwardly mobile family of lawyers as the least expensive way to safeguard his landholding. Equally, John More saw no conflict of interest between presiding over John Colt's trustees while continuing to act as the Duke of Buckingham's lawyer.

How far Thomas and Joanna were ever in love would always intrigue Erasmus. Thomas, he concluded from his extended stays with the couple, had acted rationally rather than passionately, marrying an inexperienced and diffident girl, wholly lacking in confidence and urbanity, seeing her as a blank canvas that he could mould to fit his own ideal of a perfect wife. 'He arranged,' said Erasmus, 'for her education and made her skilled in music of every kind, and had (it is clear) almost succeeded in making her a person with whom he would gladly have shared his whole life, had not an early death removed her from the scene.'

So much Erasmus purported to be fact, but he also wrote a semi-fictional colloquy about an unhappy wife, recounting how a brilliantly learned man of his acquaintance had married a seventeen-year-old country girl. 'Her lack of sophistication recommended her, because he would fashion her to his tastes the more readily. He undertook to teach her literature and music and gradually to accustom her to repeating what she had heard in a sermon; and by other devices to train her in what would be of later use.' Since Joanna was indeed seventeen, the story may relate in part to her. Thomas himself said in a Latin poem that an ideal wife needs to be educated by her husband to ensure that she will 'ever be agreeable, never a trouble or a burden . . . [and] will teach your little grandsons, at an early age, to read'.

As Erasmus relates, the unhappy wife hates reading, cries inconsolably and wishes herself dead. So her husband suggests a visit to the country to see her parents. On arrival, the husband leaves his wife with her mother and sisters and goes out hunting with his father-in-law, to whom he explains the problem. 'Use your rights and give her a good beating,' says her father. 'I know my rights,' replies the son-in-law, 'but rather than resort to this desperate remedy, I'd prefer to have her cured by your skill.' The father feigns to be so angry with his daughter that she kneels before him, begging forgiveness and swearing she will do her duty in the future. She rushes to her bedroom and tells her husband, 'You shall see me a changed person; only forget the past.' They kiss and make up. So happy is the marriage afterwards, the woman can hardly believe her luck.

And yet, despite Erasmus's personal knowledge of the couple, the story doesn't quite add up, since the only pastime Thomas More loathed and detested more than hunting was gambling. Unlike almost every other one of his contemporaries, he objected to blood sports and games of chance as a matter of principle, and the fact that the husband in the colloquy goes out hunting makes the topical allusion doubtful. Such a detail may even have been inserted to muddy the waters, leaving the whole question of Thomas and Joanna's true relationship open to endless speculation. As with so many things about the interior world of Thomas More before he wrote *Utopia*, the whole truth wasn't fully known even to the most intimate of his friends.

10

THE LIMITS OF REASON

B Y THE TIME THAT Thomas More had married Alice Middleton and embarked on *Utopia*, his character was beginning to mature. Although building a career and often absent from his wife and children on civic or royal business, he took great care to insulate his family from his role in political affairs. Whereas he doesn't compartmentalize his religious and career values, he strictly separates his private and public worlds. Margaret and the older children yearned for their father to come home and to hear about his work, but information was hardly ever shared. Barely a handful of his 132 surviving letters mingle public and private news. He would either write official letters, usually to Wolsey, that were starkly factual, rarely offering personal observations or revealing anything about himself, or else he'd send intimate, chatty, witty letters to his friends and family in which he'd seem to complain about how maddeningly distracted both from them and the liberal arts he was by his roster of public duties, but giving them no more than tantalizing hints as to what such tasks might involve or even often where his duties had taken him.

His other tendency was to worry if he felt he was enjoying himself too much. Although he and Alice revelled in banter and 'merry tales', his annotations to his Book of Hours show him asking God to give him the strength 'To abstain from vain confabulations/ To eschew light foolish mirth and gladness'. And in *A Dialogue of Comfort against Tribulation*, one of his last books written in the Tower, ostensibly a work of fiction but patently semi-autobiographical, he said he was 'of nature even half a giglot and more. I would I could as easily mend my fault as I well know it.' (A 'giglot' is excessively prone to jesting and merriment, someone whose sense of humour could lead him into wantonness.) Since his days as Cardinal Morton's page he'd adored the plays of Plautus and Terence with their slapstick scenes of vice, drunkenness and street life. He seems to have been conscious that such levity had the potential to clash with his solemnity, but had so far been able to handle the tension and deal with it in his own way.

Shortly before Christmas 1514, his iron-willed piety led him to become deeply involved in another *cause célèbre*, this time one that was completely outside his jurisdiction, but which he followed closely, attending all the hearings until he understood the matter (as he said) 'from top to toe'. The chain of events began when a suspect awaiting trial on a charge of heresy was found hanging by his silk girdle from a hook in the ceiling of his cell at the Lollards' Tower at St Paul's, his clothes drenched in blood. The man was Richard Hunne, a successful, articulate member of the Merchant Tailors' Company, who'd challenged the discipline and authority of the Church, playing for the highest possible stakes.

The facts are that the Church had accused Hunne of heresy, imprisoning him in the cell where he was found. The Church claimed that he'd committed suicide, whereas his friends were adamant that he'd been accused of heresy to force him to pay his Church dues, then murdered after bringing a test case using an obscure medieval law called *praemunire* by which those enforcing papal or Church jurisdiction in conflict with the king's prerogative should suffer life imprisonment and lose their property. A suspicious death required a coroner's inquest, and within two days a civil jury had examined the corpse and the cell.

Although Hunne was dead, the bishop's chancellor did an extraordinary thing, convening a heresy trial at which Hunne was put on trial posthumously and convicted. Witnesses testified that he'd owned some heretical books and an illegal translation of the English Bible. What caused an uproar was that the Church had been unable to produce any of this evidence while Hunne was alive. Thomas More attended every sitting of the heresy tribunal and coroner's inquest, taking notes and eventually deciding that Hunne was the author of his own destruction, brought low by his 'spirit of pride'. After hearing all the evidence, he believed the man had been 'a wily heretic', allowing his private sympathies to slip out, because Hunne, being dead, had been denied due process of law. By the strict rules of canon law, only 'obstinate' heretics could be condemned, meaning those who had been tried, convicted and allowed to recant before relapsing into heresy. First-time offenders, like Hunne, couldn't be sentenced unless they *refused* to recant after their day in court, persisting 'obstinately' in their false opinions. The Church had in fact been forced to claim that Hunne's 'obstinacy' was established by the fact that he'd committed suicide.

The coroner's jury rejected the Church's findings and committed the bishop's chancellor to stand trial for murder. He immediately claimed 'benefit of clergy' (i.e. immunity from prosecution), invoking the privileges reluctantly granted to the Church and clergy by Henry II after the bloody and public murder of St Thomas Becket at Canterbury Cathedral in 1170. The judges of the Court of King's Bench were obliged to release him to the custody of Archbishop Warham, who removed him to Lambeth Palace and gave him sanctuary.

When Parliament reassembled in February, there was an outcry. The House of Commons voted for a sweeping reform of 'benefit of clergy', but the Abbot of Winchcombe threatened that if the Church's privileges were touched, then it was sacrilege and any member of Parliament, even the king himself, could be excommunicated. He was refuted in a fiery speech by Dr Henry Standish, Warden of the Friars Minor, who attacked the notion that the clergy had immunity, calling for the law to be changed so that all felons and murderers could be tried in the royal courts. Such a reform, he said, would not contravene Church law, since the pope and clergy lacked the power to enforce laws made in their synods and convocations without the royal assent.

The idea that Henry had a right to vet canon law or papal decrees before they were accepted as valid was truly revolutionary. But it was a timely and popular argument, not least among the royal judges, angry and frustrated as they were by a growing number of criminals escaping justice. Matters came to a head when the Bishop of London, Richard Fitzjames, dared to tell Parliament that the jurors at Hunne's inquest were 'false perjured caitiffs'. Sir Robert Sheffield, the Commons' leader and mouthpiece, demanded a retraction. In reply, the bishops said they would defend benefit of clergy to the death. It was at this moment that Henry ordered Parliament to be adjourned for Easter, sending its members home while he pondered Standish's claims.

Thomas More was then sent on his embassy to Bruges, meeting Peter Gillis in Antwerp and beginning *Utopia*. Choosing the fictional Raphael Hythloday to spin the yarn, he demonstrates in stages how his vision of an ideal society isn't a predominantly secular one like Plato's in the *Republic*, but one where Christianity alone can lead the citizens towards perfection. After setting the scene in a grassy arbour at his lodgings just like one of those he'd constructed for his family at Bucklersbury, he coaxes out of Hythloday a description of the mysterious island he'd explored for several years at the end of a voyage with Amerigo Vespucci to Brazil, when he didn't return to Europe with the rest of the crew.

The island, says Hythloday, is five hundred miles long and two hundred in width at its broadest point, and has fifty-four cities, evenly distributed across the landscape, identical in language, customs, institutions and laws. Together the cities form a republic ruled by a senate. King Utopus, a conqueror in the far-distant past, laid down the form of the constitution and gave the laws, which may never be changed.

The Utopians have abolished professional lawyers and private property, considering this to be the best way to uproot pride and greed. Lawyers aren't needed, says Hythloday with a smile, because all the laws are clear and straightforward and litigants find it easier, cheaper and fairer to tell their stories to a judge sitting alone without lawyers' tricks and chicanery. This 'makes for less confusion and easier access to the truth', because the basic principle is plain-dealing. As to land and property, everything is held in common, enabling the citizens to concentrate on the things that really matter in life. No one is poor, everyone feels rich, and no beggars roam the streets. The Utopians hold wealth and ostentation in contempt. Diamonds and pearls, collected from cliffs and the seashore, are given as baubles to children, who cast them aside with their toys when they grow up. Gold and silver are considered to be inferior to ironwork: the Utopians value precious metals so little, they use gold to manufacture urinals and the chains and shackles of slaves. Gold in Utopia translates into little more than a badge of shame.

Public health provision is remarkable. Every city has four hospitals, with ample supplies of medicine, the beds well spaced apart, and as many physicians and nurses as are needed, all working shifts to ensure fully qualified staff are on call day and night. The Utopians care lovingly for the sick, sparing nothing in the way of medicine or diet to restore them to health. Healthcare concerns also dictate the ritual for choosing marriage partners. People are first allowed to inspect each other naked after the fashion used by Europeans when buying horses, then make their choice after ensuring that no hidden sores or diseases (such as syphilis) are discovered in their prospective partners that would affect their reproductive functions.

Every Utopian child receives a free education. They are first taught to read and write, before progressing to more advanced subjects. Educated from an early age to be pacifists, they despise war and engage in it only for defensive reasons or to liberate an oppressed people from tyranny. If a war is reluctantly declared, they prefer to use techniques of psychological warfare to risking their troops in pitched battles. No citizen is ever forced to fight. When engaging the enemy, they are magnanimous. Truces are honoured, massacres forbidden, cities are not sacked, nor are territories laid waste.

The Utopians understand human nature well enough to know that the love of money is the root of all evil. Agriculture is the main occupation. Farms operate on a collective basis, directing labour and resources to where they are most needed, especially at harvest time. Farming is the job at which everyone works, men and women alike, but since no one lives by bread alone, everyone also learns a trade. Some magistrates are let off manual labour, but choose not to claim the privilege, preferring to set a good example. Scholars are excused, but are reassigned to manual duties if they fail to make the grade. There are daily public lectures before dawn, compulsory for the scholars, voluntary for the rest. Hythloday is impressed that so many busy Utopians, both men and women, flock to attend.

In other words, the Utopians, by their application of reason, can discriminate between true and false values. They have no place for hollow spectacle, courtly gesture, a social hierarchy or empty titles of honour, and their clothes are of undyed wool like the habits of Carthusian monks. Inherited wealth and social status are alien to them. The only status distinctions they permit arise from intellectual ability, election to public office or punishment for crime. Sports like hunting or gambling are banned. Leisure time is organized so as to cultivate the liberal arts, and when relaxing the citizens stroll in their gardens, make music, or enjoy improving board games. One, like chess, is a battle of numbers in which one number captures another (this teaches them arithmetic). Another is a game in which the vices fight a pitched battle with the virtues.

An entirely rational, if tightly regulated, model of society has thus far been set forth. The Utopians, according to Hythloday, live well, but any notion of them as 'noble savages' must be set aside. This isn't so much because they practise slavery. The Utopian slaves, performing the dirtiest, most arduous domestic chores, turn out to be criminals undergoing social rehabilitation or volunteers from other nations who prefer living as slaves in Utopia than elsewhere as citizens. Slavery doesn't receive a systematic examination in *Utopia*; rather the yardstick is religion. Thomas More concludes his first draft of *Utopia* by tackling this subject, and immediately his tone modulates, his voice audibly adjusts, becoming less whimsical, less ironical, more homiletic. For whereas Hythloday, until now, has described, and applauded, the Utopians for creating a fair and equal society, from here onwards he carefully distances himself from them, because their values are fatally flawed. This is because they are hedonists at heart, considering pleasure alone to be the measure of happiness. Their story may have suggested that they've uprooted pride and understood justice and equality, but because they do not know Christ, their virtue will always be insufficient. On those grounds alone, their island cannot be a paradise on earth.

Their basic religion is polytheist. In spite of this, they agree on one 'supreme god' whom they call Mithra. They have no official liturgy or rituals. King Utopus, their founding father, had granted them religious freedom, but qualified it by a law requiring two specific beliefs. The first is the doctrine of the immortality of the soul. The second is that the universe is ruled by divine providence and not by 'blind chance'. King Utopus decreed that citizens denying these controlling ideas are to be ostracized, stripped of their privileges and allowed to discuss their opinions in future only with priests in the confessional. 'Obstinate' offenders are to be excommunicated by priests, then arrested and severely punished by magistrates. It seems that, even in Utopia, the articles of religion are no more optional than they were for Richard Hunne.

Hythloday then counters a series of shibboleths. It's this part of his portrayal, more so than his description of Utopian communism, that would have perplexed, even scandalized, sixteenth-century readers. Utopian society allows, and actively supports, customs diametrically opposed to the approved doctrines of Catholicism: divorce, euthanasia and women priests. True, the Utopians treat them with caution. Divorce is allowed for infidelity, but those who admit to it or are otherwise found out are punished with the harshest form of slavery. Women priests are permitted, 'but,' says Hythloday, 'only a widow of advanced years is ever chosen, and it doesn't happen often'. As to euthanasia, it is rigorously supervised, always voluntary, nor does a refusal ever lead to a denial of medical care. If anyone, even in a state of torment, ends their life without the prior approval of the priests and magistrates, their body is thrown unceremoniously into a pit.

Still, the Utopians *do* practise these customs. They condone them even if Hythloday chooses to confront them. More had obviously decided that *Utopia* was getting much too cosy. When his game with Gillis had begun, their intention was to cram in as much satire and irony as possible. Then, as they got more and more carried away with such hilarious conceits as golden urinals, the heathen Utopians suddenly begin to look more 'Christian' than the supposedly Christian Europeans, for pride and greed are uprooted in Utopia and it is the poor and meek who will inherit the earth.

Thomas saw it would be fatal if anyone concluded, mistakenly, that he was allowing reason to flourish at the expense of revelation, making it appear as if the heathen Utopians have the capacity to create a redeeming moral code on the basis of reason alone. To dispel the shame and revulsion of that heresy, he thus felt obliged to attribute beliefs to them that contradict some of the most cherished principles of Catholicism, enabling Hythloday to reject them and so proving that reason has its limits. He'd begun *Utopia* with an allusion to Plato, meaning that he was searching for the best possible model of society. But unlike Plato, his quest isn't for the best model of any commonwealth, but solely of a Christian one. The Utopians will always need Christ to perfect their ideal society. Reason must be crowned by revelation.

The Utopians are led towards Christianity in two easy stages. First, they are taught to appreciate the true significance of their belief in the immortality of the soul, seeing how they can earn eternal life and felicity in heaven by their merits and labours on earth, which encourages them to live more virtuously. Then, before leaving the island, Hythloday and his companions explain Christianity to them and show them the New Testament. Many, as a result, come forward to be baptized, identifying Christ's call to his disciples to adopt a communal way of living as validating a society very much like their own. But, although many Utopians volunteer themselves, they can't be confirmed or receive the Eucharist because, unexpectedly, several of Hythloday's companions are struck down by a fever, leaving no priest among the survivors. Still, the

Utopians 'understand what these [sacraments] are, and eagerly desire them'. They await the arrival of a Christian bishop from Europe, and it is here that Hythloday's narrative ends, for he has reached the point in the story where the Utopians know that a truly perfect society is finally within their grasp.

But before finishing *Utopia*, Thomas was stopped in his tracks, receiving a copy of a letter from Martin Dorp to Erasmus informing him that the *Praise of Folly* had been officially censured by the University of Louvain. 'Your style, your fancy, and your wit they like,' said Dorp. 'Your mockery they do not like at all.' Erasmus was accused, in turn, of frivolity, irresponsibility and sarcasm, of being witty but destructively negative. 'The easiest way to put things right,' Dorp advised, 'will be to balance your *Folly* by writing and publishing a *Praise of Wisdom*.' He called for a full retraction in which Erasmus would humbly apologize for the misunderstandings he'd caused, a public admission that he'd never meant to ridicule the pope or the Church authorities.

Dorp's salvo isn't all that it appears to be. As a newly promoted professor of theology, his confrontation with Erasmus was partly staged for effect. And to some extent, Erasmus had colluded: each was as keen as the other to magnify his own reputation. The trouble began in earnest only when the slanging-match got out of hand, for Erasmus found Dorp's letter deeply patronizing. Barely able to tolerate criticism from anyone, he was incensed when Dorp urged him to abandon work on his Greek New Testament, by this time nearing publication, which he believed would be the apotheosis of his career.

In a confident, withering reply, Erasmus invited Dorp to encourage his plodding colleagues to learn Greek themselves before criticizing others. He also rejected (really he just didn't see its significance) the most valid and constructive part of Dorp's advice that, even if the Latin Vulgate edition of the Bible did contain inaccuracies, the effects of disclosing them in print were likely to be seismic if not carefully managed, since otherwise the doctrines of the Church, relying on the Vulgate text as they had for over a thousand years, would appear to have been proved wrong, putting Erasmus at the centre of a whirlwind.

Erasmus wrote a second, more blistering answer, which he had the good sense to burn before he sent it. Instead, Thomas More raced to his defence, rushing off his own impassioned rebuttal of Dorp in a fortnight and circulating it. Perhaps judging the cause for the primacy of the Greek New Testament might be lost by default, perhaps manipulated into entering the fray by his more supple, insinuating friend, More's polemic exceeded 18,000 words, railing against Dorp and vilifying his colleagues before artfully suggesting that Dorp might have been forced by a majority vote of the Faculty to endorse views he was too intelligent to hold personally. As Erasmus's champion and the dedicatee of the *Praise of Folly*, Thomas clearly felt himself vulnerable to a charge of sacrilege. As a result, his invective exceeded anything he'd ever written before, accusing Dorp of being in love with himself and his own opinions, 'just as every man thinks his own fart smells sweet'. In the heat of the moment, Thomas drew on vocabulary he would afterwards rely on more frequently to vilify an opponent. While not charging Dorp with heresy, he rebuked him for hypocrisy and for condoning a far worse blasphemy than anything imputed to Erasmus, since his bone-headed pedantry and attack on the liberal arts could only give encouragement to heretics.

By saying this, Thomas gave a hostage to fortune. He also laid himself open to future attacks from other, more rancorous and unsavoury defenders of the Latin Vulgate Bible than Dorp, since his letter was the document above all others in which, with nitric clarity, he defended the primacy of the Greek New Testament, saying that 'the Church believes the Gospels are contained in the Latin manuscripts, while still admitting they are translated from the Greek. The Church credits the translation, but still more so the original. It credits . . . the Latin, but only insofar as it trusts the translator. And, I believe, it does not trust the translator so unreservedly as not to realize that he could have erred out of human frailty.'

Ever since he'd first met Grocyn and Linacre in 1499, Thomas's forays into Greek learning and the liberal arts had been the essence of his being. But now that idyll was about to be cruelly shattered by those sharing the opinions of Richard Hunne and Friar Standish, or by those like Dorp relying on hell-fire sermons and superstition, who cheated their audiences by peddling lies or fraudulent saints' legends, driving honest old women to tears or making them tremble with fear. And Thomas More took this personally.

His quandary shouldn't be overdrawn, but Hunne's case and Dorp's attack on Erasmus showed that the ground was beginning to shift beneath him. These were the beginning of unsettling times. Over a decade was to pass before Henry would turn against Wolsey and the Church, but by claiming that the pope and clergy lacked the power to enforce laws made in their synods and convocations without the royal assent, Standish had raised an argument that would later help to bring about the downfall of Thomas More.

Already the effect on him is discernible, for his letter to Dorp is so distant from the effervescent, laughing, bantering style of what he'd so far written towards *Utopia* that it's hard to believe the works are by the same author. Dorp's critique had made him aware that, if he didn't take counter-measures, he would be next in the firing line if he went on to publish *Utopia* in its present form. For Hythloday, like 'Folly', talks 'nonsense' to shake us out of our complacency. Thomas More realized the version of *Utopia* he had before him needed to be substantially recast. He had, in fact, to take Dorp's censure firmly into account.

11

ALTERNATIVE UTOPIAS

THOMAS MORE WASN'T THE only member of the family bubbling with ideas for the reshaping of society and his world. So was his brother-in-law John Rastell who, despite leaving Milk Street and taking his wife Elizabeth to Coventry, had afterwards returned to London to establish a printing press. Since then, he'd published over a dozen books culminating in three vast folio volumes, the *Graunde Abridgement* of legal cases: an encyclopaedia, organized alphabetically by topic and digesting 13,845 entries from the unpublished law reports, which became a landmark in legal publishing. All aspects of the book's printing and marketing were controlled by Rastell, who employed a team of legal friends to write and edit it, among them Christopher St German, whose home was near Coventry and who'd taught Rastell at the Middle Temple when he was a student.

John Rastell's early career had developed along lines not dissimilar to his brother-in-law's. In Coventry, he'd been chosen as the city's coroner, making him the youngest and most important civic lawyer after the recorder, also presiding over the Court of Statute Merchant and acting as clerk of the recognizances (of loans and debts), rubbing shoulders with the Mayor and Aldermen and attending the Corpus Christi Guild, where he would discover a flair for drama and interior design by building stage-sets for the 'miracle' or 'mystery' plays. Among this cycle of plays were three entitled *The Creation of Heaven and the Angels*, *The Creation of the World and Man*, and *The Parliament of Heaven*, which Rastell adored for their astronomical motifs around such themes as heaven, the stars and planets and 'God the Father of Heaven'. 'I am Alpha and Omega, the First and the Last,' says the Father of Heaven in one of the Coventry plays; 'first I make heaven with stars of light.'

After Rastell's return to London, his success as a printer enabled him and his family to leave their tenement near Fleet Bridge and move to a freehold dwelling on the south side of St Paul's within easy walking distance of Cheapside. They also leased a country estate at Monken Hadley, a leafy, sleepy village to the north-east of Barnet in Hertfordshire, three miles from Gobions. Rastell signed a lease for thirty years, then took a ten-year lease of a neighbouring farm. After taking possession, he brought in the builders to convert the old house, adding a ground-floor parlour and further rooms upstairs and down, with four or five bay windows 'well glazed' and 'three goodly chimneys'. New doorways were carved for the mansion, roofs tiled, and a neighbouring 'great barn' turned into a separate abode for a tenant. Three or four acres of garden were laid out, the overgrown shrubs and briar cleared away, and five fish-ponds dug and connected to a local stream. Rastell would have stocked his ponds with bream, pike and chub, the recommended species. He developed a passion for gardening, personally overseeing his project and declaring with great feeling that he wanted nightingales singing on both sides of his house. He was gregarious and hospitable, welcoming guests to enjoy sports such as archery or 'running at the ring' in which mounted competitors took aim with a lance at a circlet of metal suspended from a post intending to carry it off. In a shady corner of his garden, he built a raised bowling green, inviting his legal friends to play there. Among those joining him was a self-made lawyer, a trusted servant of Wolsey, firmly established among the London merchants and lately returned from a commission in Italy, Thomas Cromwell.

Like Thomas More, John Rastell had a utopian vision, but from a more practical, economically driven standpoint. In 1514, a whole year before Thomas would begin *Utopia*, he published his own, much shorter manifesto, calling for society to be governed and reformed by law. Although tucked away as the 'Prologue' to one of his law books, it considers what a commonwealth or 'public weal' is and ought to be. Rastell, unlike More, never envisages the abolition of lawyers or private property or the use of collective social engineering. To solve the problems of poverty and unemployment, he believes in creating the most favourable conditions for social and economic individualism. Honour and riches aren't bad in themselves, he says, unless they are abused or monopolized by the few. The best way to level the playing field 'stands in augmentation and preferring of law'. The rule of law, and respect for 'due process of law', he says, are civilizing values that when widely cultivated and shared will have the effect of encouraging equality of opportunity, and preventing the ruling class from governing capriciously.

Rastell, however, calls not just for laws, but laws in plain English that ordinary citizens can understand and read at home, and which are printed and therefore easy to verify. He wants the legal system to be fair, transparent and accessible, since only if a more general understanding of law permeates society will 'justice' cease to be a matter of how well-connected or how affluent people are. He'd been deeply affected by his experiences in Coventry, where, unlike London with its expanding commerce overseas, the city was gripped by an acute depression. While the Rastells were living there, the economic crisis was so severe that almost one in three houses stood empty in many of the streets and the taxes owed to the king could not be paid. Since the fourteenth century, Coventry's population had halved with a catastrophic impact on the local community. Some 3,300 inhabitants had died of plague or malnutrition in the 1470s alone, and the Rastells had been shocked by the stark poverty they'd encountered on arrival there.

When, shortly before his daughter Elizabeth was born, Thomas More had ridden to Coventry to visit his sister, he too must have seen with his own eyes the human consequences of a recession, although it wasn't that which he most remembered. Rather, it had been a controversy raging over religion, since a number of citizens had lately been accused of heresy. One in trouble while Thomas was there was Alice Rowley, the widow of a prominent merchant whom Rastell would have known. She was accused of reading heretical books, apparently an English psalter and an edition of the Epistles of St James, for Coventry was one of the main centres of Lollardy, a grass-roots heretical movement inspired by a fourteenth-century Oxford theologian, John Wyclif, who was in the vanguard of a campaign for access to vernacular scriptures. For over a century the threat of Lollardy had made scriptural translations risky to own, since, if not forbidden outright, they had been censored to the point of extinction. Whereas translations were allowed in France or Germany, none was lawful in England, where only the Latin Vulgate was licensed for sale. Almost certainly, when Richard Hunne went on trial for heresy, it was because the Church authorities had marked him out as a Lollard.

While living in Coventry, John Rastell had skirted the fringes of Lollardy, since what he believed about making the law transparent applied to the scriptures too. His links arose through one of the city's wealthiest grandees, Richard Cook, whose orthodoxy was in doubt after he promised to bequeath his own copies of the English Bible, all handwritten, to his fellow parishioners. Naming Rastell as one of the administrators of his estate, Cook instructed him where to send the Bibles when the time came, before introducing him to his son-in-law, John Peyto, a Warwickshire squire whose family had lived in the county since the time of the Domesday Book. Rastell afterwards became one of Peyto's land trustees, which is how he came to be reunited with Christopher St German, who was acting in the same capacity.

St German would one day lock horns with Thomas More in one of the bitterest clashes of Henry's reign over heresy trials. And yet earlier on, when Thomas had visited Coventry, far from automatically mistrusting his brother-in-law's friends for their avant-garde approach, he had shared their rejection of the sort of absurdity that put ritual and superstition ahead of plain and simple truth. Nothing better exemplified his outlook than his stinging critique of a cadaverous old friar he encountered during his stay, who'd caused a scandal by preaching that all those who said Our Lady's Psalter (i.e. the rosary) every day would be eternally saved. A few months before he was appointed Lord Chancellor, he was still able to take a positive line, saying, 'I never yet heard any reason laid why it were not convenient to have the Bible translated into the English tongue.' The 'lewdness and folly' of a small minority of ignorant trouble-makers 'were not in my mind a sufficient cause to exclude the translation and to put other folk from the benefit thereof'. But as Dorp's attack on Erasmus had shown all too clearly, the times were changing and Thomas More's defence of his friend's translation of the Greek New Testament had already given hostages to fortune. When his struggle with the king began in earnest, he would retreat from his more enlightened, optimistic view of human nature.

After it was published in 1516, Thomas More sent copies of *Utopia* to all his friends. John Rastell, given his practical, entrepreneurial bent, was always likely to interpret the book differently from those immersed mainly in the study of the liberal arts. Although fully versed in the fictional elements of the work, he found its evocation of the travels of

Christopher Columbus and Amerigo Vespucci too gripping to ignore. He and his brother-in-law would well have remembered the flurry of excitement about the time they were both still living at Milk Street when Bristol merchants, roaming the Atlantic, had discovered strange men 'far beyond Ireland', who were brought to London and paraded up and down Cheapside, 'clothed in beasts' skins, eating raw flesh, and [as] rude in their demeanour as beasts'. Rastell, in particular, used to talk to his friends of the exploits of John Cabot, or Giovanni Caboto, like Columbus a Genoese by birth, a naturalized Venetian citizen in Henry VII's employment who had voyaged from Bristol to North America. After reading *Utopia*, he was inspired to pioneer a voyage of his own to the New World as a shareholder and adventurer.

After bargaining with a financier, Rastell purchased one ship, renaming it the *Frances Rastell*, and chartered another, the *Barbara* of Greenwich, taking a half-share with a partner, and persuading a London fish wholesaler and other merchants to fit out a small flotilla of a dozen or so ships to accompany him. Their plan, licensed by the Lord Admiral, was to sail to 'the New Found land', where they would trade and fish. To this end, Rastell invested in a cargo of the finest silks, fustian (a kind of cotton velvet), frieze-cloths (made of coarse wool with a nap on both sides to keep out the cold, used for mariners' capes), canvas, hides, featherbeds, napery, pots and pans. He stocked the *Barbara* with large quantities of dried and salt beef, bacon, biscuit, wheat flour, salt, beer and other victuals. Live sheep were taken aboard, as were boxes of tools for masons and carpenters, and 'other engines' (mainly pulleys, hoists and wooden scaffolding) for construction works. He even recruited soldiers as security guards to protect his mariners and valuable cargo. He really was thinking of establishing a colony or trading post, signing up, among others, a young French apprentice, 'Thomas Bercula, printer', to join his expedition, intending to open an overseas branch of his printing-shop in America.

Thomas More and John Rastell would most likely have chatted together about *Utopia* and the projected voyage, because an intriguing link exists between the sources Thomas used in compiling Hythloday's narrative and Rastell's own research in preparation for his voyage. Hythloday's description closely paraphrases extracts from Vespucci's own writings taken from the Latin translation appended to the *Cosmographiae Introductio* (or *An Introduction to Cosmography*) of 1507. In *New World*,

Iudge More Sʳ Tho: Mores Father.

Iohn More Sʳ Thomas Mores Son.

ABOVE: Judge John More.

LEFT: Thomas More's
son, John.

Thomas More as 'the king's good servant' (oil on panel).

LEFT: Thomas More, drawing for the family-group portrait.

BELOW: Thomas More, drawing for the oil portrait.

RIGHT: Margaret Giggs
(false inscription).

Mother Iak.

BELOW: Cecily Heron.

OVERLEAF: Rowland
Lockey's version of the
family-group portrait, 1593.

Elisabetha Dancea
Thomæ More filia anno

Anna Crisacria Joannes
Mori Sponsa anno · 1 5.

Joannes Morus pater
annu · 76.

Thomas
no · 5

The Lady Barkley.

Elizabeth Daunce
(false inscription).

Anne Cresacre.

Vespucci's description of his third voyage, it is said of the indigenous Americans: 'Neither do they have goods of their own, but all things are held in common.' And in *Four Voyages*, a fuller and more reliable account of his travels: '[They] do not value gold, nor pearls nor gems, nor such other things as we consider precious here in Europe. In fact they almost despise them, and take no pains to acquire them.' Compiled by Matthias Ringmann to accompany a world map drawn by his friend and colleague, Martin Waldseemüller, the *Introductio* explains the main features of the map, itself sold either as a sheet of twelve printed 'gores' or lune-shapes to cut out and paste onto a wooden ball to make a small terrestrial globe, or less often as a spectacular, self-assembly wall-map.

When Thomas first embarked on *Utopia*, Ringmann and Waldseemüller alone had used the word 'America' to describe a separate American continent, although the name soon reached a much wider audience when it was copied by Johann Schöner, a German globe manufacturer. Rastell encountered it in one form or another, because he is the very first Englishman to talk about a continent called 'America'. His ships put to sea in July or August 1517, but never got further than the west coast of Ireland since his inexperienced crew refused to pass Dursey Head, the point where the information on their own maritime charts and pilot books ran out. Putting in at Waterford in an attempt to recruit new officers, he faced a mutiny, led by the purser of the *Barbara*, who sailed away to sell the precious cargo at Bordeaux. Rastell was left stranded for two years until he could afford to charter a vessel home, but used his enforced leisure to write a stage play, *The Four Elements*. Part-way through, one of the characters describes 'certain points of cosmography as how and where the sea covereth the earth, and of divers strange regions and lands and which way they lie, and of the New Found lands and the manner of the people', naming America as a separate continent and crediting Amerigo Vespucci with its discovery: 'This [*sic*] New Lands found lately/ be called America by cause only/ Americus did first them find.' And in his stage directions, Rastell instructs the actor whose role is to prove that the earth is round to make his grand entrance 'portans fyguram': 'carrying a globe'.

On the wall of the main hall at Bucklersbury, visible to all Thomas's family and their guests at dinner-time as they came in to eat, was 'a great map of all the world', perhaps based on a sketch of one of Waldseemüller's or Schöner's maps which Rastell or Thomas had got a London painter-stainer to illustrate. The complete story will never be known, and yet an inventory of unsold stock at Rastell's print-shop shows that, shortly after his return from Ireland, he went on to print his own edition of a *mappa mundi*, whetting our curiosity further. Sadly no known copy has survived, leaving open the question as to whether his was also the first English map to use the name 'America'.

Returning from Ireland, Rastell sued to recover damages for his stolen cargo. One aspect only of his case is significant, since it shows that before embarking for the New World he'd put his trust in his father-in-law, John More, and in Richard Staverton, the scrivener, married to Thomas More's older sister. They were to care for Rastell's wife and children while he was away, act as his attorneys for anything his wife Elizabeth 'as a woman sole' could not undertake on her own, collect his rents, and sell a valuable quantity of surplus ship's tackle on his behalf. Originally, Rastell had meant to entrust Thomas More with all these tasks, until at the last moment, when the *Barbara* was ready to depart, Wolsey sent Thomas abroad again, this time to Calais to treat with the French over piracy and the trading privileges of the English wool merchants.

As his factor for Rastell's affairs, John More hired Stephen Puncheon, a carpenter living in Fleet Street. Trouble arose first when Staverton, who had invested £40 in Rastell's venture, was obliged to sell wares and plate to finance his stake, and when Puncheon disposed of the ship's tackle for a fraction of its true value. Puncheon duly collected Rastell's rents and sold the tackle while Staverton sold his own wares and plate, but both men handed the proceeds to John More, who dictatorially chose to reimburse himself for debts he said that Rastell still owed him from the time when he and Elizabeth had left Milk Street for Coventry after quarrelling with Joan Marshall. When Rastell returned from Ireland, he found himself doubly out of pocket.

Rastell chose to postpone his day of reckoning with his father-in-law. On the back foot with creditors who were threatening a sequestration of his assets, this wasn't the moment to revive a family feud, not least since, while he'd been away, John More, at sixty-seven, had finally obtained his heart's desire and been appointed a judge in the Court of Common Pleas. With a sitting judge as a material witness to his alleged losses, it would be Rastell's word against his father-in-law's.

Rastell bided his time, for he had a new connection that might one day enable him to rebuild his career and his fortune. His guest from his games of bowls at Monken Hadley, Thomas Cromwell, was already a rising star. Whether Rastell had encountered any of Cromwell's clients in his law practice or knew of those attending a 'night school' off Cheapside where 'heretics were wont to resort to their readings' is less likely. Rastell, despite his erstwhile links to the fringes of Lollardy, still believed himself to be a devout Catholic. When a fellow Londoner tried to persuade him that the late Richard Hunne 'in his life sustained manifold intolerable injuries and wrongs, and finally against the law of God and of our said sovereign lord [was] wrongfully put to death', Rastell angrily retorted that '[he] was not wrongfully put to death, but that he was detected of heresy, and for the same heresy convicted by the law of Holy Church'. And yet for all their shared optimism and belief in setting forth the plain, unvarnished truth, John Rastell's vision of himself and the world was to lead him along a radically different path to Thomas More's, culminating in a fiery, bitter disagreement that would one day shatter family unity for ever.

12

CONVULSIONS IN CHRISTENDOM

DESPITE BUILDING A RELATIONSHIP of unusual trust with Henry after accepting a position as a royal councillor, something as close to friendship as was possible for a subject with a king, Thomas More would never feel at ease in a courtly milieu. Writing to John Fisher, Bishop of Rochester, a tall, willowy patron of Erasmus and a long-standing friend, he said: 'Much against my will did I come to Court, as everyone knows, and as the King himself in joke sometimes likes to reproach me. So far I keep my place there as precariously as an unaccustomed rider in his saddle.' Whereas the other courtiers tried to magnify their own importance, pretending their influence was greater than it really was, he did the opposite, insisting that the 'commodities of man' – worldly success, 'rooms' or offices, honour and authority – were the devil's temptations. He must have seemed more like a monk than a politician, impatient with protocol, refusing to put on a councillor's fur-lined black silk gown or velvet sleeves except at the special Easter and Whitsun festivals when the king would sit in state in his purple robes, wearing his gold crown and surrounded by his advisers. As some of his bemused colleagues sniggered, he preferred a plain woollen gown thrown 'awry upon the one shoulder'. What he yearned for wasn't the trappings of power, but a chance to put *Utopia*'s ideas into practice. His hopes were pinned on Wolsey, whom he judged to have the potential of a model statesman.

In *Utopia*, pride and greed are the chief obstacles to justice and equality. Wolsey shared many of these ideals, making 'equal' and 'impartial' justice the mainspring of his domestic policy. In and after 1516 he fined or imprisoned gentry, local magistrates and even nobles and king's councillors for economic crimes, prosecuting over 260 rapacious landlords in Chancery before hauling dozens of food racketeers before the Star Chamber. He investigated the meat trade in unusual depth, county by county, summoning seventy-four cattle farmers to make their appearance along with dozens of butchers. Those put on remand included 'Master Bond dwelling beside Barnet' and 'one Hall dwelling at North Mimms', both on the doorstep of Gobions. How did Wolsey get hold of their names? Only local knowledge could have supplied them. Thomas More, who liked to say that when rulers act corruptly, the laws could be made no better than cobwebs 'in which the little gnats and flies stick still and hang fast, but the great bumble-bees break them and fly quite through', must have heartily approved.

Except that Wolsey's attention soon flagged. His reforming forays were spasmodic: bursts of prodigious energy would be matched by periods of inertia as his mind darted elsewhere. Even this didn't deflate More, who could see that, partly from a churchman's desire for peace, partly through a chief minister's grasp of the spiralling costs of warfare, Wolsey was steering Henry into a new and uncharted role in foreign policy: less warrior-king, more arbitrator and peacemaker. Secure in his position as a cardinal, but determined to extract from the pope a wider international role, Wolsey had a vision in which Henry (and Wolsey himself) would unite the rulers of Europe in a treaty of perpetual peace, and from the vantage-point of London.

He was well aware of the dangers. Within a year of succeeding Louis XII in 1515, Francis I had led an army across the Alps, capturing Milan and Genoa. Spain, an ally of Milan, felt threatened, as did Pope Leo and the Emperor Maximilian. Charles of Castile, who had inherited the throne of Spain after Ferdinand of Aragon's death, had yet to establish his authority, but would soon make belligerent noises. Francis was willing to talk, but another war, it was clear, could erupt at any moment. Wolsey feared that Francis would retaliate against Henry for capturing Tournai, while from the east came a terrifying threat from the Turks. Fresh from conquering Anatolia, Syria and Egypt, their armies were advancing westwards, invading Hungary and laying siege to the island of Rhodes. In one daring assault, Turkish pirates had harried the coast of Italy, sailing up the Tiber and chasing Leo while he was hunting. 'It is time,' declared the pope with feeling, 'that we woke up from sleep lest we be put to the sword unawares.' In March 1518 he proclaimed a five-year truce among all Christians, sending ambassadors scurrying to and fro in Europe to rally support for a crusade.

Leo's diplomacy became Wolsey's opportunity. He neatly hijacked the pope's plan, inviting the ambassadors of all the leading powers to London and proposing a 'Treaty of Universal Peace'. To mollify Francis, Tournai would be returned in return for a pension. But Wolsey dropped the idea of a crusade. The Turkish threat was too remote for Henry, who warned of 'a certain other person than the Great Turk', someone far more dangerous, meaning Francis.

Thomas More worked furiously with Richard Pace to help bring the peace to fruition, both acting as Henry's secretaries interchangeably. Apart from them, only Wolsey and Tunstall had the necessary linguistic skills. When Cardinal Lorenzo Campeggio, the new papal nuncio, arrived in London, it fell to More to make a speech in Latin, welcoming him as he processed along Cheapside in his chariot, drawn by borrowed mules. Wolsey, meanwhile, secured from Leo the plenipotentiary powers he coveted, enabling him to preside over the formal sessions of the peace conference as a papal legate, sitting at Henry's right hand. When the final peace treaty was proclaimed in October, it was Wolsey, not Campeggio, who celebrated a solemn high mass, sung in unusual splendour.

Maximilian died in January 1519, precipitating an election among the German princes for the title of Holy Roman Emperor. Henry, Francis and Charles of Castile all declared their candidacies, Henry with quite unrealistic hopes. Charles was duly elected, styling himself Charles V. But, despite Henry's obvious disappointment, the balance of power moved in his favour, since the result made Charles and Francis more evenly matched than before. To defeat the other, each would need Henry as an ally.

By 1520, Francis had the advantage. Both he and Henry invited Wolsey to stage a crowning act of reconciliation between them. The result was a dazzling spectacle called the Field of Cloth of Gold, scheduled for June and complete with fairy-tale banquets, masques, tournaments and feats of arms, its centrepiece a meeting of the two kings in the so-called 'Golden Valley' halfway between the towns of Guisnes and Ardres beside Calais. Wolsey put Sir Edward Belknap in charge of building a temporary English palace. A design of pure Italianate magnificence, the exterior walls and roof were made of timber and painted canvas laid on brick foundations. Set within a quadrant each side of which exceeded 300 feet, the walls were pierced by oriel windows 30 feet high, glazed with clear glass for maximum effect. Inside, carved panelling and gilt bosses filled the spaces between the windows; the ceilings were of the finest white silk, fluted like the petals of a flower and embossed with roses set in lozenges of gold brocade. On display were Henry's and Wolsey's most sumptuous tapestries, their most valuable gold and silver plate. The walls of Henry's chapel, 100 feet long, were hung with cloth of gold; twelve gilded statues of the Apostles adorned the chancel, and on the high altar stood a solid gold crucifix over 3 feet high.

Belknap hired armies of craftsmen and entrepreneurs, giving his old protégé John Rastell the job of building a theatre, allowing him only two months for the work. Accompanying Wolsey and the royal party across the Channel were 1,200 lords, knights and esquires, their wives, chaplains, and 4,500 servants and hangers-on, most of them forced to sleep in tents. Wolsey alone took 150 horses; the lowliest esquires were allowed 8 each. Provisioning was a nightmare: the English contingent consumed 340 sides of beef, 2,200 sheep and 800 calves, and drank 37,500 gallons of wine and 140,000 gallons of beer, all in just three weeks.

Since Thomas More ranked as an esquire, he was allowed to bring his wife and horses with him, but not Margaret and the other children, who were left behind to continue their studies with Gonnell. But although attached to Henry's retinue, More never really took part in the festivities; he had other concerns. Charles V, seeking to forestall events, had made a surprise visit to England in late May. Behind the scenes, More had the delicate task of convincing his advisers of Henry's commitment to peace. At Wolsey's suggestion, a second meeting was hastily arranged between Henry and Charles, to be held at Calais after the rendezvous with Francis, and it was More's job to prepare for those talks.

While everyone else was feasting and carousing in between battling with violently strong winds and heavy showers at the Field of Cloth of Gold, Thomas disappeared to meet Francis's secretary, since Wolsey, already playing the French king off against Charles, wanted him to take informal soundings. Afterwards, when the Golden Valley was a mass of splinters as the temporary buildings were flattened as quickly as they had been erected, Wolsey and Henry went to meet Charles. Thomas made ready to accompany them, arranging to see Erasmus on the side, but at the last moment was sent to Bruges instead to settle commercial disputes with the merchants of the German Hanseatic League.

Arriving safely at Bruges, he despaired of seeing Erasmus, who'd turned up at the agreed rendezvous in Calais, where he'd been graciously received by Henry. Wolsey briefly looked in, but could spare the time only for the most cursory of handshakes. Then, while Thomas was still haggling with the Hanse merchants, Erasmus came on to Bruges. More greeted him with delight, bubbling with news, especially eager to tell his friend how successful Gonnell had been with his young charges. 'He took it into his head,' said Erasmus, 'to give me a demonstration . . . He told them all to write to me, each of them independently.' No topic or 'theme' was set, nor anything corrected before the samples were handed to the courier. 'Believe me,' said Erasmus, 'I never saw anything so admirable: there was nothing foolish or childish in what they said.'

Now Thomas was to be distracted from his utopian vision, but for reasons other than royal diplomacy. He had been stunned when, out of the blue and in the midst of the preparations for the Field of Cloth of Gold, a Frenchman, Germain de Brie, had published a vitriolic attack on him, poking fun at *Utopia*, before viciously attacking some lapses of style and grammar in his Latin poetry. Thomas rattled off a coruscating reply, congratulating himself on the speed with which he managed to publish it. 'What you write,' he frankly told de Brie, 'isn't just absurd and pointless, but criminal as well, and indeed as pernicious as you have been able to make it.' Men of learning would be insulted 'that you should contaminate them with such a tract as yours, as if setting jewels in the mire'.

What he'd overlooked was that Erasmus was an admirer of de Brie, and so refused to take sides. 'I am not so ill-informed or so blindly devoted to More,' said his best friend, looking through his fingers, 'that I cannot see the difference between them.' He warned Thomas that he risked overstepping the mark, causing him to run out to every London bookshop and buy up all unsold copies of his diatribe.

No other episode shows quite so starkly or how easily Thomas could be overawed by Erasmus. He tried to excuse himself with a joke: 'I still dwell in this mortal abode,' he said, 'and have certainly not yet been entered in the number of saints – let me laugh at a laughable notion.' But he declined to cloak his true feelings, lapsing into scatology as he had with Dorp. He wrote, rather scandalously, that de Brie should have someone 'fart in his face' and 'piss or worse' into his 'open mouth', then published two more highly offensive tracts. One, already circulated as an open letter, rebuked his old childhood friend, Edward Lee, the brother of Joyce, the dedicatee of his translation of the *Life of Pico*. The other laid into John Batmanson, son of the Doctor of Laws of Seville hired to assist Thomas in the case of the papal alum and a recent convert of the London Carthusians. For several years both men had been sniping at Erasmus, whose edition of the Greek New Testament had first appeared in 1516, saying it contained over 300 errors. Erasmus dismissed their claims as 'hairsplitting trifles', provoking them into calling him a 'tramp', 'fake theologian', 'slanderer', and the 'herald of Antichrist'. Since mud sticks, More couldn't stay silent, lashing out when Batmanson went so far as to accuse Erasmus of heresy.

Thomas felt he'd been a recipient of a double betrayal – in one case of an old friendship, in the other of Carthusian moral values – but on discovering that Lee and Batmanson were in league with the same Friar Standish who'd made the revolutionary claim for the king's right to vet canon and papal law, he convinced himself that he'd stumbled into something far more sinister: a 'faction' or 'conspiracy', stirred by malice and ambition, which had to be nipped in the bud.

Batmanson's charge of heresy was predictable given the challenge to the Church three years earlier by an Augustinian friar and professor at the University of Wittenberg, Martin Luther. On the eve of All Saints, 1517, Luther had nailed up ninety-five theses attacking the sale of indulgences. By 1520, as Henry prepared to sail to Calais to meet Francis, the convulsions had been felt across Christendom. Luther's forthright defence of his arguments, his inspired use of the printing press to reach out to millions, had made his name known everywhere. He and his adherents taught that good works and the sacraments of the Catholic Church alone were insufficient. Grace, and therefore redemption, was solely at the will of a just, if merciful God: the good (or 'elect') receive a gift of faith that has nothing to do with their own actions or those of the pope or the clergy. This, said Luther, was the true gospel of Christ.

Erasmus prevaricated over Luther for too long, because his own new ways of thinking had been based on methods and approaches so very close to this rebellious friar's. 'I am in favour of the man,' he typically said in answer to embarrassing questions, 'as far as one can be.' He even praised Luther as a fellow evangelical sharing his 'simple philosophy of Christ', wanting to reform the prelates and the monasteries, and rooting his theology in the Greek New Testament, parodying Lee and Batmanson as 'maniacs' and 'paranoids'. This played right into Batmanson's hands. As he cried triumphantly, 'the pot matches the lid.'

In June 1520, even as Henry and Francis disported themselves at the Field of Cloth of Gold, Pope Leo excommunicated Luther in the bull *Exsurge Domine*. Fully aware of the bull's significance, Pace, Fisher, Tunstall and Thomas More joined forces to ensure that Lutheranism was kept out of England. Gaining Wolsey's and Henry's support was their chief priority, but a victory was won when Henry agreed to send Tunstall, now a royal chaplain, to the imperial Diet of Worms, from where, in January 1521, he wrote an alarming report to the king of the spread of Lutheranism in Germany. He attended the Diet until 11 April, missing Luther's appearances on the 17th and 18th, but sending Henry a copy of *The Babylonian Captivity of the Church* in which Luther claimed that only three of the seven Catholic sacraments had been instituted by Christ and the others were spurious. With his secretaries Pace and More on the spot to advise him, Henry decided to refute the book personally, convening a conference of theologians in London led by Fisher.

Leo's bull was promulgated in London after the conference. On Sunday, 12 May 1521 Wolsey processed in state along Cheapside to St Paul's, to be met by a deputation of clergy and footmen bearing a golden canopy 'as if the Pope in person had arrived'. Entering the chancel in the presence of the bishops, members of the King's Council, nobles, and the Venetian and imperial ambassadors, he read out the papal decree. Everyone then trouped into the churchyard, where Wolsey mounted a dais raised on a stage, sitting in his golden chair. Flanked beneath him in serried rows, the bishops and royal councillors faced crowds so large it seemed as if half of London's population was there. Thomas More sat with the most important councillors, because ten days earlier he'd been appointed Under-Treasurer of the Exchequer and knighted. He found his new title of 'Sir Thomas' mildly, if pleasantly, ridiculous, even if his wife, now to be correctly addressed as 'Lady Alice', couldn't share in his usual self-deprecation.

When everyone had taken their places, Fisher preached a sermon. Within days it had been printed in English and in a Latin translation for the pope's benefit. Fisher, whose exalted view of the papal primacy was modelled on Gianpietro Carafa's, censured Luther for two hours. Anyone tempted to slumber would have been roused when Fisher gave the startling news that Henry would himself write a book denouncing Luther. A murmur of approval ran through the crowd which Wolsey acknowledged by waving aloft an unfinished copy of the king's manuscript, before signalling to a torch-bearer to light a bonfire of Luther's books. As the flames soared high into the sky, Wolsey rose and solemnly intoned the words of the papal anathema against Luther, cursing him and all heretics and schismatics for their wicked obstinacy, pride and malice.

Pace, exultant at the day's events, sent a copy of the sermon to Erasmus, but found him keen to distance himself from all such affairs. Before long, his caution was taken for cowardice by both sides. 'Erasmus is an eel,' said Luther. 'Only Christ can grab him. He is two-faced.' The Catholics were almost as perturbed, but Erasmus knew his own strengths and weaknesses. 'Mine,' he told Pace, 'was never the spirit to risk my life for the truth. Not everyone has the strength needed for martyrdom. I fear that, if strife were to break out, I shall behave like Peter.* When popes and emperors make the right decisions I follow, which is godly; if they decide wrongly I tolerate them, which is safe.'

Erasmus had looked into the future and was afraid of what he saw – unlike Thomas More, altogether tougher and fast discovering a taste for public confrontation if he believed the cause was just.

* St Peter three times denied Christ after leaving the Garden of Gethsemane.

13

A UTOPIAN DILEMMA

W HEN, ONLY WEEKS AFTER the book-burning, Thomas More was sent by Henry to threaten the Londoners for mourning the executed Duke of Buckingham, he must have known in his heart that he might have to contemplate resigning. His graphic fictionalized account of a 'great Duke' secretly accused of high treason and sentenced to death against the evidence in a show trial is suggestive of his inner turmoil. His choice of his daughter Margaret, rising sixteen, as a confidante encouraged to write beside him on the Four Last Things also indicates that in a crisis he could find it hard to keep his public and private worlds apart, and that Lady Alice, despite her love, worldly wisdom and feisty wit, was unable to meet all his intellectual demands. With friends like Erasmus, Grocyn or Colet to confide in, Thomas had rarely noticed this gap in his life before, but now these three were beyond reach. Grocyn and Colet were dead, and Erasmus, although for several years in the Low Countries after leaving Cambridge where Thomas could occasionally meet him, had sought refuge at Basel in Switzerland.

Dismayed and disillusioned at the rise of sectarianism in Europe, Erasmus sensed a smothering of free intellectual enquiry. 'Satan,' he said, 'is already singing his song of triumph.'

> Things have been brought to such a pass by the bitterness of Luther's party and the stupidity of some who try to mend this evil with more zeal than sense, that I for one can see no way out, short of a great tumult and confusion in human affairs. What evil spirit spread this frightful seed through the world of mortals . . . Luther seems to me to behave as though he did not wish to be kept alive; on the other side some

people handle their case in public so clumsily that you might think they are in collusion with Luther and only pretending to be advocates for the pope.

For Erasmus, the tragedy was that he'd himself laid down the foundations of Luther's heresy in his championing of the Greek New Testament and in his *Praise of Folly*. For Thomas More, whose study was crammed with books from floor to ceiling, and who couldn't even enter his own 'counting-house' without tripping over the overflow piles, the sad irony was that he should now be helping to burn Luther's.

The combative, steelier side to Thomas More had first been seen during his embassy to Bruges when he'd defended Erasmus from Dorp's calumnies. He'd returned to London early, claiming lack of funds and how much he was missing his family, but in reality scuttling back as soon as Henry had recalled Parliament to give his verdict on Hunne's case. Still an undersheriff and not then a royal councillor, Thomas may have feared rioting in the streets because Friar Standish, who'd made the claim for the king's right to veto canon law and papal decrees, had since given an inflammatory course of lectures at St Paul's. The bishops had closed ranks against him, summoning him to appear before Convocation, the most important council of the English Church, to answer on oath to a set of questions drawn in such a way as to be the prelude to a heresy trial.

With Hunne's fate looming before him, Standish had appealed to Henry. Oblivious as to what might be in store for them, the bishops had called on the king to defend the Church and the Catholic faith as he'd sworn to do in his coronation oath, thereby provoking the Lords and Commons to unite in a petition to Henry to uphold his oath by safeguarding the rights of his crown.

Henry had summoned Parliament to Blackfriars, a Dominican monastery in London, one of a number of alternative settings for Parliament, before moving it to Baynard's Castle, a luxurious riverside mansion where he could lodge overnight. Early in the proceedings, the judges had ruled that Standish was correct in strict law, agreeing with him that the pope and clergy lacked the power to enforce laws made in their synods and convocations without the royal assent, adding that anyone who tried to prosecute one of Henry's subjects for saying so would be guilty of *praemunire*. If necessary, the entire bench of bishops could be imprisoned and forfeit all their property.

Wolsey had knelt before Henry attempting to mollify him, but the king was impassive, slowly but surely beginning to glimpse the wealth and power he could obtain if he applied these sorts of principles to his regular dealings with the Church.

Henry had risen to speak at last. 'By the ordinance and sufferance of God,' he said, 'we are king of England, and the kings of England in times past have never had any superior but God alone.' He had warned the bishops: 'You make interpretation of your decretals at your pleasure. Therefore we will not agree to your desire now any more than our forebears have in times past.'

The judges had then ruled on the verdict of the coroner's jury in Hunne's case. After an hour's deliberation, they had decided that the crown lacked enough evidence for a murder conviction, and so the bishop's chancellor was freed.

Thomas More had seen and heard everything from a gallery, where the undersheriffs were sitting behind the Mayor and Aldermen in reserved seats. It seemed to be the end of the affair, except that for him it was really just the beginning, because he would soon be investigating Friar Standish on his own account and writing to Erasmus warning him against the friar, whom he said lay at the heart of an international 'faction' or 'conspiracy' to discredit the Greek New Testament.

Although ill for two months after Parliament had been adjourned, Thomas had begun his final revisions to *Utopia* the following spring, taking Dorp's censure of Erasmus and the display of royal power in Standish's case very much into account. He knew by then that Hythloday's 'nonsense' had to be less destructively negative and impractical than Erasmus's biting satire in the *Praise of Folly*, less a game and more a manifesto for change, but also that, unlike an imaginary island of Utopia which was a republic and ruled by a senate of wise and equal members, England was a monarchy ruled by a powerful, implacable Henry. Only, it seemed, if the king himself could be won over to the cause of reform could beneficial change begin.

Thomas had concluded on the basis of what he'd seen of Henry that what would count for most in real-life politics would be an honest man's ability to tell the truth to rulers and survive. Had he not had his own bruising experience of speaking out against Henry VII's taxation in 1504? To help refine his ideas, Thomas experimented with a gloriously vivid and dramatic 'History of King Richard III', a manuscript which, despite being left unfinished, would a generation later shape the backbone of William Shakespeare's own classic play. More's manuscript isn't a genuine history: his models were those pioneered by ancient authors putting characters and drama ahead of factual accuracy, and a third of his manuscript is in the form of invented speeches. By writing 'history' in this semi-fictionalized way, he found he was free to examine monarchy and politics from every conceivable angle, getting inside the heads of his characters, the good and the bad together. What fascinated him was how good, honest, innocent men are corrupted by 'the serpent of ambition', then laid low when monarchy totters into tyranny. Richard III is a worst-case example, but More uses it to illustrate a maxim from Seneca, a councillor to the Emperor Nero, who said: 'A tyrant differs from a king not in the name but by his deeds.'

He also borrows a metaphor from Lucian, saying, 'these matters be king's games, as it were stage plays, and for the more part played upon scaffolds . . . And they that wise be will meddle no further. For they that sometime step up and play with them, when they cannot play their parts, they disorder the play and do themselves no good.' Cardinal Morton is the story's hero, the closest thing Thomas knows in real life to Plato's ideal in the *Republic* of a philosopher-prince. Morton alone of the few honest men in Richard's reign is able to step onto the stage and play his part in the right way. He knows it's vital to be prudent as well as honest, for a naive councillor will quickly get his head cut off. According to him, it's crucial to know which lines to speak, and when. If necessary, he'll use every ploy, every trick of deceit or dissimulation in a moral cause, for it's only by resorting to 'crafty ways' to 'prick' the old Duke of Buckingham into a revolt that he can begin to dissipate the wickedness brought about by Richard's evil deeds. Such conduct on Morton's part, says Thomas More, is morally justifiable, because Richard's methods had been literally diabolical and by acting as he did, he outwits the devil at his own game.

When, however, a real-life Duke of Buckingham, son of the old duke, was charged with treason by Henry in May 1521, Thomas would abandon his manuscript. He stopped at the point where he'd written his own version of the very speech in which Morton tempts the old duke to rebel by telling him one of Aesop's *Fables* in which a Lion King, whose word is law, subverts and alters the law to suit himself in order that he may deceive, and devour, the other beasts at his pleasure. But despite consigning his 'History' to a bottom drawer, Thomas had already factored many of these same concerns into the final version of *Utopia*. He'd done so chiefly by recasting much of the first half of the work around the theme of whether an honest man should enter a king's service, grabbing the reader by setting up an intriguing, compelling, near-theatrical debate by characters speaking their lines in the first person to persuade us that good, honest men can be champions of truth, while keeping their heads on their shoulders.

Thomas, when revising *Utopia* for publication, had split the draft he'd composed in Bruges into two unequal books or parts. Hythloday's description of the island and its people was left largely intact, becoming Book II, but was set into an entirely fresh context by the addition of Book I. In this greatly expanded version, Gillis re-enters the conversation after More's account of his rendezvous after mass in the market-place at Antwerp and everyone moves into the grassy arbour at More's lodgings.

'My dear Raphael,' says Gillis, 'I'm surprised that you don't enter some king's service; for I don't know of a single prince who wouldn't be very glad to have you.'

His suggestion triggers a debate on candid counsel. A real-life Thomas More speaks for himself in the new dialogue, while Hythloday plays the part of the detached spirit, the uncorrupted philosopher whom life cannot bamboozle. Hythloday says it's pointless to search for wisdom at the courts of princes, where favouritism, sycophancy and hierarchy flourish like weeds. Why, he asks More, would he even consider putting himself in servitude to kings, when they habitually prefer war to peace and are obsessed with power and conquests instead of governing responsibly the lands they already possess? In any case, a ruler's councillors will be so proud, envious and self-opinionated, the ruler himself so narcissistic and susceptible to flattery, an honest man wouldn't stand a chance.

To clinch his point, Hythloday recounts a fable, a purported account of his experiences as a guest in Cardinal Morton's household on a visit to England. Almost half of the new material in Book I is given over to this apparent digression, the equivalent of a play within a play. Hythloday explains how at a dinner at Lambeth Palace where Thomas More had been a page, his fellow guests, a lawyer, a flunkey and a friar, turned out to be typically nasty courtiers for their fawning flattery, agreeing with anything Morton might say in their efforts to ingratiate themselves. Hythloday, entering their conversation, tries to show how poverty is made worse by the greed and profiteering of the rich. If, when food prices soar and wages fall, the poor are cruelly evicted from their homes, they will have no alternative but to turn to begging or crime.

The lawyer pricks up his ears, priding himself on his tough line on crime. He's indignant when Hythloday argues that it might be better for individuals as well as the state if petty thieves were set to work for the public good and not hanged. He simply can't envisage a possible link between economic destitution and crime.

When Hythloday cites the good example of the commonwealth of the Polylerites ('talkers of much nonsense'), a country where thieves make restitution in full to their victims and pay their debt to society as labourers on public construction projects, his fellow guests pull faces and shake their heads until Morton says he thinks the idea could be worth a try. Morton proposes an experiment. It would be no more unjust or risky than the English system, he observes, and even if it didn't work, no lasting danger could come of it. He even elaborates on Hythloday's suggestion: 'I think it wouldn't be a bad idea to treat vagabonds this way too, for though we've passed many laws against them, they've had no real effect as yet.'

As soon as Morton says this, the onlookers heap praise on the plan in spite of their earlier doubts. Hythloday, predictably, derides them for their obsequiousness, his indignation blinding him to the fact that Morton is willing to take his ideas on board.

Thomas More seizes on this golden opportunity. 'Your friend Plato,' he tells the fictional Hythloday, relishing his chance to incorporate his real-life thoughts and feelings into the dialogue, 'thinks that commonwealths will be happy only when philosophers become kings or kings become philosophers. No wonder we are so far from happiness when philosophers do not condescend even to assist kings with their counsels.'

Hythloday replies that intellectuals have offered their advice through the medium of published books; the trouble is that kings ignore them. Plato, he says, had been right to forecast that kings will never be guided by wise men short of changing into philosophers themselves. Kings are inherently wilful: sleeping tyrants with no space for honest councillors.

But Thomas is ready with his answer. While conceding that 'academic philosophy' will be useless in politics, he advocates 'another philosophy more suitable for statesmen': a 'practical philosophy' that knows its place, adapts itself to the circumstances at hand, and acts its part sensitively and appropriately.

> That's how things go in the commonwealth and in the councils of princes. If you cannot pluck up bad ideas by the root, or cure long-standing evils to your heart's content, you must not therefore abandon the commonwealth. Don't give up the ship in a storm because you cannot hold back the winds. You must not deliver strange and out-of-the-way speeches to people with whom they will carry no weight because they are firmly persuaded the other way. Instead, by an indirect approach, you must strive and struggle as best you can to handle everything tactfully. What you cannot make wholly good, you may at least make as little bad as possible.

An honest man should follow Morton's example in Richard III's reign, colluding in politics, and even (potentially) in lies and deceit, but to a strictly moral end.

Hythloday cannot agree. For an honest man to mangle the truth to make it palatable to the wicked, he contends, is to invite madness. Such an approach would be unethical, unchristian and impractical. 'At Court there is no room to dissemble or look the other way. You must openly approve the worst proposals and endorse the most vicious policies. A man who praised wicked counsels only half-heartedly would be suspected as a spy, perhaps a traitor.'

Thomas More completes his revisions to *Utopia* at this point, and his strategy works, since his proposals for how the champions of truth and reform are meant to function in the real world sidestep Dorp's complaints that Erasmus's satire had been witty but irresponsible. When finally published at Louvain, Dorp's own university town, a few days after Christmas 1516, *Utopia* had been acclaimed as much for its wisdom as for its satire. If anything, its realism had been a trifle too perfect. Jean Desmarez, the university's public orator who'd helped Erasmus to devise a woodcut map of the mythical island, didn't seem to realize the work was fictional, making himself appear a complete fool by calling for a bishop to be sent to the Utopians without delay. Peter Gillis, to whom

More had decided, after all, to dedicate *Utopia* in preference to Wolsey, had been unable to contain his glee at this, and at the naivety of those Antwerp readers who were poring over maps of the New World, vying with each other to pinpoint Utopia's precise location. Such misunderstandings are blissfully comic, but their effect at the time was profound, heightening the impression of realism and so further insulating More from Dorp's spleen.

Almost five years later, when Thomas and Margaret, father and daughter, were working side by side on the Four Last Things, the message he'd so graphically and indelibly scripted into the published version of *Utopia* must have seemed more urgent than ever. For when he'd inserted his new dramatic scenes, inventing Hythloday's rebuttals as a counter-weight to his own opinions on the merits of honest councillors at the courts of kings, he was far too intelligent, and knowledgeable in the lessons of history, not to know that, however wrong Hythloday appears to be, he is ultimately right. 'Practical philosophy', as Buckingham's trial and execution must have shown Thomas More only too clearly, will carry an honest councillor only so far, and even his hero Cardinal Morton had failed in Richard's reign, being forced to flee into exile until he could join Henry Tudor in organizing a foreign invasion. The dilemma for Thomas was that, despite those harsh facts, he still saw it as his moral duty to take the risk. After publishing *Utopia*, he had taken the plunge, accepting Henry's offer of a place in the King's Council and there, he believed, he had to stay.

PART III

THE ROPERS

14

SHIFTING SANDS

L ITTLE DID MARGARET GUESS when John Roper, her father's old
teacher from Lincoln's Inn and the Chief Clerk of the Court of
King's Bench, had renewed his acquaintance with her family that
his eldest son, William, would be her future husband. Possibly Jane,
William's mother, daughter of Chief Justice Fyneux, had first broached
the question of marriage with Lady Alice when both sets of parents were
together at the Field of Cloth of Gold.

Jane, a wealthy heiress in her own right, was as much accustomed to
getting what she wanted from her husband as Lady Alice. She had three
sons, William, Edward and Christopher, and six daughters, one of whom,
Agnes, was a nun. Edward, a sickly child, was her second son. Christopher,
her youngest, was her favourite whom she adored. William she came to
find ungrateful, resentful, aloof and indifferent to his studies at Lincoln's
Inn. Stockily built with curly dark brown hair, large brown receding eyes,
a slight squint, a protruding nose, thick lips, bushy eyebrows and a beard,
William was smooth and brash with a taste for high fashion, but of no
more than average intelligence. Now twenty-two,* he had independent
means and wished to leave home. For at his coming of age, his father had
arranged for the Chief Clerkship, that valuable sinecure, to be settled on
him, expending roughly a third of his fortune in the process. And since
the bulk of the Chief Clerk's work was done by salaried officials, William
was in clover. All he had to do was to deduct their wages before pocketing
his share of the court fees.

---

* William twice gave his date of birth as 1498 as a witness in the Court of Chancery. Although
conflicting with the age he gave when he made his will, and the age inscribed on his portrait
miniature, it is likely to be correct because witnesses in Chancery deposed on oath.

If only he'd been satisfied with this. In Kent his father's landholding included the delightful moated manor of Well Hall, set in idyllic rolling countryside near Eltham, surrounded by barns, stables, gardens and an orchard; lands and manor houses near Sittingbourne and in the parish of St Dunstan's, Canterbury; and rental properties in East Greenwich and Candlewick Street in London. William demanded assurances that every-thing would be his when his father died, whereas his mother wanted all her sons to have fair and equal shares.

Marriage alliances were harshly commercial, easiest to arrange between families of equivalent status, and the Mores and Ropers had reached a par. In November 1520 Henry had given a half-share in the keepership of the foreign exchanges to Thomas More, a grant tantamount to a monopoly, to be shared with a Genoese merchant, George Ardeson, who subcontracted the concession to a genuine foreign exchange dealer, Antonio Vivaldi. Already well known to Thomas as a friend of his dining companion, the merchant banker Antonio Bonvisi, Vivaldi handled all the transactions and paid More and Ardeson a fixed annual sum of £200 a year each. When added to More's councillor's fee and salary in his appointment as Under-Treasurer of the Exchequer, his income rose to almost £500 a year, close to that of the richest London merchants. And this was before Henry granted him the manor of Southborough, near Tonbridge in Kent, out of the lands forfeited by the Duke of Buckingham.

The marriage talks were under way by the spring of 1521. John Roper would have expected around £200 for Margaret's dowry, a sum he would consider appropriate for his own daughters but rather a lot for the Mores to find in cash. Lady Alice, who'd by now given up hope of marrying Margaret to Edmund Shaa to recover her own ancestral home, had to face the fact that she was dealing with a family as adept in the ways of the world as she was. As Margaret was not quite sixteen, her father in any case wouldn't allow her to leave home. She could sleep with William Roper after they were married if she wanted to, but not yet move out.

On 2 July, the eve of the announcement of John Roper's promotion as the next Attorney-General, a special licence was obtained for Margaret's wedding. To end the dowry haggling, Thomas fell back on the template that his own father, Judge John, had once established for Elizabeth and John Rastell. Margaret and William would receive free board and lodging at Bucklersbury for five years. Margaret's dowry would be payable at a later date by mutual consent. Only then would her jointure lands be legally assigned to her and William.

As a special marriage licence was used, wedding banns weren't needed, saving at least three weeks. Margaret and William exchanged their vows at St Stephen's Church where she'd been baptized, across the street from her home. Around eight or nine o'clock in the morning, the bride and groom met in the church porch, where Richard Staple, a priest hired by the churchwardens to take the place of the absentee rector, and his assistant, Harry Fynck, were waiting to greet them. The ceremony began on the threshold, rather than inside the sacred space, to symbolize the intermingling of the spiritual and secular worlds. Margaret and William stood side by side in front of the open door, the bride on the left and the groom on the right, watched by their families and friends. They exchanged their vows, after which the celebrant blessed the ring with holy water. He gave it to William, who took Margaret's left hand in his own.

'With this ring I thee wed, and this gold and silver I thee give; and with my body I thee worship, and with all my worldly chattels I thee honour.'

William repeated the hallowed phrases after the priest before placing the ring on Margaret's thumb, saying, 'In the name of the Father'; on the second finger, saying, 'And of the Son'; then on the third finger, saying, 'And of the Holy Ghost'; and lastly on the fourth finger where he left it, saying, 'Amen'.

The priest made the sign of the cross with his right hand, blessing the couple before inviting everyone inside the church for the nuptial mass. Leaving their guests in the nave which had lately been refurbished, Margaret and William followed the priest into the chancel as far as the steps before the high altar, where they knelt in prayer. An acolyte stepped forward with a thurible, the perfumed, acrid smoke of the incense fast engulfing them in a ritual of symbolic purification. Then, as the cadences of the 'Sanctus' died away, Margaret and William prostrated themselves on the stone floor, while four deacons in surplices stretched a fine linen cloth or 'pall' over them, one at each corner, ready for the concluding blessing and to remind them that marriage wasn't just a legal contract, it was also one of the holiest sacraments of the Church.

The benedictions over, the deacons lifted the pall and asked Margaret and William to stand. The celebrant handed William a pax or osculatory, normally a tablet of gold, silver or ivory depicting the Crucifixion, which he kissed, before passing it to Margaret, kissing her. The six bells in the tower would have rung out, and a magnificent new organ, standing in a gallery beside the rood screen, its case studded with hundreds of tiny jewels donated by wealthy parishioners, would have been played to the families and their guests.

After the wedding banquet at Margaret's home, the priest returned to bless the bridal chamber and sprinkle holy water. Margaret and William were left alone, perhaps for the very first time, since when a woman barely sixteen was courted by her suitor, protocol required them to be constantly chaperoned. A fiancé was, however, allowed to visit and share in his future wife's family meals. Margaret may have taken her opportunity at the dinner table, because she'd left William under no illusion that from the moment they were married, his attendance at lessons in her father's 'school' would be obligatory. Unsure as to how he would behave as a husband, how far he might try to curtail her freedom to read exactly what she chose, she treated him with mild disdain, but with an air of possession. Or so it appears from the first of her father's letters to reach her after Henry recalled him to Court. 'I am delighted,' he gently teased her, 'that your husband is following the same course of study as yourself. I am ever wont to persuade you to yield in everything to him, except now I give you full leave to strive to surpass him in astronomy!'

Margaret's father had bought a special licence for her wedding, because with a European war looming, he knew he could be sent abroad at any moment. As early as February and March, he'd warned Frans van Cranevelt, the new city clerk of Bruges whom he'd met after the Field of Cloth of Gold, to expect him. 'Please,' he wrote, 'give some thought to a house, and perhaps the one that I had before would not be the worst, but the price was the worst. Find out at what price it could be rented for two months from May 1, and thereafter by the week.' Then, on 9 April, he said: 'As for your very friendly offer to me of your own home, I find no thanks adequate to it.' But 'there is many a slip, my dear Cranevelt, between the cup and the lip.' It seemed he might not be going after all. 'In a few days I will know for certain and once I know I will write to you on the spot.'

Francis I, the aggressor, had begun mobilizing troops for another invasion of Italy, terrifying Pope Leo, who promptly allied with Charles V. Opportunism then played its part. When a catastrophic explosion at an ammunition dump delayed Francis's plans, Charles decided to strike at

France, urging Henry and Wolsey to join him. Henry was sorely tempted, but only if the pope stripped Francis of his title of 'Most Christian King' and granted it to him. He took advice from his secretaries, from Richard Pace on tactics and from Thomas More on the manuscript of his attack on Luther. The book, *Assertio Septem Sacramentorum* (or *A Defence of the Seven Sacraments*), contains little of significance on theology, but was hugely important in diplomacy since Henry extolled papal power, defending Leo against Luther who, thundered Henry, had slandered the pope by calling him a usurping tyrant.

In his intoxication against Luther, Henry had forgotten his revolutionary claim to be able to vet canon and papal law. Thomas spotted the inconsistency, turning to Henry and asking him what he would do if, one day, he were to quarrel with the pope. But Henry wouldn't listen, so keen was he to win the coveted title.

On 25 July Thomas kissed goodbye to his family once again. Henry was sending him with Wolsey to Calais and Bruges to mediate between Francis and Charles. It was a defining moment, for More had so far considered Wolsey to be a model statesman, a worthy successor to Cardinal Morton. Not any longer, for during this embassy he began to mistrust him, suspecting him of abandoning his vision of a perpetual European peace in exchange for power and self-advancement.

After ostensibly courting both sides, Wolsey made a secret alliance with Charles, pledging to invade France before two years were out. After several months of shuttling to and fro, the deal was done, during which time Leo had awarded Henry the title of 'Defender of the Faith', which (as Wolsey artfully advised) trumped that of 'Most Christian King'. Thomas More saw all too clearly where this was leading: back to the days of the 'Holy League', when Henry had joined Julius II and the emperor in a bloody, futile war against France. Had he seen Wolsey's ciphered correspondence with Leo, he would have been even more dismayed, for in it Wolsey revealed that he was not trying to bring about a lasting peace in Europe, but had taken on the role of mediator chiefly to hoodwink the French.

Before returning from Bruges, Thomas commissioned an oil painting of the Virgin Mary, leaving a deposit and arranging for Cranevelt to settle the balance. The artist drove a hard bargain, which More found distasteful. 'As for the people of Bruges,' he complains, 'I was disturbed by such meanness in the midst of such extravagance: when they have consumed immense wealth in such a way that whatever is spent is lost, they are forced to set things right by bits and pieces.'

Arriving in London, he withdrew to Gobions to relax, but fell gravely ill of a fever. He had a severe headache and a dry, acrid mouth, lots of aches and pains, and was alternately shivering, then consumed by burning heat as the fever peaked on the third day. A week or so later and convalescent, he felt an obsessive curiosity about his illness, believing he'd experienced something scientifically impossible. 'Fell there on me one fit out of course, so strange and so marvellous,' he said, 'for I suddenly felt myself verily both hot and cold throughout all my body, not in some part the one and in some part the other . . . but the self-same parts I say, so God save my soul.'

He knew that English medical textbooks denied that this could happen. So did his two physicians, each saying that he must have been delirious. The puzzle was solved by Margaret Giggs, who spotted that in one of Galen's treatises a whole chapter dealt with exactly her foster-father's symptoms. More couldn't suppress his elation that a member of his 'school', and a woman, had put two qualified, experienced male physicians to shame. Giggs was, he said, 'very wise and well learned and very virtuous too . . . [with] more cunning than both [his] physicians beside'.

Still trying to rest, Thomas can't have been sorry, when news arrived of Leo's death in December, that it was Pace, not himself, whom Wolsey sent to lobby for his election as pope. But if Wolsey aspired to a papal tiara, he would be disappointed, for Adrian of Utrecht, Charles's viceroy in Spain and former tutor, was elected. Promises flowed like quicksilver in the election: Giulio de Medici, long retained by Henry and Wolsey as their agent at Rome, blithely assured Pace, a personal friend from his days as Henry's envoy to the Vatican, that he would vote for Wolsey in every scrutiny and get all his friends to do the same. All this was to string Wolsey along, ready for the war against France.

Fully restored to health, More returned to Court early in 1522, where he found the atmosphere poisoned by Wolsey's accusations of leaks and plots. Wolsey, on the defensive over the treaty, had for several weeks allowed no one except himself access to Henry's in-tray. He'd then appointed Richard Sampson, Dean of the Chapel Royal, once his own chaplain and a safe pair of hands, to replace Pace as a royal secretary.

More trod warily, working with Sampson before continuing alone as secretary when Wolsey sent Sampson on an embassy to Spain.

Thomas, who suspected Wolsey's bad faith over the treaty, said nothing until, asked one day to coax Henry into writing urgently to Charles, he dared to voice his own opinion of foreign policy. This followed an interview between Henry and Charles in June, when Charles had landed at Greenwich and he and Henry made a grand ceremonial entry into the capital across London Bridge. More spoke his mind after Wolsey told Henry about fresh intelligence that the Duke of Bourbon, Constable of France, was plotting to overthrow Francis. Henry was overjoyed, because if Bourbon's conspiracy resulted in Francis's defeat, Henry himself might succeed him.

'I pray God,' said Thomas, speaking his mind, 'if it be good for his Grace and for this realm that then it may prove so, and else in the stead thereof, I pray God send his Grace one honourable and profitable peace.' He had foreseen Bourbon's unreliability, but even if Wolsey or Henry had been willing to listen, it was too late. Henry's claim to the French throne, the old ambition, was driving events forward. Unwilling to summon Parliament unless he had to, Wolsey demanded substantial, urgent loans from all taxpayers. London, where many merchants had to sell their stock to raise sufficient liquidity to pay in a hurry, was hardest hit. Even this wasn't enough, so in April 1523 Wolsey reluctantly called Parliament. More was chosen as Speaker and, remembering his ordeal under Henry VII, secured (as he honestly believed) a concession of absolute free speech for members.

Despite boycotting Parliament's opening ceremony, Wolsey, nevertheless, strode arrogantly into the House of Commons, calling for a levy of £800,000 and declaring 'he would rather have his tongue plucked out of his head with a pair of pincers' than ask Henry to accept a lesser sum. He tried to bludgeon the Commons into submission, but met 'a marvellous obstinate silence'.

Seventeen weeks later, he got less than half of what he wanted, and so, to compensate for the funds he believed Parliament had denied him, withheld repayment of the earlier loans, breaking a promise, which Thomas found deeply disquieting. Nobody had argued more eloquently against Wolsey's exactions than John Bridgeman, one of the representatives for Exeter. In a reprise of More's own misfortune, only worse, Wolsey sent for Bridgeman and tried to silence him. Relying on Henry's grant of absolute free speech, Bridgeman carried on. At the next reading of the tax bill, he repeated all his criticisms, only to be arrested, then confined to his lodgings, where he fell sick and died.

Wolsey, irritated with More for his lukewarm support, sent for him and, pacing up and down his newly built, stylishly fashionable long gallery at Westminster, said, 'Would to God you had been at Rome, Master More, when I made you Speaker.'

'Your Grace not offended, so would I too,' answered Thomas, changing the subject. He began to speak of Wolsey's interior decorations, saying, 'I like this gallery of yours, my Lord, much better than your gallery at Hampton Court.'

And yet, despite these mutations, Wolsey kept up outward appearances. Aware that the Speaker, in addition to his ordinary fee of £100, was due to receive the same sum again as a bonus at the end of the session, he reminded a forgetful Henry to authorize the payment.

In August 1523 Henry's second major war began after Wolsey shipped an army of 11,000 troops led by the Duke of Suffolk to Calais. Suffolk's orders were to march on Paris, for the campaign held out the prospect of huge profits if the capital fell. Wolsey masterminded the strategy, reassuring an initially sceptical but now exultant Henry that with Bourbon in open revolt, 'there shall be never such, or like opportunity given hereafter for the attaining of France.'

As Suffolk led the army closer towards Paris, More, closeted with Henry at Woodstock in Oxfordshire, received Margaret's excited letter telling him that she was pregnant. His mood lightened, sheer exhilaration swept over him as he realized he was shortly to become a grandfather: 'I pray most earnestly for you,' he answered by return of post. His spirit was so lightened, he couldn't resist another tease: 'May God and the Blessed Lady grant you happily and safely to increase your family by a little one like to his mother in everything except sex. Yet let it by all means be a girl, if only she will make up for the inferiority of her sex by her zeal to imitate her mother's virtue and learning. Such a girl I should prefer to three boys.'

It was indeed a girl. Born about Christmastide, she was baptized Elizabeth after her aunt, Margaret's younger sister. Erasmus, keeping safely out of trouble at Basel and tidying up the notes and commentary to a forthcoming edition of the Christmas hymns of Prudentius,

dedicated that work to mother and baby on hearing the news, and sent
the baby a kiss. 'The Christ-child,' he told Margaret in a flourish of his
pen, 'will not scorn to be celebrated by such a couple as you and your
husband, whose purity of life, peace, concord and simplicity are such
that few, even from among the professed monks or nuns, would dare to
compete with you.'

Since Erasmus had not, and never would, set eyes on William Roper,
this accolade is deeply ironic, for the Roper family quarrel had entered a
fresh phase. John Roper, while still of sound mind and in good health,
decided the time had come to make his will, overruling his wife Jane
for the first time in her life, and causing her to increase her lobbying,
especially for Christopher, her favourite son. A witness saw her pleading
with her husband: 'Would God,' she had said, 'you would let Christopher
your son have your manor in St Dunstan's, Canterbury, and your eldest
son some other thing.'

John Roper, increasingly irritated and impatient with his eldest son's
greed, finally snapped. He decided to cut William almost completely
out of his will. His younger sons would instead divide his principal
landholding between them. William would receive only the residue of
the estate, purchasing lands of his own, if he wanted them, out of the
accumulated profits of his Chief Clerkship.

William rebelled at this, telling his father frankly that unless the terms
of the will were altered in his favour, he would contest its legality in court.
John Roper did not blink, telling his son, 'All trust and familiarity is set
apart between thee and me,' and adding a clause to his will stating that
if either William or his descendants did anything 'to let [i.e. hinder],
interrupt or disturb the performance of this my testament and last will
in any parcel thereof', then the entire estate would pass to Edward and
Christopher, and William would be stripped even of the residue. At this,
a furious William stormed from the room.

15

HEAVEN IN CHELSEA

MARGARET ROPER'S PIETY WAS as sincere and intense as her father's. Every morning and evening, she knelt beneath the 'great Crucifix' in the family's private chapel, saying her prayers before the portable images of the saints on the altar, reading her octavo-sized illuminated Book of Hours with its cycles of devotions to fit the liturgical calendar, before closing its green leather covers and retying their thin vellum strings. Every day she and Margaret Giggs crossed the street to hear the priests say mass at St Stephen's. Twice a year at least she went to confession, unburdening her conscience to her parish priest after testing herself privately for days and hours beforehand in case she had broken any of the Ten Commandments in thought, word or deed. And at family meals in the great hall, she and her sisters would take it in turns to read aloud from the Bible or one of the Church Fathers, continuing until her father signalled for them to stop and return to their places, after which a general discussion could begin.

After marrying William, it was sometimes Margaret, rather than her busy father, who wrote to Erasmus to pass on all the family's news. She even stepped in as a surrogate host, entertaining Juan Luis Vives, a Spanish-born scholar living in the Low Countries, whom her father had invited to stay but then was unable to receive. Vives, one of Frans van Cranevelt's best friends, had first met her father at the Field of Cloth of Gold. Twelve years older than Margaret, he was descended from a family of *converso* Jews, a brilliant rhetorician also trained in medicine: his sobriquet was 'Vives the physician'. He sought a new position and a salary after his patron had been killed in a riding accident.

On van Cranevelt's recommendation, More had arranged for Vives to be paid to write a book on women's education. When, in April 1523, he had submitted his draft, he dared to believe it might lead to a resident post as tutor to Princess Mary, Henry and Queen Katherine's only living child. Travelling to England to deliver his manuscript in person, he gained an audience with Wolsey, who appointed him a lecturer at Oxford. He visited the Mores four or five months later, correcting the proofs of his book at Bucklersbury and inserting a brief eulogy of Margaret and her sisters.

Vives had arrived just as their father was called away by Henry to write a revised version of an *Answer to Luther*. As before with *Utopia*, he greatly expanded on his first attempt, inserting material that was to shape many of his subsequent ideals, shifting the attack on Luther away from the Bible and the Greek New Testament towards upholding the Catholic Church and its authority. Whereas Luther believed in *sola scriptura* (the 'Word of God' alone) and judged the Church and clergy by how far they conformed to the Bible, More defended Church tradition. The 'true gospel of Christ', he said, had been 'inscribed on the heart of the Church' since the Apostles had walked on earth. The 'true Church' wasn't Luther's schismatic one but the Church of the Apostles, and only this Church had the right to interpret scripture. When, in its General Councils lawfully convened at Rome or elsewhere, the Church had distinguished between true and false doctrines, those present had been 'inspired by the Holy Spirit'. Church Councils, said More, had enabled Christians to reach a true and valid 'consensus'. The Church was never to be judged, or scripture interpreted, by single individuals like Luther. The 'common faith of Christendom' was rooted in 'consensus', even if foul, vile, detestable heretics claimed otherwise.

Margaret, already washing her father's hair-shirt with her own loving hands, wanted to know more. Laying aside Seneca and Galen, she read for herself the authors the king and her father had been discussing. One was St Cyprian, who'd converted to Christianity in AD 246 and was elected Bishop of Carthage. Steadily working through his letters in a version edited by Erasmus, she spotted that one of them contained a nonsense. The letter, strongly rebuking pastors allowing apostate Christians to be received back into the Church, included the phrase '*et nisi vos severitatis . . . dissolvere*', which is untranslatable. Erasmus, burning the midnight oil, had erred. Reading like her father with an eye to the meaning and significance of whole sentences, not the individual words, Margaret guessed what the text should say: '*nisi vos*' was a mistake for '*nervos*'. In translation, it should say, 'Far be it for the Church of Rome to relax its vigour . . . *and to weaken the nerves of discipline* in a manner so detrimental to the majesty of faith.'

She also discovered this letter wasn't by Cyprian as scholars believed, but by Novatian, a heretic and schismatic, an opponent and rival of the holy saint, an excommunicate denying the authority of Church Councils. She knew the gist of the story from Eusebius, one of the early Church historians used by her father, who showed how, driven by insatiable pride and ambition, Novatian was led into schism, splitting the Church for a century. Heretics like that, said Eusebius, were blasphemers and sexual perverts, corrupting faith and morals.

Margaret sent word of her discoveries to Erasmus, who – a trifle shamefacedly but genuinely impressed – acknowledged her to be one of Europe's leading women intellectuals, rattling off a glowing tribute in the shape of a thinly veiled colloquy about her.

The dialogue, between a foolish abbot, Antronius ('ass'), and Magdalia, an erudite, eloquent wife and mother, whose name evokes both 'Meg' and Mary Magdalen, shows that her speciality is breezy one-liners.

'It's not feminine to be brainy' [begins the foolish abbot]. 'A lady's business is to have a good time.'

'How do you measure good times?'

'By sleep, dinner parties, doing as one likes, money, honours.'

'But if to these things God added wisdom, you wouldn't enjoy yourself?'

'What do you mean by wisdom?'

'This: understanding that a man is not happy without the goods of the mind; that wealth, honours, class make him neither happier nor better.'

'Away with that wisdom!'

'What if I enjoy reading a good author more than you do hunting, drinking or playing dice? You won't think I'm having a good time?'

'Distaff and spindle are the proper equipment for women . . . I could put up with books but not Latin ones.'

'Why not?'

'Because that language isn't fit for women.'

'I want to know why.'

'Because it does little to protect their chastity . . . They're safer from priests if they don't know Latin.'

'Very little danger from you in that respect!'

'I'm sure I wouldn't want a learned wife.'

'But I congratulate myself on having a husband different from you. For learning makes him dearer to me, and me dearer to him.'

'God forbid.'

'No, it will be up to you to forbid. But if you keep on as you've begun, geese may do the preaching sooner than put up with you tongue-tied pastors. The world's a stage that's topsy-turvy now. Every man must play his part or – exit.'

'How did I run across this woman?'

Before the colloquy could arrive, a rapid succession of events threw the family into disarray. At thirty-one, Thomas Elryngton, husband of Margaret's stepsister Alice, suddenly died. Taken ill at Hoxton near Shoreditch, he was given the last rites around 15 January 1524. Alice, heavily pregnant, already caring for three young children, two boys and a girl between one and three, was distraught. After burying her husband in the tomb of his ancestors, she came straight back to her mother, Lady Alice, at Bucklersbury, where she could have her baby and she and her children could be comforted.

When the baby was stillborn, her mother took the strain. Thomas More, too, had much to do. As Elryngton's executor, he found that he'd inherited a run of lawsuits begun by his stepson-in-law over alleged waste and mismanagement of his lands. The crisis was sufficient to bring Judge John More over from Milk Street for a family conference. As down-to-earth as ever, he had the answer. The grieving widow would be betrothed without more ado to Giles, the wealthy son and heir of the recently deceased Sir Giles Alington of Horseheath, whose estate Judge John just happened at that very moment to be settling. The elder Alington had died of 'the sweat', caught while sitting as an assize judge at Cambridge. The prisoners had got infected in the castle gaol, causing everyone attending these assizes to fall 'sore sick'.

Sir Giles, who spent lavishly on luxuries, died in debt despite owning thousands of acres of prime agricultural land in Cambridgeshire and a manor house at Willesden, five miles north-west of London. Selling his son's marriage to the highest bidder to raise cash-in-hand to pay his creditors was a task Sir Giles had entrusted to Judge John. In June 1524 Alice and Giles, both twenty-three, were married after the judge brokered a masterly deal in which Giles accepted full rights as legal guardian over his stepchildren in lieu of a dowry, enabling him to scoop £2,000 in profits over the period of his guardianship, an offer too good to refuse. Giles, decent, intelligent and well-liked, a husband whom Alice in time came to love, moved temporarily into the Barge while the lawyers set about their tasks, Judge John taking the lead and calling on William Roper to assist.

Next came the bad news of a break-in by vandals at the Mores' country estate at Gobions. The intruders had torn down the palisade surrounding the park, before massacring the deer, ripping unborn fawns from the wombs of the does, one a much-loved family pet, before they killed them, and pinning the severed head of the finest buck to the front door of the manor house with a stake. Not content, they'd returned next day, riding and hunting over the estate. The ringleaders came from St Albans; maybe Judge John had sentenced a local man to the gallows and his relatives wanted revenge, maybe the Mores had quarrelled with their neighbours over hunting rights. To stop further incursions, Judge John complained to Wolsey, who hauled the marauders into court.

Then, Richard Staverton the scrivener, Margaret's uncle, scandalized the family. Judge John, unrelenting in his efforts to advance his favourite son-in-law's career, had at last persuaded Thomas to nominate him for a post of secondary (or deputy) in the Sheriffs' Courts, only for Staverton to withdraw at the last moment. He'd been found out for swindling his young niece, a spinster and heiress, by taking her to church at nine o'clock at night and forcing her to sign two documents, one making over a valuable estate near Bray in Berkshire in trust to him, the other a written covenant never to marry without his consent, or else forfeit £300. When, in spite of this, she married her lover, Staverton sued her for the money, and when she died leaving a younger sister as her heir, he went to the judges in the Court of Common Pleas to register his title to the estate, which is when the swindle was discovered.

Staverton's case came immediately after the attack on the deer park. Queen Katherine, lord of the manor of Bray, informed of his unsavoury tricks, reported him to Wolsey, who called Staverton to account before the Court of Star Chamber, hanging all his dirty washing out to dry. After this, Judge John, himself lately promoted from the bench of the Common Pleas to that of the King's Bench, could have had no further illusions about Staverton as the family's black sheep.

Still suckling her baby, which it seems she preferred to employing a wet-nurse, Margaret had to help her stepmother cope with these and yet more unexpected changes. Henry, delighted with the progress of the *Answer to Luther*, had granted her father the wardship of Giles, eldest son of Sir John Heron, heir to his father's estates in Lincolnshire, Essex and Oxfordshire, with a newly built mansion at Hackney. At first the Mores saw little of their charge, since he was studying at Cambridge with two of his younger brothers, staying in a hostel under the supervision of a priest. Then, when almost twenty, Heron had been forced to leave university because no one had remembered to pay his fees. Arriving at Bucklersbury in time for the Alingtons' wedding, it was decided that he would attend More's 'school' instead until he came of age. A handsome, gregarious young man whose marriage prospects were excellent, he enjoyed the good things of life and soon became a friend of William Roper.

A month later, Margaret acquired a second adopted sister in an extraordinary way. Among all his other duties, her father still sat as a judge in the court of 'poor men's causes', a workload made all the heavier by the fact that Wolsey rarely had much time for his judicial duties. But a case taking up several weeks of both men's time concerned a brutal abduction and rape. A Yorkshire squire, Edward Cresacre, from Barnborough, near Doncaster, had died young, leaving an infant daughter, Anne. As most of her inheritance was freehold, a sly lawyer, marrying her mother, had conspired with a neighbouring squire, Ralph Rokeby, to marry Anne to Rokeby's bastard son, John, and steal her lands. When the parties were no older than six and despite flagrant illegality, they were brought before a priest and forcibly wed.

The plot appeared to have succeeded, until Anne one day pulled her wedding ring from her finger and said loudly before witnesses, 'I utterly refuse John Rokeby . . . I would rather never have husband than have him.' Her disavowal alerted a local knight and magistrate, a military man and royal servant, a man said to be of 'a dangerous disposition', Sir Robert Constable. He turned informer, but, coveting Anne's inheritance for himself and believing himself secure in Henry's favour, violently abducted her when she was still under twelve, betrothing her to his own son, who raped her.

Constable meant to force Anne into a second illegal marriage, but instead the Rokebys triggered a battle royal, reporting Sir Robert to Henry. Proud, arrogant and presumptuous, Sir Robert dared to ignore a royal summons to appear in court and apologize. Instead, he had to be dragged by royal pursuivants before Wolsey in the Star Chamber, where he was forced to kneel and beg for mercy.

Wolsey fined him 1,000 marks (£666). The investigation continued, but despite Wolsey's best efforts, the case was dropped after Constable apologized and Henry granted him a pardon. As to Anne herself, Henry and Wolsey gave her on a whim to More and Lady Alice as a foster-child.

Poised and vivacious, spirited and spry, Anne was a teenage minx, no more an intellectual than Lady Alice herself. Warmly welcomed by her new family, she quickly acclimatized to life in London, relishing the latest fashions and badgering her foster-mother to buy them for her as soon as she was old enough, especially sleeves and French hoods: long, showy, designer over-sleeves of satin or brocade, and slim, elegant hoods with a row of glittering pearls along a golden headband, chic and flattering in comparison to the old-fashioned gable-headdresses.

Over the ensuing years, Anne and Lady Alice would forge the closest of bonds. And yet, however happy and at ease Anne was made to feel, her new surroundings must have seemed strange at first. Bible readings at mealtimes, prayers morning and evening, regular church attendance weren't things she'd encountered much during her chequered childhood. Maybe it was during this, her first summer with her adopted family, that she was spotted giggling at Thomas More's hair-shirt creeping out from beneath his linen shirt as he relaxed in his shady arbours in the cool of the evening. Saying nothing to Anne, Margaret spoke discreetly to her father, who took no action beyond ensuring his hair-shirt was never, ever seen by anyone except his eldest daughter again.

Scarcely had autumn leaves begun to fall than the family moved house, a step they'd been considering for some time. Maybe anticipating more grandchildren or maybe on an impulse, Thomas More bought first the lease of a fine mansion called Crosby Place in Bishopsgate Street. Built of limestone and timber, large and beautifully proportioned, one of the tallest, grandest houses in London, some fifty years old, and with the largest garden in the city still in private hands, this was where Richard III had lodged while plotting to usurp the throne. Determined to have as much outdoor space as possible if they were really going to live there, Thomas and Lady Alice then leased nine adjoining properties to ensure their privacy, before changing their minds completely and selling on all their purchases to More's friend, Antonio Bonvisi.

They resumed their search in Chiswick, a delightful spot five miles upstream from Westminster on the north bank of the Thames, but after leasing from St Paul's Cathedral the manor of Sutton, which included a spacious house and meadows, pasture, arable land and woods amounting to 150 acres, the couple again got cold feet. Perhaps the awkward commute into London was a worry. If so, it was third time lucky. Keeping the Chiswick estate as a farm and an investment, they turned their quest to Chelsea, just as green and verdant and on the same side of the river, but half the distance from the city, accessible by a cart-track along the riverbank, but fastest by barge or wherry. Of course, a barge had to be readily available, since the tides and currents could be treacherous on the approach to Chelsea Reach, so Thomas decided from the outset to allow himself the luxury of owning his own barge with eight oarsmen to speed him on his way.

Property in Chelsea was expensive and hard to find. Searching assiduously throughout the spring and summer of 1524, Margaret's father needed all his silver-tongued persuasion, all his legal acumen, to get value for money, securing what to a casual observer would have looked like a ragbag of insignificant, disparate plots, before expertly aggregating and rationalizing them to carve out a country estate rivalling in size and setting the nearby Chelsea Manor, owned by the courtier Sir William Sandys, a man in a far higher status league than Thomas More.

First purchasing a house, garden, seven acres of arable land and half a meadow, he added twenty-four more acres of arable and three of meadow. Next, paying in cash for a quick sale, he bought a two and a half acre plot called Butts Close overlooking the west door of Chelsea Church, a space once used by the parishioners for military training, before acquiring a private wharf from the same seller, plus an adjacent field. The transaction almost misfired: the vendor took the money, then gazumped Thomas, who was forced to hire an experienced land agent as well as London's leading expert in contract law to rescue the deal. Finally, he leased another, smaller farm from the executors of John Meautis, one of the clerks of the King's Council, who'd died leaving property in Chelsea.

The family ended up with a riverside 'mansion' or 'place', rambling and dilapidated, with a wharf reached (after some modifications) via the garden through a wicket gate, set in an estate comprising garden and orchards, the Butts Close property, seventy-seven acres of arable land and twelve and a half of meadow, and a dozen other lesser fields and buildings. Landscaped afresh by the Mores, the garden, a couple of stone's throws to the rear of the mansion – according to a relative of John Rastell who strolled there – was idyllic. Perhaps a third of a mile in depth and three or four hundred yards in width, it came complete with a viewing platform, set on rising ground, enjoying a breathtaking vista of the London skyline to the north-east, with its tall church spires, clusters of houses and carefully tended fields, and of the rolling Thames to the south-west, its banks flanked by trees and meadows subtly refracting the light as in a living Arcadia.

Since transporting bulkier, heavier items of furniture from houses into which they had been custom-built was impractical, many of the family's possessions would have remained at the Barge regardless of whether Thomas and Lady Alice would decide to continue their lease there. In fact, they kept their old house on, possibly to see how things worked out, more likely because Thomas still needed an overnight base in the city from time to time. The rooms were mothballed; it was just books, selected artworks, clothes, pewter and plate, household utensils and bed linen that were moved. Exactly how long the carriers took to complete their work is unknown, but the family was safely at Chelsea by 1 October.

Then the builders moved in.

16

'OUR FATHER'

AMID THE TOPSY-TURVY OF 1524, Margaret still found time to finish one of the projects that meant most to her, a translation of Erasmus's meditations on the Lord's Prayer. Completing her manuscript just a few weeks or days before the family started loading their clothes and books onto carts for the move, she aimed to popularize Erasmus's ideals for the mass market, crafting her translation to be read aloud so that as many people as possible could share and enjoy it in a domestic setting. Very few Englishwomen had dared to go into print like this before. Those who did had either been members of the royal family or their work had been published posthumously. Margaret didn't contemplate publishing under her own name, or not in so many words. Fully aware of the risk to her modesty, she meant to conform broadly to the expectations of her father and his society, even if more in the letter than in the spirit. But now that she was married, she was free to act provided her husband didn't object, and she was giving him little say in the matter. Nothing would be allowed to stop her getting at least one of her own manuscripts into print.

Erasmus's *Precatio dominica*, first published at Basel in 1523, had been a soliloquy upon the meaning and significance of the Lord's Prayer. He'd paraphrased and interpreted the prayer, proceeding step by step in small, easily manageable bites or sections, keeping to the structure of the original. Intended as a model for private devotion, Erasmus wished to encourage ordinary people to apply his methods in their own prayers, persuading them to forgo immediate, selfish requests in favour of a concern for the spiritual welfare and salvation of all God's children, but by writing in Latin, he had little, if any, chance of reaching out to his intended audience.

Seeking to remedy this deficiency, Margaret explained her guiding principles in advice she gave to other women wanting to write vivid, readable English prose. Her chief aim as a translator, she said, was to convey as far as possible the true 'sense and meaning' of the source, not to leave any passage 'abstruse and dark' for the sake of a slavish, literalist accuracy. She sought to replicate the original author's voice and tone, whether soft or loud, grave or light-hearted, in such a way as is 'most decent and best beseeming him'. 'I strove,' she said, 'to set out that same style and effect in English, somewhat accordingly as the gravity and importance of so notable a story required.'

Margaret's translation isn't literal or even exact. She captures the true spirit of Erasmus's evangelical piety, his 'simple philosophy of Christ', by 'expressing lively the Latin'. Her work is longer than the original, for she often amplifies single words for greater effect by turning them into phrases or sub-clauses, and by using doublets such as 'unity and concord', 'head and ruler', 'verity and truth'. Avoiding arcane, esoteric idioms and vocabulary, her syntax, with the rarest of lapses, is natural, conversational, cumulative. She can soften Erasmus's language to make it more intimate or sharpen it to drive home her point. And she knows just as surely as her father in Hythloday's scenes in *Utopia* how to dramatize her writing so as to inveigle her readers into believing that a voice speaks personally to them.

One of her most inspired techniques is the use and positioning of vocatives. 'Hear O father' or 'O father' or 'good father', she says, where Erasmus has only *pater*, evoking an atmosphere of intercession. Her translation is peppered with self-contained collects:

> O Father in Heaven, which of thy exceeding goodness most plenteously feedest all things that thou has so wondrously created, provide for us thy children, which are chosen to dwell in thy celestial and heavenly house . . . some spiritual and ghostly food, that we obeying thy will and precepts, may daily increase and wax bigger in virtue, until after the course of nature we have obtained and gathered a full and perfect strength in our Lord Jesus Christ.

She instils a familiar, cosy, domestic idiom into the idea of a loving, merciful God: 'Thou desirest rather to be called a father than a lord or master. Thou would'st we should rather love thee as thy children, than fear thee as thy servants and bondmen.' She paints a radiant, tender image of heaven as 'our father's house', contrasting 'heavenly felicity' with the fear and dread of 'foul and wicked devils', the 'tyranny of sin', the depravity of Lucifer, that 'tyrannous fiend'. She pinpoints pride and ambition as the root of all evil. 'For it is not fitting nor agreeable that brethren whom thy goodness hath put in equal honour should disagree or vary among themselves by ambitious desire of worldly promotion.'

Margaret fully shares her father's otherworldliness. 'Jesus taught us,' she says, that 'we should despise the realm of this world, which standeth all by riches, and is held up by garrisons of men, by hosts and armour . . . by pride and violence, and is both gotten, kept and defended by fierce cruelness.' She believes, also as her father believed, that suffering, even persecution, is a gift of God able to lead his true disciples towards a stronger, deeper faith. 'For who,' she asks, 'might abide to be had in derision of the world, to be outlawed and banished, to be put in prison, to be fettered and manacled, to be spoiled of all his goods, and by strong hand be deprived of the company of his most dear wife and well-beloved children, but, if [only] now and then, he were heartened with thy heavenly and ghostly bread.' In a passage that, when Henry sent her father to the Tower ten years later, would acquire an extraordinary poignancy, she appeals for God's grace that, 'albeit we be not imprisoned nor tormented, though we be not wounded nor burnt, although we be not crucified nor drowned, though we be not beheaded, yet notwithstanding, the strength and clearness of thy realm may shine and be noble in us.'

A moniker cloaks Margaret's identity as author, for however much she may have wished to emulate Hortensia, she remembered her father's cautionary words. Unwilling to defy him but reluctant never to be allowed to write for an audience wider than her husband and father, she resorted to a ruse. Her book is called *A Devout Treatise upon the Pater Noster, made first in Latin by the most famous doctor Master Erasmus Roterodamus, and turned into English by a young, virtuous and well-learned gentlewoman of xix years of age*. Still nineteen when she completed her manuscript, she celebrated her twentieth birthday soon after moving to Chelsea, where she found a young, impressionable graduate, Richard Hyrde, employed by her father as a physician. A man 'singularly learned' in both Greek and medicine, so valued for his skills that he would attend English ambassadors in Italy, Hyrde had been hired to translate Vives's book on women's education, and also appointed as a resident doctor, caring for the elderly occupants of a row of almshouses. Margaret had been put in charge of these almshouses, which stood beside the gatehouse of the family's estate. And as an inventory of the family's provisioning shows, it must have occupied much of her time, since they needed food for a hundred people a day. Allowing for the forty or so indoor and outdoor servants now managed by More's steward, John Watson, that means there could have been as many as thirty or forty people in these almshouses.

Margaret got Hyrde to find her a publisher: one 'Thomas Berthelet', a newcomer to the trade in his own right, very possibly the same man as the young apprentice taken on by her uncle Rastell at the time of his Atlantic adventure. After also helping her to choose her moniker, Hyrde wrote a dedication and preface addressed to her cousin and fellow student, 'the most studious and virtuous young maid Frances Staverton', packed with clues enabling readers easily to unpack Margaret's true identity. And if that isn't enough, within ornamental borders on the title page is a woodcut of a woman resembling Margaret, seated at a reading desk and turning the pages of a folio.

Dating his preface 1 October 1524, Hyrde seeks to preserve decorum, painstakingly and unnecessarily explaining about 'the labour that I have had . . . about the printing', but the fiction is wafer-thin. As to the 'young gentlewoman', she is, he says, both 'erudite and elegant' and of 'such discreet and substantial judgement' as can scarcely be matched even by the best of 'rightwise and very well-learned men'. Her work unites scholarship and art. And of course, art encompasses artfulness, for by using Hyrde as an intermediary, by securing a laudatory preface from a male scholar already noted for his moral and literary distinction and holding an acknowledged position of trust in her father's household, Margaret had beaten the system. Or so she thought.

Idyllic as the family's Chelsea estate may have been, their house still needed refurbishment. In particular, Thomas More called for extra space, commissioning a large annexe – the 'New Building' as William Roper calls it – set 'a good distance' from the mansion with a private chapel, a library and a gallery. His builders were on site for the best part of two years, arriving with ladders, ropes, pulleys, hoists and wooden scaffolding, and requiring regular deliveries of bricks, tiles, timber, flagstones and sand which came by river, with cartloads of lime, prefabricated window jambs, and rolls of lead for cisterns and gutters arriving by road. Panes of glass were manufactured to order, most likely carried by boat and stored away safely in outhouses until required.

The New Building, when completed, gave Thomas the privacy he cherished. He used it, says Roper, 'for godly purposes': to be alone, to write and pray in peace. Since he meant to build his annexe from scratch, his choice of Chelsea makes even greater sense. Just across the river at Battersea lay the brickworks belonging to Westminster Abbey. As a judge in the court for 'poor men's causes', Thomas sat regularly with the abbot, John Islip, a devout Benedictine, but a man in tune with the ways of the world. Abbot Islip entertained judges, courtiers and royal councillors at his table, among them Judge John More, who dined on salmon, plaice, fresh lampreys, conger eel and red mullet followed by custard. Islip had lately retained Thomas More 'of council' for the abbey, also selling him bricks at cost price. All Thomas had to do was to send his builders across the river in a boat. Since bricks, depending on the distance involved, cost between four and ten times more to transport than to manufacture, he was able to build on a scale far above his means. Clay was dug at Battersea, while sand was readily available from a sandbank on More's side of the river at the entrance to Chelsea Reach: Abbot Islip's labourers could regularly be seen there wiping their brows.

Thomas saved on architect's fees too. Among the books discussed by his circle of friends was the first printed edition of Vitruvius's *De Architectura*, which had templates for floor plans, internal decorations and classical ornaments. Although we cannot prove he too owned this book, we do know that his alterations to his dilapidated mansion closely follow Vitruvius's description of the Greek arrangement of rooms. Male and female servants were to occupy separate wings of the house, and only in case of fire or emergency were the women permitted to enter the men's wing. The New Building's prospect and design were also classically inspired. A free-standing structure on the north bank of a river where (it was believed) buildings catch the light and sun more easily than on the south bank, and on a site at 'a good distance' from neighbouring buildings on gently rising ground with open views, matches Vitruvius's advice to the letter.

More's gallery would have been a long portico or hall with windows on each side looking out towards the vista of the garden and the river. Probably built over a loggia of oak pillars with sculptured limestone bases, it would have been used for exercise, for the reception of distinguished visitors and special friends, and for showing off art objects. Since Thomas, even at his most affluent, could never have afforded to buy Flemish tapestries, he would have displayed his diptych of Erasmus and Peter Gillis by Massys, his oil painting of the Virgin Mary purchased in Bruges, other lesser paintings on classical, historical and religious subjects, perhaps a few sculptures, and his collection of antique coins and gems. Usually galleries had an extra function as a corridor connecting different parts or wings of a much larger building, but not at the New Building. Thomas's 'goodly gallery' was, from Roper's description, more like the one built by the Earl of Shrewsbury at his house at Sheffield, a freestanding affair leading to a 'chamber' surmounted by a tower-room, or in More's case to his library and study from which a stone spiral staircase led up to a chapel or secret oratory. The New Building's chapel would have been small, since the mansion house already had a largish one. Good Friday, says Roper, was the only day of the year when everyone gathered in the New Building. They would have met in the gallery, where (according to a family tradition) Thomas or his secretary read aloud the biblical accounts of the Last Supper and Crucifixion.

Thomas rarely called in favours but, stretched financially by his building works, asked Abbot Islip for another. Wishing to found a chantry or private family chapel in Chelsea Parish Church, he first sought Islip's approval as patron of the church, then sent his own workmen in to hew out part of the retaining wall of the south aisle nearest to the chancel before building an extension. When finished, the More Chapel had an altar with a frontal of the finest Bruges satin, a window with a stained-glass panel of Thomas's coat of arms – a chevron between three moorcocks – and was lit by oil lamps and candelabra. Islip, however, baulked at dismissing the incumbent rector in favour of Thomas's own nominee, and it took another six years for a vacancy to arise.

  More's desire to replace his parish priest may explain why the double wedding of Margaret's sisters, Elizabeth and Cecily, wasn't held at Chelsea. Instead, by another special licence, the nuptials were held at Alice and Giles Alington's private chapel at Willesden. The licence, granted on 29 September 1525, was followed a week or so later by the weddings themselves. Although originally planned as one happy event, the bureau-crat dealing with the application in the vicar-general's office found the idea of a double wedding so novel, so liturgically unsound, he consulted his superiors, who consented only on condition Thomas promised that two separate services would be held.

Elizabeth was nineteen, Cecily eighteen. Cecily married Giles Heron, who'd come of age two months before. Delighted to be out of wardship, he recovered possession of his lands, then raised a mortgage to finance his extravagant lifestyle. As he doesn't appear to have asked for much of a dowry, his relationship with Cecily is likely to have been a romance.

The same is true of Elizabeth, who married William Daunce, an earnest young man, son and heir of Sir John Daunce of Thame in Oxfordshire, a goldsmith and royal treasurer. Aged twenty-four, William had little money of his own, but Elizabeth wasn't to be discouraged. The dowry negotiations would be tough and protracted, for the families, although acquainted, were never close. The sticking-point was financial, for although William owned a modest estate in Oxfordshire, it was rented out to a farmer on a long lease. His father, meanwhile, was soon to remarry a much younger woman well above his station and needed to retain whatever assets of his own he could. He also kept a mistress, Agnes, who bore him a love-child. How much Thomas More and Lady Alice knew about Sir John's lurid private life is impossible to fathom. What counted was that he refused to help his son purchase a home. Lady Alice was content to allow the newly-weds to live at Chelsea, but wanted provision made for Elizabeth in case she ever had to face life on her own. To break the deadlock, Thomas, his own coffers bled dry by his builders, went cap-in-hand to Wolsey, whom he knew to possess an empty house at Battersea, too small for a cardinal and without development potential since the vast estates of Westminster Abbey encircled it. Wolsey gave the young couple the use of his house on one condition. The caretaker's wife, one of his own distant relatives, and her immediate family were to be allowed to continue living there as sitting tenants until they died. Thomas willingly agreed, sending William to Wolsey to give his word that they should never be evicted.

Two months later, Margaret and her two sisters put on their very best clothes. For the one and only time in their lives, their father had invited them to Court. The summons came while Henry was at Richmond Palace on his way to spend Christmas at Eltham. The excited young women would have been rowed the seven miles upstream in their father's barge, a journey lasting an hour or more depending on the tide. Henry had education very much on his mind, because his illegitimate son by Elizabeth Blount, Henry Fitzroy, was now rising seven. Six months before, Henry had created him Earl of Nottingham and Dukes of Richmond and Somerset, and president of the Council of the North, a surrogate for Prince of Wales. Now he was beginning Latin, but a bitter wrangle had erupted as to whether he should start Greek as well and, if so, which authors he should study. Most of Henry's courtiers still believed that too much learning made boys soft and cowardly, and that a prince, after acquiring the rudiments of French, Latin and arithmetic, should concentrate on the 'nobler', more manly arts of riding, hunting and shooting. What Henry wanted to know, and see in action, was whether Greek learning could do all its advocates claimed it could to sharpen and improve young minds.

Margaret would have had an extraordinary day. 'When your daughters disputed in philosophy afore the King's Grace,' said Fitzroy's school-master enviously, 'I would it had been my fortune to be present.' When 'disputing' before the king, each sister would, in turn, have delivered a speech arguing 'for' or 'against' a motion – as if before the judges in a law-court – a technique Vives had watched them practising during his brief stay. They chose their 'themes' out of Quintilian, then invented speeches of their own, just as their father and Erasmus had done twenty years before. One of their favourites was the case of a man with a blind son whom he'd made his heir. After marrying for the second time, the man set aside a room for his son in a far-flung corner of his house. Next morning the father was found murdered in his bedchamber. The son's sword was in the body; the wall from his room to the scene of the crime all bloody with the prints of a hand. Had the murder been committed by the son or the wicked stepmother?

When Elizabeth and Cecily had finished, Margaret stepped forward. She may have chosen the same subject, but also had a *pièce de résistance*. It was the case of a rich man who, driven to distraction by his poor neighbour's bees, sprinkled pesticide in his own garden to kill them when they flew over the wall. Quintilian had taken the poor man's side. One of the biggest challenges in classical oratory was to find a winning defence for the rich man. Margaret had her arguments ready: she had made notes which still survived fifty or sixty years later. One of the family's earliest biographers saw them, but, maddeningly, failed to make a copy.

According to Quintilian, when accosted by the poor man for killing his bees, the rich man claimed there was no damage to property because bees were wild, roving and winged, under no man's authority or command. He said he'd only sprinkled a small amount of pesticide on a very few flowers. The bees flew over his wall at their peril.

When such a case came before the English courts for the first time on record in 1984, the defence counsel said that a man applying pesticide on his own land has no duty of care to insects that might come or go. Such insects are trespassers, or, if it is unreal to treat them as trespassers, the law should not place them in a more favoured position than if they were human trespassers. The 'duty of common humanity' of a man to his neighbour doesn't encompass forgoing the right to avoid a nuisance, especially if one acts reasonably, applying only a moderate amount of pesticide. The bee-keeper, especially if given prior notice, could have been expected to have taken precautions for the safety of his swarm, and by failing to do so had contributed to his loss.

Whether Margaret said this or something far more elegant, she rose to the challenge with style and panache: 'the more difficult such a defence is,' says the writer who'd had access to her notes, 'the greater the scope for [her] eloquence and wit.' He reckoned hers to have been a bravura performance.

As winter ended and the first signs of spring reappeared in 1526, Margaret had a sudden, bruising jolt. Dr Richard Foxford, the Bishop of London's vicar-general, called in three books on suspicion of heresy, one being her own. Thomas Berthelet, her publisher, found himself threatened with prosecution for selling 'a certain work called *The Treatise of the Pater Noster* translated by the wife of Master Roper'. Questioned as to whether he'd submitted the book to the Church authorities for approval, Berthelet replied that he had not. Foxford forbade him to sell any more copies, ordering him to appear in the consistory court on the third day after the feast of St Monica (4 May).

Margaret was suspected because, with the Church in a state of high alert, scriptural translations were vulnerable to accusations of Lollardy, as her uncle Rastell had discovered in Coventry. With Cuthbert Tunstall newly appointed as Bishop of London, systematic print censorship came into force. On 12 October 1524 all printers and booksellers were forbidden to market any religious texts or translations until each imprint had been licensed, but Berthelet for some reason had disobeyed. Maybe he was misled by Hyrde, who possibly assumed that Margaret's book would be automatically approved by Tunstall, her father's friend. Or more likely he took the date of Hyrde's preface to be the date of publication, in which case the book had appeared eleven days before Tunstall's order was made. When, however, Margaret's book sold out and a reprint was needed, Berthelet lacked a licence, falling foul of the rules.

Thomas More would never have interfered in the proceedings of a Church court even to protect his own daughter. It was Hyrde who came to her rescue. His friend, Stephen Gardiner, a brilliant Cambridge academic, had lately secured a post as Wolsey's secretary. Hyrde 'was wont to resort much to me', said Gardiner, who explained Margaret's predicament to Wolsey. The result was that Berthelet got his reprint in record time, and with a unique addition. A woodcut of Wolsey's coat of arms as cardinal and papal legate boldly appears on the reverse of the title page. True, the image is crudely drawn and has mistakes: a lion and two crows inside a shield are back to front. It's an amateur production made in a hurry, and yet nobody dared challenge its authority. Margaret's book had acquired Wolsey's *imprimatur*, trumping the vicar-general. When St Monica's Day arrived, Berthelet had no need to appear in court, leaving Foxford red-faced and humiliated.

But Margaret would learn her lesson. Although the Church had begun to see the relevance of teaching the people the Creed, Lord's Prayer and Ten Commandments in English instead of Latin, it was essential to follow the correct procedures. According to Erasmus, Bishop Fitzjames had once threatened another author of an unofficial translation of the Lord's Prayer, and a similar fate had befallen the one man in England whose talent for scriptural translation equalled, and with further practice would come to better, that of Margaret. This was a Gloucestershire man educated at Wolsey's old college in Oxford, an ardent admirer of Erasmus's Greek New Testament, William Tyndale. After leaving university and translating Erasmus's *Manual of the Christian Knight* for private circulation, he had called on Tunstall, offering to translate the New Testament, but was roundly rebuffed. Refusing to accept defeat and privately sponsored by a sympathetic London merchant, he left for Cologne, where he vowed to bring England over to Luther's side. Forced to flee to the safe Lutheran city of Worms in 1525, he watched the first-ever complete English New Testament roll off the presses a year later.

Tyndale's New Testament was slow to take off, but was unstoppable once it did. The English Reformation had begun. The tragedy, from the official Church's viewpoint, is that Tyndale lacked competition. The Church authorities were unable to see that the one person in England who knew Latin and Greek to the point where she could correct Erasmus, who could match Tyndale as a translator and stylist, and could be relied on to conform to Catholic teaching and doctrine, was Margaret Roper. But, of course, she was a woman, so it never entered their heads.

17

THE DEVIL MAKES WORK

Despite asking for the loan of a house for the Daunces, Thomas More found it ever more difficult to conceal his growing rift with Wolsey. The catalyst for his disillusion with the man he'd once seen as a latter-day Cardinal Morton was foreign policy.

Bourbon's revolt against Francis I, upon which Henry had pinned so many hopes, had fizzled out, with Bourbon himself retreating to Italy and the Duke of Suffolk, sent to capture Paris, forced to return home ignominiously with an army decimated by plague and frostbite. Wolsey's and Henry's policy had miserably failed and for the reason that More had anticipated: Bourbon's unreliability. Wolsey, however, blamed the emperor for the fiasco, realizing that Charles had little interest in helping Henry achieve his dream of the French crown. After digesting the full extent of the disaster in France, Wolsey came to regret the support he'd given to Charles's staunch ally, Giulio de Medici, in a second papal election following the sudden death of Adrian VI shortly after Suffolk had begun his initial advance. Clearly, the priorities of Charles and Clement VII, the title taken by de Medici, lay in Italy and Germany.

Henry took a little longer to repudiate Charles, even renewing the imperial alliance, despite Wolsey's misgivings, when Bourbon laid siege to Marseilles. This campaign went the way of the first, but it was Charles who finally triumphed. On 24 February 1525 his commanders defeated and captured Francis at the Battle of Pavia after leading the French army into an ambush. Francis had paid the price for deciding to invade Italy, an invasion that had so alarmed Pope Clement that he'd fatally switched sides at the last moment, allying with Francis and antagonizing Charles. As to Henry, he rejoiced in Charles's victory, believing that France was ripe for partition, but his excitement turned to anger, and anger against Wolsey in particular, when it became clear that Charles regarded his triumph at Pavia as complete and would not back him.

So Wolsey performed a hasty volte-face, joining Clement in allying with France. He made the treaty with Louise of Savoy, Francis's mother, the regent of France while her son was a prisoner. He had little choice, because a fresh attempt to raise extra taxes for a resumption of the war had triggered revolts in East Anglia and riots elsewhere. Forced to abandon his demands for taxation, and ostentatiously disowned by Henry, who'd backed the taxes until the scale of resistance became clear, Wolsey saved face by flaunting the new alliance but at a heavy cost to his reputation. Openly in London and Rome, it was said that Henry's minister cared more for his own wealth and position than for peace or the unity of Christendom.

The moment of truth for Thomas More was surely this desperate treaty, for while Wolsey had managed to stave off Henry's displeasure by obtaining indemnities from France to make up for the taxes he had failed to secure, the alliance was mainly about Wolsey rescuing his reputation as a fixer. Self-interest – rather than idealism for peace – was driving Wolsey forward, and the treaty ignored the economic sanctions likely to follow from Charles. Addressing the King's Council, Wolsey said he thought the terms so reasonable 'that all the world would allow them'. He got a shock when they were criticized, flying into a rage. 'By the mass,' he told one unnamed diplomat, probably More himself, 'thou art a very fool.'

Margaret always remembered her father talking about this incident, saying how Wolsey had rebuked his fellow councillors with one of Aesop's *Fables*. A group of 'wise' men, believing rain made fools of all whom it soaked and seeing storms approaching, sheltered in caves so they could rule when the sun reappeared. But when the skies cleared and the 'wise' men tried to rule, the fools pounced on them and beat them up. For fools, said Wolsey testily, are not willing to be ruled by wise men. The English would suffer more as pacifists than as warriors, since the French and imperialists would join forces to attack them and divide the spoils. He would not make so crass a blunder.

To reassert his authority, Wolsey announced a reshuffle at Court and More was among those demoted. Sir Richard Wingfield, Chancellor of the Duchy of Lancaster, had died, giving Wolsey the opportunity to take away More's most lucrative post of Under-Treasurer and give him Wingfield's old job, but minus the usual salary supplement. More's income dropped by £100 a year, causing Lady Alice to search the ledgers anxiously, worried (as it turned out unnecessarily) that he'd been forced to borrow from Henry to finance the New Building.

More's final verdict on these years, delivered from his cell in the Tower, was that Wolsey had squandered his talents. 'Vainglorious was he very far above all measure,' said Thomas, 'and that was great pity, for it did harm, and made him abuse many great gifts that God had given him. Never was he satiate of hearing his own praise.' For all his glitzy rhetoric, for all his talk of fair and impartial justice for the poor, Wolsey had turned into a proud, vain opportunist who had promised much and delivered little, failing the people and the king. The French alliance wasn't even stable, since Wolsey had scarcely finished his reshuffle than Francis, held at Madrid since his defeat at Pavia, was released once a ransom was paid, meaning the treaty had to be ratified all over again.

Despite becoming Chancellor of the Duchy, More found that Henry refused to relinquish him as his secretary, leaving him to commute several times a week between the royal palaces and the Duchy offices in London. The Duchy of Lancaster owned land all over England and it fell to Thomas to manage the portfolio and resolve disputes over leases, tenants, boundaries, feudal taxes or grants of mineral rights, relying on out-of-court settlements rather than hearing cases in full. He tried to nurture the career of Margaret's husband William Roper, now a qualified barrister, by offering him work, but found him dilatory and unresponsive. Whether feeling eclipsed by his more talented wife or simply lazy, William showed little interest in his career, content to live on the income from his sinecure.

Much of William's energy, in fact, was consumed by his family feud. When John Roper died without reinstating his eldest son as his principal heir, William carried out his threat to contest the will, appealing to Wolsey as a papal legate. The dispute grew ugly, as William fought his mother and younger brothers in court, and Wolsey seized the opportunity to flaunt his jurisdiction over Archbishop Warham, who thought he should be in charge of the case. Warham complained of William's 'sinister means' in drawing the case as far away as possible from the reach of his mother or her Kentish relatives, and of Wolsey's bullying, for Wolsey could be ruthless in probate cases, once allowing Warham to be arrested and imprisoned overnight in a common gaol in London, meaning to show once and for all who was in charge.

With his affairs in limbo until this gladiatorial contest was played out, William's disenchantment led him to mope and brood 'even until sick at heart'. Rejecting books recommended by his wife, he purchased instead one of the earliest copies of Tyndale's New Testament to be smuggled into England. Just upstream of London Bridge on the north bank of the river lay the Steelyard, the centre for the expatriate German Hanseatic community. (The name comes from *Staalhof*, a hall where cloths were sealed or stamped to prove they met the regulations of the guild.) The merchants, whom Roper got to know well, also supplied him with Luther's *The Liberty of a Christian Man* and *The Babylonian Captivity of the Church*, which 'bewitched' him.

He then read the *Image of Love*, intended like More's own *Life of Pico* as a New Year's gift for nuns. The author, a preaching friar, declares his wish to donate an 'image of love' to their nunnery, then describes his fruitless searches in the shops of 'nature', the 'world', the 'flesh' and the 'artificers' before finally discovering the 'only true image of love' in the Bible. Although inspired by Erasmus's attack on Church abuses in the *Praise of Folly*, the author's arguments – as far as the Church authorities were concerned – smacked of such Lollard and Lutheran heresies as judging the institutions of the Church according to scripture and preferring living images to dead ones. Sitting in the Lady Chapel at St Paul's on 19 December 1525, Bishop Tunstall's vicar-general pro-scribed the *Image* and summoned its printers to answer a charge of heresy, ordering all copies to be handed in whether sold or not.

Before William could comply, his wife and father-in-law discovered his apostasy in the most searing way, after More, at Tunstall's request, led a series of armed raids on the Steelyard, ostensibly in his capacity as joint keeper of the foreign exchanges. The first, three days after the *Image* was put on the index of prohibited books and three before Christmas, was followed by two more raids in the New Year, when More burst into the Steelyard precincts and posted guards at all the exits. He warned the Germans of the penalties for debasing English coinage before searching their rooms looking for Tyndale's New Testament and other Lutheran books. Enough was found to implicate four of the merchants and put them on trial before Wolsey's own commissaries. After interrogation on oath, they confessed and were ordered to do penance at another public book-burning at St Paul's.

The merchants informed on William Roper, who was forced to join them in court. Luckily for him, Wolsey could be lenient, discharging him with a stern but friendly warning. Margaret's father had less sympathy for his errant son-in-law, and according to a devoted admirer, writing thirty years later, 'Sir Thomas More during that time' was the man 'whom then of all the world' William Roper 'did most abhor'.

Finding her husband remote and utterly intractable, Margaret, in a state of fear and apprehension for herself and her child, but mainly for her husband's immortal soul, went to her father, who took her for a walk around the garden at Chelsea. 'Meg,' he finally said when they were alone, 'I have born a long time with thy husband. I have reasoned and argued with him in those points of religion, and still given to him my poor fatherly counsel; but I perceive none of all this able to call him home. And therefore, Meg, I will no longer argue nor dispute with him, but will clean give him over [i.e. leave him alone], and get me another while to God and pray for him.'

With God's help, William would come to his senses. The devil had found work for idle hands, and there was nothing either Margaret or her father could do about it except pray that he could find peace with himself.

Christmas 1525, sandwiched uncomfortably between Thomas More's first and last raids on the Steelyard, would have been a bleak occasion for the family had not his servant, Walter Smyth, a jovial Londoner, a remarkable amateur actor with a taste for beer and Chaucer in equal measure, scripted twelve 'merry jests', one each for the Twelve Days which he performed solo in the great hall of the mansion house. Smyth, who also did voice impressions, imitated to perfection the salty, scurrilous dialogue, the clowning, burlesque and gutter-jokes so beloved of Thomas when in that mood. His script, a mixture of fact and fiction enlivened especially on the last three nights with bawdy innuendo and topical allusions, was preserved because John Rastell, who'd moved again, this time to Old Street in Finsbury Fields beyond Cripplegate where he'd opened a public theatre as his latest commercial venture, enjoyed it so much he chose to print it.

Called *The Widow Edyth*, the story chronicles the wiles and adventures of Edyth, daughter of a yeoman of Exeter. When her thrice-married father dies of a cough, Edyth's stepmother, a young woman of the world, marries her off, giving her some shrewish advice: 'Daughter, make merry whilst thou may/ For this world will not last away.'

Quickly tiring of her lacklustre husband, Edyth runs off with the servant of an earl by whom she has a child. The liaison doesn't last and, after a series of scrapes, all involving sex and swindles, Edyth meets a pilgrim couple in Fulham, upstream from Chelsea on the way to Chiswick. She feigns to be about to drown herself, gulling the couple into carrying her back to London and paying a scrivener to lodge her and write her will. Her property, she says, is at Kingston-upon-Thames, but the scrivener uncovers the truth. That night, 'when he rose to piss', he casts Edyth into the street in her petticoat.

Step by step, Smyth insinuates Edyth into the heart of the family circle. She seduces, in turn, servants of Sir Thomas Neville – a former undersheriff of London, ex-Speaker of the Commons and royal councillor, one of Thomas More's colleagues in the court for 'poor men's causes' – of John Fisher, Bishop of Rochester, and of Wolsey himself. She fools the Earl of Arundel into believing she has a daughter, an heiress living at a fine house at Foots Cray in Kent. When Arundel's men visit the house, they find it really belongs to Giles Heron's younger brother. Edyth then escapes in disguise to Croydon, where she lives with a cook before stealing his money and, passing the door of the Daunces' home in Battersea, takes a wherry 'and over Thames [is] rowed full merry' to Chelsea.

At Thomas More's house she has 'best cheer of all', for there she finds three indoor servants – all real-life characters, Thomas Croxton, Thomas Arthur and Walter Smyth himself – each of whom lusts after her. Croxton, tall, brash, thick-chinned with long arms and broad shoulders, is Giles Alington's servant, suggesting that Margaret's stepsister and her husband were in the audience. Arthur, handsome, well-spoken and of middle height, is William Roper's man. Both they and Smyth, who heaps more ridicule on himself the longer he performs, are horny with desire. Croxton is so smitten, he stands as close as possible to Edyth's chair, smelling nectar 'every time she farts'. Arthur is shyer, but no less ardent. He asks Margaret Roper to put in a good word for him, which she promises to do, after which he and Edyth canoodle by candlelight.

Next day, Arthur saddles his horse and rides pillion with Edyth to Brentford near Chiswick to fetch her money. But doubts enter his mind when she tells him that her wealth, after all, is at Kingston. They return to Chelsea, where his suspicions grow. Edyth, meanwhile, is irrepressible, and in her chamber 'the next night following/ There was the revel and the gossipping/ The general bumming as Margaret Giggs said.' Arthur sits musing in a chair, casting lascivious glances at Edyth, who kisses him and sits on his lap, farting like thunder and telling him, 'If I loved you not, I would not give you this.'

The following day, a fine Sunday, Edyth leads a party to mass at the convent of Holywell near Shoreditch, some four miles away. Insisting on refreshing herself at every wayside inn, she arrives late and when the offertory bell rings looks knowingly at Croxton, saying she has no change. The poor man gives generously, but, strolling with him in the cloisters, Edyth slips away for a tryst with Smyth, who professes his love and proposes.

Disaster strikes when Edyth returns to Chelsea. Arthur, who hasn't gone to the convent, has been checking her story and finds her 'not worth the sleeve-lace of a gown'. The scales fall from the eyes of the beguiled lovers, who plot their revenge. At supper, they drop a powerful laxative into Edyth's soup and ale, so that she rushes from the table to relieve herself. As in a classic Roman farce, one 'Brown', another servant, comes running into the great hall, half dressed, to tell 'Thomas More' and 'Lady Alice' – Smyth is now playing all their parts at once and imitating their voices – that their coal-house is on fire.

'I saw no light,' says 'Brown', 'just a stinking smoke.'

'Bonus deus, bonus deus' – 'good God man, will this gear never be left?' cries 'Lady Alice', uttering her favourite oath. 'Get thee fast and look . . . go look, go look, get thee hence.'

'Brown', of course, finds no fire in the coal-house, merely Edyth, who emerges 'well eased' to howls of derision. She tries to brazen it out – Smyth can hardly lay it on enough – blaming a rabbit she ate for dinner. She retires to bed, but on awakening is led in chains to the assizes. Three weeks later, says Smyth, taking his final bow, she is acquitted, resuming her life of crime as if everything had been a midsummer night's dream.

How Margaret and her father greeted this racy performance is impossible to judge, except there was nothing in Smyth's rendition not readily available in Chaucer or Boccaccio, or in classical dramatists such as Plautus or Terence, whose work they are known to have enjoyed. Smyth was happy to entertain his audience with coarse ribaldry, but the fact that he was allowed to lead the family's revels, mocking them, their friends and servants without shame or embarrassment, suggests that the view of life attributed to Giggs – a 'general bumming' – was all along theirs as much as his. Given the breakdown in relations between William Roper and his father-in-law that Christmastide, what everyone needed most of all was a diversion. Smyth had provided it, and there was, it seems, little conflict, even in so pious a household, between religion and innocent fun.

18

ILLUSION OF REALITY

AS THE SEASONS PASSED in 1526, Margaret won her husband back to the Catholic faith in a series of faltering steps. It can't have been easy, since William had rebelled because he was smarting over money and his place in society as much as over religion. He and Margaret had been married for five years, meaning that under the terms of their marriage settlement her dowry was due and the couple should have been free to leave Chelsea and buy their own house. William, whose lofty sense of dignity and tendency to sulk were the flaws in his character, wanted to be his own master. But until he had voluntarily purged himself of his heresy, his father-in-law seemed reluctant to release the money, nor was Margaret as eager to leave home as her younger sisters. Even were she to change her mind, the couple had to face the fact that William couldn't raise sufficient capital to buy a suitable property without saving or obtaining probate of his father's will of which there was little sign, as probate had become the chief stumbling-block in the quarrel between Wolsey and Warham over their respective, conflicting jurisdictions.

Margaret began to see her world change around her, for besides her sisters moving out, she had to bid farewell to her beloved Margaret Giggs. Shortly before her twenty-first birthday, Giggs was betrothed to John Clement, Thomas More's former page, who'd returned from Italy after qualifying as a physician. Clement had known Giggs ever since he'd briefly stood in as her tutor and it's likely the pair were in love. The wedding was held at St Stephen's Church, and not Chelsea.* A week or so

---

* To avoid confusion, Margaret Giggs will continue to be identified by her maiden name in later chapters.

after Epiphany, the whole family was rowed downstream for a joyous ceremony with extra singers hired by the churchwardens. Giggs is described in the parish records as 'my Lady More's maid', which may not accurately reflect her status but makes sense of a cryptic note by the astronomer, Nicholas Kratzer, describing her as Lady Alice's 'familiar'.

As a wedding present the Mores let the couple take over the lease of the Barge at Bucklersbury. The arrangement was perfect; in his new post of Chancellor of the Duchy, Thomas had to spend an ever-increasing number of nights in London, when it wasn't always possible to return by barge to Chelsea. Now he could lodge at his old home in comfort and with congenial company, without having to hire a resident caretaker and cook. And yet, the fact that the house was given to the newly-weds and not the Ropers, who could surely have asserted a prior claim, tends to confirm that Margaret, although the same age as Giggs, had made a resolution not to leave her father's house.

And there were other changes. Richard Hyrde left for Paris, his lodging at the mansion house taken by Henry Patenson, nicknamed 'Master Harry', another of More's servants recruited about the time he was appointed Under-Treasurer of the Exchequer. 'A man,' said More, tongue-in-cheek, 'of known wisdom in London and almost everywhere else . . . a man of special wit by himself and unlike the common sort', Patenson had a hot temper and a two-handed sword with a sharp point he loved to show off. He'd got himself into a series of spectacular scrapes when he'd accompanied his employer with Wolsey to Bruges in 1521, culminating in an unsightly brawl. Master Harry, whose face and gesture, as well as taste in headgear, had a remarkable, if uncanny, resemblance to Henry VIII's, especially when both wore full beards, lived in an alley off Milk Street. He found it impossible to commute to Chelsea, forcing him to lodge there. Given that Harry had a penchant for clowning and More loved to intro-duce him to his guests as his 'fool', it may not be a coincidence that about the time he joined the household, John Rastell scripted a comic scene for his Finsbury theatre requiring a Henry VIII look-alike to perform a song-and-dance routine to a ditty called 'Time to pass', parodying a famous song the king had written himself called 'Pastime with good company'. Wolsey at least had a sense of humour, since he knew all about the ditty and didn't disapprove, not denying Rastell a gift of thirty yards of slightly battered, but still fine red buckram once adorning his presence chamber, which Rastell asked for as a backcloth for his stage.

The family's happiest news was that Margaret gave birth to her second daughter, Mary. The baby's godmother was her great-aunt, Joan Staverton, from whom she later received a ring with a diamond. Otherwise, the big event was the betrothal of young John More, Margaret's brother, to the bubbling Anne Cresacre. This occurred around the time of Anne's fourteenth birthday and John's sixteenth. Judged not to be ready to marry yet, the couple were 'espoused *de futuro*', not '*de praesenti*' as was usually the case. John would have said in the presence of witnesses, 'I will marry thee' or 'I will take thee to be my wife', and Anne would have replied, 'I will contract marriage with thee', or 'I will take thee to be my husband'. Although a solemn pledge on either side, this exchange of vows wasn't considered binding and many such 'espousals' came to grief when the parties, on reaching adulthood, changed their minds, but it did signal their intentions, sparing Anne, an heiress to a considerable fortune, the attentions of unwanted suitors.

A chain of events now led up to what can be seen as among the family's finest, most enduring monuments. In August, Erasmus sent an extraordinarily gifted painter, Hans Holbein the Younger, to England. Arriving penniless, he sought out Thomas More, already aware that he adored the style of portraiture of which this artist, along with Albrecht Dürer and Quentin Massys, were acknowledged masters. More chuckled with delight at such naivety, writing back: 'Your painter friend, my dear Erasmus, is a wonderful artist. I fear he will not find English soil as rich and fertile as he hoped. But I shall do my best to make sure it is not completely barren.' A genuine connoisseur, More knew that patrons had as yet only a barely formed appreciation of portraiture other than in altarpieces, preferring tapestries and opulent displays of precious metalwork or jewellery. Little did he guess how far he would be able to help Holbein change that in a relatively short space of time.

Either he dropped a word to Sir Henry Guildford, Comptroller of the Royal Household and Master of the Revels, or else to his brother-in-law Rastell, who'd been fortunate enough to win Guildford's patronage himself. On 8 February 1527 'Master Hans' started work alongside Rastell inside a large, canvas-roofed temporary building on a plot of land adjacent to Greenwich Palace, where revels were planned for May to entertain a visiting delegation of French diplomats. Similar in scale and purpose to the English palace at the Field of Cloth of Gold, it consisted of a banqueting hall and a theatre, each featuring a majestic triumphal arch.

When the day of the visit arrived, Henry first presided over a gourmet dinner served on solid gold plates in the banqueting hall, then led the ambassadors through the larger of the two arches towards the theatre, amusing himself by making his guests turn and gaze up at the back of the arch where Holbein had depicted the English victory at the siege of Thérouanne. Arriving at the candle-lit theatre, the delegates beheld a smaller, costlier proscenium arch, but what made them gasp aloud was the ceiling, made of stretched linen on which was painted a vast *mappa mundi* showing land and sea with the names of all the principal territories legible, and overlaid by a glittering, transparent gauze which, by means of ingenious lighting, created the illusion of the heavens with all the stars and planets and signs of the zodiac. In devising this spectacle, Holbein was assisted by Kratzer, his friend and interpreter since the artist as yet spoke no English, and by the man who did the scenery and lighting for Rastell's Finsbury theatre.

With the ceiling such a resounding success, Holbein, free to take on other work, headed for Chelsea, and before the year was out had received two commissions: one for a single half-length portrait of Thomas More, now in the Frick Collection in New York, in which he appears in his official, public capacity; the other for a life-sized group portrait in which the family is placed in its more intimate domestic setting.

In the single portrait, in oils on a panel of oak, Thomas poses wearing the attire he was normally said to shun: his fur-lined black silk gown, red velvet sleeves, and 'S'-patterned gold collar of state, the 'Ss' signifying 'service' and allegiance to Henry. He stares into the distance, his greyish-blue eyes clear, serious, focused as one might expect of a statesman and politician. His expression is one of steely determination, perhaps too of overwhelming sadness. Light glances off the edges of the folds of his sleeves and is subtly reflected in the glinting hairs of the stubble on his cheek. On his left forefinger is a gem-set ring, in his right hand a petition in the Court of Duchy Chamber. Wisps of curly black hair creep out of the front of his wide black hat; his white linen shirt is just visible at the neck. X-radiographs give insights into Holbein's technique. Beneath the visible colour, the outline of the sitter in the oil painting doesn't exactly match the lines of the preliminary cartoon, suggesting More chose to return for a second sitting. Also part-way through,

Holbein moved the hat to show a little more of Thomas's forehead, adjusting his shirt, and making a number of refinements to his mouth and eyes and especially to his right hand, so that he relaxes his grip on the petition for a moment.

The family-group portrait, once a wall-hanging about nine feet high and twelve feet wide, belongs to a different medium. Painted on linen, it relied on water-based pigments and techniques of illusion like those on the ceiling at Greenwich. Unlike the panel portrait, it doesn't survive today. Dispersed with the rest of More's sequestered property, it was eventually sold to art dealers and had reached the Bishop of Olmütz's collection by 1671, very probably perishing in a fire at Kremsier Castle (now in the Czech Republic) in 1752. In the 1590s Rowland Lockey, a pupil of Nicholas Hilliard, made various reproductions of it before it left the country, adding extra (later) sitters, close friends or descendants of Thomas More, to suit the wishes of his patrons. Fortunately, Holbein's preparatory sketch of the group scene survives, as do most of his working drawings of the individual sitters, making possible a fair impression of what the original wall-hanging must have looked like.

Two working drawings are of More himself. Only one is linked to the group scene; the other is the cartoon for the panel portrait. The revelation is in the comparison, for the drawing in readiness for the group scene is a world apart in that Thomas appears more at ease, more open; the hat is softer and reveals even more of his forehead. His long hair flows out freely from beneath it on either side. His expression is animated, unguarded, enquiring, vulnerable, less bleak and remote, and there's a disarming hint of mirth and the suppressed smile of someone who finds the whole idea of posing for a portrait pleasantly ridiculous. He looks here as Erasmus describes him: 'always friendly and cheerful, with something of the air of one who smiles easily, and (to speak frankly) disposed to be merry rather than serious or solemn'. Even the lack of colour in his gown adds to the effect, for we cannot tell this man's worldly status: he's as likely to be dressed in undyed wool like a Carthusian monk as in the finest silk.

Holbein's preparatory sketch for the group scene is set in one of the family's finer reception rooms, maybe that in which the picture itself was meant to hang. It seems as if the onlooker, when entering the room, would first have seen the painting on the opposite wall before coming to stand in front of it. Substituted for the wall itself, the picture would have conveyed a sense of gazing into space on the far side of the room where life-sized figures take their parts as if in a play. Thomas holds centre stage. As Holbein drew the scene, he shows (from left to centre) Elizabeth Daunce and Margaret Giggs standing, Judge John sitting next to Thomas on a bench, with Anne Cresacre standing behind them. Continuing to the right are young John More and Harry Patenson (standing), Cecily Heron and Margaret Roper seated on cushions or low stools in front of Patenson, with Lady Alice (far right) kneeling at a prie-dieu. Lady Alice wears a crucifix; Cecily, who is heavily pregnant, has a rosary in her left hand. Margaret Giggs, wearing a fine gable-headdress, leans across to Judge John to point out something in a book she holds. Books are central to the iconography, for they are everywhere. Lady Alice looks down as she reads, about to turn a page; Margaret Roper holds a book open on her lap; Cecily's is in her lap, but not yet unclasped; young John is also reading; Elizabeth carries a book under her arm. As all these books seem to be quite small, they may be prayer books. Larger books lie on a shelf by the window, temporarily laid aside. Everyone is quiet, almost solemn, as if family prayers are about to begin.

But a transformation follows, toning down the religious emphasis dramatically. Holbein had shown his sketch to More, who called for changes. Notes and amendments in the artist's handwriting, conveniently in a different, lighter ink, make them readily identifiable. Against Lady Alice he scribbles: 'she is to be seated'. Between the clock on the wall and the adjacent buffet or sideboard, he draws a viol de gamba and reminds himself to put a clavichord and other musical instruments on the sideboard. He draws the family's pet monkey climbing up Lady Alice's skirts, then crosses out a lighted candle on a windowsill. Using the same lighter ink, he scatters a pile of books, and a singleton, about the floor, untidily, but within easy reach of Margaret Roper and Margaret Giggs. Although a line runs vertically across one of these new and larger books, it isn't a crossing-out. The 'scoring' is a long inverted caret, for besides Holbein's annotations are those of Kratzer, identifying the sitters and giving their ages using the formula 'anno aetatis' ('in the year of his or her age'), so that someone 'anno aetatis 50' (like Thomas More) is forty-nine, or 'anno aetatis 20' (like Cecily Heron) is nineteen. In Cecily's case, there is insufficient space left on the page, so that Kratzer has to improvise a caret to squeeze in his note.

The family didn't 'sit' for an artist in the way that a family would sit today for a photographer. Holbein's alterations reveal that, far from merely stepping in and out to rearrange the composition here and there, the illusion is deeper and subtler, controlled by the patron and leaving the artist little discretion over the looks of the sitters or the story the picture was meant to tell. As to looks, the giveaway is Margaret Giggs. She poses (as it appears) confidently, prominently in the preparatory sketch, but at that time Holbein had never seen her. This is certain, because when he came to add her likeness to his set of working drawings, she looks quite different. In the sketch she is older, more staid, wearing more expensive clothes, assumed to be a middle-aged aunt. In the working drawing she is younger, slimmer, more simply dressed, wearing a soft fur cap with ear-flaps of a sort often worn by women of the lower middle class, no longer a costly gable-headdress. Perhaps when Holbein had met the sitters some had posed together, but if so Giggs was absent or her place taken by a stand-in. She'd already left the household and was living with her husband, where Holbein must have gone afterwards to draw her.

The effect of these changes on the final (now lost) version of the wall-hanging can be gauged by comparing Holbein's preparatory sketch with the best of Rowland Lockey's reinterpretations, dated 1593 and now hanging at Nostell Priory in West Yorkshire. There, the monkey stares out at us, bold as brass. Lady Alice is seated, her prie-dieu gone. Musical instruments and a pile of books rest on the sideboard. The candle has disappeared, replaced by flowers. Cecily no longer holds a rosary, although Giggs has acquired one. Giggs has the likeness of her true self and still reads, but no longer leans forward and her position is changed. She is sidelined in favour of Elizabeth, who stands beside her grandfather. As an adopted member of the family, Giggs would not have expected to usurp the position of a blood relative.

But far more is at stake than who is standing or sitting where; the painting's meaning lies in the story it tells, something More had first learned when Erasmus and Gillis had presented him with their diptych commissioned in honour of *Utopia*. Thrilled by the vivid, living, three-dimensional images, he'd written back to say 'the painting speaks', and in the Nostell Priory version Margaret Roper holds open on her lap two facing pages from the Chorus of the fourth act in Seneca's *Oedipus*. Those pages aren't randomly chosen. The text is legible and, when compared to all the known printings of Seneca's tragedies between 1500 and the date of Lockey's commission, matches only one: the Aldine Press edition, published in Venice after Erasmus had corrected the proofs. The representation is exact other than that the passage comes from two consecutive, but not facing pages in the genuine book. Such minor doctoring is typical in Renaissance art, and in his most famous painting, *The Ambassadors* in the National Gallery in London, Holbein does the same with a Lutheran hymnal, where he reproduces on facing pages two hymns, except that in the genuine hymnal those pages are differently arranged.

What Margaret holds up to view is no less than Seneca's classic defence of the 'middle way' or unambitious life, the passage in which he counterpoints the security of lack of ambition with the dangers of a public career. His message is about the relationship of human beings and fate. No one can predict what will happen to those who enter the counsels of princes. Fate is an irrevocable series of causes and effects with which not even the gods can interfere. Rather than urge an honest man to take the plunge, Seneca points out to him the perils of high office and the inevitability of fate. Using Plato's metaphor in the *Republic* of the ship of state, he says if he were left to his own devices, he would trim his sails to the light westerly winds: 'May soft breezes, gently blowing, unvarying, carry my untroubled barque along; may life bear me on safely, running in middle course.' Most compellingly, Seneca cites the example of Icarus who, attempting to escape from prison with his father, Daedalus, flew too close to the sun so that the wax melted on his wings and he fell into the sea, where he drowned. And it is to the very line in which Seneca describes how Icarus 'madly sought the stars' that Margaret points with her finger.

The Aldine text of Seneca's tragedies is linked intimately to the lifelong friendship between Erasmus and Thomas More. It was not long after Erasmus had left Venice that he travelled to England, staying at More's house. There, he says, 'I made a fresh recension of Seneca's tragedies'. His interest in *Oedipus* dates to a period when his friendship with More was at its most creative and productive. On top of this, Erasmus's letters are crammed with allusions to the passage held up by Margaret: 'We are driven by fate,' he says, paraphrasing Seneca, 'and fate we must obey.' Rowland Lockey, making his copy of the wall-hanging, couldn't have known any of this. He was, in any event, a notoriously weak Latinist, and so it can only be the case that the book he reproduces is the one he'd also seen in Holbein's original painting.

* * *

Margaret's part in the story still wasn't over after the paintings went on display. Whether, during one of her father's lengthy absences, she had supervised the hangings or discussed Holbein's commissions earlier with him cannot be known, but she it was who, a year after they were delivered, had in her possession the artist's preparatory sketch for the group scene. In August 1528 she decided to send it as a gift to Erasmus, asking Holbein to deliver it when he returned to Basel to see his wife and children, and causing Erasmus to exclaim:

> I'm scarcely able to express in words, my dear Margaret Roper, ornament of Britain, the pleasure I felt in my heart when the painter Holbein depicted for me your entire family like this, so skilfully that even if I'd been present among you, I could hardly have seen you all more clearly. How often I've found myself privately wishing that, just once more before I die, I could have the pleasure of seeing that little circle of friends that is so dear to me, and to whom I owe a good part of my fame and reputation.

Through her cherished gift, he said, Margaret wasn't just able to make absent friends present, enabling him to evoke and reawaken their mutual conversations, she (and the artist) had also made it possible for him to see a reflection of their very souls. He knew that, according to classical art theory, 'pictures' – like 'statues' if they were carved by a clever enough artist – are able to 'talk' to us. One of the most quoted maxims was that of Isocrates, an adviser to Philip of Macedon, father of Alexander the Great, who had counselled a ruler to 'leave behind him statues and images that shall represent rather the figure and similitude of his mind rather than the features of his body'. It isn't so much the physical appearance of the sitters that counts, it's what they feel and keep hidden in their hearts and minds.

Margaret, greatly touched, wrote back to acknowledge with love and gratitude everything Erasmus had said, adding that there is 'nothing for which we desire more ardently than to be able to see and speak face-to-face with our mentor again, he whose learned labours have taught us everything we know about the liberal arts, and one who is also the oldest and truest friend of our father'.

But if Erasmus could claim, as he did, that Holbein could evoke the feelings of hearts and minds, it had to be done by encoded instructions, and this Thomas More had achieved through the artist's use of diagonals as well as through the book to which Margaret is pointing. Ascending to the right in the preliminary sketch is a line on which the artist arranges the figures from Judge John to Harry Patenson. Descending from the left is another beginning with Elizabeth Daunce that follows her gaze towards Margaret. Thomas More's head is immediately above where the two lines intersect, and about where they meet is his collar of state which reappears (as it seems at first) as in the oil painting. Except that this time, the 'Ss' in the collar are back-to-front. That can't be a mistake, because a pair of portcullises at the clasp are the right way round. Only the 'Ss' are affected, and since Holbein knew how to portray them accurately in the oil painting, someone – it has to be More himself – is playing one of his games, poking fun at the ostentation of his gold chain. Just as the Utopians had regarded gold as the most appropriate metal for urinals and had forced criminals to wear gold chains as badges of shame, so More will invert his own collar.

Here is the most pungent, defiant insistence on the reality of personal, non-political life in his imagination of himself so far, an unequivocal rejection of 'worldly' success for its own sake. The family-group portrait is a deliberate counterweight to the image in the oil painting, where the 'story' is of Thomas as 'the king's good servant', perhaps suggesting he had already looked into the future and seen his fate.

PART IV

THOMAS'S CHALLENGE

19

'FATE WE MUST OBEY'

THE FAMILY-GROUP PORTRAIT might reveal Thomas More's interior world, the world that he and Margaret shared, but it was 'the king's good servant' of the oil painting that was to be catapulted into the maelstrom of politics. 'My thoughts and heart had long been set upon a life of retirement,' he wrote to Erasmus in 1529, 'when suddenly, without any warning, I was tossed into a mass of vital business affairs.' Refusing to take no for an answer, Henry had demanded that Thomas should succeed Wolsey and accept the post of Lord Chancellor, the highest office of state. Thomas's reaction was no false modesty; his promotion had been an extraordinary turn of fate. Nobody had expected him to be Lord Chancellor, least of all himself.

On 8 October Henry had decided to be rid of Wolsey, unleashing a struggle for power. The Duke of Suffolk, who'd seized Pope Leo's shipment of alum and led the English march on Paris, coveted Wolsey's preferments. A royal in-law since Mary, the young but far from grieving widow of Louis XII, had held Henry to his promise that she might choose her second husband for herself and married him, Suffolk's semi-literacy was his handicap. No one believed he could cope with the Chancellor's legal work, so he was fobbed off. The Duke of Norfolk, eldest son of the man who had blubbed while sentencing the Duke of Buckingham, had a surer grasp of politics and a courtier's role. He'd befriended More in the Council: the two were similar in age – More fifty-one, Norfolk fifty-six – and both had understood Wolsey's limitations. Norfolk didn't seek to be Chancellor himself, unwilling to be encumbered by judicial office. Archbishop Warham reappeared at Court, but was said to have refused the position from which Wolsey had driven him. The lawyers called for a professional judge, but in the end it was Wolsey's own recommendation that was accepted. Publicly disgraced, but not yet bereft of all influence, he told Henry that Thomas More was the 'aptest and fittest man in the realm'.

Thus it was that on Monday, 25 October Henry handed Thomas the great seal of England at a private audience at Greenwich, appointing him Wolsey's successor. Next day, the two dukes led him down the winding stairs from the Star Chamber into Westminster Hall to be officially installed in his seat as Lord Chancellor. Norfolk made a speech explaining how England was indebted to him 'for his good service, and how worthy he was to have the highest room [i.e. office] in the realm' and 'how dearly' the king 'loved and trusted him, for which . . . he had great cause to rejoice'. The bustle of the hall – judges, lawyers, court officials and litigants about their daily business – was abruptly silenced. Thomas replied that 'although he had good cause to take comfort of his highness's singular favour towards him . . . yet nevertheless . . . he had done no more than was his duty'. Protesting himself to be 'unmeet for that room', he took his oath of office after which the ceremony was concluded. The dukes and councillors withdrew, leaving him to begin his first day's work as the presiding judge in the Court of Chancery.

Thomas, barely catching his breath, wrote to his friend again. Choosing his words with care, fully aware that diplomatic correspondence was already being intercepted by the king, Thomas confided: 'The more I realize that this post involves the interests of Christendom, my dearest Erasmus, the more I hope it all turns out successfully.' We know exactly what he meant by this. Henry wished to divorce his wife, Katherine of Aragon. When in 1525 he'd elevated Henry Fitzroy, his illegitimate son by Elizabeth Blount, to the dukedoms of Richmond and Somerset, he was, in effect, admitting that Katherine had passed the menopause and all hope of a living son by her was gone. Fitzroy's ennoblement, and to titles so closely associated with the royal family as these, was the first of Henry's attempts to settle the dynastic succession. The hopes long ago expressed in Thomas's coronation speech that Katherine would be a 'mother of kings' had come to nothing. Her only healthy child was her daughter Mary. Katherine doted on her, but for Henry she would always be a disappointment. After her last stillborn daughter was born in 1518, Katherine had failed to conceive again.

By 1526, Henry was head over heels in love with a younger woman. Rumours abounded of his mistresses after he discarded Blount and married her off to a wealthy landowner, but nothing could be proved. Then he met Anne Boleyn, great-granddaughter of the same Sir Geoffrey Boleyn who'd commissioned the rood-loft and screen at St Lawrence's Church where Thomas had prayed in his youth. She was an unremarkable brunette, lacking the pale, translucent skin so in vogue. As the Venetian ambassador said, she 'is not one of the most beautiful women in the world. She is of middling stature, swarthy complexion, long neck, wide mouth, bosom not much raised.' Her chief assets were Henry's lust 'and her eyes, which are black and beautiful'. Brought up at the French Court, Anne had unmistakable chic. Her sharp wit and vivacity, her willingness to answer men back on equal terms, marked her out from other women.

If Katherine had disdained to notice Henry's other mistresses, she couldn't ignore Anne, who had vowed to supplant her. Unlike Fitzroy, Anne insisted, her child would be legitimate because she and Henry would be married. Faced with Anne's demands, it was natural for Henry to find the answer to his prayers in the Bible. Thomas was among the first to hear of it, since it was in the gallery of Wolsey's (and now Henry's) magnificent palace at Hampton Court that the king had first broached his doubts to him in the week beginning 13 October 1527. Thomas had lately returned from Amiens, where he'd assisted Wolsey in ratifying one of the Anglo-French treaties. More tells us that, much to his surprise, 'his Highness, walking in the gallery, brake with me of his great matter', explaining that his marriage to Katherine 'was not only against the positive laws of the Church and the written law of God but also in such wise against the law of nature'. The defects of the marriage were so serious that 'it could in no wise by the Church be dispensable'.

Katherine had married Henry on the strength of Pope Julius II's dispensation of the impediment of affinity which her former marriage to his deceased elder brother, Prince Arthur, had created between them, and it was the validity of this dispensation that Henry sought to contest. All prospects of a quick annulment had evaporated after Pope Clement had made the terrible mistake of allying with Francis I on the eve of the Battle of Pavia. Charles V retaliated against the papal lands, his forces commanded by the feckless Bourbon, and despite yet another last-minute switch by Clement, nothing could stop their southward march. Bourbon's men, who had not been paid, raced towards Rome, intent on grabbing the loot they had been promised, sacking the city in an orgy of violence, murdering the citizens, raping nuns, burning down churches and using the holiest of images for target practice. Clement fled, taking shelter in his stronghold of Castel Sant'-Angelo, where he signed a truce making himself Charles's prisoner. The news had arrived in England a month before Wolsey embarked for France. And with the pope a puppet of Katherine's nephew, he was stymied.

By the time Wolsey was home, Henry had changed tack, seeking a divorce on the grounds that the Old Testament prohibition on marriage to a brother's wife (Leviticus 20:21) was a precept binding on Christians which no pope could dispense. Henry rejected a seemingly contrary text (Deuteronomy 25:5), denying its relevance on the grounds that it merely reflected a Jewish tradition known as the 'levirate' by which the brother or next of kin to a deceased man was bound to marry the widow. Soon afterwards, he went much further, claiming that sexual intercourse with a brother's wife amounted to incest and 'in such high degree against the law of nature'. Thomas More had first heard that argument at Hampton Court, where Henry read aloud verses from Leviticus that, in the king's view and those of his supporters, proved his case.

Asked for his opinion, Thomas had replied that he was not in a position to confirm or deny Henry's interpretation of the scriptural texts without deeper study. 'Accepting benignly my sudden unadvised answer,' he said, Henry had 'advised him to commune further' with Edward Foxe, the provost of King's College, Cambridge, one of the king's advisers compiling the first of a series of royal dossiers on the divorce. More read Foxe's manuscript, which was later shown to a committee of bishops and theologians, but his opinion was unchanged. And Henry, for the moment, hadn't pressed the point, leaving Thomas alone until shortly after he was sworn in as Lord Chancellor.

The biblical texts had naturally been considered by the Vatican long before. What had changed wasn't the Church's understanding, but Henry's. At the suggestion of Richard Pace, Henry had summoned Robert Wakefield, the foremost Hebrew expert at Cambridge, who encouraged him to think that the divine retribution threatened against illicit marriage partners according to Leviticus – 'they shall be childless' – was to be understood solely in the male gender. The passage, said Wakefield, should read: 'If a man shall take his brother's wife, it is an impurity. He hath uncovered his brother's nakedness: they shall not have sons.' This, at a stroke, removed the major stumbling-block from Henry's case as his daughter Mary was alive and well.

After two long years of intricate diplomacy, and a few months before More had stepped in as Lord Chancellor, Wolsey had obtained delegated powers from a reluctant Pope Clement to hear Henry's case, sitting jointly with Cardinal Campeggio at Blackfriars. Katherine had made an emotional appeal for justice, throwing herself at Henry's feet, begging him to consider her helpless position as a foreigner, her obedience as a loyal and devoted wife, her own and her daughter's honour. She'd appealed to Rome as the only tribunal before which her case could properly be judged, and then withdrawn. The legates overruled her; she was recalled, and on refusing to return, was pronounced delinquent. But the court had to be adjourned before a final sentence could be given. At the last moment, Clement had revoked the case to Rome after which the battle-lines were drawn, for Henry took the line that a Christian who became aware that he had married unlawfully and was living in sin was obliged to do something about it. When the Holy Spirit had so touched a man's heart, he said, that he knew his marriage was incestuous, his 'conscience' was aroused.

Henry, in his comments and annotations on Foxe's dossier, had slowly but surely begun to define 'conscience' as the 'private law' written in the hearts of individuals by the Holy Spirit, something that wasn't just a moral force, but which could be turned into a set of written principles and used to justify resistance against the pope. Henry's evolving view of 'conscience' was, however, diametrically opposed to the Catholic Church's teaching. It had been held for centuries by the Church that what someone should rightfully think in 'conscience' could be valid only if it were cross-referenced against those doctrines and beliefs that the Church in its lawfully convened General Councils had previously judged to be valid. It was only Luther and his supporters who believed that a man's 'conscience' could be shaped by reading the Bible alone.

A few days after Thomas had been sworn in as Lord Chancellor, Henry entreated him in the name of friendship to 'look and consider his great matter' again. If, he said, it were to turn out that he could now persuade his most loyal servant to support his cause, then, recounted More, 'he would gladly use me among other of his councillors in that matter'. If not, 'he graciously declared unto me that . . . I should perceive mine own conscience should serve me.' Thomas found it reassuring that Henry had remembered their conversation at Reading Abbey after all these years, once more telling him to 'first look unto God and after God unto him'. Keenly aware of the ways in which the ground was shifting under his feet and that Henry's favour came at a price, he agreed to revisit the divorce.

Henry asked Foxe and his team of researchers to update his new Lord Chancellor. With Foxe came Thomas Cranmer, a Cambridge theologian and chaplain to the Boleyns, assisted by Nicholas de Burgo, a Franciscan friar from Florence, and Thomas More's old antagonist in the battle over Erasmus's Greek New Testament, Edward Lee. It must have been a bitter blow for Thomas to have to take instruction from Lee, but he had no choice. These advisers tried to convince him of the justice of Henry's suit for divorce, but in vain.

Thomas returned to Henry, offering his excuses and explaining that 'to do him service', he would 'have been more glad than of all such worldly commodities as I either then had or ever should come to', if only he could have agreed with his opinion. And Henry accepted defeat with considerable grace, saying that he would never 'put any man in ruffle or trouble of his conscience'. He would, he said, use only those councillors in his suit for divorce 'whose conscience [he] perceived well and fully persuaded upon that part'. After that, as More was careful to record, he did nothing else towards the divorce himself. He neither wrote to prejudice Henry's case, nor did anyone else by his 'procurement'. He settled his mind to serve the crown 'in other things'. He would not read the numerous treatises in favour of Katherine by his friend Bishop Fisher. And when he discovered in his study a treatise in her favour which someone had sent him, he promptly burnt it.

Although self-preservation from this point onwards would force Thomas to conceal his private thoughts on the divorce, it didn't stop him as Lord Chancellor from taking his own advice in Book I of *Utopia*: 'Don't give up the ship in a storm because you cannot hold back the winds . . . Instead, by an indirect approach, you must strive and struggle as best you can to handle everything tactfully. What you cannot make wholly good, you may at least make as little bad as possible.' For the first time in his life, he found himself not simply praising Cardinal Morton for having set the gold standard for wisdom and honesty during Richard III's reign, but also stepping into his hero's shoes, ready to engage in politics, to collude if necessary in distasteful acts, but to a strictly moral end. Morton, as Thomas believed, had outwitted the devil at his own game. Now it was his own turn to face the challenge. There could be no hope of release, no chance of a quiet life if he were to fulfil his duty as an honest councillor.

Ever since his stay at the Charterhouse, Thomas had shaped much of his world-view around his belief in God's providence. Morton had pointed the way, and even the heathen Utopians know that the universe is ruled by divine providence and not by 'blind chance'. Many Catholic theologians already imagined Luther to be the Antichrist, whose appearance on earth presaged the Second Coming. Thomas sometimes talked himself of 'concealed prophecies' and other matters 'not to be disclosed until the times appointed by God's providence'. Shortly before accepting the Chancellorship, he let slip his opinion that Antichrist was 'the head of all heretics' and Luther was his harbinger. Whole books were pouring from the presses discussing the 'tokens of Antichrist', several making bizarre apocalyptic predictions in which events like the Turkish victories in Hungary and the Mediterranean, or natural disasters such as floods, famine and pestilence, were seen as 'signs' or 'scourges' sent by God. Two incidents affecting the lives of those he held dearest to him allow a rare glimpse inside Thomas's state of mind around this time.

In the spring of 1528 the sweating sickness had returned, rampaging through London and the south-east. Judge John More, still living at Milk Street and fearing the worst at the age of seventy-seven, had made his will. He was spared, but at Chelsea Margaret had fallen gravely ill. Her fever was so extreme, says William Roper, that she fell into a coma, causing her physicians to despair of her life. Sleeping victims had to be roused by shaking them if necessary, because an unconscious patient wasn't able to sweat properly. When everything had failed in Margaret's case and her physicians had given up all hope, Thomas wouldn't yield. He retreated to his secret oratory to pray for her, beseeching God with tears in his eyes to spare her. A few minutes later, he remembered how Galen had recommended as a means of arousal the use of a 'clyster' (or enema), usually made from oil of violets with the leaves of red roses dried in an oven and the yokes of two eggs, or else of crushed aloes, saffron and myrrh blended in a thick astringent syrup. The physicians administered the purgative and Margaret's life was saved.

Then, while Thomas was travelling in Oxfordshire with Henry a month before Wolsey's dismissal, Giles Heron brought him news of a disastrous fire at Chelsea. A wing of the mansion house and all the family's barns and those of their neighbours had been destroyed. Losses were huge, with no easy way of replacing the lost grain except by purchasing it in the market at barely affordable prices. Far from cursing his luck, Thomas sat down and wrote to Lady Alice: 'I pray you be with my children and your household merry in God.' The fire, he said, was an act of divine providence, brought about to teach the family the insignificance of material, worldly values. God worked in mysterious ways. Everyone should go to church and give thanks, and Thomas would make good his neighbours' losses. Money must have been tight, because he asked Lady Alice to consider whether, in future, it would be better to share the risk by subletting all the family's cultivated fields, to avoid the worry and expense of farming. If, however, Alice agreed, Thomas insisted that alternative employment be found for all the family's labourers, so that none should be put out of work.

Perceiving the hand of God in such incidents led Thomas More to toughen his resolve, reinforce his ascetic streak, and see with nitric clarity that an honest councillor had to seize his opportunities if he were to have any chance of improving the society in which he lived. Margaret's brush with death and the fire, like his Charterhouse meditations, were among the life-experiences teaching him what really mattered to him. Providence was a greater force than heathen 'fate' because God stood behind it. If Henry's infatuation with Anne meant that, for the moment, Thomas couldn't influence the divorce, 'other things' could be just as important, and perhaps more so. His conversations with Foxe's team had disclosed to him the full extent of the impending threat to the Church. As long as Henry was flirting with Lutheranism, the issues underlying the divorce could prove to be even more damaging to the 'true faith' than the Hunne affair. For the divorce had changed Henry's character and for the worse. Now thirty-eight, he was turning into a bully, more wilful and impervious to advice or criticism than before, fuming that he 'would be obeyed whosoever spake to the contrary'. Abrupt and dictatorial, he insisted on having his own way over the interpretation of the Bible; very soon it would be a matter of 'conscience' for him to impose his will on Parliament and the nation if the pope disagreed. He had only to begin a sentence with the word 'Well' for all around him to understand that his mind was made up and it was safer not to argue.

When Thomas walked to mass in his scarlet robes lined with white fur as Lord Chancellor to mark the opening of Parliament on 3 November 1529, he knew that his questions about the role of honest councillors in Book I of *Utopia* were deadly serious, and that he stood at the crossroads of history.

20

GRAPPLING WITH THE DEVIL

DESPITE CALLING PARLIAMENT WITH the intention of impeaching Wolsey, Henry's mind changed after the fallen cardinal voluntarily confessed that, on the authority of bulls from Rome making him a papal legate, he had unlawfully vexed, and taxed, the king's subjects. Stripped by Henry of his wealth, Wolsey, sick, humiliated and defeated, would be suffered to travel to his diocese of York to undertake pastoral work until, within a year, he would start to recover some of his old confidence, attempt to stage a comeback, and be recalled south to answer trumped-up charges of treason, dying of dysentery (and fright) on his journey.

In his opening speech to Parliament as Lord Chancellor, More urged members to direct their efforts towards reforming outdated laws and correcting 'new errors and heresies sprung up among the people'. His exhortation the laity interpreted, wrongly, as a mandate to attack Church abuses. After lively debates, the Speaker of the Commons, Thomas Audley, appointed select committees to consider these abuses, including mortuary fees for burying the dead, and prepare draft legislation. A clever lawyer, Audley had been catapulted into the Speakership for one reason alone: he was efficient and unquestioning in his loyalty to Henry, as nimble and adaptable as a chameleon. And as time went by, he attached himself to Thomas Cromwell, once Wolsey's right-hand man and now in his mid-forties, who would soon be gliding effortlessly into an equivalent role in Henry's innermost circle.

The Commons' grievances were quickly turned into draft laws and petitions meant for Henry. Led by Warham and Fisher, the bishops 'frowned and grunted', saying the draft laws showed 'lack of faith' and would bring the Church 'into servile thraldom'. On Henry's orders, fresh drafts were made, for the king was happy to play snakes and ladders in Parliament until he got his way on the divorce. Some members of the Commons, remembering Friar Standish's feisty speech, had already begun challenging the Church's privileges as conceded by Henry II after St Thomas Becket's murder. Happy to assist, Henry repeatedly intervened, skewing the votes and debates so that all the reforming laws passed.

For Thomas More, the anticlerical measures were a crushing defeat, although the churchmen weren't letting their case go by default. Despite losing in Parliament, they appealed to Rome, asking Pope Clement to annul the reforms, calling them 'invalid' because Parliament had 'exceeded its powers' by contravening canon and papal law. Henry and Cromwell knew nothing of their appeal, which was kept a closely guarded secret. As to More, he had vowed to steer clear of anything relating to the divorce, but to serve the crown 'in other things'. It was with that very much in mind that he turned on his own account to attacking the 'errors and heresies' that he'd mentioned in his speech.

Strolling along the riverbank at Chelsea, taking his ease not long after Parliament began its work, Thomas spoke to William Roper of his hopes and fears for the session. Thanks to Margaret's painstaking work, her husband and father had been reconciled. William had purged himself of Lutheranism and, on returning to the Catholic fold, his father-in-law had secured him a seat in Parliament as one of the representatives for Bramber, a Sussex borough controlled by the Duke of Norfolk.

Although Thomas always tried to avoid mingling public and private business even when relaxing, he was finding it increasingly difficult. If just three things could be settled the way he wanted them, he confided to William as they enjoyed the view, he would be well content to be 'put in a sack and here presently cast into the Thames'.

'What great things be those?' asked Roper.

'In faith,' answered Thomas, 'the first is, that where the most part of Christian princes be at mortal war, they were all at a universal peace. The second, that where the Church of Christ is at this present sore afflicted with many errors and heresies, it were settled in a perfect uniformity of religion. The third, that where the king's matter of his marriage is now come in question, it were to the glory of God and quietness of all parts brought to a good conclusion.'

In Thomas's eyes, the divorce and the Lutheran threat were connected, because as long as Henry insisted on defending his own interpretation of the Old Testament Book of Leviticus, then his view of 'conscience' would be Luther's. As Parliament got down to business, Henry grew ever more brazen in his posturing, inviting the papal nuncio and Charles V and Francis I's ambassadors to dinner, then mischievously telling them that wars and heresies alike were the fault of the pope and cardinals. Had the Church paid more attention to the Word of God, he said, Christendom would have been governed less scandalously. Luther had been right to say so; his theological mistakes were 'not a sufficient reason for reproving and rejecting the many truths he had brought to light'.

Thomas completely disagreed. In his literary feuds he'd shown he could be utterly intransigent, that attack was the best form of defence. He'd been utterly scandalized when Luther, a monk, broke his vow of chastity by marrying Katharina von Bora, a nun, calling him 'a fond friar, an apostate, an open incestuous lecher, a plain limb of the devil, and a manifest messenger from hell', a 'lewd, lousy lover in lechery'. It wasn't the first time he'd crossed the line into scatology: when defending Henry in the *Answer to Luther*, he'd berated Luther's own vulgar claim to 'a prior right to bespatter and besmirch the royal crown [i.e. Henry's] with shit', retorting, 'Will we not have the posterior right to proclaim the beshitted tongue of this practitioner of posteriorities [i.e. Luther] most fit to lick with his anterior the very posterior of a pissing she-mule?'

Thomas had most fully developed his thoughts and feelings on heresy in *A Dialogue Concerning Heresies*, published four months before he became Lord Chancellor. It is a work of far-reaching importance; a family production, since printing had been undertaken as a favour, and at short notice, by John Rastell, upon whom his brother-in-law had made unusually exacting demands, rewriting long sections of the text in proof and so incurring extra costs, absorbed within the family. Rooted in purportedly real-life conversations with an interlocutor known as 'the Messenger', Thomas creates a dramatic structure in which the Messenger sets forth his Lutheran beliefs, enabling More to refute them. The family link is ever stronger, for a character called 'the Messenger', an ardent youth, performs a similar role in Rastell's play *The Four Elements*, written after the failure of his Atlantic expedition. In Thomas's *Dialogue*, the Messenger evokes uncannily William Roper's lapse into apostasy: he is a headstrong, brash and arrogant student who, when too lazy to finish his studies, becomes infatuated by Lutheranism, his ear open to all the grievances and gossip of the street. He is 'deceived by the devil in his blind affections'.

In the *Dialogue* Thomas vigorously defends Catholic traditions against Luther and Tyndale, but still hopes to see the Bible accessible to everyone. 'I would not,' he protests, 'withhold the profit that one good devout unlearned layman might take by the reading [of it], not for the harm that a hundred heretics would fall in by their own wilful abusion.' A true English Bible translation, he says, should be undertaken as soon as possible. To refuse would be to imitate a 'lewd surgeon' amputating a leg as a cure for gout or cutting off a man's head 'to keep him from the toothache'.

But Thomas and the Messenger can agree on little else. Among the most emotive passages are those lumping together heretics, Turks and Saracens as malignant, evil subversives, as bad as – and in Luther's case considerably worse than – pagans and pornographers. While explaining to the Messenger that 'the burning of heretics . . . is lawful, necessary, and well done', Thomas argues that the use of violence is as justifiable, as essential against heretics as it is against infidels, not least because heretics themselves had first turned to violence in the days of St Augustine. 'Heretics', he says, are 'worse than Turks', and history proves that violence is always necessary to restrain the 'great outrages committed against the peace and quiet of the people in sundry places of Christendom by heretics rising of a small beginning to a high and unruly multitude'. For these reasons, 'many sore punishments' had been devised for them, 'and especially by fire'.

With Parliament adjourned throughout 1530 and 'sore punishments' for heretics at the forefront of his mind, Thomas, in May, chivvied Henry into issuing a royal proclamation bringing print censorship for the first time within the jurisdiction of the Court of Star Chamber. Over a hundred titles were to be placed on an officially proscribed index of heretical books, with Tyndale's New Testament at its head.

Then, on 25 October, presiding in Star Chamber, Thomas examined four Londoners on oath before sending them to do public penance for possessing forbidden books. They were paraded on horseback through the streets, facing their horses' tails and wearing pasteboard hats bearing the legend 'For sinning against the king's proclamation', their clothes festooned with confiscated New Testaments. Forced to throw the books onto a bonfire before a large crowd rattling pewter pans and basins with their spoons, the four men were then set in the pillory. Except that the charivari backfired, for these men held their heads high, knowing that no better advertisement could be found for their beliefs. One of them, riding a 'lofty gelding and fierce' that pranced on its hind legs at the cacophony of sounds, boldly sported his English Bibles as a ruff.

The youngest of the four was an apprentice, the others established citizens. John Purser was a vintner, Thomas Somer a fishmonger and John Tyndale (the reformer's brother) a merchant tailor. Purser and Somer had attended a 'night school' off Cheapside with the late Richard Hunne, and were among Cromwell's regular clients in his law practice, becoming his friends when Cromwell himself turned towards Lutheranism after studying Erasmus's Greek New Testament. John Tyndale had sent money to his brother abroad and helped to market his publications.

After the four were taken from the pillory, they were sent to the Tower, where Somer made his will and died. Purser too suffered from the harsh conditions. He became seriously ill, but was released to die at home, surrounded by his Lutheran friends. He sent his young son, Dick, whom (his enemies said) he had 'nurtured up in heresy', to be apprenticed with another merchant, but Dick was evicted as soon as his father was laid in his tomb. Thomas More, his conscience touched, had him brought to Chelsea, employing him as an indoor servant, but when the boy showed another servant a copy of Tyndale's New Testament, he was whipped and cast out, whereupon Cromwell, in a highly symbolic gesture, hired him as the keeper of his pet leopard at a salary of £12 a year with an extra 4d a day for the animal's food.

The *cause célèbre* in Star Chamber is that of John Petyt, a warden of the Grocers' Company and cloth exporter, a man who'd shot to wealth and fame as the proprietor of the wharfs and landing-stages closest to London Bridge where all goods arriving by sea had to unload even if they were to continue their journey from the other side of the bridge. Shortly after the index of prohibited books had been proclaimed, Petyt, a member of the House of Commons, a Lutheran and a defender of Richard Hunne, heard a knock on his door. His wife, Lucy, seeing More and the lieutenant of the Tower outside, hastened to fetch her husband 'being in his closet at prayers'.

'Come, come, husband,' she said. 'My Lord Chancellor is at the door and would speak with you.'

When Petyt looked up, he found More already inside. Refusing a drink, Thomas asked him if he had any of the forbidden books and Petyt answered that he had none. The conversation shifted to other topics, but before taking his leave, Thomas asked again, 'Ye say ye have none of these new books?'

'Your lordship saw my books and my closet,' Petyt answered.

'Yet,' said Thomas, 'you must go with Master Lieutenant.'

Petyt, unable to protest further, was led away to the Tower, where (said his wife) he was cast into a dungeon. Not perhaps without reason, since a copy of Tyndale's New Testament had all along lain undiscovered beneath his desk. A priest afterwards came forward, offering to testify that Petyt was the owner of the book, but when called by Thomas as a witness, he denied all knowledge of the affair.

Petyt was released when the case collapsed, but the strain had been too great, and within a year, a pain 'came over his chest like a bar of iron' and he was to die in Lucy's arms, leaving her his wharfs and the bulk of his property.

By the terms of Petyt's lease from the Mayor and Aldermen, his interest in one of his wharfs was not transferable, so to fight this and other battles connected to her late husband's estate, Lucy married a draper and friend of Purser and Somer: John Parnell. And no sooner had Parnell put the ring on Lucy's finger than he hired, first, Cromwell to petition the city for the renewal of the lease, and next John Rastell to assist Cromwell by suing for the money spent on improvements to the wharf and its warehouses.

Gradually it would emerge that, since the failure of Rastell's Atlantic expedition, Parnell had been helping him, supplying all the timber needed for the construction and repair of his public theatre at Finsbury Fields and so making it financially viable. But Parnell, for some years known to be a Lutheran, was said to be slippery in his business dealings, a man who never did anything without a hidden agenda. What his motive might be in cultivating the Lord Chancellor's brother-in-law would shortly become clear.

On 11 July 1531 Henry separated from his wife Katherine, exiling her to one of Wolsey's abandoned, empty houses. He went hunting openly with Anne Boleyn, whom he allowed to 'keep state' at the royal palaces.

Flanked by her own almoner and other household officers, Anne processed to mass in the Chapel Royal, 'loaded with jewels' as if she were already queen, sitting close to Henry and surreptitiously scribbling love notes to him in her psalter.

Spurred into action by Anne, Henry invited two influential Protestants, Robert Barnes and Simon Grynaeus, to visit him under the promise of safe-conduct. The olive branch to Barnes, an exiled Cambridge friar, was especially galling for Thomas More, who regarded him as a dangerous, perfidious heretic. Barnes certainly had a colourful past. Hauled up long ago by Wolsey for dubious preaching, he'd been given sanctuary by John Parnell, who'd introduced him to Purser and Somer. Tried for heresy, he'd recanted and made a public penance. Sent under house arrest to Northampton, he'd staged a spectacular escape, leaving a pile of clothes on a riverbank and a suicide note, before fleeing to join Luther at Wittenberg.

Grynaeus, a pillar of the Swiss Reformation, arrived first. Meeting Henry several times, he offered to canvass support for the divorce abroad. More had no choice but to greet him civilly, inviting him to Chelsea and showing him round his garden. But he sent his own newly appointed secretary, John Harris, to follow Grynaeus wherever he went, as far as Oxford, where the reformer travelled in search of ancient manuscripts. As a mark of esteem towards the author of *Utopia*, Grynaeus offered to dedicate a forthcoming edition of Plato to More, but Thomas found the idea of a tribute from so notorious a heretic too repulsive, and graciously declined.

When Barnes arrived, Cromwell entertained him and introduced him to those advising Henry on the divorce. More was incensed that Henry and Cromwell allowed Barnes to shave off his beard and walk freely about London, disguised as a merchant, chatting to all his old Lutheran friends. Thomas used his authority to have him watched night and day, even having his spies drink with the heretic in an alehouse, but was unable to arrest him while Henry's safe-conduct was valid.

Out of frustration, perhaps even displaced aggression at Henry's supping with the devil, Thomas started rounding up suspected Lutherans and imprisoning them. Up until this point, he'd largely reacted to what was laid before him by the bishops. The correct procedure was clear: the bishops and their officers might arrest suspects and put them on trial, calling for assistance if required. If convicted by a Church court, a heretic would be required to recant and do penance, processing to church in a white sheet carrying a faggot or wearing badges painted with faggots. A heretic refusing to recant or relapsing into heresy would be delivered to the secular magistrates for punishment, but no heretic could be put to death until the Lord Chancellor had issued a writ.

Thomas had issued the first of the writs for which he is responsible on 16 February 1530, after Archbishop Warham certified that Thomas Hitton, captured after stealing wet washing from a hedge near Gravesend, was a relapsed heretic. Without hesitation, More condemned Hitton to the stake. Rather shockingly, he calls him 'the devil's stinking martyr' who 'hath taken his wretched soul with him straight from the short fire to the fire everlasting'. Hailed by Tyndale as a true and worthy martyr, Hitton, says More, was nothing of the kind, for 'martyrs have died for God, and heretics have died for the devil'. Determined to defend the Church and canon law, Thomas didn't mince his words, describing heresy as 'poison' and 'treason to God'.

Although denied a voice as a woman and obliged to whisper, echoes of Margaret's opinions can be detected to show that she condoned her father's stand. What she said privately to William Roper when she won him back from his apostasy can never be known, but in her *Devout Treatise on the Pater Noster* she anticipates her father's idioms, equating those 'obstinate and rebellious spirits' in the Church sowing discord rather than behaving as 'members of one body' with Jews and infidels. Such people 'never cease', she says, 'from despiteful and abominable backbiting'. Already an expert on Eusebius after correcting Erasmus's mistake in his edition of the letters of St Cyprian, she would have been familiar with his key idea that heretics were the forerunners of Antichrist. Her rhetoric (like Erasmus's own) is more anti-Semitic than her father's, since Thomas took care in his *Dialogue* to avoid comparing heretics to Jews, whom he depicts as God's chosen people before the coming of Christ. But the innuendo against schismatics is the same.

After Henry split with his wife, Margaret watched as her father, clearly despairing of the churchmen's inability to organize surveillance of the Lutheran community, made his moves. Iron-willed as she'd never seen him before, she would have observed him depart with his constables to arrest George Constantine, an artful dodger privy to the secrets of the Lutheran lawyers and involved in shipping Tyndale's books. Locking him up in the gatehouse beside the almshouses at Chelsea, Thomas put him in the (indoor) stocks he kept there. They can't have been in good repair since, a week or so later, Constantine splintered the wooden frame and wriggled his legs free, scaling More's garden wall and fleeing to rejoin Tyndale in Antwerp. Chagrined but willing to admit he'd been outwitted, Thomas joked he must have fed his prisoner properly, his black humour disguising the importance of the intelligence he'd secured, since while in custody Constantine had boasted of a major shipment of books due to arrive, setting Thomas on the trail of what he judged to be a conspiracy.

Constantine's information enabled More to lie in wait for, and trap, one of Barnes's closest friends, the book dealer Richard Bayfield. Interrogated by Thomas at Chelsea, Bayfield was handed over to the Church courts for trial, and the Lord Chancellor, following the strict letter of the law, withdrew until a conviction was obtained, after which he issued a writ. At the stake, the fire took an abnormally long time to catch hold, and Bayfield, bound in chains, died with excruciating slowness. Challenged by the Protestants to justify such cruelty, Thomas retorted that Bayfield, a relapsed heretic, was 'like a dog returning to his vomit' and 'worthily burned'.

And so the trail led on. John Tewkesbury, a leather-seller, was another Lutheran kept in Thomas's gatehouse and tried by the Church court. According to the bishop's register, the court's decree convicting him was 'read and pronounced . . . in the house of Sir Thomas More, high Chancellor of England in the parish of Chelsea', suggesting that, on this occasion, the Church court itself was convened here. 'The poor wretch lieth in hell,' said Thomas after the victim died in agony, with 'a hot firebrand burning at his back that all the water in the world will never be able to quench'. He believed that justice had been done, but was equally keen to ensure it was seen to be done. In spite of this, Tewkesbury's friends complained that when the doomed man was cast into the fire, no writ had been issued and the burning was illegal. As no copy of the writ has ever been found, it is conceivable that More, in his eagerness to put the sentence into effect, issued verbal orders but the paperwork slipped his mind.

In straining every nerve against heretics, Thomas believed he was serving God and Henry equally. He'd long ago explained in *Utopia* that, even in an ideal society, those denying the essential articles of faith must be excommunicated, stripped of their citizenship and severely punished.

The Protestants grasped at once that he was making martyrs for their cause. 'Of the ashes of one heretic springeth up many,' is what they said. But no one could persuade Thomas. His earliest mentors, Grocyn, Colet and Linacre, were dead, and Erasmus was a broken man, forced to flee from Basel to sanctuary at Freiburg im Bresgau, a remote Catholic city on the slopes of the Black Forest, to escape the fury of a Protestant iconoclasm he had himself helped to unleash. The one person whom Thomas might have allowed to influence him, whom he genuinely respected for her learning, his 'dearly beloved Meg', was already convinced he was right.

His intransigence cut the ground from under his feet, as opinions were changing as rapidly as the times. Erasmus fell into a state of denial over it, unable to credit that what the Protestants were saying could be true, refusing to believe that anyone so talented as Thomas could have ended up debasing his genius in such an evil cause, because for all his moral cowardice, Erasmus was on the side of the angels where heresy trials were concerned, accepting the burning of books, but rejecting as barbaric the burning of people. In his inability to acknowledge, even to comprehend, the truth, he was twice forced to claim, inaccurately, that no heretic had been put to death while More was Lord Chancellor. Thomas afterwards put him right, wanting all his friends abroad to know that he'd been 'grievous to thieves, murderers and heretics', saying: 'I wrote that with deep feeling. I find that breed of men absolutely loathsome, so much so, that unless they regain their senses, I want to be as hateful to them as anyone can possibly be.'

Distraught and disillusioned with the way in which Luther and his followers had ravaged Christendom and his own ideals, Erasmus drew inwards into himself. It was a defining moment, after which his correspondence with his lifelong friend all but ceased.

21

THE PRESS OF SUITORS

WILLIAM ROPER WASN'T THE only member of the family to sit in Parliament while his father-in-law was Lord Chancellor. When Thomas took his place in the House of Lords, his father Judge John sat nearby with other senior members of the judiciary to advise on legal points. And besides finding Roper a seat, the Duke of Norfolk nominated William Daunce and Giles Heron as representatives for Thetford in Norfolk, Giles Alington was returned for Cambridgeshire, and John Rastell for Dunheved in Cornwall. Only young John, betrothed to Anne Cresacre, wasn't elected, having a year to wait before he was twenty-one and old enough to put his name forward.

While the Commons were busy attacking the Church, Roper lost no time in pursuing his own advantage. Five long years after he'd first begun to contest his father's will, he had still not secured probate. The Roper family feud, meanwhile, was notorious, with accusations of perjury, violent quarrels and provocation hurled by both sides. Under cover of the Commons' grievances about abuses of probate jurisdiction, William introduced a private member's bill to rewrite his father's will to suit himself and obtain probate by a special Act of Parliament. His trump card was that his father had bequeathed the bulk of his landholding to his younger sons, flying in the face of the legal doctrine of primogeniture by which land was inherited by a man's eldest son. To most members of Parliament, primogeniture was a sacred trust and, whenever they had the opportunity, they would vote for legislation to prevent the splitting of inheritances.

Partly, then, to end 'great trouble, strife and variance' between the Ropers, but mainly to bolster primogeniture, Parliament set John Roper's will aside in favour of a settlement giving William a much larger share of his father's estate than either of his brothers. And by promising to pay his father's debts and settle all his bequests promptly, William was granted immediate possession of his lands. He emerged victorious, scooping the lion's share of the freehold lands, including the most desirable properties at Well Hall near Eltham and in the parish of St Dunstan's, Canterbury, which the will had assigned to others. His mother, Jane, was the biggest loser, stripped of a life interest in a large proportion of her late husband's lands and given little more than her jointure. Christopher, her youngest son, fared almost as badly, losing the manor of Well Hall and being forced to accept Linstead, a smaller manor near Sittingbourne. A young law student at Gray's Inn where his maternal grandfather, Chief Justice Fyneux, had been a bencher, Christopher nursed a grudge against his eldest brother and in-laws for the rest of his life.

The sources are silent as to what Margaret thought about her husband cynically using his position in Parliament for personal gain. Whatever she may have thought, William took no notice. Far from keeping a low profile, he traded on his status as the husband of the Lord Chancellor's favourite daughter to lecture others. He sneered, for instance, at William Daunce for complaining that opportunities for kickbacks and bribes had been frustrated by Thomas. When Wolsey had been in charge, said Daunce, even grooms and porters had 'got great gain'. More, by his scrupulous dealings, had ruined such lucrative opportunities.

Thomas, hearing of the complaint, first poked fun at Daunce. Why, he asked, get caught up in anything so unsubtle as bribery? There were many other ways in which a judge could help his family: by granting favours here and there; by choosing one-sided arbitrators to settle their lawsuits or those of their friends; by urging parties who could have won their case outright in court to settle for less out of court. He then upbraided his son-in-law. 'I assure thee on my faith,' he said, 'that if the parties will, at my hands, call for justice, then, all were it my father stood on the one side, and the devil on the other, his cause being good, the devil should have right.' He was scandalized by Daunce's behaviour, having lately received a horrifying report that his son-in-law, contrary to his solemn promise, had evicted the caretaker and his family from the house at Battersea that Thomas had secured for them as a favour. Deliberately biding his time until the caretaker was absent overnight, Daunce had ordered the poor man's wife and children to leave with all their goods, and when they refused, knowing they would be homeless, had bundled up their possessions and dumped them outside in a heap.

Roper also jeered at Giles Heron for bringing two lawsuits to his father-in-law, expecting to win. When More had rejected his pleas, Heron had thrown a tantrum, leading to 'a flat decree against him'. One of Giles's suits was to recover sixty acres of arable land and sixty of pasture that he claimed to have inherited in Lincolnshire. He was trying it on, having already begun the case in the Court of Common Pleas, then, seeing his father-in-law arrive in the Court of Chancery, switching his case there. More wasn't fooled, ignoring that particular case. The 'flat decree' arose over Heron's other suit to occupy the manor of Woodford Hall in Essex. Giles had inherited a mere twenty acres, and was attempting to buy out the other stakeholders, making promises he failed to honour. More first heard the case on 7 November 1530, deciding against Heron and ordering him to pay damages. Heron refused, and after waiting in vain for a year, Audley, the lawyer for the opposing party, filed a motion that he be recalled, which More willingly granted. This time, Heron was judged to be in contempt of court and bound in a penalty of 1,000 marks (£666) to appear in the Court of Star Chamber to account for his presumption on pain of imprisonment in the Tower. Threatened with the Tower, Heron paid the damages, borrowing from Cromwell to do so.

Thomas, by now, was realizing that he couldn't escape the press of suitors, least of all his own friends and relatives. He was well on his guard by the time the name of the black sheep of the family, the disgraced scrivener Richard Staverton who'd swindled his young niece, appeared on his court list. Sued by a London grocer for reneging on a deal for the sale of a house, Staverton must have been shocked to find his brother-in-law ordering him to be hauled into court on the Friday of the very same week as the grocer made his complaint, under threat of a ruinous fine. Faring a great deal better was John Rastell, who in a typically forthright way arrived in Chancery at eight o'clock in the morning asking Thomas to deal as soon as possible with someone he claimed to be a sly, disreputable attorney who was suing him in Yorkshire, alleging a debt that Rastell said he'd long repaid. Convinced of his brother-in-law's sincerity, Thomas issued an injunction on the spot, and without seeking further proof, forbade all other courts from deciding the case, boldly signing his order 'Tho[mas] More, King's Chancellor'.

Margaret got a personal taste of her father's approach to justice when, one day, a disgruntled suitor arrived at the mansion house to see Lady Alice about a case he was pursuing before her husband. A trickster who'd tried to defraud a neighbour's wife by selling her a wardrobe of old

clothes, pretending they were new, the suitor had successfully deceived
her until her angry husband, taking legal advice, had used a loophole in
the law to keep the clothes without paying for them. When the biter
found himself bitten, he sued in Chancery, only to find that instead of
dismissing the case, Thomas decided on a 'merry jest', a prank of the sort
he could rarely resist when at home. Somehow managing to keep a
straight face, he told the suitor to go to Chelsea and seek his remedy from
Lady Alice. It's hard to see how anyone could have taken him at his word,
but the trickster did. He took his case to her, only to find that she dealt
with him exactly as she saw fit, giving him the rough side of her tongue.

Just as when he'd been an undersheriff, Thomas freely applied his
discretion in the cause of justice, dismissing cases that he considered to be
frivolous out of hand, expecting suitors to settle out of court wherever
possible, and requiring them to be governed by the golden rule of equity –
'Do as you would be done by' – as Christ had commanded in the Sermon
on the Mount. A lawyer who loved justice more than he loved lawyers, his
jokes and pranks were his means of emancipating himself from a barrage
of pettifogging litigation, but naturally rankled with the professionals, who
said he was turning himself into a superior judge of appeal, interfering
with due process of law in other courts, and making snap decisions after
listening to *ex parte* claims to the detriment and loss of honest citizens.

A dispute, before long, arose over equitable injunctions of exactly the
type that he'd awarded to John Rastell. As Thomas saw the matter, they
were an essential weapon in the Chancellor's arsenal, enabling him to
halt litigation, often permanently, in any other court of law, and he
decided to confront his critics, inviting them to dine with him. When the
meal was over, he 'broke' with them 'what complaints he had heard of
his injunctions', explaining 'both the number and causes of every one of
them in order'. This he did 'so plainly' that, following a full discussion,
they 'were all enforced to confess that they in like case could have done
no otherwise themselves'. This part of the meeting ended in a triumph.

Not so the rest of the debate. Thomas went on to argue that 'if the
justices of every court . . . would, upon reasonable considerations, by
their own discretions, as they were as he thought in conscience bound,
mitigate and reform the rigour of the law themselves, there should from
henceforth by him no more injunctions be granted.' Some of the younger
judges may have supported More, but the older ones would not tolerate
any outside interference in their courts.

According to William Roper, Thomas said afterwards of the judges, 'I perceive . . . why they like not so to do, for they see that they may by the verdict of the jury cast off all quarrels from themselves.' He had looked into the heart of the dispute, for there were no juries in the Court of Chancery, where a single judge decided the cases. In the Courts of King's Bench and Common Pleas, and throughout the country at the assizes, verdicts in criminal and a majority of civil cases were given by juries of 'twelve good men and true' and not on the basis of a single judge's discretion.

Judge John couldn't be at the dinner to advise his son. Sitting in court until his final illness, he drew his last instalment of salary on 5 November 1530. A month later, he was dead aged seventy-nine. Coinciding with Advent, the dirge and funeral were held at St Lawrence's, the mourners congregating in the same porch where the judge had married three of his wives, before entering the church for the requiem mass. Judge John had prepared his tomb in the Lady Chapel on a spot next to that of John and Joan Marshall. In death, as in life, his second wife continued to exert her baneful influence over him. His widow, Alice Clerk, inherited a life interest in Gobions, where she moved and lived quietly for the rest of her days. Although Thomas had inherited all the furniture and kitchen utensils there, he gladly gave them back to his stepmother. The property at Milk Street was sold, the profits ploughed back into the estate at Chelsea, where costs had soared after the fire a year before.

Despite clashing with the judges over injunctions, Thomas still considered it his duty to teach arrogant or discreditable litigants a lesson. Power and wealth would not protect them, as Richard Gresham, a rich mercer and future Mayor of London, was to discover. Once a neighbour of Judge John, Gresham was investing the profits of his trade in land, and at New Year, the season for gift-giving, he sent 'a fair gilt cup' to Thomas, even though one of his lawsuits was pending. He was buying a manor from a young heir who'd lately come 'of age', who had the right as heir to sell the freehold, but whose stepfather and trustee was refusing to release the title-deeds or vacate the manor house. On its merits, the case was a perfect illustration of the points Thomas had already been making to the judges, since if they had decided the case, and not the Chancellor, Gresham would have lost his investment as only the Court of Chancery gave legal protection to the beneficiaries of trusts. Gresham would probably have won the case if he'd been willing to wait his turn, but More knew he couldn't accept what was manifestly a bribe, blocking the case and venting his wit on Gresham. Despite being a connoisseur's dream, the cup's 'legal' worth had nothing to do with its aesthetics, arising purely from its value as scrap. What better, then, than to return an uglier but more valuable cup? By making a swop, Thomas refused the bribe, rebuked the donor, but kept a beautiful object. At the time it must have seemed like something straight out of *Utopia*, reminiscent of the fable of the golden urinals. But was it wise?

A more damaging encounter, as it would turn out, involved John Parnell, whom Thomas had already marked out as a slippery Lutheran. The bare facts are uncontested. Parnell had contracted to sell Richard Vaughan, a mercer, 1,000 woollen cloths for £1,216, with the supply to be made by Whitsuntide. Vaughan promised to pay £840 in cash and the rest in bales of woad, and to deliver 303 bales on account. While waiting for the cloths, Vaughan resold them for export at the next Antwerp fair, which, as he told the court, should have been to his 'great lucre'.

Vaughan sailed for the Netherlands, leaving his factor to arrange the shipping. Here the story is disputed. Vaughan claimed that Parnell failed to deliver the cloths, despite repeated offers to pay him. Parnell counter-claimed that he'd delivered 560, and then stopped as the woad he'd received was of poor quality, worth only a fraction of Vaughan's valuation.

When the deal fell apart, Richard Vaughan was arrested in Antwerp. After escaping from a debtors' prison and returning to London, he demanded damages. Parnell, said Vaughan and his father, Geoffrey, who joined him as co-plaintiff in the lawsuit to More, had milked the family of working capital. The Vaughans applied for a speedy return of the woad they had supplied and hefty compensation for their losses.

Parnell, all the while trying to use his friendship with John Rastell to ingratiate himself with Thomas More, used every legal trick to delay the Chancery hearing, for which Thomas reprimanded him in open court. His patience exhausted, his irritation barely concealed, he ruled that in the cause of justice, the Vaughans should be allowed to resubmit testimony taken during previous litigation under Wolsey against Parnell, a controversial move because, by law, all the witnesses ought to have been recalled to give their evidence all over again.

More then called in expert valuers. Although a prudent decision, he wrong-footed himself by not reading their reports in full, commissioning instead a summary from John Kite, a part-time arbitrator in Chancery. He was probably trying to steer the parties towards an out-of-court settlement, but might have thought twice about it, because Kite was none other than the absentee rector of St Stephen's and afterwards Bishop of Carlisle, the same man who'd been missing from his post when Thomas had turned up late on a Sunday night to arrange his wedding to Lady Alice.

According to Parnell, Kite gave a false account to More. That isn't credible, but knowing Kite it is likely to have been a sloppy piece of work. When More gave his final judgement, only fifteen months after the Vaughans had presented their petition which was very fast for a complex commercial case, he ruled that all contracts between the parties should be annulled, and that Parnell should pay the Vaughans £128 for the woad and £50 in damages for their loss of profits. Seemingly the height of fairness, the decree would look very different if a part-load of cloths really had been delivered, or if the bartered woad was worthless, as Parnell swore on oath it was. More's decree could only be as good as Kite's certificate. There lay the problem. To his dying day, Parnell would maintain that Kite had got it wrong, leaving him out of pocket. He even wrote a clause into his will, demanding that Kite pay restitution to salve his conscience.

Alarm-bells should have rung in More's head when Geoffrey Vaughan, after the case was over, sent him 'a great gilt cup' by the hands of his wife in gratitude. Thomas returned it, but the damage was done, since Parnell was not a man to be short-changed. By now, he had a profitable sideline as a vintner, and was supplying wines to the Boleyns. In fact, Anne Boleyn's father, Thomas, Earl of Wiltshire, was one of his best customers. For sure, there would be consequences of the decree for the Vaughans.

Seeking as Lord Chancellor to manage the press of suitors in the interests of justice and common sense, Thomas More aimed to provide a simpler, faster, fairer judicial system, not unlike the one Hythloday describes in *Utopia*, where professional lawyers aren't needed because the laws are clear and straightforward, litigants tell their stories directly to a judge sitting alone, and the basic principle applied by the judges in giving their verdicts is plain-dealing. But while streamlining the judicial system he had inherited, Thomas underestimated how far his methods could be seen to be unaccountable, since, however desirable an abstract conception of 'justice' might be on the island of Utopia, it veered away from the values of 'due process of law' dating back to Magna Carta. Parnell, for one, now turned to his friends in high places, especially Cromwell. The decree in favour of the Vaughans, he believed, had been the result of a bribe, and by making it Thomas had exposed himself to a vendetta.

22

RESIGNATION

ENRY RECALLED PARLIAMENT IN 1531, and he meant business. He wanted swift action on his divorce, and also money, demanding £100,000 from the Church and threatening that if payment wasn't made quickly, he'd indict the higher clergy for *praemunire* en masse as a punishment for recognizing Wolsey as a plenipotentiary papal legate. Next, he insisted that the bishops acknowledge him as the 'protector and supreme head of the church and clergy in England'. A mouthful in more ways than one, the new title hit Convocation like a thunderbolt. Bishop Fisher, lean and grim, protested, but after weasel words from Cromwell, it was granted with the saving clause 'as far as the law of Christ allows'.

These were Henry's opening shots in his campaign to become Supreme Head of the Church. He'd decided to reconvene Parliament after Edward Foxe, Thomas Cranmer and the scholars working on the divorce had shown him a collection of precedents from (especially) histories and chronicles to 'prove' that the Anglo-Saxon kings had always been head of the English Church. According to this not entirely fraudulent, but highly selective research, the pope, before the Norman Conquest, had been a pastoral bishop, a spiritual leader enjoying a primacy of honour but lacking any legally binding powers over foreign princes, whereas God (as they said) had invested the kings of England at their coronations with an 'imperial', inalienable sovereignty.

Cromwell seized on this formula, recommending it to the nobles in the King's Council. Thomas More knew it would be a struggle to reverse the tide, but there was still hope. He tried to warn Cromwell against awakening a sleeping giant, for Henry had started talking as if God had exalted him above Parliament, the Church and the law, as if no one but himself could be a lawful intermediary between the people of England and Christ. When Cromwell arrived one day at Chelsea with a message from Henry, Thomas took him quietly aside. 'Master Cromwell,' he said, 'you are now entered into the service of a most noble, wise and liberal prince. If you will follow my poor advice, you shall, in your counsel giving unto his Grace, ever tell him what he ought to do, but never what he is able to do. So shall you show yourself a true faithful servant and a right worthy councillor. For if a lion knew his own strength, hard were it for any man to rule him.' On the threshold of power himself, Cromwell wouldn't listen.

No sooner had Henry got his £100,000 than Cromwell discovered how Fisher had appealed to Pope Clement to annul the Acts passed by Parliament in 1529. He advised Henry to retaliate, prohibiting all future bulls or decrees arriving from Rome, but when proclamations were posted up in Cheapside to this effect, the citizens tore them down. Henry was becoming as unpopular in London again as after the trial of the Duke of Buckingham. Cromwell had to be careful not to stir up a mutiny.

He needn't have worried, since the churchmen made all the mistakes. While Parliament and Convocation were still sitting, the bishops debated the case of William Tracy, who'd died after making a will in which he expressed belief in the Lutheran doctrine of justification by faith alone. Copied and circulated to the point where it had become one of the reformers' favourite texts, the will was judged to be scandalous and full of errors. A grant of probate was refused, and the bishops condemned Tracy as a heretic. His corpse would be exhumed and burnt at the stake, creating another Protestant martyr.

More kept silent on the case, but the clergy's zeal in refusing probate incensed Christopher St German, John Rastell's old teacher at the Middle Temple. Another ex-Coventry man, St German had known Tracy personally. He argued in *Doctor and Student*, an influential legal textbook, that to deny probate was to leave a dead man unable to discharge his conscience by paying his debts or making his final bequests. He questioned whether the clergy were acting legally in enforcing the heresy law, already knowing the cases of thirty or forty Lollards and reformers put on trial in Warwickshire, eight of whom were burnt in Coventry alone, a greater number than anywhere else in the country.

St German, a fervent opponent of capital punishment for crimes of the mind, wasn't leaving it there. Seventy-one years old but with a razor-sharp intellect and the eyes of a hawk, he knew that, according to strict canon law, one of several ways in which heresy suspects in a Church court were permitted to clear their names in cases where the evidence was lacking or ambiguous was by swearing an 'oath of innocence'. He discovered that, following an erroneous interpretation by the English authorities, canon law was being interpreted, wrongly, in such cases to mean that suspects could be given 'penitential pains' regardless of whether they were proved guilty. St German took his criticisms to Cromwell, sending him a raft of ideas for remedial legislation. Only after a full investigation by members of both Houses of Parliament, he said, should the bishops be allowed to conduct any more heresy trials on their own.

St German had no seat in Parliament, and Thomas More may well have believed he could fend off such initiatives. What he couldn't have foreseen was that the knife would be turned from within his own family. For his brother-in-law, John Rastell, slowly gravitating towards Cromwell and a lifelong friend of St German, sat in the Commons and, in a dramatic, heartbreaking split with the Mores, introduced a private member's bill making the law of heresy accountable to the judges of the common law and to Parliament, a revolutionary reform as it would have stripped the bishops of their independent rights to conduct trials. The draft was read once by the Commons, but made no further progress in this session. It would have been impossible to get it through Parliament as long as the Lord Chancellor opposed it, denying it parliamentary time in the House of Lords. So the Commons filed the document away, waiting for another opportunity.

John Rastell's move triggered a permanent family rupture: one his wife Elizabeth would rue until the day she wrote her last will and testament. After introducing his private member's bill, John never spoke to his brother-in-law or Lady Alice again. The shattering of a relationship between in-laws who'd known and trusted each other for over thirty years must have been all the more painful, the more decisive, because for so long both families had shared similar ideals. Both Thomas and John, at heart, were men of action. Ever since they'd lived together at Milk Street and first qualified as lawyers, both had sought to reshape society and their world according to principles of 'justice' and equality. The difference was that whereas Rastell's experience of the severe economic depression in Coventry had led him to take a practical approach, fostering social and economic individualism and emphasizing law and 'due process of law' as the foundation for equality of opportunity, Thomas's more theoretical standpoint in *Utopia*, based on Plato's *Republic*, had given him a vision that depended on the wisdom and discretion of a ruling élite.

No one knows what Margaret thought of the family estrangement, except that it didn't extend to her cousin, William Rastell, who after finishing his education alongside the younger children in her father's school had left home and set up his own printing press. A protégé of her adopted sister, Margaret Giggs, and her husband, John Clement, with whom William was lodging at Bucklersbury, it was to him, and not his father, that Thomas More would turn to print a revised edition of the *Dialogue Concerning Heresies*. So impressive would be the result that Thomas's printer of choice, from then onwards, would be his nephew. Only in one small matter did William Rastell's youth and inexperience let him down. By failing to consult the errata sheet appended to the first edition of the *Dialogue*, he'd allowed a number of his father's misprints to go uncorrected.

On Thursday, 30 March, the day before Henry prorogued Parliament, Thomas More strode into the House of Lords to make a statement. Visibly uncomfortable and acting on royal instructions, he explained that he was there to squash the rumour that Henry wanted a divorce 'out of love for some lady'. 'This is not true,' said Thomas, 'for he is only moved thereto in discharge of his conscience.'

More asked Brian Tuke, the clerk of Parliament, to read out the favourable opinions of Henry's case that Cranmer had solicited from a number of European universities, together with a summary (annexed to these opinions) of his and Foxe's latest research on the divorce. Tuke's speech would have taken him two hours, but afterwards Henry's supporters lost no time, introducing a motion in favour of the divorce. Hearing this, Queen Katherine's allies baulked, intervening on a point of order to say that as the hour was so late, there would be insufficient time for them to reply adequately.

Fearing a clash, the Duke of Norfolk closed the debate, saying that Henry had sent the documents to Parliament for information and not discussion. He turned to leave, but not before a quick-witted speaker managed to ask More for his opinion. He answered evasively: 'I have many times already declared it to the king.'

More then led a deputation of councillors and peers before the waiting Commons. 'You of this worshipful House,' he said when he arrived, 'know well that the king our sovereign lord hath married his brother's wife . . . If this marriage be good or no, many clerks do doubt. Wherefore, the king, like a virtuous prince, willing to be satisfied in his conscience . . . hath sent . . . to the chief universities of all Christendom to know their opinion and judgement in that behalf.'

He asked Tuke to read the opinions again, saying afterwards, 'Now you of this Common House may report . . . what you have seen and heard, and then all men shall openly perceive that the king hath not attempted this matter of will or pleasure, as some strangers report, but only for the discharge of his conscience and surety of the succession of his realm.'

William Roper guessed from his seat in the Commons that his father-in-law had been bludgeoned into this, but was he also right that the duty was compromising enough for him to consider resigning? He was anxious, says Roper, 'lest further attempts after should follow, which, contrary to his conscience, by reason of his office, he was likely to be put unto'. Although Henry had promised not to 'put any man in ruffle or trouble of his conscience', excusing More from involvement in the 'great matter', within eighteen months he'd been forced into a parliamentary charade.

Thomas, behind the scenes, was striving to steer Henry into wiser counsels. As he'd learned the hard way in opposing Henry VII's taxation and said himself in Book I of *Utopia*, speaking the truth was a matter of finding the right time and place.

Eustace Chapuys, Charles V's ambassador to London, commented that More was Henry's one honest councillor and among Queen Katherine's very few genuine friends. He was taking dangerous risks given his promise not to meddle in the divorce and serve the king 'in other things'. So much so that Chapuys asked Charles to write him a letter of thanks. Signed in Brussels on 11 March and addressed in friendship to 'The Chancellor of England, my cousin', the letter had arrived in England by the 22nd. Chapuys waited until Parliament had been prorogued before attempting to deliver it, but More, ever prudent and still determined to keep his family out of politics whenever he could, was sensitive about his oath of loyalty to Henry and refused him permission to visit Chelsea. 'He begged me,' said Chapuys, 'for the honour of God to forbear, for although he had given already sufficient proof of his loyalty that he ought to incur no suspicion, whoever came to visit him, yet, considering the time, he ought to abstain from everything which might provoke suspicion.'

Thomas chose to stay in office to fight for what he believed in. He refused to bow to that dark influence which seemed to be growing more unbearable and unjust with every passing day. Never before had it been clearer to him that, if truth is the one great principle, then what matters in life is an honest councillor's ability to speak the truth to rulers and survive. Like his hero, Cardinal Morton, after the tyrant Richard III had usurped the throne, he has to play his part in the right way, for as he and Erasmus had confessed so often, 'We must obey our fate.' Whatever the outcome, Thomas knew he was playing a real-life game for the highest possible stakes, not joking with Erasmus in the comfort of his study.

Henry's inner circles had no place for any woman except Anne Boleyn, but on Tuesday, 12 September an extraordinary ceremony took place in the choir at Chelsea Parish Church within a few paces of the More family chapel, enabling Margaret to witness at first hand her father's deep discomfiture and Henry's vindictiveness. An academic opinion on the divorce from the Faculty of Law at Paris, one highly favourable to Henry and Anne, had arrived three weeks before, while the royal lovers were hunting in Oxfordshire. Finding the parchment awaiting him on his return, Henry decided that it must be registered, and sealed, in a form suitable for Parliament and the Vatican. He instructed his notaries and scribes to perform this task, and – on a whim – sent everyone down to Chelsea with orders to perform a public registration in the chancel of his recalcitrant Lord Chancellor's own church in full gaze of the parishioners and his own family.

Cromwell was now expediting the divorce, his preparations centring on a menu of alternatives. One, set out in a draft law prepared by Audley, aimed to bypass the uncooperative Warham by authorizing the Archbishop of York to investigate 'finally and summarily' whether Henry was married or not. After reaching a verdict, he would have 'full power and authority' to publish it as binding, leaving Henry free to marry 'at his pleasure'. Another draft, mostly Cromwell's work and a variant of the same idea, envisaged a trial of Henry's case before the whole of Convocation, where the bishops would judge his marriage by the principles of Leviticus, leaving him free to remarry.

Such drafts had seemed feasible when, a month earlier, Edward Lee, one of More's earliest antagonists in the battle over Erasmus's Greek New Testament and Henry's nominee to replace Wolsey as Archbishop of York, had been consecrated in York Minster after, startlingly and on his own initiative, renouncing the pope's supremacy and swearing that he would hold his archbishopric 'immediately and only from the king'. The snag was that, even if Lee would annul Henry's marriage, Katherine could appeal to Rome. As this unpalatable fact slowly sank in, Henry realized that, with Charles V ascendant in Italy, his dilemma lay in the much bigger, intractable conundrum of whether to break once and for all with the pope.

As he wasn't ready for that yet, he went ahead with the third of Cromwell's options, a compromise measure stopping the payment to Rome of annates or 'first fruits' (the taxes exacted by the pope from each new appointee to a Church living amounting to the equivalent of one year's salary). The dynamite lay in a clause that if Pope Clement issued an interdict against England or excommunicated Henry in retaliation for his lost taxes, then he might 'lawfully' be resisted. And to force the measure through Parliament, Henry came three times in person to the House of Lords, cutting short the debate and telling anyone who disagreed with him to stand up and be counted in a vote.

But although the new legislation deprived the pope of income and threatened future reprisals by Henry if progress did not ensue on the divorce, Cromwell and Audley were still hamstrung since the new Act couldn't block Katherine's appeal to Rome. Cromwell's solution was to manoeuvre Henry ever closer towards a definitive break with the past, skilfully resurrecting the Commons' anticlerical petitions of 1529 and merging them with the main thrust of John Rastell and St German's critiques of the heresy law, and then turning them into a grand 'Supplication' to Henry, an omnibus of grievances to be laid before him in Parliament. In this way, Cromwell hoped to make the bishops accountable to Henry, to strip the Church courts of their ancient, independent jurisdiction, thereby giving Henry and his advisers, men like Cromwell and Audley, a final say in all cases including heresy and matrimony alike.

The 'Supplication', for all Cromwell's subtle orchestration, failed to catch Henry's eye at first. Receiving it from the members of a Commons' delegation, he seemed bored by it and them, referring it to Convocation for a reply. No more was heard of it before Henry adjourned Parliament for the Easter recess. What sealed Convocation's fate was its official 'Answer', a document full of high dudgeon and pedantry, delivered on 27 April. The danger for the prelates had always been that Cromwell would tempt them too far. Now they outraged and incensed Henry by informing him that their autonomy was ordained by God alone, a divine prescription that neither he nor Parliament could touch without committing sacrilege. Canon and papal law, they rashly said, might not even be submitted to him for his *opinion*.

Henry flew into a fury, and Cromwell had an unexpected stroke of luck when, in an Easter sermon before the king and Court at Greenwich Palace, Friar William Peyto, a friend of Bishop Fisher and a loyal supporter of Katherine, dared to warn Henry that it was the affliction of princes to be abused by flatterers, and that if his divorce went ahead, the dogs would lick his blood as they had Ahab's.

Henry struck back, sending Foxe to Convocation, demanding that the Church submit to three conditions instantly. No new Church laws were to be enacted or put into effect without royal assent. A standing committee of Parliament was to review the existing canons to see if any conflicted with the royal prerogative or annoyed the people, and if so, to annul them. Lastly, canon law or papal decrees judged to be consistent with the royal prerogative could stand, but only if Henry explicitly assented to them.

The bishops dithered, but Henry kept up the pressure, summoning Audley and twelve of the Commons' leaders, and telling them (quoting from a script written by Cromwell): 'We thought that the clergy of our realm had been our subjects wholly, but now we have well perceived that they be but half our subjects, yea, and scarce our subjects, for all the prelates at their consecration make an oath to the pope.' Handing Audley a copy of the oaths of the prelates, he invited the Commons to 'invent some order that we be not thus deluded of our spiritual subjects'.

Determined, for their part, to focus on repealing the heresy laws once and for all, the Commons eagerly began work. But Henry hadn't reckoned with Thomas More, who in the House of Lords supported the bishops in outright opposition to the king's demands, 'at which,' reported Chapuys, Charles V's ambassador, 'he is exceedingly angry'. Speaking out alongside More was Stephen Gardiner, now Bishop of Winchester, the author of the 'Answer' of the prelates, and the same man who had once spared Margaret the embarrassment of seeing the publisher of her *Devout Treatise upon the Pater Noster* arraigned for heresy.

On 13 May Henry lost control of the House of Lords for the first time in his reign as More and Gardiner defied him. His reaction was to dissolve Parliament, ordering the lay members back to their homes next day, but instructing the prelates to stay on and continue to debate his terms in Convocation. Facing the full force of Henry's wrath alone on the 15th, the bishops and abbots finally capitulated. A vote was taken among the very few left in their seats after a majority staged a walk-out, enabling Henry to dismiss Convocation too.

At three o'clock in the afternoon of Thursday, 16 May, in the garden at Whitehall Palace, Thomas More, watched by the Duke of Norfolk, handed back to Henry the white leather bag containing the great seal and resigned as Lord Chancellor. The ironical inflexion of his voice, his piercing gaze, his dignified composure all gave the lie to his excuse that he was 'not equal to the work'. Resigning just a few hours after an official ceremony marking Convocation's surrender, he knew, said Chapuys, that 'if he retained his office he would be obliged to act against his conscience'. According to William Roper, resignation wasn't a soft option: Norfolk had been obliged to plead with Henry on Thomas's behalf.

Outward appearances were preserved. According to More's own account, he'd made his 'poor humble suit' to Henry, asking 'to bestow the residue of my life in mine age now to come about the provision for my soul in the service of God, and to be your Grace's beadsman* and pray for you'. And Henry had answered, 'that for the service which I before had done you ... that in any suit that I should after have unto your Highness ... I should find your Highness good and gracious lord unto me.'

It was a bitter, poignant moment. Thomas had stayed in office after his humiliations at Henry's hands in the hope that he could steer the king into gentler, wiser counsels. He'd fought for what he believed in, but could do no more without putting his head on the block. Resignation wasn't just his admission of defeat, it was his acknowledgement that the 'indirect approach' he'd advocated in Book I of *Utopia* had failed. 'Practical philosophy' was no use any more. He could no longer

---

* I.e. one who prays for a benefactor.

'strive . . . to handle everything tactfully'. 'Practical philosophy' might have worked while Wolsey had been Chancellor, but the king's 'great matter' had ushered in a cut-throat world where evil counsels were measured only by the standard of success.

And yet, Thomas had kept his head. He could return to his family, whom he'd scarcely seen in the last thirty-one months. It was they, and especially his own 'dearest Meg', whom he loved more than anyone else except God, who could comfort and reassure him.

Four days later, Henry took the great seal out of the same white leather bag and handed it to Audley, appointing him More's successor. Audley used it immediately to seal a valuable grant to Henry's chief gentleman of the privy chamber, who would shortly accompany the king and Anne Boleyn to Calais on a state visit to France. His next highly symbolic act was to release twenty heretics from prison, earning him the resounding accolades of the Protestants.

Cromwell knew better than to gloat, conniving to soften the impact of More's resignation and playing down its significance. On 14 June Thomas was able to explain in a letter to Erasmus (and intended for publication) that he'd left with Henry's warmest approval. Audley, he said, had paid him a most generous tribute in his maiden speech in Parliament. Any hint of disgrace was shrouded. It was a dissimulation, but a necessary one. Failing his political conversion, More's very continued presence in England was a threat to Henry's view of monarchy. By dint of his moral authority as an honest man, Thomas was, in fact, more likely to succeed out of office than in it, freed of his greatest liability, since he could play no further part in censoring books or burning heretics.

'Kings', Hythloday had said in *Utopia*, are no better than 'sleeping tyrants'. Finally it was time to put the matter to the test.

PART V

TWO AGAINST A TYRANT

23

A KNOCK AT THE DOOR

SHORTLY AFTER THOMAS'S RESIGNATION, Margaret and William Roper joined the rest of the family at a conference in the mansion house. No longer, said her father, who'd called everyone together, could he and Lady Alice afford to live in the ways to which they'd become accustomed, nor could they hope to assist the children financially any more. Most of their indoor staff would have to leave, and economies had to be found, especially in the kitchens. Least affected by these changes were the Daunces, Herons and Alingtons, established as they were in their own houses. John Clement and his wife, Margaret Giggs, were still occupying the family's old house at Bucklersbury, but offered to pay their way by taking over the lease. They'd settled in happily, and had two children, Winifred aged five, and Thomas, godson to Thomas More, who was four. Alice Clerk, the widow of Judge John, fast approaching seventy-five, had enough to live on at Gobions, where she alone paid for the upkeep. That left Thomas's son and heir, John, by now twenty-three, who'd taken the plunge and married Anne Cresacre. No longer just 'espoused' but genuinely in love, John and Anne had wished to marry for a year or so, but to satisfy Lady Alice had first been required to overcome the last legal hurdle to recovering Anne's lands in Yorkshire worth £100 a year.

Despite her father's sombre tone, Margaret could see that he was keeping up his spirits. As always when he came under pressure, his defence against inner turmoil was his puckish wit. He began to make jokes about how he and Lady Alice would find savings, suggesting they eat like lawyers, but if that proved too costly dropping down to student menus as eaten at Oxford colleges. At worst 'may we yet,' he said, smiling broadly, 'go a begging together'. He noticed, as he spoke, that Lady Alice, shocked by her unexpected loss of dignity, had a furrowed brow, and as if to warn her of the perils of worldly pride and 'vainglory', the following weekend he played a prank on her. He'd continued even as Lord Chancellor to sing in the church choir, when, after the service had ended and he was ready to depart, his servant had used to come to Lady Alice's pew to say, 'Madam, my lord is gone.' So on the Sunday next after parting with the servants, Thomas came to her pew himself, bowing low and mimicking the servant.

Margaret, who alone continued to wash her father's hair-shirt, is likely to have been the only member of the family to whom he disclosed that he was beginning to suffer the early, painful effects of angina. 'I pray you,' he begged Cromwell when sending him a dictated rather than a handwritten letter, 'pardon me that I write not unto you of mine own hand, for verily I am compelled to forbear writing for a while by reason of this disease of mine, whereof the chief occasion is grown, as it is thought, by the stooping and leaning on my breast that I have used.' Margaret would have worried about the possible repercussions of her father's quarrel with the king on his health, but there was at least some compensation: he could now get to know his grandchildren properly. The elder Roper children, Elizabeth and Mary, were nine and rising six respectively, and the youngest, Margaret, a toddler. They were very much on hand, since Margaret and William hadn't left the mansion house, despite inheriting the manor of Well Hall, as Margaret refused point-blank to abandon her father in his hour of need.

Not all the servants had been discharged. Thomas's secretary, John Harris, stayed, as did his assistant John Wood, and Margaret's maid, Joan Alleyn. John Watson, the family's faithful steward, was retained, as was Lady Alice's chaplain, 'Sir Edmond'. What must have taken a heavier emotional toll than letting the others go was John and Elizabeth Rastell's absence from the discussion. Once Margaret's favourite uncle, John Rastell was no longer speaking to his relatives after trying to reform the law of heresy in Parliament. Worse, he had sensationally converted to Protestantism. The family felt doubly betrayed, because Rastell was also suing them in the Court of Chancery. Seething with resentment, he'd decided that the day of reckoning had come for his ancient feud with Judge John, whom he believed had swindled him, and he wanted his executors and descendants to pay. Rastell brought two lawsuits before Audley, both designed to cause maximum embarrassment. One demanded that Alice Clerk pay £30 in compensation for her late husband's pretence that Rastell had owed him money, the other that she and Stephen Puncheon, the carpenter and Judge John's factor, should return the funds allegedly misappropriated while Rastell was at sea. Since Thomas More was his father's co-executor, the effect was to force him into court too. Rastell, meanwhile, demanded that Puncheon and the Mores submit itemized accounts for the surplus ship's tackle they'd sold on his behalf.

Audley, keen not to fan the flames, dismissed the suits, but not before the irrepressible Lady Alice, observing the proceedings, to her great chagrin, discovered that Puncheon had used the inside information he'd gleaned from the family to marry his own daughter to Thomas Shaa, the nephew and heir of Edmund Shaa, the owner of Lady Alice's ancestral home at Markhall in Essex. So that when Edmund Shaa died, an upstart carpenter's daughter would become lady of the manor, leaving Lady Alice unable ever to realize her life's ambition to return there.

John Rastell, rebuffed at law, turned to Cromwell and proposed another of his entrepreneurial schemes. Building on information he'd acquired about mining for gold and silver ore, Rastell asked Cromwell to license a syndicate to exploit mines in the forest of Dartmoor. A petition was sent to the General Surveyors of the King's Lands with the result that Cromwell and Rastell obtained shares. In return for the favour, Rastell took on a series of printing projects overtly (and also sometimes surreptitiously) at Cromwell's behest to advance Henry's divorce and the break with Rome. Although Rastell still had to earn a living, he was no longer printing for money, as his zeal for Lutheranism spurred him on.

'Sir,' he said to Cromwell in a rare burst of candour, 'I am an old man, I look not to live long, and I regard riches as much as I do chips [i.e. wood-chippings] save only to have a living to live out of debt. I care as much for worldly honour as I care for the flying of a feather in the wind.'

For another year or so the Ropers lived at the mansion house with Thomas and Lady Alice in genteel poverty, since it never seems to have occurred to William to use his own money to help his father-in-law. After settling his debts and selling his silver plate, Thomas found he had been left with around £100 in cash and his gold collar of state, ironically his to keep. His pension of £100 a year from Henry, awarded for life at his first appointment to the King's Council, would continue to be paid, if irregularly, but wasn't enough to maintain such a large house and garden. It seemed for a while as if Henry might leave his ex-Lord Chancellor alone, but this was because his tactics, during these months, switched to European diplomacy. Crossing the Channel to meet Francis I at Calais and Boulogne, Henry and Anne believed that they'd won French support for the divorce, finding the French king in a receptive frame of mind and willing to follow Henry's example in teaching the pope a lesson. Jubilant at the prospects of a French initiative at Rome, and feeling more confident with every passing day, Henry sent Anne's brother, George, as his special envoy to Paris, pledging his troth to Anne the day after the couple returned home. Anne, believing the divorce was all but secured, chose this moment to give way to Henry and sleep with him, with the result that she became pregnant. Henry, utterly confident that God would give him a son, urged Francis to hurry, but all the pope would do was issue the requisite bulls for Cranmer to become Archbishop of Canterbury after the eighty-two-year-old Warham conveniently died.

On 24 or 25 January 1533 Henry and Anne were secretly (and bigamously) married at Greenwich Palace. And after Henry recalled Parliament, Cromwell set about drafting an Act in Restraint of Appeals to Rome, which passed in April. From now on, all appeals on whatever grounds from the Church courts to the pope were prohibited, stopping Katherine in her tracks. Everyone at Chelsea became apprehensive again, since Henry had finally made his break with the past.

While Parliament debated the Act of Appeals, the bishops ruled Katherine's marriage to be unlawful. On 23 May Cranmer annulled it and pronounced Anne's marriage valid. Henry was already planning a glorious coronation for his new queen. The celebrations were to begin on the holy feast of Whitsuntide and last for five days: no expense was to be spared. Anne herself was determined that everyone who mattered should attend. And since she could be as spiteful and vindictive as her husband where anything affecting her reputation or family was concerned, she was particularly looking forward to flaunting herself before all Katherine's allies and supporters.

'God give grace,' Thomas confided to William and Margaret Roper when he heard that Anne was to be crowned queen, 'that these matters within a while be not confirmed with oaths.' With Anne married to Henry and her coronation imminent, people had to choose which side they were on. Whole families found themselves divided, and the Mores were no exception. John Rastell chose to declare, publicly, that he'd entered Cromwell's service, and was joined by Christopher Roper who, after taking possession of the portion of his late father's lands allocated to him once William had secured a private Act of Parliament and buying wood cheaply from Cranmer to renovate his dilapidated manor house, was appointed Cromwell's building-surveyor and paymaster of works. A further crack in family unity occurred when Giles Alington accepted a place of honour at Anne's coronation banquet as her cupbearer.

Thomas More's conscience wouldn't allow him to attend the coronation of a queen he believed to be living in adultery. He didn't recognize the validity of Cranmer's annulment; didn't believe that Parliament had the power to break with Rome. Like his friend Bishop Fisher, he held that the 'common faith of Christendom' transcended the opinions of individuals or national states, that 'conscience' had to fall into line with Catholic tradition. He'd said so in his *Answer to Luther*, writing (then) at Henry's request. And when afterwards he'd refused to support the divorce on similar grounds, the king had answered that he would never 'put any man in ruffle or trouble of his conscience'.

But times were changing. Not for nothing would Margaret's descendants compare Anne to Salome, who'd called for the head of St John the Baptist on a plate. Incensed by More's boycott, Anne thirsted for revenge after discovering that, although some of his friends had urged him to attend her coronation and he'd accepted £20 from them to buy a new gown, he'd stayed at home, jesting with his benefactors; telling them that as he'd granted them the second of their requests by taking their money, he thought he might the more readily deny them the first. He'd even told his friends a fable justifying his refusal. A tyrannical emperor, he said, wishing to put a maiden to death but having himself decreed that no virgin should suffer the death penalty, asked how he should proceed. 'Suddenly arose there up one of his Council,' said Thomas, 'a good plain man . . . [who] said: "Why make you so much ado, my Lords, about so small a matter? Let her first be deflowered, and then after may she be devoured."'

Thomas had revelled in such quips ever since Erasmus had first introduced him to Lucian's dialogues, but this time he'd overstepped the mark. His jokes, admittedly his natural defence mechanism and the only way he knew to protect his self-esteem, could easily be mistaken for insolence. He'd asked Henry when he'd resigned to be allowed 'to bestow the residue of my life in mine age now to come about the provision for my soul in the service of God', but it seemed he could also be determined to score moral points; to have the last word; to set the record straight. By boycotting Anne's day of triumph, he put a sword in his enemies' hands.

John Parnell was first to grasp it, appearing before the King's Council to accuse Thomas of accepting a bribe from the Vaughans and calling for his impeachment. The Earl of Wiltshire, Anne's father and one of Parnell's customers, jubilantly exclaimed, 'Did I not tell you, my Lords, that you should find this matter true?' Summoned to justify himself, Thomas explained that, having received the 'great gilt cup' from Geoffrey Vaughan's wife after his Chancery decree in favour of the Vaughans, he'd filled it with wine, drunk the donor's health, then sent it straight back. 'Thus,' said William Roper, 'was the great mountain turned scant to a little molehill.'

Except that mud sticks, and Thomas was called in again to refute an allegation relating to Richard Gresham's New Year's gift. This time his task was harder, since he'd chosen to exchange that most elegant of standing-cups for an aesthetically inferior, if more valuable substitute, with the result that Wiltshire, a 'good plain man' if ever there was one, was quite unable to grasp that this didn't mean he'd taken a bribe.

The Protestants, too, raised an outcry, alleging that, to extract confessions, Thomas had resorted, illegally, to flogging them in his garden. The worst of these charges were later to be retracted and Thomas in any case denied them, although he did admit to having used violence twice. He'd flogged young Dick Purser, he said, before casting him out to become Cromwell's leopard-keeper. He'd also whipped a mentally deranged man who'd fallen into 'frantic heresies' and lifted up women's skirts in church. Otherwise, he protested, no heretic had received so much 'as a fillip on the forehead'. 'I hate that vice of theirs,' he said in rueful reflection, 'and not their persons, and very fain would I that the one were destroyed, and the other saved.' But by railing on the record against Hitton as 'the devil's stinking martyr', Thomas had made his position all too clear.

On 7 September a daughter, Elizabeth, was born to Henry and Anne, but after setting his heart on a son, and under sentence of excommunication from Pope Clement for breaking with Rome, Henry was looking for scapegoats. Bent on securing obedience to himself and his new queen by fear and threats, he found his first victim in a Canterbury nun, Elizabeth Barton. Famous for her mystical visions, many people had revered her as a 'holy maid'. Eight or so years before, Henry had sent Thomas to interview her, who found her to be 'a right simple woman', honest if naive, although he'd worried a little about her prognostications, warning her how the greatest peer in the realm, the Duke of Buckingham, had been destroyed by the prophecies of a monk.

Barton, regardless, went on to denounce Henry's divorce, predicting his death in a deadly plague, even claiming to have seen the place reserved for him in hell. After Anne's baby was born, Henry, until then pretending to ignore Barton, ordered her and her associates to be rounded up, blaming them for conjuring up all his disappointments. The Attorney-General, Sir Christopher Hales, himself from Canterbury, was sent there to find them. 'As I can catch them, one after another,' he promised Cromwell, 'I will send them to you.'

Henry asked Cromwell to draw indictments for treason, but the judges, not yet completely overawed, took the line that no treason had been committed. Barton could be indicted for inciting sedition, but no more. Only plots involving deeds against the king, not words alone, were specified in the Treason Act of 1352. Henry fumed, but Hales bravely stood his ground. The sole alternative was for Parliament to pass an Act of Attainder, proscribing the nun as a traitor, and over Christmas and New Year Cromwell set his mind to the question of how to draft one.

Shortly after Christmas, he received an anonymous tip-off that Thomas More was preparing a broadside against Henry. Unable to take the risk, Cromwell raided William Rastell's printing-shop, expecting to find a stinging reply to the *Articles Devised by the Whole Consent of the King's Most Honourable Council*, a pithy government tract justifying Henry's divorce, denouncing his excommunication, and accusing the pope of heresy. More told Cromwell in a letter that the scare had been unfounded. His most recent book, he said, had been one defending the theology of the mass, since when he'd given nothing else to his nephew to print.

The trouble was that, a month before Anne's coronation, he'd published what was tantamount to his self-defence against the Protestants: *The Apology of Sir Thomas More*, a defence of the old order in response to a fresh onslaught by John Rastell's mentor Christopher St German. But with Cromwell (and Rastell) behind him, St German, a terrier snapping at More's heels, fought back, laying into the *Apology* in a tirade called *Salem and Bizance*, a punning title deploring the fact that Christendom was rent by futile internal squabbling like that between

More and the Protestants while Jerusalem and Constantinople, the holiest Christian shrines, lay in infidel hands.

In his haste to see off his critics, Thomas let slip remarks in his *Apology* subversive of Henry and his new Church, advising 'every good Christian man and woman' to 'stand by the old, without the contrary change of any point of our old belief for anything brought up for new'. He'd exhorted all Henry's subjects 'to stand to the common well-known belief of the common-known Catholic Church of all Christian people, such faith as by yourself, and your fathers, and your grandfathers, you have known to be believed, and have (over that) heard by them that the contrary was in the times of their fathers and their grandfathers also taken evermore for heresy'.

On 21 February 1534 Cromwell's draft of Barton's attainder was laid before Parliament. Thanks to Anne Boleyn, the names of More and Fisher were added to it for 'aiding and abetting' treason. In the event, More's name (but not Fisher's) was to be removed, but only because he was quick enough to enter a legal challenge. Although denying his request to appear in person before the House of Lords, Henry allowed More to put his defence to a committee, exonerating himself and leaving Henry, as William Roper tells us, 'highly offended'.

Hearing the news in a corridor beside the Commons' chamber, Roper sent his servant, Thomas Arthur, to Chelsea with a message for Margaret, who kissed her father in delight on his return. 'In faith, Meg,' said Thomas, quite unmoved, '*quod differtur non aufertur*' ('what is postponed cannot be laid aside'). Was his irony so deep that it has escaped explanation for 500 years? Nobody save Margaret appears to have noticed that her father's response is a quotation from the *Chronicle* of Salimbene de Adam, a thirteenth-century Franciscan celebrated by the Church for castigating the Emperor Frederick II as the Antichrist in his struggle with Pope Innocent IV.

Now Margaret understood. Her father may have won a battle, but would lose the war. On 26 March Henry got Parliament to approve an Act of Succession, settling the inheritance of the crown on his heirs by Anne with a clause requiring any subject to swear an oath affirming the 'whole effects and contents' of the Act, including a paragraph saying that Anne's marriage was legally valid. Deeds or writings threatening the king or slandering his marriage were to be adjudged high treason, with the same offences by words alone punishable with life imprisonment and loss of property. One day encountering Thomas in London, the Duke of Norfolk said to him, 'By the mass, Master More, it is perilous striving with princes. And therefore I would wish you somewhat to incline to the king's pleasure. For by God's body, Master More, the wrath of the prince is death.'

'Is that all, my Lord?' Thomas replied. 'Then, in good faith, is there no more difference between your grace and me, but that I shall die today, and you tomorrow.'

The day before the Act of Succession came into law, More put all his property into a trust, naming John Clement, William Rastell and John Watson, his steward, among his trustees. Should he die, they were to distribute his assets in accordance with a set of sealed instructions deposited for safekeeping with his secretary, John Harris. What he'd done was technically legal, but might be regarded as the equivalent of a debtor setting up a trust on the eve of an insolvency claim. His chief concern was for Margaret, his favourite child, remembering that he'd never got round to giving her dowry to William Roper. Plainly troubled as to whether his settlement would hold, two days later he signed a second conveyance removing the two and a half acre plot known as Butts Close from the trustees, throwing in a house, barn and garden, and making them over to the Ropers unconditionally. They moved to Butts Close, barely five minutes' walk away from the mansion house, a few days later, enabling Margaret to stay beside her father, but with her future at Chelsea secure.

The rest of the family must have been oblivious to the danger since, according to the eyewitness recollections of Harris and Margaret's new maid, Dorothy Colley, Thomas decided to give them a visceral, macabre warning, inviting them all to dinner, then arranging for one of the king's messengers to call in the middle of the meal. The man knocked at the door, entered the hall, and pretended to summon More to appear before the king's commissioners administering the oath. Pandemonium ensued, before Thomas confessed that this was a dress rehearsal. He'd wanted, he explained, to prepare those dearest to him for what fate was about to bring; it would be the more devastating for them to be taken unawares.

Once everyone was calm again, Thomas spoke of his own fears and doubts, of the joys of heaven and the pains of hell. Only with the blessing of his wife and children, he said, did he think he could find the strength to refuse the oath, for after over twenty years of doing everything he could to keep his public and private business separate, he'd finally been forced to concede that he was too gregarious, too emotionally dependent on his family, to face Henry's terrible wrath alone, and that far from screening them from what was to come, he could only achieve his aims with their constant love and support.

The birth of new grandchildren may have helped him to settle his nerves: a long-awaited son for the Ropers, christened Thomas after him, and two sons for John More and Anne Cresacre – another Thomas, whose godparents were Margaret and her father; and Augustine (nicknamed 'Austen' by his grandfather), whose godparents were Lady Alice and Antonio Bonvisi. Godparents took their duties seriously, and on the Sunday after Easter, 12 April, Thomas went to visit his other godson, Thomas Clement, at Bucklersbury. It was while dining there, after hearing the sermon at St Paul's with William Roper, that the blow fell. A royal pursuivant arrived to order him to appear next day before the commissioners at Lambeth administering the oath of succession.

He returned at once to Chelsea to prepare himself and say goodbye.

24

THE HEART OF THE MATTER

FIVE LONG, ANXIOUS DAYS after her father was called before Henry's commissioners, Margaret received a letter from him, written from the Tower of London. From now onwards, she would be his main channel of communication with the family and outside world as, instinctively, he followed the pattern he'd adopted as one of Henry's busy secretaries, when, finding it impossible to keep up a regular flow of letters to every member of the family, he'd sent his bulletins to his beloved Meg, using her as his intermediary for relaying information back and forth.

He'd risen early, taking a wherry from Chelsea to Lambeth just upstream from Westminster on the opposite bank near a public horse ferry, perhaps touched by nostalgia as, around a corner, through the morning mist, he caught sight in the distance of the magnificent brick gatehouse with its five-storey towers built by his old patron, Cardinal Morton, for this was the spot where he'd lived and worked as a page in his youth. Now the place was bustling, because all the London clergy had been summoned to take the oath that day. It was a scorching spring, and More spotted many of the priests and chaplains he knew so well skylarking about Archbishop Cranmer's lawns, laughing and talking, and ordering drinks at his buttery bar. More was the only layman among them, and was the first person to be interviewed.

Led up a flight of stone stairs beside the north-east corner of the great hall to a large antechamber, fifty-six feet by twenty-seven, that he knew extremely well, since it had been used by Morton's esquires and body servants for dining and conversation while he was a page, Thomas found himself facing Cranmer, Audley and the Dukes of Norfolk and Suffolk. After greeting him and attempting to put him at his ease, they showed him the oath on parchment, sealed with the great seal of England, and the Act of Succession in a printed roll. After reading both through carefully and comparing them word for word, perhaps for as long as an hour, More said he could swear to the dynastic succession of Anne Boleyn's children, but not to the oath as it stood.

'My purpose,' he explained to Margaret, finally abandoning all pretence of not mingling public and private news in his letters and conversations with her, 'was not to put any fault either in the Act or any man that made it, or in the oath of any man that sware it, nor to condemn the conscience of any other man. But as for myself, in good faith, my conscience so moved me in the matter that, though I would not deny to swear to the succession, yet unto the oath that there was offered me, I could not swear without the jeopard[iz]ing of my soul to perpetual damnation.'

His reasons may readily be guessed, even if he dared not give them for fear of the dire penalties of the Act. The order of succession to the crown was a secular matter within Henry's and Parliament's competence, whereas annulling Henry's marriage to Katherine and authorizing his second marriage to Anne were matters solely (in More's opinion) for the Church to decide. To swear an oath against his conscience, he knew, was to commit perjury, for which the penalty was damnation in hell. Reflecting on this many times afterwards in his cell, he jotted down a chilling memo to himself: 'Every act of perjury is, as it seems to me, a mortal sin without any exception whatsoever.'

Faced with his refusal, the commissioners showed him the names of those who had previously taken the oath. The list included every member of Parliament in attendance when Henry had given his royal assent to the Acts passed during the session before adjourning it. Among those swearing were William Roper, William Daunce, Giles Heron and Giles Alington. All wanted to keep their positions and property: none, it seemed, dared to risk Henry's reprisals.

Thomas, unwavering, was asked to wait in the garden, but as it was approaching noon and unseasonably warm, he preferred to stay indoors, tarrying 'in the old burned chamber that looketh into the garden and would not go down because of the heat'. Able from this vantage-point to witness many of the comings and goings, he watched, eagle-eyed, as Dr Nicholas Wilson, once a royal chaplain and Henry's confessor, an intimate of Richard Pace and Bishop Fisher and an ardent supporter of

Katherine, was first led up, and then escorted back down the stairs by two gentlemen, then conveyed directly to the Tower. Later, Fisher was sent for, but did not reappear. As the day wore on, More lost count of the time and, not seeing him again, did not know what had happened to him. When the turn of the London clergy finally arrived, they were sworn and treated with such favour 'that they were not lingered'.

By then it was dusk and More was brought in again, the commissioners delighting in letting him know how so many men had taken the oath that day and with none quibbling over the wording. For then, as he told Margaret, 'was it declared unto me what a number had been sworn . . . without any sticking'. He answered as before, only to be accused of 'stubbornness and obstinacy', a sinister move, since 'obstinacy' implied malice, even seditious intent. He denied the charge, saying that, since he might not safely give his reasons for refusing the oath because of the Act, 'then to leave them undeclared is no obstinacy'.

Cranmer, riled by this, seized on More's professed reluctance to pass judgement on others for taking the oath. Surely that must mean that he considered 'the swearing or not swearing' to be 'a thing uncertain and doubtful'? In which case, continued the primate, 'you know for a certainty and a thing without doubt that you be bounden to obey your sovereign lord your king.' Describing their battle of words to Margaret, her father, with lashings of irony, said that in refuting Cranmer's question – 'so subtle' and replete 'with such authority coming out of so noble a prelate's mouth' – he had brought himself to the edge of an abyss, admitting: 'I might not well do so, because that in my conscience, this was one of the cases in which I was bounden that I should not obey my prince.'

As night fell, Cromwell arrived, accompanied by William Benson, Islip's successor as Abbot of Westminster. Benson, an unashamed careerist earning his promotion by celebrating Anne Boleyn's coronation mass, cautioned More that he was opposing the 'great council of the realm' in Parliament, but Thomas, who had no time for men like that, snubbed him by invoking the higher authority of the General Council of the Church. That cut straight to the heart of the matter, for Thomas More believed that the 'common faith of Christendom' transcended the opinions of individuals or national states, and that 'conscience' had to fall into line with Catholic tradition. His response brought him face to face with Cromwell – 'he that tenderly favoureth me' in More's ironical vignette – since when he said that no one could oblige him to mould his conscience 'to the council of one realm', Cromwell 'sware a great oath that he had liever [i.e. rather] that his own only son . . . had lost his head than that I should thus have refused the oath. For surely the king's highness would now conceive a great suspicion against me.'

Cromwell openly resorted to threats. If More refused to budge, Henry's wrath would be unleashed. Twice More repeated his offer to swear to the succession alone, but to no avail. He was put into the abbot's custody, to be kept for a few days under arrest at Westminster Abbey in the hope that he might reconsider. In the interim, a further consultation took place. Cromwell returned to Henry's Court at Greenwich; Cranmer to his country house at Croydon, from where he wrote sympathetically and moderately, urging Cromwell to allow More and Fisher, as exceptional cases, to swear to the dynastic succession alone provided both swore to uphold it against all foreign powers and potentates, including the pope. Wouldn't that be sufficient for the king?

It was an eminently sane compromise, which Henry angrily rejected. As Cromwell reported back to Cranmer, 'I have received your letters and showed the same to the king's highness, who . . . thinketh that if their oath should be so taken, it were an occasion for all men to refuse the whole.' If that happened, it would be to the 'utter destruction of his whole cause and also to the effect of the law made for the same'. It was to be all or nothing, for Henry was turning into a monster. He was king, he said, his will as expressed in Parliament was law, and More and Fisher must conform to it like everyone else.

After spending four days and nights with the monks at the abbey, More was taken by river to the Tower. Cromwell's nephew, Richard, took charge of him until he was handed over to Sir Edmund Walsingham, the lieutenant, and locked in a cell on the ground floor of the Bell Tower, adjacent to Walsingham's lodging. A day or so later, Fisher was put in a cell on the upper floor. Situated in the south-west corner of the inner ward of the Tower, the Bell Tower, its stone walls between nine and thirteen feet thick, was surmounted by a small wooden turret containing the alarm bell rung at five o'clock as a signal for outsiders to leave the inner ward unless they wanted to have the gates shut on them. More's cell, roughly circular in shape and with deep recesses in the walls, had an unusually high vaulted roof, a small fireplace and a privy in a corner. Straw mats covered the floor. High up in the walls, narrow embrasures, or loop-holes, let in shafts of daylight. By standing on a stool or chair and craning his neck, he was able to look out across the outer ward towards the Byward Tower with its iron portcullis leading to the moat and on towards the drawbridge and the Lion Tower, where the slumbering lions, lionesses and leopards of the king's menagerie were housed.

Before long, the lieutenant came to visit him. Well known to Thomas as a fellow honorary member of the Mercers' Company, Walsingham found an awkward reunion unexpectedly relieved by his prisoner's merry jests. More knew that among his very few remaining weapons was his murderous wit, which he proposed to exercise liberally in order to boost his confidence. Finding Walsingham stumbling his way badly through an apology for his inability to grant favours to old friends, he cut him short, saying, 'Master Lieutenant, I verily believe, as you may, so you are my good friend indeed, and would, as you say, with your best cheer entertain me, for the which I most heartily thank you; and assure yourself, Master Lieutenant, I do not mislike my cheer, but whensoever I so do, then thrust me out of your doors!'

Like all Tudor prisons, the Tower was expected to be self-financing and prisoners themselves had to pay for their board and lodging. More was charged fifteen shillings a month, ten for himself and five for his servant. Allowed a single attendant, he'd sent to Chelsea for John Wood, assistant to his secretary, John Harris. Sworn by Walsingham to inform him of anything that he might hear spoken or written against the king, Wood was a shrewd choice, since (ostensibly) he was illiterate and therefore could not be expected to report on what his master was reading or writing, but was used to handling books, paper, quills and ink for Harris, all items particularly desired by More. Before a fortnight was out, Wood had cleverly managed to obtain a pass to enter and leave the Tower at will on the pretext of fetching money for More's prison fees, enabling him to smuggle out at least two letters to Margaret. The first was the long one describing the proceedings at Lambeth; a second, hastily scribbled on a single sheet, advised her that her father was 'in good health of body and in good quiet of mind', but hinted broadly at his urgent need for paper and ink, for the letter ended: 'Written with a coal [i.e. charcoal stick] by your tender loving father, who in his poor prayers forgetteth none of you all, nor your babes . . . nor our other friends. And thus fare you heartily well for lack of paper.'

Margaret, at twenty-nine, had reached her sovereign maturity. Her more worldly-minded husband, after taking the oath in Parliament, was gradually distancing himself from his father-in-law, actively pursuing his own career for the first time in his life. Keen to freshen up his image, William Roper persuaded Holbein to return to Chelsea, commissioning individual portrait miniatures of himself and his wife in which he poses as a cosmopolitan man of affairs, exuding affluence and success, clutching his luxurious lapels, his dark beard and hair flecked with grey, and yet the wisps creeping out from under his cap across his forehead are thinning suggestively.* He lets no clue slip as to his religious affiliations, unlike Margaret, who sets her own priorities, choosing to wear an exquisitely embroidered pendant collar to draw our eyes down from her contemplative gaze to her medallion where St Michael grapples with Lucifer. When Holbein came to draw her, we can see at a glance that he'd caught her while reading her cherished Book of Hours: her left thumb still marks the place for the liturgy of the day.

Now she took her courage in both hands. Of the two sitters in the diptych by Quentin Massys that her father had treasured all his life, Erasmus had all but abandoned him and Peter Gillis was dead. She knew that to keep up his spirits she had to gain entry to the Tower, to play the part of her patron saint, Margaret of Antioch, who'd routed the devil in the shape of a dragon in her prison cell. It was her most fervent desire, she now told her father in a clandestine message carried by Wood, 'above all worldly things to be in John Wood's stead to do you some service'. Although her father would protest to her that he understood his danger and accepted it, 'counting,' as he said, 'many a restless night . . . what peril was possible for to fall to me . . . but yet for all that, I never thought to change', she understood him well enough to know that he would struggle if left indefinitely on his own. He was simply too gregarious, too

---

* Although the exact date is uncertain, Holbein records Margaret's age as 'anno aetatis 30', i.e. she was 'in her thirtieth year' (and thus still twenty-nine), implying 1534 or 1535.

emotionally dependent on those dearest to him. Who was there to support him now that his friends and even close family members were racing for the exits, because for all his blithe outward assurance, he was prone to deep bouts of worry and uncertainty, racked by his congenital self-doubt?

Partly he agonized over the dangers in trusting too much in himself for fear of acting out of vanity or spiritual pride. He did not willingly court martyrdom. 'I have not,' he later wrote to Margaret, 'been a man of such holy living as I might be bold to offer myself to death, lest God for my presumption might suffer me to fall, and therefore I put not myself forward, but draw back.' He was afraid of being an overly 'eager' martyr, aware that, while the Church expected its martyrs to be confident, it also condemned those who, by prematurely inviting death, lacked humility and in effect committed suicide. Partly, the thought of a traitor's death terrified him. He feared the extreme physical pain it was likely to entail, being dragged alive by horses on a hurdle over the bumpy ground from the Tower to the usual place of execution at Tyburn, a journey of some four miles. He had no way of knowing whether Henry would grant him the 'privilege' of decapitation. He suspected that he'd receive the standard treatment that royal justice afforded: to be hanged from the gallows by the neck, his body brutally mangled, and only then beheaded.

Partly, he worried about the repercussions for his family. But his greatest battle wasn't with the most tangible threats and dangers, but with fear itself. Most of all, he feared the desperation that might come to him, especially at night, from the greatest of all demons, fear of his own fear, which might tempt him to yield to Henry's tyranny.

Margaret knew that her father needed her help. She therefore sent him a letter, folded but unsealed, knowing it would be intercepted by Cromwell. In it she announced her intention of following her husband's example by taking the oath. She then presented herself voluntarily before the commissioners, although when her turn came to say the words of the oath, she slipped in a proviso 'as far as will stand with the law of God'. It was a concession she knew that Cromwell, grudgingly, had already made unofficially, and without telling Henry, to some of the London Carthusians. None of the commissioners thought it important enough to question in her case either. The stereotyped assumption was that a married woman was subject to her husband's authority. If William Roper had sworn the oath unreservedly, and without blinking, as indeed he had, that would be sufficient.

Margaret, in her intercepted letter, pretended not to think the oath a cause worth dying for, urging her father to save his life. Cromwell was hooked, believing that if she could inveigle him into swearing, the propaganda value would be huge and Henry's victory complete. He granted her free access to the Tower: she could come and go as she pleased during the hours of daylight. It was an ingenious coup. Her intervention meant that her father's conditions were at once relaxed: his cell was left unlocked except at night, and he was allowed to walk and talk with her in the gardens of the inner ward and to attend mass in the Chapel of St Peter ad Vincula or the Chapel of St John. He watched the progress of the builders as they worked on repairing the roof of the White Tower. He was even allowed to receive gifts. Antonio Bonvisi sent him brewer's beer, stewed meat and a bottle of white wine every week, and Wood was allowed to carry his books and writing materials in and out of the Tower unchecked.

Discovering what Margaret had let Cromwell believe, More was shaken and appalled. 'If I had not been at a firm and fast point,' he sharply rebuked her, 'your lamentable letter had not a little abashed me.' Nothing, he said, could be 'so grievous' to him, as for her 'in such [a] vehement piteous manner' to labour to persuade him to change his mind about what he had emphatically told her he had to do to save his immortal soul.

But his mood softened when he kissed her and heard her side of the story. Her aim had been to hoodwink the devil just like Cardinal Morton in Richard III's reign, and so was his. Margaret, for her part, would have rejoiced as he explained to her how he and Fisher, whose cell on the upper floor of the Bell Tower could be reached from the ground floor by a narrow spiral staircase, had successfully suborned Walsingham's servant, George Gold, who was no admirer of Cromwell, to carry letters for them, relieving the pressure on Wood. Initially doubtful as to what he should do if he were caught and questioned, Gold was informed by both More and Fisher that he should deny everything as by English law he was not bound to incriminate himself, but 'that if he were sworn upon a book [i.e. on oath], that then . . . he should discharge his conscience and say the truth.' Dissimulation and deceit were morally justifiable in the face of Henry's cruelty, except on oath. The trouble was that Margaret's dissimulation *had* involved an oath, albeit one with a saving clause.

For the rest of that whole summer, Margaret commuted from Butts Close to the Tower as often as she could, staying with Margaret Giggs and John Clement at her old home at Bucklersbury when the evening tides were against her. Clement had lately become one of Henry's own physicians, but his loyalty was to More and Fisher, so that when the sixty-five-year-old bishop fell ill of liver disease, rapidly losing weight and suffering from severe aches and pains, he was called in to treat him, prescribing goat's milk and a course of pills, with Bonvisi defraying the costs.

More, too, was unwell: his angina was getting worse and he began complaining of 'gravel and stone' in his kidneys, and of 'the cramp that grippeth me in the legs', but he rallied whenever Margaret appeared. 'I found him out of pain,' she joyfully informed her stepsister, Alice Alington, after one of her regular visits. They had knelt and said the seven penitential psalms and the litany together as they'd so often done at home during family prayers, before 'sitting and talking, and being merry' together, catching up on all the gossip from Court about how Queen Anne did, and sharing the news of Lady Alice, the family and the neighbours. Margaret also brought her father a clutch of gifts from his friends and admirers: 'a picture in parchment' – most likely a devotional miniature – from Lady Conyers, and 'an algorism stone' for multiplying and dividing arabic numbers from Margaret Giggs.

During August More was hard at work on a new manuscript, *A Dialogue of Comfort against Tribulation*, doing what he loved best, recovering much of the singular imagination that had so inspired him when he'd laughed and joked with Peter Gillis in that other glorious summer when he'd dreamed of *Utopia*. With Margaret around and his cell unlocked during the day, he was barely affected by prison. Part of him even found it liberating, reminiscent of his formative years in the Charterhouse. He was as eager as ever to make a difference: but now for the spirit and not the world, concentrating on how all honest men and women should respond to evil and oppression. No longer was attacking heresy a priority: the intransigence marking (and so often marring) many of his earlier writings had evaporated.

Margaret would become central to the new *Dialogue*. As with *Utopia*, readers find themselves eavesdropping on adaptations of real-life conversations, this time imagined as set in war-ravaged Hungary during the lull between two devastating Turkish invasions. Fear and death encompass everyone. A fictional Vincent ('he who overcomes') has come to visit his aged Uncle Antony on his deathbed. Margaret's contributions are delivered through the mouth of Vincent, while More plays Antony, giving advice to an audience more likely to be the future victims of the 'Great Turk' Henry VIII than of the all-conquering Suleiman the Magnificent. The work, like the earlier *Dialogue Concerning Heresies*, is crammed with 'merry tales' and pithy allusions to More's own household. And yet, the allegory is extremely loose, for Antony means to offer moral support to victims suffering persecution in cases of faith and conscience everywhere.

The 'merry tales' lighten the tone. A few are an acquired taste, the sort of stories Walter Smyth, impresario of the *Widow Edyth*, would have loved, like the ones about a woman so fiendish, the devil tempts her to goad her husband into cutting off her head so that he'll be hanged, or the one about a 'lusty lady' who vomits into her lover's face in the bedroom. Others are animal stories adapted from Aesop's *Fables*. One is a tale of an ass, a wolf and a fox. The ass and the wolf come before Easter to confess their sins to 'Father Reynard' the fox. The ass has a scrupulous conscience. He's done nothing wrong, but feels obliged to own up to the most inconsequential, trivial offences. The fox, on a whim, punishes him for gluttony, ordering him to fast. Then enters the wolf, whose appetite is gargantuan, but the fox excuses him as he is just as greedy himself.

'Eat your fill,' he quietly counsels, but 'secretly in your chamber, out of sight of anyone who might be offended in their conscience'.

'So shall I,' replies the wolf, 'making sure that those with me have weak consciences, but strong stomachs.' Meanwhile, the ass is starving, not daring to eat a single straw for fear of mortal sin.

Until, that is, 'Father Reynard' returns and tells him to behave like everyone else, allowing him to 'cast off that scruple and fall mannerly [i.e. properly] to his meat'. And all live happily ever after.

Margaret herself had inspired this fable after receiving a letter from Alice Alington, reporting a chance conversation with Audley, whose country house on the Essex and Cambridgeshire border lay close to hers. Audley, said Alice, had been hunting a buck in her park. Next day she went to see him, to plead for her stepfather, but Audley peremptorily dismissed her by telling her two fables. One was Wolsey's old tale of the wise men who sought to rule over fools, the other about a lion, an ass and a wolf.

Margaret brought her stepsister's letter to the Tower, provoking riotous mirth and revelry as she and her father paced up and down, competing with each other to tell bigger and better animal stories, adapting them to contemporary events, and lampooning Audley and those of his ilk as third-rate timeservers who rejoiced in their own ignorance, laughed at their own feeble jokes, and callously refused to help anyone unable to help themselves. But neither dared to go so far as Thomas had once done in his unfinished 'History of King Richard III' and include a lion in their stories, for nothing could have been more dangerous than to have been overheard poking fun at the central character in Aesop's gallery, the Lion King, whose word is law, who subverts and alters the law to suit himself and who, when angry, deceives and devours the other beasts.

And then father and daughter had an inspiration. They went one stage further, putting together a long 'letter' of Margaret Roper to Alice Alington, not a genuine answer to her stepsister, but a semi-fictional dramatic realization of what Margaret's exchanges with her father might have sounded like had she really gone ahead and tried to coax him into taking the oath. They had both realized how the classical art of 'letter'-writing as so brilliantly rediscovered by Erasmus could be turned to their advantage. For besides being 'a mutual conversation between absent friends' and a unique and cherished way of reuniting friends and family members whom fate has parted, 'letters' enable their writers to reach out to generations that are yet to be born. Drawing on all their combined experience, they therefore set out to describe, and justify to the world and for posterity, why it was that Thomas More had no choice but to take his stand as a conscientious objector. After trying out their lines like impromptu actors at Christmas or Twelfth Night revels, just as Thomas had so triumphantly done as Morton's page, they put together an inflammatory political testament brilliantly camouflaged as an innocuous family letter.

Margaret (who'd learned her father's part besides her own) wrote out the script. The action is a temptation scene, played out in her father's cell. 'Conscience' is the key word, repeated over forty times, and Margaret's role in the story is that of Eve in the Garden of Eden, invoking every subtle wile, every slippery art, every blandishment she can think of to test and cajole her father to yield to the oath, which in turn allows Thomas More to play himself. From the outset, handwritten copies would be made and circulated like samizdat literature: the 'letter' is the most convincing, most exhilarating, most persuasive defence of her father's cause that could possibly be imagined, and yet, in every possible sense, Margaret is its co-author.

'Have you not always found the King so singularly gracious unto you,' she soothingly and insinuatingly begins, 'that if you should stiffly refuse to do the thing that were his pleasure . . . it would both be a great blot in your worship in every wise man's opinion and, as myself have heard some say . . . a peril unto your soul also?'

'Daughter Margaret,' he replies, 'we two have talked of this thing oftener than twice or thrice, and that same tale in effect that you tell me now therein, and the same fear too, have you twice told me before, and I have twice answered you too, that in this matter, if it were possible for me to do the thing that might content the King's Grace, and God therewith not offended, there hath no man taken this oath already more gladly than I would do.'

'But so many [people] . . . as well spiritual as temporal, [those] that for their learning and virtue you yourself not a little esteem . . . have taken the oath.'

'Verily, Daughter, I never intend (God being my good lord) to pin my soul at another man's back, not even the best man that I know this day living.' One simply doesn't, he explains, using another of his jaunty fables to clinch his point, take anything as momentous as an oath just to keep other people company.

'But Father, they that think you should not refuse to swear . . . mean not that you should swear to bear them fellowship, nor to pass with them for good company, but [for] the credence that you may with reason give to their persons.' Had not so many high in rank and character taken the oath? Why should he disdain to follow their example?

'Marry, Margaret,' he retorts, preparing to deliver his longest, most explicit speech, 'for the part that you play, you play it not amiss.' Some people, he tells us, may imagine that in difficult cases the scriptures or Church doctrine are clear-cut, while other folk venture to differ, just as in one part or region of Christendom a law might be made that some think is lawful while others 'of equal learning and goodness' strongly disagree. In such a doubtful case, no one can be bound 'upon pain of

God's displeasure to change his own conscience' or compelled to swear on oath that the 'local' law of a specific region or nation is legitimate 'standing his own conscience to the contrary'. In doubtful or disputed cases, 'I can see none that lawfully may command and compel any man to change his own opinion, and to translate his own conscience from the one side to the other.'

In other words, More develops forcibly his opinion, already expressed during several of his conversations with Henry about Luther while he was still a royal secretary and councillor, that 'conscience' has to be shaped in line with the decrees of the General Council of the Church and the 'general faith' of Christendom as a whole.

'But Margaret,' he adds, covering his tracks for fear of the Act, 'for what causes I refuse the oath, the thing (as I have often told you) I will never show you, neither you nor nobody else . . . I have refused it, and do [so] for more causes than one.' The drama enters its climax as he avows, 'But as concerning mine own self, for thy comfort shall I say, Daughter, to thee, that mine own conscience in this matter (I damn none other man's) is such, as may well stand with mine own salvation, thereof am I, Meg, so sure, as that is, God is in heaven.'

Margaret sits quietly abashed. Seeing her 'very sad' and 'full heavy for the peril of his person', her father smiles broadly. He gently chides her: 'How now daughter Margaret? What how Mother Eve? Where is your mind now? Sit [you] not musing with some serpent in your breast . . . to offer Father Adam the apple yet once again?'

'In good faith, Father,' she answers, 'I can no further go, but am . . . even at my wits' end.' All that is left to her, she weakly (but tellingly) concedes, is the solution of 'Master Harry' Patenson. 'For he met one day one of our men, and when he asked where you were, and heard that you were in the Tower still, he waxed even angry with you and said, "Why? What aileth him that he will not swear? Wherefore should he stick to swear? I have sworn the oath myself!" And so I can in good faith go now no further neither . . . but if I should say like "Master Harry", "Why should you refuse to swear, Father? For I have sworn myself."'

Poignantly, Margaret in her real-life persona has behaved like Patenson 'the fool'. Like him, she has taken the oath, although with a qualification. Does her father really approve of this? Would that reservation be enough? Would she be damned for ever in hell? Margaret has her private fears too.

But there is nothing else left for 'Mother Eve' (at least) to say or do. All she has left to her, all she can contrive, is to entreat her father one last time to reconsider before it is too late.

'Too late, Daughter Margaret? I beseech our Lord, that if ever I make such a change, it may be too late indeed.' His mind, he insists, will not change. 'I pray God,' he says, 'that in this world I never have good of such change.' And then he prays aloud for strength to bear the suffering he may shortly expect 'patiently, and peradventure somewhat gladly too', asking God that 'we may meet together in heaven, where we shall make merry for ever, and never have trouble after'.

Margaret turns and leaves, and the door of her father's cell slams sepulchrally shut behind her.

25

FIGHTING BACK

THE WEATHER IN THE autumn of 1534 was vile. Winds and driving rain were so strong that ships attempting to cross the Channel were constantly beaten back and some vessels lost. The tempests were as bad at Henry's Court, where opposition was mounting to Cromwell's taxes besides the divorce. Ordinary citizens cried out that the king was 'an extortioner, knave and traitor', and that Queen Anne was 'a goggle-eyed whore'. A group of friars led by William Peyto, who had preached that Henry's blood would be licked by dogs, had gone into exile. Others stayed behind and refused the oath. Their houses were ransacked and two cartloads of friars taken to the Tower. Some were kept in chains, others tortured before they died in prison: all were denied lawyers or a hearing in court.

Cromwell warned Margaret that little time was left if her father was to save himself. 'Parliament,' he said, 'lasteth yet,' meaning it would reconvene on 3 November, when Henry intended to take the definitive step in his break with Rome, laying before it a draft law ratifying his powers as Supreme Head on Earth of the Church in England.

On 17 November the legislation passed. Henry received his title with full authority to redefine the duties of 'his' clergy, summon Church councils, revise canon law, redress and reform heresy, found or dissolve monasteries, and decide the articles of faith. Next came a draft making it high treason to threaten the royal family even by words, or deny their titles (especially Henry's as Supreme Head), or call the king a heretic, schismatic, tyrant, infidel or usurper. The draft, the most draconian of Henry's reign, was resisted: there was 'never', an eyewitness said, 'such a sticking at the passage of any Act'. A Commons committee, including John Rastell, considered it line by line, making sure it only covered words spoken 'maliciously'. Rastell, who had long opposed capital punishment for crimes of the mind, found the measure repugnant, and yet, as Cromwell's servant, was compelled to vote for it.

Rastell salved his conscience with an adverb, after which Parliament approved the new law. Members were too afraid of Henry, who then rounded on More, calling for an Act of Attainder imposing on him the penalties of the Act of Succession. Fast losing the will to think for itself, Parliament complied: More was to stay in prison for the rest of his life and all his property was to be seized.

Shortly before the new Acts were printed and perhaps as the result of a final, desperate attempt by Cromwell to exert pressure on More, Lady Alice came in a wherry from Chelsea to see her husband. It was the one and only time she would make the effort, because she simply couldn't fathom how the man she'd married, and who'd risen to such heights of power and influence as a royal councillor and Lord Chancellor, had ended up a prisoner like this.

'What the good-year, Master More,' she began as she strode into his cell, barely pausing for breath.

> I marvel that you that have been always hitherto taken for so wise a man will now so play the fool to lie here in this close, filthy prison and be content thus to be shut up among mice and rats, when you might be abroad at your liberty and with the favour and good will both of the King and his Council, if you would but do as all the bishops and best learned of this realm have done. And seeing you have at Chelsea a right fair house, your library, your books, your gallery, your garden, your orchard, and all other necessaries so handsome about you, where you might in the company of me your wife, your children and household be merry, I muse what in God's name you mean here thus fondly to tarry.

The feisty granddaughter of the owner of Markhall in Essex and widow of a wealthy mercer who'd taken such elaborate precautions to provide for the material comforts of his unborn child and the rest of his family in his will, Lady Alice was flummoxed, and even bitter, as to why Thomas couldn't just say a few simple words and sign his name on a piece of paper. The most that she was willing to concede was that her husband had 'a long continued and deep-rooted scruple as passeth his power to avoid and put away', but she was unable to grasp what it could be or why it could be so, for their own sons-in-law, and especially William Roper and Giles Alington, had taken the oath the moment it was laid before them.

'Is not this house as nigh heaven as my own?' asked More, unfazed by his wife's rebuke.

'Tilly vally, tilly vally,' retorted Alice, meaning nonsense, fiddlesticks! It isn't moral principles that pay the bills and feed the family.

As Thomas More's heroic struggle against Henry entered the beginning of its next, and still more gruelling, phase, it was increasingly clear that a symmetry existed whereby both he and Margaret were married to spouses who could only dimly glimpse what their own partners felt and truly believed in their hearts, and that father and daughter needed each other more than ever before for mutual support. His lifelong soul-mate Erasmus wasn't even prepared to take the risk of sending a message of comfort to a political prisoner. Juan Luis Vives, the Spanish scholar whom Margaret had once entertained, had written from Bruges to explain More's case to him, but all he got in return was silence. As to Margaret herself, she had to live with a husband who'd taken the easy option as soon as it was offered to him to keep on the right side of Henry, and her brothers-in-law had done the same.

Margaret's visits to the Tower had been stopped shortly after Parliament reopened, when her father had been returned to solitary confinement, his cell door locked day and night. He was allowed to walk for an hour or so a day in the lieutenant's garden and to keep his books and writing materials; otherwise his freedom was drastically curtailed. Cromwell's men then raided the Chelsea estate, arriving, as Lady Alice had feared all along, armed with quills and notebooks to survey the assets and make an inventory of items of value. They made lists of how much rent could be obtained for the mansion house, the outbuildings, the garden, orchards and fields, which lands were freehold and which leased, tabulating the grants and rewards that More had received from Henry over the years so that everything could be legally revoked. All the family owned, apart from Butts Close which had been conveyed to the Ropers, and the lands in Yorkshire belonging to Anne Cresacre, had become Henry's. Or so Cromwell thought: no one as yet dared tell him that a single day before the Act of Succession had become law, More had put all his lands and property into a trust. Even the house and park at Gobions were included in the inventories, although with a scribbled note in the margin saying that Alice, the widow of Judge John, had a life interest. For the moment, no one was evicted, but all the rooms were searched. The men were looking for hidden cash and incriminating letters, especially in the New Building, and took away bundles of documents. Little was found. More had exhausted his savings on building renovations after the fire, and must have weeded his papers before he was summoned to take the oath. All that was left were his estate or business records. Among a pile of documents confiscated in error were Elizabeth Daunce's marriage articles, obliging her father-in-law, Sir John, to petition Henry to give them back.

But if Lady Alice kept her house and furniture for the moment, the loss of her husband's pension left her in vastly reduced circumstances. Apart from £30 a year from her rents in Hitchin and the income she received from letting out two farms, she was forced to rely on Anne Cresacre's charity. Fully convinced and not a little indignant that Thomas More had spent the ready cash she'd inherited from her first husband in renewing and extending the family's lease at Bucklersbury, she decided to petition Henry to pardon and release her husband into her safe-custody to live out his days on an annuity that she was bold enough to claim in lieu of the 'fair substance' she had brought to her second marriage.

Although Lady Alice's petition was to fall on deaf ears, it gave Margaret a second opportunity. She offered to take it to Audley as Lord Chancellor shortly after New Year's Day in 1535, when snow blanketed the ground. In the damp, freezing Tower, her father had sent apples and oranges and a miniature or medallion depicting the Adoration of the Magi as seasonal gifts to Fisher. He'd also sent him the last of his few remaining gold coins, for Fisher's worldly wealth had been stripped out of his house at Rochester, with Henry taking the money and plate, and Cromwell's servants sharing out the books and furniture, leaving the bishop with nothing to pay his servant or buy food. His liver failure meant that he was unable to eat the prisoners' meals and had to have a special diet sent in at inflated prices from a nearby tavern in Thames Street.

When Margaret visited Audley at his London house near Aldgate, he told her, 'Your father is a great deal too obstinate and self-willed. There be no more in the realm that stick in this matter but him and the blind bishop.'

Sly and cunning as a fox, Audley lied that Fisher 'is now content with much ado to take the oath. And so I wish your father to do, for otherwise I can do him no good.' So desperate were Cromwell and Audley to get results, they first tried to dupe Fisher, and then More, by interviewing them separately and pretending that the other had given in. They must also have started false rumours, since by 16 January Oliver Leder, one of the Six Clerks of Chancery, who had assisted the ex-Chancellor with the drafting and enrolling of court documents and was now acting for Lady Alice as an unpaid legal adviser, had written to More expressing great relief that he had taken the oath, and so was safe. Thomas was at pains to refute all these stories. 'The tale that is reported,' he countered, 'albeit I cannot but thank you though you would it were true, yet I thank God it is a very vanity.'

Nicholas Wilson, who had refused the oath at Lambeth and whom More had seen being led to the Tower on that day, did succumb. 'Whereas I perceive by sundry means that you have promised to swear the oath,' More wrote to him in a scribbled note delivered by George Gold, 'I beseech our Lord give you thereof good luck.' He then admitted, 'Whether I shall have finally the grace to do according to mine own conscience or not hangeth in God's goodness and not in mine.' With Margaret's visits forbidden, the pressure had returned and so had his doubts about his ability to conquer his own inner demon, fear.

Over the next four months, father and daughter were unable to meet, but managed to resume their clandestine correspondence. Gold was their postman, for the lieutenant's servant was only occasionally searched and, given his dislike of Cromwell and sympathies for his prisoners, wasn't likely to turn informer. More's first letter from this part of the sequence is lost, but judging from Margaret's reply, he told her that, besides being locked up securely, he was prevented from attending mass. His confidence had been severely dented: conditions during the previous summer when they'd talked and laughed and acted out the lines of Aesop's *Fables* now seemed like a distant dream.

She tried to keep up his spirits. 'Mine own most entirely beloved father,' she began, 'I think myself never able to give you sufficient thanks for the inestimable comfort my poor heart received in the reading of your most loving and godly letter, representing to me the clear shining brightness of your soul . . . Father, if all the world had been given to me . . . it had been a small pleasure in comparison of the pleasure I conceived of the treasure of your letter, which though it were written with a coal is worthy of mine opinion to be written in letters of gold.'

She recalled some of their happier moments together, saying that he'd himself predicted that his persecutors would one day decide that the only way to try to coerce him was by denying him a priest and her visits.

He answered: 'If I would with my writing, mine own good daughter, declare how much pleasure and comfort your daughterly, loving letters were unto me, a peck of coals would not suffice to make me the pens. And other pens have I, good Margaret, none here: and therefore I can write you no long process, nor dare adventure, good daughter, to write often.' He had received news of the Acts of Supremacy and Treason from Robert Fisher, a member of the Commons, who'd crept into the Bell Tower in disguise to tell his brother. The bishop had then sent out for copies of the printed Acts, after which Gold had carried a message to More.

As death seemed to loom ever closer, Thomas More was increasingly afraid. He made almost 150 marginal annotations in his psalter and Book of Hours around this time calling for 'patience in tribulation' and the grace to resist 'tribulation and the fear of death'. Where the psalmist laments that he is forsaken by friends and surrounded by slander and vanity but keeps his silence, Thomas wrote: 'Thus ought a meek man to behave during tribulation: he should neither speak proudly nor retort to wicked words, but instead he should bless the evil-speakers and suffer patiently either for the sake of justice if he has deserved it, or, if he has not deserved it, for the sake of God.'

'Surely Meg,' his letters to his daughter continue, 'a fainter heart than thy frail father hath, can'st you not have . . . My reason showeth me that it were great folly for me to be sorry to come to that death which I would after wish that I had died . . . And yet I know well for all this mine own frailty.'

Margaret wasn't just an outside observer. Her father had always said that he would be able to overcome his tribulations only if he could be sure of his family's blessing. But all except his eldest daughter, and especially Lady Alice and William Roper, thought the way forward was to steer him into taking the oath to save his life. Margaret alone understood what it was that her father had to do, and why. The sad irony is that after all those years as a child and a teenager when she had yearned for her

absent father to return home, she knew now that she must steel herself
to give him over to a higher cause. She was his rock, his anchor, his true
comfort in tribulation, and without her help, he didn't know if he would
manage to hold out. 'I am,' he candidly confessed to her, 'of [a] nature so
shrinking from pain.'

She decided to send him a copy of a special prayer she'd written for
them both to say at the same time each day, one not unlike several of the
collects she had included in her *Devout Treatise upon the Pater Noster* ten
years before:

> O Lord, give us grace of your tender pity so firmly to rest our love in you
> with little regard of this world, and so to flee sin and embrace virtue, that
> we may say with St Paul, 'To me, to live is Christ and to die is wealth', and
> again 'I wish to be discharged and to be with Christ'. Send me, O Lord, the
> grace, wretch that I am far, far, farthest of all other from such point of
> perfection, to amend my life, and continually to have an eye to mine end,
> without grudge of death, which to them that die in God is the gate of a
> wealthy life to which God of his infinite mercy bring us all, Amen.

As she knelt on a cushion in the private chapel in the mansion house
at Chelsea or in her own chamber repeating the words she had so
carefully composed to bring her father comfort, and which she knew he
was also saying at that very moment in his bleak stone cell, Margaret
could never have felt so close to him. She knew that, no matter how
impenetrable they seemed, prison walls were no barrier to the power of
God and the power of love.

'Your daughterly loving letter, my dearly beloved child,' he wrote in
deep appreciation, 'was and is, I faithfully assure you, much more inward
comfort unto me than my pen can well express you . . . especially for that
God of his high goodness giveth you the grace to consider the incompar-
able difference between the wretched estate of this present life and the
wealthy state of the life to come for them that die in God.'

Nothing Meg had ever done in her life had pleased him more. He
could see at once from her prayer that she'd fully grasped the point, that
it wasn't just the oath, or any single idea, principle or doctrine that had
made him defy the tyrannical Henry, but his belief in a redeeming Christ.
More (as he and Margaret saw it) could willingly accept death under an
unjust law because he had his Saviour's example before him.

He sat down to write his own, longer meditation in which the key passage is: 'Good Lord, give me the grace in all my fear and agony to have recourse to that great fear and wonderful agony that thou my sweet Saviour had'st at the Mount of Olives before thy most bitter passion.' He then wrote, and at the greatest speed, his last major work, *De Tristitia Christi* ('On the Sadness of Christ'), a commentary on the Gospel accounts of Christ's agony in the Garden of Gethsemane, sublimating his own fears and feelings, his terror of what lay before him, into a dramatic realization in which the Gospel characters speak to us in the first person, like actors in a play.

'O faint of heart,' he writes in a scene in which he visualizes Christ addressing those who are afraid of torture, 'take courage and do not despair. You are afraid, you are sad, you are stricken with weariness and dread of the torment with which you have been cruelly threatened. Trust me. I conquered the world, and yet I suffered immeasurably more from fear, I was sadder, more afflicted with weariness, more horrified at the prospect of such cruel suffering . . . Follow my leadership; if you do not trust yourself, place your trust in me. See, I am walking ahead of you along this fearful road.'

'And thus,' he said to Margaret to whom the manuscript was smuggled out of the Tower, 'have I mine own good daughter disclosed unto you the very secret bottom of my mind.'

So the spring went by, and then Henry began a savage attack on all those denying his claim to be Supreme Head of the Church. He meant to pick off his opponents one by one, and hang them from the gallows. With the friaries already purged, he turned to the monasteries, starting with the London Charterhouse. Cromwell sealed off the Great Cloister with guards, ordering the monks to stay in their cells, permitting nobody to enter or leave without his say-so. He then sent in his servant John Rastell to convert the monks to the royal supremacy, which was utterly fruitless, for the Carthusians mocked him as the Judas of the More family, laughing him to scorn as the man content to break faith with his brother-in-law in return for Cromwell's wages.

Cromwell struck back. After arresting two Middlesex priests, John Hale and Robert Feron, for calling Henry 'a great tyrant . . . the cruellest, capital heretic puffed with vainglory and pride', he began to uncover a trail of dissidents leading to John Houghton, the prior of the Charterhouse.

He and two more Carthusian priors, along with Dr Richard Reynolds of Syon Abbey, were promptly taken to the Tower in irons.

Devising a new oath, Cromwell put it to the monks. 'Will you,' he asked them in turn, 'swear to obey the king as Supreme Head on Earth under Christ of the Church in England, according to the statute?'

'I cannot,' each replied, 'for there is one Catholic Church of which the pope is head.' They meant no malice, they said, but the pope had been head of Christ's universal Church for centuries, recognized by untold generations, and they could not swear to something they knew to be manifestly false.

Henry put the monks on trial, commissioning a special court to 'hear and determine' their 'damnable treasons' in Westminster Hall, packing the bench by appointing to it Cromwell, the Duke of Norfolk, Anne Boleyn's brother George, and her father, the Earl of Wiltshire, among others, so that the professional judges were outnumbered by courtiers eleven to ten. Beginning on 28 April, the proceedings lasted two days. Houghton, speaking for the Carthusians, confessed that they had denied the king's title, but not 'maliciously'. The meaning of the adverb inserted by Rastell's committee was about to be tested. The jurors retired, but were unable to agree on a verdict, several maintaining that 'in their consciences', they didn't think the prisoners had acted 'maliciously'.

The court ruled that the word 'maliciously' was 'a void limitation'. To all intents and purposes, it was meaningless. When the jurors still refused to convict, Cromwell, in a rage, stormed into the jury room, threatening them, after which they brought in a verdict of guilty out of fear.

Next, Feron and Hale were tried for inciting sedition. After their 'not guilty' pleas, fresh jurors were sworn in, one of them William Roper. As the new owner of Butts Close, he was a freeholder in Middlesex, eligible for jury service, so Cromwell made sure he was chosen for this case.

Roper's humiliation would be another of Cromwell's ways of dividing the family and getting back at Margaret for her inaction after he'd allowed her free access to the Tower the previous summer. As to William, his mind was in turmoil, but he chose to keep on the right side of Henry, turning up as he was asked to do, not feigning illness as others did. On 29 April he entered the jury room, expecting to have to send the priests to a harrowing death. 'Then,' the official trial record tells us, 'after the jurors were sworn in, but before they had reached their verdict, they were called back into court, because the said Robert Feron and John Hale, voluntarily, and of their own mind . . . pleaded guilty.'

Roper had been reprieved, but for ever after shrouded his role in the trial in secrecy. Whenever his property and his principles were in conflict, he always chose to protect his property, lacking the moral fibre of his wife and father-in-law.

On the following day, Cromwell went to see More in the Tower, for Henry was fuming that his ex-Chancellor's 'obstinacy' was 'making other men stiff' in their opposition to his new title. Cromwell brought with him the law officers: the Attorney-General, Christopher Hales, who'd refused to indict the Canterbury nun, Elizabeth Barton, only to be overruled, and Richard Rich, whom Audley had lately helped to vault into the post of Solicitor-General. An ambitious young barrister from the Middle Temple, Rich was a man with a query against his name. Lodging for many years in Bucklersbury and attending St Stephen's Church while the Mores were still parishioners, he'd once run for civic office in London. The contest had been too close to call, until, on the eve of the vote, Henry had unexpectedly intervened to pass Rich over. No one knew why, but Rich believed he could guess the name of his detractor. He suspected Thomas More, then Henry's secretary, for casting doubt on his character.

Two notaries accompanied Cromwell and the law officers. Invited to sit at the table in the lieutenant's dining room, More said he would rather stand. Without further ado, Cromwell broached the topic of the Act of Supremacy, asking More for his opinion, which he flatly declined to give.

'I have,' he answered, 'from the beginning well and truly from time to time declared my mind unto his Highness . . . And now I have in good faith discharged my mind of all such matters, and neither will dispute king's titles nor pope's, but the king's true faithful subject I am and will be, and daily I pray for him and for all his, and for you all that are of his honourable Council, and for all the realm, and otherwise than thus I never intend to meddle.'

Cromwell warned him of Henry's resolve, to which he replied, 'I have fully determined with myself neither to study nor meddle with any matter of this world, but that my whole study should be upon the passion of Christ and mine own passage out of this world.'

After that, Thomas fought back by evading Cromwell's demands. 'I do nobody harm,' he said, 'I say none harm, I think none harm, but wish

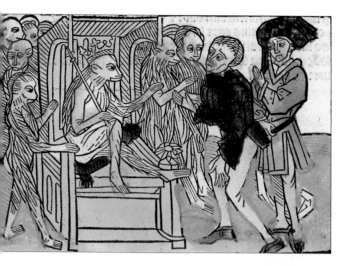

LEFT: 'The King of the Apes' from *Aesop's Fables.*

RIGHT: Map of Utopia, 1516.

BELOW: Panorama of London, 1588.

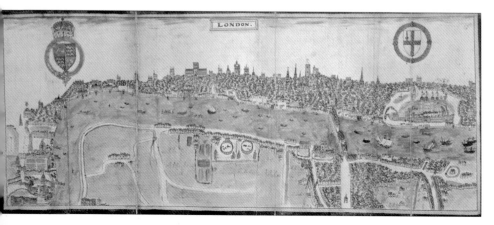

Katherine of Aragon.

Erasmus of Rotterdam.

The death of Richard Hunne.

Hans Holbein (self-portrait).

Title page of Margaret's *Devout Treatise*.

Peter Gillis.

Nicholas Kratzer.

Margaret's holograph letter to Erasmus.

More's letter to Erasmus about Holbein.

William Roper.

Margaret Roper.

Anne Boleyn.

The burning of Thomas Hitton.

THE vvorkes of Sir

Thomas More Knyght, sometyme Lorde Chauncellour of England, wrytten by him in the Engļysh tonge.

Printed at

London at the costes and charges of Iohn Cawod, Iohn VValy, and Richarde Tottell.

Anno. 1557.

Title page from *The Works of Sir Thomas More, Knight.*

Annotated folio of Thomas More's psalter.

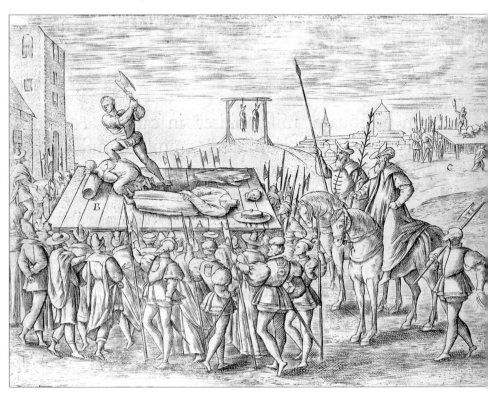

More and Fisher on the scaffold (1592 engraving).

everybody good.' He kept repeating these same words and phrases over and over again like a mantra until ordered to return to his cell. Next day, Cromwell sent a messenger to Chelsea, granting Margaret a visit to her father on Tuesday, 4 May. After being kept apart from him for so many months, she must have been fearful as to why Cromwell had selected this particular date.

It was two days before Ascension Day. Thomas and Margaret, after saying their usual prayers and psalms together, would have been talking animatedly, if apprehensively, when a noise outside the Bell Tower interrupted them. Standing on stools and craning their necks, they watched in awed silence as the Carthusians, with Dr Reynolds and John Hale, were led in chains through the portcullis of the Byward Tower. All except Feron, who'd turned informer and secured a pardon, were about to be dragged on hurdles to Tyburn. Arriving there dirty and exhausted, and before a vast crowd including many of Henry's councillors, they were to be butchered, still clad in their religious dress. Suspended from the gallows by the thickest ropes that could be found so that their agony would last as long as possible, their hearts and bowels were to be cut out and burnt before their eyes. To stifle their last prayers, the hangman would cram their severed genitals into their mouths to choke them. Only then would they be lowered from the gallows and decapitated, their bodies cut into quarters, their heads parboiled and tarred ready for display on poles from the parapet of London Bridge.

Seeing the victims disappear from sight, Thomas said, 'Lo, doest thou not see, Meg, that these blessed fathers be now as cheerfully going to their deaths as bridegrooms to their marriage?' He understood the true horror of what Henry had in store for him, but did not flinch. His bouts of angina were ever more painful, and he'd made up his mind to die. 'I am dying already,' he'd told Cromwell on 30 April, 'and have [been] since I came here . . . Divers times I thought to die within one hour, and I thank our Lord I was never sorry for it.'

Before kissing him goodbye, Margaret told him that she was pregnant again. If the child was a boy, she said, he would be baptized Antony after the hero of the *Dialogue of Comfort*, whose ringing benediction, 'Blessed be they that suffer persecution for justice, for theirs is the kingdom of heaven,' was a perfect epitaph for the Carthusians. Her baby, born later in the year, would indeed be a son. She named him as she'd promised, making sure that it would be he, and not his older siblings, who one day would inherit two silver bowls 'commonly called Sir Thomas More's bowls', a gift he would cherish for the rest of his life and pass on to his own son, another Antony.

Greatly concerned that she might succumb to one of the outbreaks of plague in and around London that year, More urged her to take care of her body as well as her soul. She had growing children, he said, who were depending on her. He sent his love to Lady Alice and the rest of the family, but probably had more than an inkling of his wife's harsh opinion of his New Year's generosity to Fisher. Having given away the last of his money, he'd left his bills for board and lodging at the Tower unpaid, forcing Lady Alice to start selling her clothes to satisfy the debt collectors. She tried to petition Cromwell, complaining 'of my great and extreme necessity', begging him 'for the love of God . . . to show your most favourable help to the comforting of my poor husband and me'.

But Cromwell could do nothing. No one knew better that Henry's mind was a volcano. If it erupted, it could bring down his ministers as surely as his opponents, as had happened spectacularly to Wolsey. Cromwell, largely at Cranmer's behest, had so far treated More with as much compassion as he felt he could justify. But with the Carthusians out of the way, Henry had given him a six-week deadline to 'solve' the problem of More and Fisher, making it likely that he would have to adopt equally brutal tactics in their cases.

26

'MERRILY IN HEAVEN'

ENRY, AFTER SETTING a deadline, was never likely to honour it. On 20 May 1535 Clement's successor as pope, Paul III, created Fisher a cardinal at Rome, the news reaching the French embassy in London on the 28th. Antonio Bonvisi, dining there, sent Margaret a message to pass on through George Gold. 'A cardinal!' cried Fisher in astonishment, but Henry forbade his hat to be delivered and called on Cromwell to force both More and Fisher to give way immediately. On 3 June Cromwell led a delegation including Cranmer, Audley and the Earl of Wiltshire into the Tower, demanding their submission. Henry, he said, had decided that More, in particular, was the 'occasion of much grudge and harm in the realm', showing 'an obstinate mind and an evil will'. He commanded him on his allegiance 'to give a clear opinion on the Act of Supremacy one way or the other'.

More's reply was taken down verbatim. The Act, he said, 'is like unto a sword with two edges, for if I say that the same law is good, then it is dangerous to the soul, and if I say contrary to the said statute then it is death to the body. Wherefore I will make thereto none other answer, because I will not be the cause of the shortening of my life.'

Cromwell, still lacking what he needed, said that Henry might compel him 'by his laws' to make a 'plain answer', to which More answered that, although he didn't dispute that, 'it seemed to me somewhat hard'.

The duelling got personal when Cromwell jibed that More, as Lord Chancellor, hadn't shown such scruples when examining suspected heretics. Hadn't he forced John Purser and Thomas Somer, the distributors of Tyndale's New Testament, both Cromwell's clients in his law practice, to answer questions on oath, and didn't the bishops do the same in the Church courts? Where was the difference? Why couldn't Henry, now that the Act of Supremacy was passed, put questions on oath?

More had his answer ready. The two cases weren't alike. An oath could only be used in cut-and-dried cases. 'I said,' he told Margaret in a letter afterwards, 'there was a difference between those two cases because . . . at that time [i.e. when he'd been Lord Chancellor] as well here as elsewhere through the corps of Christendom, the pope's power was recognized for an undoubted thing.' It was not 'a thing agreed in this realm and the contrary taken for truth in other realms'.

Cromwell's riposte was swift and devastating. 'They were as well burnt for the denying of that as they be beheaded for denying of this, and therefore as good reason to compel them to make precise answer to the one as to the other.'

But More didn't think he was applying double standards. 'The reasonableness or the unreasonableness in binding a man to precise answer,' he countered, 'standeth not in the respect or difference between beheading or burning, but because of the difference in charge of conscience, the difference standeth between beheading and hell.' Ever since he'd first examined the matter at Henry's request in order to refute Luther, he'd realized that 'conscience' had to be shaped in line with the 'consensus' of Christendom as a whole.

Audley cut in, offering More 'an oath by which I should be sworn to make true answer to such things as should be asked me on the king's behalf, concerning the king's own person'. This was slippery, treacherous ground and More declined to cooperate. 'Verily,' he said, 'I never purpose to swear any book oath more while I live.' Audley, undeterred, handed him a paper containing two clear and simple questions, demanding answers one way or the other. Had he read the Act of Supremacy? If so, was it lawful? To the first, he answered yes, to the second he refused to reply.

Thomas wrote to Margaret the same day recounting the scene, but not before dispatching Gold with a hastily scribbled note to Fisher, urging him to be vigilant, and explaining that, to avoid creating an impression that they were colluding, he would no longer keep him abreast of what he was telling Cromwell as he had thus far. Despite such exemplary caution, when Fisher himself was later questioned, he used, inexplicably, the same metaphor of a two-edged sword as his friend, causing Cromwell to suspect a conspiracy. He immediately had the Tower servants rounded up, interrogating Gold, John Wood and Richard Wilson, Fisher's servant, repeatedly and on oath. As soon as they were put on oath, they ceased in their denials, just as More and Fisher had advised them to do if they were caught smuggling letters, confessing the whole truth. By 11 June, Cromwell knew not only that More and Fisher had been conducting a clandestine correspondence, but also of More's letters to Margaret, exactly how many had been sent and when, which were written in ink and which in charcoal, whether they were sealed or open, and who had delivered them. He also knew that More and Fisher had burnt each other's letters.

Next day, Cromwell sent Richard Rich to strip More's cell of all his books and writing materials, a move the eager young Solicitor-General chose to interpret as a job opportunity. He'd done it before, visiting Fisher on his own initiative on the pretext of inviting him to send Henry a confidential message, and then cajoling him into revealing his true opinions. Believing his methods could succeed where Cromwell's had failed, Rich struck up a seemingly innocent conversation with More while his flunkeys trussed up the books. Starting off ingratiatingly by saying that to offer such a distinguished man advice would be like 'taking a bucket of water and casting it into the Thames', he exchanged pleasantries and banter for a while before introducing the subject he really wanted to discuss.

Batting legal conundrums to and fro in the way that professional lawyers always did to show off their learning, and pretending throughout to be speaking off the record, he asked first whether Parliament could pass a law making him, Richard Rich, king of England.

Yes, of course, said More, because Parliament could determine the dynastic succession. Wasn't that too obvious a case, just as clear-cut as asking whether Parliament could declare that God wasn't God? Or did Rich actually think Parliament could unfrock God?

No, replied Rich, because 'that act is not possible'. Seizing his opportunity, Rich asked More about the case that 'is [known] to you and me'. Could Parliament make the king head of the Church in the same way as it could make him king?

'The cases,' parried More, 'are not [a]like, because that a king may be made by Parliament and a king deprived by Parliament, to which act any subject being of the Parliament may give his consent, but to the case [you've just put] a subject cannot be bound because he cannot give his consent [in] the Parliament.' He then added, 'Although the king were accepted in England [as Supreme Head] yet most utter [i.e. foreign] parts do not affirm the same.'

Although still thinly veiled, this was only fractionally more explicit than telling Cromwell that the Act was 'a two-edged sword' that could either kill him or send him to hell. Thomas More hadn't crossed the line yet, as Rich made plain in delivering his parting shot.

'Well Sir,' he sallied, 'God comfort you, for I see your mind will not change, which I fear will be very dangerous to you, for I suppose your concealment to the question that hath been asked of you is as high offence as other that hath denied it.'

Rich saw that More's opinion had not changed, and yet under the Solicitor-General's infinitely flexible reading of the legislation and knowing Henry's mind, it wouldn't make any difference whether Thomas kept silent or denied the title, since silence, in Rich's interpretation, meant 'concealment' that would be adjudged treasonable.

At this presumption, all More's old hackles were raised. Perhaps irresistibly, he mocked Rich for his remark, believing it to be an empty threat that 'it was all one not to answer and to gainsay [i.e. deny] the statute'. Thomas gave no further thought to their exchange, but when Cromwell was sent a handwritten transcript of the conversation by Rich, he decided it might just be enough.

On 14 June Cromwell sent a final delegation to the Tower to question More about his clandestine communications. Asked to explain and disclose their contents, he answered with disarming candour about his letters to Fisher, but kept those he'd written to Margaret under a shroud, deflecting his accusers by saying that, since he believed her to be pregnant, he'd sought to allay her natural fears about his welfare; turning the tables by reminding them that it had been Cromwell, all along, who had granted her permission to visit him at the Tower.

On 17 June Fisher, so weak and lame he was barely able to walk unaided, stood trial in the full public glare, accused by Rich of asserting that 'The king our sovereign lord is not Supreme Head in Earth of the Church of England.' Now emaciated and nearly blind, the bishop was so sick he couldn't even have made his way to court had not Henry laid out £40 in doctors' fees and sent a royal barge to fetch him. Although he pleaded 'not guilty' and tried to explain how Rich had trapped him, his trial was short. The judges instructed the jury to convict him as a matter of law, since he'd admitted speaking the words. 'The most part of the twelve men,' said an eyewitness, 'did this sore against their own conscience.' Five days later, the frail old man was carried on a mule to Tower Hill and beheaded.

Cromwell rode to Windsor to see the king. 'Item,' he put into his notes, 'to know his pleasure touching Master More, and to declare the opinions of the judges therein, and what shall be the king's pleasure.' After brooding for a week and despite the risks since More hadn't spoken out unequivocally, Henry decided he wanted him tried in Westminster Hall too. He authorized the necessary writs on 26 June, but was taking no chances, appointing only eight professional judges, including Audley as Lord Chancellor, to the bench beside eleven courtiers. Cromwell, meanwhile, began vetting the names of those Middlesex freeholders who would be eligible for jury service.

On Thursday, 1 July More entered the packed hall with its magnificent oak hammerbeam roof and carved angels, a place where he and his father had spent many of the best years of their working lives. Looking grey and wan, his eyes darting about to see who was there, he would have visibly stiffened on seeing who was sitting in the jury box: Sir Thomas Palmer, Henry's favourite dicing partner; Sir Thomas Spert, the Clerk Comptroller of the Royal Navy; Gregory Lovell and Geoffrey Chamber, both minor courtiers; and, most disconcertingly, his old enemy John Parnell, the fast-talking Lutheran and vintner to the Boleyns who had tried to have him impeached, clearly enjoying every minute of his day of triumph.

When the court was called to order, Hales as Attorney-General opened the case for the crown. The prisoner was expected to stand while the charges were read out, but in More's case this took so long, at least half an hour, that he was overcome by tiredness part-way through and had to ask for a chair. The indictment charged that he'd compared the Act of Supremacy to a two-edged sword, said he 'would not meddle with that matter', and also engaged in a treasonable confederacy with Fisher, a convicted traitor, by writing him letters, which he and Fisher had burnt to conceal their intentions. Lastly, he was accused of 'maliciously' depriving the king of his new title in a conversation with Rich, denying that it was within Parliament's power to declare Henry to be Supreme Head of the Church.

More was offered a pardon if he would confess and recant, which he refused. Asked to enter his plea, he instead filed a series of demurrers. He argued, first, that none of the charges constituted an offence, since the element of 'malice' specified by Parliament in the Act of Treason hadn't been disclosed. When, predictably, Audley overruled him, he maintained that all but the last of his 'offences' didn't amount to a constructive denial of Henry's title as defined by the Act. As to the alleged confederacy, Fisher was dead and the letters were burnt. Since Fisher couldn't be called as a witness, the crown had no admissible evidence on that score.

This was brilliant extempore advocacy, as if all More's training in law and the liberal arts had been to prepare him for this day. It triggered the first of two electric moments, since the professional judges upheld his plea in law. Now only one charge remained alive, the one relating to his conversation with Rich, to which he pleaded 'not guilty', paving the way for Rich to give his evidence.

The official court records have a gap at this point. Our only source is William Roper, who didn't risk showing his face at the trial but claimed to have eyewitness reports. According to these, Rich testified that, after discussing in the Tower whether Parliament could unfrock God and agreeing that such an act wasn't possible, More had retorted, 'No more could the Parliament make the king Supreme Head of the Church,' which, if the reports are true, means Rich perjured himself, contradicting his own handwritten transcript of the conversation still lying among Cromwell's papers.

Called to the witness stand to corroborate their master's evidence, his flunkeys, embarrassingly, excused themselves by saying they hadn't been listening in. It made not the slightest difference. Sent out to consider their verdict, the jurors took less than a quarter of an hour to convict. Then came the second electric moment. When a 'guilty' verdict was received, it was open to the prisoner to enter an exception to the indictment, arguing that it was invalid on the grounds that it was insufficient in law or because the Act upon which it was based was void. And this More did, speaking now unambiguously.

Audley fumbled with the procedure. He had haltingly begun to pass sentence, but More brusquely interrupted him, saying his indictment was invalid because the Act of Supremacy was repugnant to God's law and the beliefs of the Catholic Church: 'Forasmuch as, my lord, this indictment is grounded upon an act of Parliament directly repugnant to the laws of God and His Holy Church . . . it is therefore in law, amongst Christian men, insufficient to charge any Christian man.'

When Audley protested that the Act of Supremacy had been approved by the bishops, universities and 'best learned of this realm', More answered that Parliament's power was to be judged by God's law and the law of reason as determined by 'a competent majority'. And 'a competent majority' was framed not by reference to the 'well-learned bishops' and 'virtuous men' who happened to be alive at any one time in any one particular state, but by reference to Catholic tradition since the time of the Apostles: both those who were alive and those who were dead, 'of whom many be now holy saints in heaven, who had kept the faith while they lived'.

More then addressed the conflict of laws. He held that 'this realm, being but one member and small part of the Church', could not legislate in a manner 'disagreeable with the general law of Christ's universal Catholic Church'. A local or national law couldn't override the general law of Christendom in a matter of belief. The fact that there happened 'to be made in some place a law local to the contrary' made no difference. 'No more,' said the former undersheriff and Speaker of the House of Commons, 'than the City of London, being but one poor member in respect of the whole realm, might make a law against an act of Parliament to bind the whole realm.'

He did not shirk from attacking Henry directly, citing the king's coronation oath and suggesting that Henry had committed perjury himself by allowing Parliament to attack the very Church that he'd sworn to defend and uphold.

But the crux was 'conscience' as in the long 'letter' of Margaret Roper to Alice Alington. For the very last time and in the most public arena imaginable, perhaps aware that copies of his words would be circulating in Paris, Brussels, Rome and Valladolid within a fortnight, Thomas More reiterated his conviction that neither individuals nor national states were competent to decide what others should believe in 'conscience'. Only Lutherans and other heretics, he said, believed that consciences could lawfully be shaped like that.

Audley seems to have been dumbfounded. No precedent could be found for such a plea. Turning to Chief Justice Fitzjames, a staunch royalist, a known stickler and the judge most deeply affected, and offended, by More's clash with the profession over equitable injunctions, he called for a ruling as to whether the indictment was sufficient in law, only to receive the clumsiest of replies.

'My lords all,' said Fitzjames to an audience hanging on his every syllable, 'I must needs confess that if the act of Parliament be not unlawful, then is not the indictment in my conscience insufficient.'

A deafening silence ensued while Fitzjames and the other judges looked uneasily at one another. Even the most senior of Henry's judges had his own conscience to worry about, and yet which of them, in Henry's court, would dare to say that Parliament had acted illegally? Fitzjames had given a hedging reply, a veiled question to the other judges, but he elicited no response.

Audley's discomfort must have been acute. 'Lo, my lords, lo,' he finally said, 'you hear what my Lord Chief Justice sayeth.' He then proceeded to pass sentence which, in the words of the official court transcript, was that More should be dragged on a hurdle to the gallows at Tyburn to be hanged until almost dead, then taken down and disembowelled, his entrails burnt before his eyes while he was still alive, his head cut off, and his body divided into four quarters, his head to be displayed on a pole wherever Henry should choose.

A phalanx of armed guards stepped forward from the sides of the hall to escort the condemned man back to the Tower. Swiftly placed in a waiting barge, More was rowed downstream to the Old Swan Wharf, half a mile short of his destination, so that he could finish his journey on foot. Now following an executioner, the blade of an axe pointing towards him, he walked along Thames Street until he reached the curtain wall of the Tower, where he turned right onto Tower Wharf, making for a narrow drawbridge used solely by important prisoners and already lowered into position. When almost there, he suddenly caught sight of Margaret, who'd been waiting, patiently, anxiously, for hours, knowing he must pass that way. Seeing him, she rushed forward, forcing her way through the soldiers, oblivious to her own safety. Throwing her arms around her father's neck, she kissed him again and again, so overcome by emotion she could hardly speak.

'Margaret,' he said, 'have patience, do not torment yourself any more. This is God's will. You alone have long known the secrets of my heart.'

Ordered to step aside and let the men pass, she reluctantly withdrew, but scarcely had her father set a foot on the drawbridge than she ran back to kiss him again for the very last time. Holding her tight and fighting back his tears, he begged her to pray to God for the salvation of his soul. Then, his face impassive, he released her and walked into the fortress. He didn't look back.

Henry, still at Windsor when the jury gave its verdict, saw Cromwell later that night. He decided that More, like Fisher, would be beheaded on Tower Hill rather than disembowelled at Tyburn. He chose Tuesday, 6 July as the date, when the Court would uproot itself to spend the summer travelling in the Valley of the River Severn. Henry would sign the execution warrant, addressed to the lieutenant of the Tower, on the 5th, and it would arrive late that same night.

Despite Cromwell's dire warnings about unauthorized letters, Walsingham turned a blind eye so that More, on the 5th, could write a final farewell to Margaret and send her his hair-shirt so that no one, seeing him on the scaffold, would know that he usually wore one. He had guessed when he would die, and on reflection relished the idea, for in the liturgical calendar 6 July was the eve of the anniversary of the day that the bones of St Thomas Becket had been restored to Canterbury Cathedral. For an honorary member of the Mercers' Company, whose patron saint was Becket, it was the most important festival of the year. It had also been Cardinal Morton's favourite day, and as Chancellor of Oxford he'd made it into a public holiday, as More would have discovered as a student.

Writing lovingly but unsentimentally, serene in mind and spirit, he wanted Margaret to reassure his children of his love:

> Our Lord bless you good daughter and your good husband and your little boy and all yours and all my children and all my godchildren and all our friends. Recommend me when you may to my good daughter Cecily, whom I beseech our Lord to comfort, and I send her my blessing and to all her children, and pray her to pray for me. I send her a handkerchief and God comfort my good son[-in-law] her husband. My good daughter [Elizabeth] Daunce hath the picture in parchment that you delivered me from my Lady Conyers; her name is on the back side. Show her that I heartily pray her that you may send it in my name again for a token from me to pray for me . . . I send now unto my good daughter Clement [Margaret Giggs] her algorism stone, and I send her and my godson and all hers God's blessing and mine. I pray you at time convenient

recommend me to my good son, John More. I liked well his natural
fashion. Our Lord bless him and his good wife my loving daughter
[-in-law], to whom I pray him be good . . . And our Lord bless Thomas
and Austen* and all that they shall have.

They all knew, he said, that he had to leave them, and he wanted it to
be soon. 'I cumber [i.e. trouble] you, good Margaret, much, but I would
be sorry if it should be any longer than tomorrow.' He was ready to die.
She had always been his favourite and his rock, dedicating herself to him
and his cause after his arrest. Lady Alice, his wife, isn't even mentioned
in this last letter, and no other letter was smuggled out of the Tower that
day. No one except his beloved 'Meg' had understood him well enough to
know why he had to do what he did, none save her could help him
conquer the worst of his often self-inflicted fears. A daughter's love meant
letting him go, and as the person he loved more than anyone else except
God, he had needed her to tell him in the Tower that she did so willingly.
He'd been spiritually uplifted by her courage on the wharf. 'I never
liked your manner toward me better than when you kissed me last, for
I love when daughterly love and dear charity hath no leisure to look to
worldly courtesy. Farewell, my dear child, and pray for me, and I shall
for you and all your friends that we may merrily meet in heaven. I thank
you for your great cost.'
Was he beginning to glimpse how great that cost was? For next day he
would die, but she would be left behind. She'd been his anchor and
confidante in the Tower. But instead of accompanying him on that same
'safe' journey to share in the joys of paradise, she'd sworn the oath of
succession to help him win his moral victory against a cruel tyrant. True,
she'd slipped in a proviso: 'as far as will stand with the law of God'. Some
of the bravest of the Carthusians had done the same. But would it be
acceptable to God? Would she and her father 'merrily meet in heaven' as
he had said, or would their embrace on the wharf be their last for all
eternity? She could only hope and pray.

* Sons of John More and Anne Cresacre.

27

TELLING THE STORY

S UCH WAS CROMWELL'S VIGILANCE in stage-managing Thomas More's execution that it didn't arouse anything like the popular resentment or disorder that had greeted the Duke of Buckingham's. When the axe fell, no one rushed forward to dip their handkerchiefs into the victim's blood. None of Henry's subjects was allowed to publish anything approaching an eyewitness account during his lifetime. Perhaps no more than a dozen civic dignitaries and twenty or thirty ordinary citizens turned up, but not even Cromwell could stop some representatives from the French embassy, who had also attended More's trial, joining them and taking notes. Here lay the danger for Henry, for within weeks he was being pilloried abroad in print for murdering the author of *Utopia*, being called 'a cruel, vicious tyrant', and compared to the Emperor Nero for his sacrilege and bloodthirstiness. Already a plan was being hatched in the Vatican for a Catholic crusade against England, causing Cromwell to send a prepared speech to the English ambassador in Rome denouncing More as a condign traitor and falsely claiming that, in proof of his malice, Henry had the evidence of his letters 'in charcoal and chalk when ink was not to be found'.

Margaret didn't come to Tower Hill to watch her father die. Maybe she couldn't bear to, maybe he couldn't bear the thought of her being there. Most likely it wasn't feasible. The news that Henry had signed the warrant and that the execution would take place 'before nine of the clock' on 6 July wasn't released until dawn, so that even if John Wood had set out at once for Chelsea to fetch her, the tide would have been against him one way or the other. He went instead to Bucklersbury for Margaret Giggs. So anxious had Cromwell been to avoid last-minute hitches, he'd sent his own messenger to tell More when he would die and to induce him to say as few words as possible on the scaffold. Offered a favour if he would curtail his remarks, More asked that Giggs should be allowed to take his headless corpse to the Chapel of St Peter ad Vincula, ready for Margaret to bury.

In a brief, but nitric speech, Thomas asked the bystanders to pray for him in this world, saying he would pray for them in the next, before exhorting them to pray for Henry that it might please God to send him good advice. Unable to forget who it was that had commanded him to 'first look unto God and after God unto the king', he said that, therefore, in obedience to Henry's own wishes, 'he died the king's good servant, but God's first'. Cromwell chose to overlook this taunt, but when Margaret afterwards retrieved her father's skull from its pole on London Bridge, he took no chances. Examined before the Privy Council, she was able to exonerate herself from the charge of attempting to propagate a cult.

Now Margaret's ingenuity and resilience came to the fore, for she'd inherited her father's steely determination as much as his intellect and charm. Already she'd pushed back the frontiers by publishing her *Devout Treatise upon the Pater Noster*, overcoming all obstacles, not least the threat of a heresy trial. From her father, her uncle Rastell before his betrayal, most recently her cousin William, and most of all from her study of Erasmus over many years, she knew how printing could shape memories and reputations in much the same way as art. With the last of her children, Antony, safely delivered and baptized, she decided to devote all her energy to preparing a collected edition of her father's works, a monument to learning in which each item would be memorialized by a short explanation putting it into context, making his life and example a beacon for others. She also meant to include a carefully chosen selection of her father's letters, knowing from Erasmus that not only are letters a cherished way of reuniting friends and family whom fate has parted, they are in themselves the original, pristine source for biography. No longer did she worry about decorum, since no longer had she any interest in gaining recognition for herself. All that mattered was that her father's name should never perish.

Her first step was to re-employ John Harris, her father's secretary, happily married to her maid, Dorothy Colley. His task would be to make accurate copies of as many of More's manuscripts as could be tracked down. Rummaging through his own old notes and drafts, Harris was even able to reconstruct the contents of two of More's longest and most important letters to Henry and Cromwell, setting out his standpoint on the 'great matter' from its inception under Wolsey, and justifying his conduct after his resignation. Harris added these letters to what was soon to become a bulging file.

Margaret next recruited her foster-sister to help her. This came to light when Cromwell, in the summer of 1537, learned that Giggs, disguised as a milkmaid 'with a great pail upon her head', was keeping alive the last ten survivors of the London Charterhouse in Newgate prison by secretly feeding and washing them through the bars of their cell. Torn between Henry's venom and his own desire to avoid bad publicity, he hushed up her role, but the trail led back to Margaret Roper. Interrogating Sir Geoffrey Pole, brother of the exiled Reginald, and his servants on suspicion of treason, Cromwell demanded: 'How often within this twelve months or two years have you been in company with Mrs Roper or Mrs Clement [i.e. Margaret Giggs], and at what places have you met with them? . . . What communication have you had with either of them touching the death of Sir Thomas More and others, and the causes of the same? Have you heard of any letters, writings or books sent to them or their friends? What have been the contents of such letters?' Pole's admission that besides talking to the women, he had been reading a precious manuscript of the 'History of King Richard III', alerted Cromwell. He summoned 'Mistress Roper' again, perhaps detaining her this time at the house of a privy councillor overnight, discovering that 'she meant to set her father's works in print'. But 'because she was a woman', Cromwell didn't have the stomach to prosecute her, and she 'was not so hardly dealt withal, but only threatened very sore . . . [and] was at last sent home to her husband'.

The stereotype that a woman's learning, to be socially acceptable, had to be appropriately unbelievable worked, for once, in Margaret's favour. If only William her husband could have given her the love and support she needed, she might have recovered a sense of inner peace, but his grasping, restless mind was fixed on worldly advantage. Belatedly uncovering Thomas More's attempt to avoid forfeiting his Chelsea estate, Henry had insisted on a special Act of Parliament annulling the family trust. Except that two small farms had slipped through the net. One lay across the river in Battersea, leased from Westminster Abbey and worth £20 a year. Hearing that it was safe, William falsely claimed that it had all along belonged to Margaret's dowry. He tried to evict Lady Alice and farm the lands himself, until she threatened to sue. He then bided his time until Henry dissolved the abbey and seized all its property, when (as an eyewitness said) 'being moved by a covetous desire to enjoy the said lands', he misled the sequestrators and 'secretly obtained a new lease'.

William's greed led to a family feud, lasting five years and distracting Margaret from her labour of love. Despite not caring a jot for the farm herself, she had no say in the matter, since her dowry belonged legally to her husband. But William hadn't reckoned with the redoubtable Lady Alice, who asked Giles Alington to defend her against Roper. The result was acrimonious litigation in which her two barrister sons-in-law fought each other. Alington won, forcing Roper to pay Alice compensation. A witness in the case, Phyllis Parker, once a servant in the mansion house, testified: 'The same Dame Alice was greatly displeased with the said William Roper for getting the said lease . . . This she knows to be true for that she was at that time continually resorting to the said Dame Alice [at] her house and . . . by that occasion ha[d] heard the said Dame Alice many times talk thereof and was very angry whensoever she chanced to speak of the same.'

Chatting to an old friend and Battersea resident, Margery Hillary, Margaret tried to minimize the quarrel, but her husband was embarrassingly visible, throwing his weight about in the manorial court at Chelsea, telling others how they should manage their affairs. Lady Alice, savouring her victory and, after finally securing a backdated pension from Henry, more solvent than at any time since her husband's troubles began, reasserted her independence by moving to a smaller, more manageable property along the river. Less dependent on her stepchildren than she'd once expected to be, she lived there quietly for the rest of her days.

Margaret got her first inkling that it would be impossible to publish her father's collected works while Henry was alive when her brother-in-law, Giles Heron, heavily in debt and selling land, was denounced for treason by a disgruntled tenant and sent to the Tower. Denied a hearing in court, he was attainted in Parliament and disembowelled at Tyburn. Cecily and her three children were forced to petition Henry, lamenting that 'we now have no friends in the world to help us, but only to depend on the King's Majesty's goodness'. Seizing what remained of Heron's estates, Henry grudgingly paid the salary arrears of the children's tutor and gave them money for food and clothes, but left Cecily to eke out a living or find a new husband.

Henry's malice towards the Mores would be unrelenting, his leniency towards Lady Alice exceptional, moulded by a desire to persuade her to vacate the mansion house voluntarily to make way for a favoured courtier, Sir William Paulet. Margaret knew she must look to her children to complete her task. She'd already founded a 'school' modelled on her father's, its nucleus being her elder daughters. Harris taught them the rudiments, after which she asked Giles Alington to invite Roger Ascham, the most illustrious classicist of his day, to coach them. When he refused to leave Cambridge, she brought in Henry Cole. He was known to be less versatile but, as Ascham was rumoured to have Protestant leanings, safer.

By then, the youngest of the Roper daughters, Margaret, was twelve, and her brothers Thomas and Antony rising eight and seven. Elizabeth, nineteen, had finished her lessons. Mary, sixteen, alone had a talent within striking distance of her mother's. And yet, it seems she disliked Cole, for when, towards the end of her life, she remembered her bene-factors, it was only Harris whom she thought of with affection.

With the quarrel between Roper and Lady Alice over, the family could reunite at William Rastell's wedding to Winifred Clement, held at St Stephen's in Bucklersbury. Despite a twenty-year gap in their ages, they'd fallen in love, and Margaret couldn't have been more delighted, not least since (in effect) her co-editor's daughter had married her designated printer. For despite silencing his presses shortly after Cromwell's raid on his printing-shop and pursuing a less hazardous career as a lawyer, William, too, was awaiting better days, having already proved his ability to turn out large folio editions of the sort Margaret had in mind.

And then disaster struck. Royal pursuivants arrived at Butts Close to arrest William Roper and take him to the Tower for plotting to discredit Cranmer. Detailed charges had been levelled by the plotters, citing names and places, but Henry refused to listen, turning the tables and appointing Cranmer to investigate the accusations himself. He unmasked a network running deep into the More circle: joining Roper in the Tower were William Daunce, Margaret's brother John, and John Elryngton – Alice Alington's son by her first marriage. Others questioned, but freed, included John Clement and Henry Cole.

Roper, in solitary confinement for up to four months, was released with a severe reprimand after paying a fine of £100. Daunce was pardoned, and so was Margaret's brother, but with a proviso. Somehow overlooked when other males in the family had been required to take the oath, he was offered the choice of taking it now or facing a treason trial. He quickly chose to swear.

Margaret, who must have been terrified by the swoop, fell mortally ill before the year was out. Margery Hillary reports what happened. She and Margaret, she said, had been 'very great and familiar together in so much that they called each other sisters'. Her death at the age of thirty-nine, from unknown causes and in the midst of the Christmas celebrations, had been a terrible shock. Carried the short distance to Chelsea Parish Church in a winding sheet through the freezing snow, her body was interred in the family tomb where her father 'did mind to be buried', his skull resting beside her. A candle-lit requiem followed, but must have been the bleakest of occasions.

She bequeathed her father's gold cross set with diamonds and pendant pearls to her daughter Mary, to whom she also left those of her father's autograph manuscripts in her possession, including his Tower letters. The fair copies transcribed by Harris she left to Margaret Giggs with her father's hair-shirt. William Roper received two silver bowls 'commonly called Sir Thomas More's bowls' on Antony's behalf, but got nothing else belonging to his father-in-law. He certainly had no copies of the Tower letters, for when he wanted to consult them later on, he had to go elsewhere.

Widely mourned throughout the world of learning, Margaret was to win a reputation transcending sectarian boundaries, mainly thanks to Erasmus's colloquy about her. Among her greatest admirers would be Protestants seeking to advance the cause of women's education. John Leland, Henry's poet laureate and in his student days a close friend of Richard Hyrde, who'd helped her to find a printer for her *Devout Treatise*, was unstinting in his praise, publishing a Latin epigram comparing her to a second Hortensia. Ascham, expressing regret for declining her invitation to tutor her children, also left a glowing tribute. An enthusiast all his life for *Utopia*, he called her achievements 'truly worthy of her great father'.

Once Margaret would have revelled in such accolades, but since that final, lingering embrace with her father on Tower Wharf, she'd lived only for his memory and her own children. Her love, her fidelity, was such that this pious and high-principled woman had been prepared to risk her immortal soul on his behalf. Her equivocation over the oath, the very thing her father had refused to do – a refusal dependent on her prayers and support – is an extraordinary act. She had loved him so much that she was prepared to make the ultimate sacrifice should God will it. She could only pray that she should be forgiven, and on her deathbed had yearned to be reunited with her father in the paradise that, in her *Devout Treatise*, she tenderly depicts as 'our father's house', where everyone is safe.

She was hardly cold in her grave than Butts Close was deserted. Within six months William Roper had moved to his manor of Well Hall near Eltham. If he needed to visit London afterwards, he lodged at Crosby Place with Antonio Bonvisi.

Now Roper was lord of his own domain, refurbishing his ancestral home and gardens, quarrelling with his neighbours and tenants over who owned a footpath called Cakehill Lane leading to the highway between London and Canterbury that spoilt his view. He married off his two eldest daughters as soon and as cheaply as he could, Elizabeth to John Stevenson, perhaps a local landowner, and Mary to Stephen Clerke, son and heir of Walter Clerke, a clothier living at Hadleigh in Suffolk, whose daughter, Agnes, had married one of Roper's nephews. Obliged to share a house with her domineering father-in-law, Mary spent her time translating Eusebius's *Ecclesiastical History* out of Greek, and her grandfather's *De Tristitia Christi* out of Latin. Calling the latter 'Of the Sorrow, Weariness, Fear, and Prayer of Christ', her translation is as clear as it is eloquent. Like her mother, her chief aim is to capture the flavour of the whole text, rather than the meaning of each individual word.

Henry died in 1547, and was succeeded by his nine-year-old son, Edward, his legitimate male heir by his third wife, Jane Seymour. A dark shadow seemed to have been lifted from the More circle, until Cranmer, after two years of in-fighting, took control of the boy-king's religious policy, introducing full-blooded Protestantism. Fearing for their lives, John Clement and Margaret Giggs, William and Winifred Rastell, and Antonio Bonvisi fled across the Channel, settling at Louvain. There, backed financially by Bonvisi, Margaret Giggs and Rastell strove to bring Margaret Roper's project closer to completion. Manuscripts were carefully deciphered and collated, while partly for commercial reasons, partly to expedite the project, Rastell decided to redefine its scope. Where

Utopia was concerned, the Protestants had scooped him by publishing a mass-market translation to drum up investors for a voyage of exploration to China and the East Indies in which several privy councillors had bought shares. But the slapstick *Merry Jest, Life of Pico*, unfinished treatise on the Four Last Things and 'History of King Richard III', *Dialogue Concerning Heresies, Dialogue of Comfort* and the Tower letters, especially the soul-stirring long 'letter' of Margaret Roper to her stepsister, could all be expected to sell as long as investors could be found to pay the typesetters. With Cranmer's iconoclasts vandalizing the statues and stained-glass windows of the London parish churches and selling their rood-lofts, ornaments and jewelled vestments for scrap, even More's attacks on the heretics acquired a fresh, contemporary relevance.

William Roper took the oath to Edward as Supreme Head of the Church, unwilling to share the fate of the exiles, whose property was confiscated and granted to eager Protestants. If they chose never to surrender, he preferred to live at home and keep his status as a magistrate in Kent and Middlesex. By 1553, however, it seemed that providence had smiled. After a severe attack of measles, Edward fell sick and died. Henry and Katherine's daughter, Mary, took the throne and the exiles prepared to return in triumph. England was to have a devout Catholic queen once more, soon to be married to Philip II of Spain. And since Mary was already planning to appoint Reginald Pole to replace Cranmer and restore the old order, the auspices couldn't have been more favourable.

In a cruel blow a few days after Edward's demise, Winifred Rastell died of a fever, aged only twenty-six. She was buried in the church of St Pierre at Louvain, her husband heartbroken at the loss of his beloved wife. But he returned to London with the others apart from Bonvisi who was too old and sick, more determined than ever to succeed, seeking out all his old friends in the printing trade and arranging with them for the *Dialogue of Comfort* to be published on its own to test the market.

After that, it took many weeks and months of arduous negotiations, and four more long years, to coordinate and adequately finance a syndicate of printers ready to publish the bulky folio needed for the collected works. Margaret's daughter, Mary, eventually stepped in, for she had become a gentlewoman of the privy chamber and a personal friend of the new queen. When her first husband, Stephen Clerke, had died, she'd married James Basset, the queen's private secretary and King Philip's chief gentleman, the royal couple's most trusted confidential agent. And Basset was already known to the More circle, described as the 'right trusty friend' of William Rastell and William Roper, and making a gift of a 'great gilt cup' to John Clement and Margaret Giggs.

When Mary had Cranmer burnt for heresy, the primate's lands were given to Pole along with a regular income. With over £25,000 a year at his disposal, he was soon handing out in excess of £900 a year in 'gifts and rewards privily to divers of his kin and others'. With some gentle nudging from John Clement and the Bassets – for Clement was one of Pole's oldest friends – he gave his blessing to Rastell's syndicate. In grateful acknowledgement of her role as an intermediary, Rastell added Mary Basset's translation of *De Tristitia* to the folio, then wrote a preface in which he humbly dedicated the entire project to Queen Mary. On 30 April 1557 *The Works of Sir Thomas More, Knight, Sometime Lord Chancellor of England, Written by him in the English Tongue,* and running to a total of 1,458 pages, was put on sale, bringing Margaret Roper's project to fruition after twenty years.

In November 1558 Queen Mary died and was succeeded by Anne Boleyn's daughter, Elizabeth I, whom the Protestants hailed as their saviour. William Rastell and his parents-in-law returned to Louvain, where William died of a fever in 1565, and was buried beside his wife. Margaret Giggs died at Mechlin in 1570, and John Clement two years later. The one who lived the longest and enjoyed himself the most was William Roper. He stayed in Kent, still a magistrate and pillar of the establishment, at least until he was suspected of plotting again. He didn't contribute to Rastell's syndicate; in fact just as the last pages of the folio were rolling off the presses, he was clinching the deal of his life, paying £1,500 in cash for the lordship and manor of Farningham, extending his landholding by 1,200 acres of arable land and 160 acres of woodland, with gardens, orchards, barns, stables, dovecotes, and the right to hold markets and fairs. An equivalent sum would have funded the syndicate several times over, but Roper had always known his priorities. If Henry VIII had believed in the divine right of kings, then William Roper believed in the divine right of property-owners.

He did commit his reminiscences to paper, sitting down in the safety of Mary's reign to recount everything he could remember about his father-in-law after an interval of twenty years. History would be kind to Roper, because he meant to dictate it. He exaggerates, egregiously, his own role and importance in the family story, and yet was so ignorant of many of the basic facts he was forced to ask William Rastell to send him copies of the Tower letters. He even tailors his account of his father-in-law's opinions of the papal primacy to suit the times, putting words into his mouth to match what Mary and Pole expected to hear. His memoir was circulated in manuscript and printed in 1626 as *The Life of Sir Thomas More, Knight*, becoming a benchmark for every biographer of Thomas More.

One thing is in William Roper's favour: he kept faith with his wife's memory. He held her in honour for the rest of his days, never remarrying. Making his will in 1578, he asked to lie beside her in the More family tomb, but the descendants of the Paulets, who by then had remodelled the Chelsea estate, refused. He was taken instead to a vault under the Roper Chapel in St Dunstan's Church, Canterbury, to be buried close to his father and grandfather. Then, to satisfy family dignity, his son and heir, Thomas, dug up Margaret, carrying her bones and her father's skull to Canterbury. He put an inscription on their tomb-chest, recording that 'William Roper and Margaret his wife lie here', then had a niche set into the wall of the vault, placing More's skull behind an iron grille as a holy relic.

Although Margaret had never been able to persuade Cromwell to release her father's headless corpse from the Chapel of St Peter ad Vincula, father and daughter are today reunited on Fifth Avenue in New York City. A few blocks apart on opposite sides of the street, but within easy walking distance, Holbein's portrait of Thomas More as 'the king's good servant' and his miniature of Margaret bring their characters hauntingly back to life. As to how they would have wanted to be thought of now, their ideas would have radically diverged. She would have wished to be remembered for telling his story, since in this way he would triumph from the grave. Without her, and certainly without her visits to and correspondence with her father in the Tower, his collected works would be a completely different book and perhaps not exist at all. He, on the other hand, for all his railings against the heretics, would have been more diffident about it, preferring to be known as an honest Londoner, born and bred, with the ability to make people laugh.

REFERENCES AND ABBREVIATIONS

The Harvard system is used in citing references to sources in the following notes. Abbreviated citations of printed primary and secondary materials identify the works listed in the Bibliography, where full references are given. For example, Baker (2000) refers to J. H. Baker, *Readers and Readings in the Inns of Court and Chancery* (Selden Society, Supplementary Series: London, 2000); Derrett (1964a) refers to J. D. M. Derrett, 'The Trial of Sir Thomas More', *English Historical Review*, 79 (1964), pp.449–77. Manuscripts are cited by the call numbers used in the relevant archive, record office or library. In citing manuscripts or printed books, the following abbreviations are used:

ASV	Vatican Secret Archives
BL	British Library, London
BNF	Bibliothèque Nationale de France, Paris
Bodleian	Bodleian Library, Oxford
BUV	Biblioteka Uniwersytecka Wroclawski
CLRO	Corporation of London Record Office
CPR	*Calendar of Patent Rolls*, 69 vols (London, 1891–1973)
CSEL	*Corpus Scriptorum Ecclesiasticorum Latinorum*, 87 vols (Vienna, 1866–1976)
CSPM	*Calendar of State Papers and Manuscripts Existing in the Archives Collection of Milan, 1359–1618*, 1 vol [series not completed] (London, 1912)
CSPSp	*Calendar of Letters, Despatches, and State Papers Relating to the Negotiations between England and Spain, Preserved in the Archives at Vienna, Brussels, Simancas and Elsewhere*, 13 vols in 19 parts (London, 1862–1954)
CSPSp Supp	*Further Supplement to Letters, Despatches and State Papers Relating to the Negotiations between England and Spain*, ed. G. Mattingly (London, 1940)

CSPV	*Calendar of State Papers and Manuscripts relating to English Affairs in the Archives and Collections of Venice and in other Libraries of Northern Italy*, 38 vols (London, 1864–1947)
CUL	Cambridge University Library
CW	*Yale Edition of the Complete Works of St Thomas More*, 15 vols (New Haven, Conn., 1963–97)
CWE	*Collected Works of Erasmus*, 76 vols (Toronto, 1974–)
ERO	Essex County Record Office
EW	*The workes of Sir Thomas More Knyght, sometyme Lorde Chauncellour of England, wrytten by him in the Englysh tonge* (London, 1557), *STC* 18076
FF	Ancien Fonds Français
Folger	Folger Shakespeare Library, Washington DC
Guildhall	Guildhall Library, London
HEH	Henry E. Huntington Library, San Marino, California
HLRO	House of Lords Record Office, Palace of Westminster
KCAR	King's College, Cambridge, Archives Centre
Lambeth	Lambeth Palace Library, London
LP	*Letters and Papers, Foreign and Domestic, of the Reign of Henry VIII*, ed. J. S. Brewer, J. Gairdner and R. H. Brodie, 21 vols in 32 parts, and Addenda (London, 1862–1932)
MMA	Metropolitan Museum of Art, New York
MS	Manuscript
NA	National Archives, Kew
NAF	Nouvelles Acquisitions Français
NPG	National Portrait Gallery, London
ODNB	*The New Oxford Dictionary of National Biography*, ed. Colin Matthew and Brian Harrison, 60 vols (Oxford, 2004)
OE	*Opus Epistolarum Des. Erasmi Roterodami*, ed. P. S. Allen, 12 vols (Oxford, 1906–58)
Rogers, *Corr.*	*The Correspondence of Sir Thomas More*, ed. E. F. Rogers (Princeton, N.J., 1947)
Rogers, *SL*	*St Thomas More: Selected Letters*, ed. E. F. Rogers (New Haven, Conn., 1961)
RSL	Royal Society Library, London
STC	*A Short-Title Catalogue of Books Printed in England, Scotland and Ireland, and of English Books Printed Abroad*, ed. W. A. Jackson, F. S. Ferguson and K. F. Pantzer, 2nd edn, 3 vols (London, 1976–91)
VCH	Victoria County History
WAM	Westminster Abbey Muniments, London

Manuscripts preserved at NA are quoted by the call number there in use. The descriptions of the classes referred to are as follows:

C 1	Chancery, Early Chancery Proceedings
C 3	Court of Chancery, Six Clerks' Office: Pleadings, Series II
C 4	Chancery, Six Clerks' Office, Answers etc.
C 24	Court of Chancery, Examiners' Office: Town Depositions
C 47	Chancery, Files, Miscellanea
C 54	Chancery, Close Rolls
C 65	Chancery, Parliament Rolls
C 66	Chancery, Patent Rolls
C 78	Chancery, Decree Rolls
C 82	Chancery, Warrants for the Great Seal, Series II
C 85	Chancery, Significations
C 142	Chancery, *Inquisitiones Post Mortem*, Series II
C 193	Chancery, Miscellaneous Books
C 244	Chancery, Files, Corpus Cum Causa
C 263	Chancery, Files, Legal Miscellanea (Injunctions)
CP 25	Court of Common Pleas, Feet of Fines
CP 40	Court of Common Pleas, Plea Rolls
DL 5	Duchy of Lancaster, Entry Books of Orders and Decrees
DL 6	Duchy of Lancaster, Draft Decrees
DL 28	Duchy of Lancaster, Various Accounts
E 36	Exchequer, Treasury of the Receipt, Miscellaneous Books
E 39	Exchequer, Treasury of the Receipt, Scottish Documents
E 40	Exchequer, Treasury of the Receipt, Ancient Deeds, Series A
E 41	Exchequer, Treasury of the Receipt, Ancient Deeds, Series AA
E 117	Exchequer, Church Goods Inventories and Miscellanea
E 101	Exchequer, King's Remembrancer, Various Accounts
E 133	Exchequer, King's Remembrancer, Barons' Depositions
E 150	Exchequer, King's Remembrancer: Escheators' Files, *Inquisitiones Post Mortem*, Series II
E 159	Exchequer, King's Remembrancer, Memoranda Rolls
E 163	Exchequer, King's Remembrancer, Miscellanea
E 179	Exchequer, King's Remembrancer, Subsidy Rolls
E 315	Exchequer, Augmentation Office, Miscellaneous Books
E 356	Exchequer, Lord Treasurer's Remembrancer, Customs Accounts
E 404	Exchequer of Receipt, Warrants and Issues
E 405	Exchequer of Receipt, Rolls of Receipts and Issues
E 407	Exchequer of Receipt, Miscellanea
IND 1	Public Record Office, Indexes to Various Series

KB 8	Court of King's Bench, Crown Side, Bag of Secrets
KB 9	Court of King's Bench, Ancient Indictments
KB 27	Court of King's Bench, *Coram Rege* Rolls
KB 29	Court of King's Bench, Controlment Rolls
KB 145	Court of King's Bench, Files, *Recorda*
LC 2	Lord Chamberlain's Department, Special Events
OBS	Obsolete Lists and Indexes
PRO 31/3	Public Record Office, Transcripts from French Archives
PROB 2	Prerogative Court of Canterbury, Inventories
PROB 11	Prerogative Court of Canterbury, Registered Copy Wills
PSO 2	Warrants for the Privy Seal, Series 2
REQ 1	Court of Requests, Miscellaneous Books
REQ 2	Court of Requests, Proceedings
SC 2	Special Collections, Court Rolls
SC 6	Special Collections, Ministers' Accounts
SC 12	Special Collections, Rentals and Surveys
SP 1	State Papers, Henry VIII, General Series
SP 2	State Papers, Henry VIII, Folio Volumes
SP 6	State Papers, Henry VIII, Theological Tracts
SP 9	State Papers, Williamson Collection
SP 46	State Papers, Supplementary
STAC 2	Star Chamber Proceedings, Henry VIII
STAC 10	Star Chamber Proceedings, Miscellaneous
WARD 7	Court of Wards and Liveries, *Inquisitiones Post Mortem*

Writings of Thomas More

For critical editions of Thomas More's writings, scholars are indebted to the *Yale Edition of the Complete Works of St Thomas More* (New Haven, Conn., 1963–97) and related projects. More's writings fall into four groups: (1) humanistic; (2) controversial; (3) devotional; (4) letters. (1) The humanistic writings comprise: *Translations of Lucian* (Yale Edition, Vol. 3, Part 1, ed. C. R. Thompson); *Latin Poems* (Yale Edition, Vol. 3, Part 2, ed. C. H. Miller et al.); *Utopia* (Yale Edition, Vol. 4, 4th edn, ed. E. Surtz and J. H. Hexter); *Historia Richardi Tertii* and *History of King Richard III* (Latin and English versions: Yale Edition, Vol. 2, ed. R. S. Sylvester; Vol. 15, ed. D. Kinney); *Letter to Martin Dorp, Letter to the University of Oxford, Letter to Edward Lee, Letter to a Monk* (Yale Edition, Vol. 15, ed. D. Kinney). (2) The controversial works comprise: *Responsio ad Lutherum* (Yale Edition, Vol. 5, ed. J. M. Headley); *Dialogue Concerning Heresies* (Yale Edition, Vol. 6, ed. T. Lawler et al.); *Confutation of Tyndale's Answer* (Yale Edition, Vol. 8, ed. L. A. Schuster et al.); *Apology* (Yale Edition, Vol. 9, ed. J. B. Trapp); *Debellation of Salem and Bizance* (Yale Edition, Vol. 10, ed. John

Guy et al.); *Answer to a Poisoned Book* (Yale Edition, Vol. 11, ed. S. M. Foley et al.).
(3) The devotional writings comprise: *English Poems, Life of Pico, The Last Things*
(Yale Edition, Vol. 1, ed. C. H. Miller et al.); *Dialogue of Comfort against
Tribulation* (Yale Edition, Vol. 12, ed. L. L. Martz et al.); *Treatise on the Passion,
Treatise on the Blessed Body, Instructions and Prayers* (Yale Edition, Vol. 13, ed.
G. E. Haupt); *De Tristitia Christi* (Yale Edition, Vol. 14, ed. C. H. Miller). (4) More's
letters are published in *The Correspondence of Sir Thomas More*, ed. E. F. Rogers
(Princeton, N.J., 1947); *St Thomas More: Selected Letters*, ed. E. F. Rogers et al.
(New Haven, Conn., 1961); *Sir Thomas More: Neue Briefe*, ed. H. Schulte
Herbrüggen (Münster, 1966); C. H. Miller, ed., 'Thomas More's Letters to Frans
van Cranevelt', *Moreana* 31 (1994), pp.3–66.

Correspondence of Erasmus
Modern critical editions and translations of Erasmus's correspondence are
published in *CWE*, vols 1–12. Vols 1–6 are translated by R. A. B. Mynors and
D. F. S. Thomson. Vols 1–2 are annotated by Wallace K. Ferguson; vols 3–4 by
J. K. McConica; vols 5–7 by Peter G. Bietenholz. Vols 7–8 are translated by
R. A. B. Mynors, and annotated by Peter G. Bietenholz. Vol. 9 is translated
by R. A. B. Mynors, and annotated by James M. Estes. Vol. 10 is translated by
R. A. B. Mynors and Alexander Dalzell, and annotated by James M. Estes. Vol. 12
is translated by Alexander Dalzell, and annotated by Charles G. Nauert, Jr.

Dates
In giving dates, the Old Style has been retained, but the year is assumed to have
begun on 1 January, and not on Lady Day, the feast of the Annunciation (i.e. 25
March), which was by custom the first day of the calendar year in France, Spain
and Italy until 1582, in Scotland until 1600, and in England, Wales and Ireland
until 1752.

Transcription of primary documents
The spelling and orthography of primary sources in quotations are always given
in modernized form. Modern punctuation and capitalization are provided
where there is none in the original manuscript.

Translation from Latin writings
In translations of Latin writings, I have occasionally substituted my own translation where this better matches the sense of the original, avoids an anachronism
or is more colloquial.

NOTES

Prologue

The wharf at Butts Close is from NA, C 1/540/78. Wherry fares and comparative values are worked out from costs itemized in WAM, MSS 33324–30, 63509. For the weather and the plague in August and September in London, *LP* IX, nos.41, 47, 74, 85, 99, 106, 116, 119, 132, 137, 152, 172, 178, 259, 341, 358, 370, 383–4, 413, 484. Henry's and Cromwell's itineraries are NA, OBS 1419; Merriman (1902), II, pp.279–82. London Bridge and its environs are fully described by the Elizabethan antiquary, John Stow, in *STC* 23341; modernized edition is Stow (1956); Barron (2004). Margaret Roper's description is from the Holbein miniature *c.*1534–5: MMA, Rogers Fund, 1950 (50.69.2); I gratefully acknowledge the kindness of the Department of European Paintings for allowing me to examine it in New York with a strong magnifying glass. Dr Susan Foister, the leading Holbein expert, who used a microscope, suggests St Michael or St George: Foister (2006), p.46. I believe St Michael to be likelier: the saint appears to have wings closely matching his description and woodcut illustration in *STC* 17973.5, sigs.BBiii–CCi. Henry VIII's black humour, which varies slightly according to the source, is taken from Van Ortroy (1893), p.164. See also the Rastell fragments in Harpsfield (1932), p.235. Another variant is from Hall's Chronicle, in Whibley (1904), II, pp. 264–5. Stapleton (1928), p.213 is the best source for Margaret's surreptitious recovery of More's head. The quotation illustrating More's objection to taking Henry VIII's oath of succession is from Rogers, *Corr.*, p.505; quotations from Whittinton's exercises are from *STC* 25569.7 and 25576 (where the misprint is corrected), fos. 15ᵛ, 17ᵛ. The Privy Council proceedings and Margaret's defence are from Stapleton (1928), p.215. William Roper's appeals are described in NA, SP 1/95, fo. 134 (*LP* IX, no.133); that they concerned the forfeiture of the More estates, and that Roper was finally sent for, is clear from Cromwell's note in BL, MS Titus B.1, fo.431 (old fo.423). The jury list for the trials of the Middlesex priests, John Hale and Robert Feron, is from NA, KB 8/7, Pt1, fo.6 (see chapter 25). Roper's taking the oath of supremacy is from Roper (1935), p.xxxvii. The Roper feud is discussed in chapters 14, 17. Christopher Roper's position in Cromwell's household is from *LP* VIII, no.415; *LP* IX, no.66; *LP* XI, no.1015; *LP* XIII.i, no.585; *LP* XIII.ii, no.857; discussed by Robertson (1975), p.552. The quotation from Erasmus is from *CWE* 8, no.1218. Her father's words to Margaret at their last embrace on Tower wharf are from the 'Paris Newsletter', in Harpsfield (1932), appendix 2, p.265. The first 'official' Catholic biography of More by Nicholas Harpsfield had been completed by 1557 or 1558: Harpsfield (1932), pp.9–218.

Chapter 1

The birth dates of the Mores, some less problematic than others, are discussed in the historical notes to Harpsfield (1932) and Roper (1935); by Hastings in Sylvester and Marc'hadour (1977), pp.92–103; and by Chambers (1935); Marius (1984); Ackroyd (1998). The likelihood is that Thomas More was born in Feb. 1478, given the fact that in the Holbein family-group drawing at Basel, his age is '*anno aetatis* 50', meaning he was in his fiftieth year and thus still forty-nine when the drawing was made. The drawing's date is discussed in chapter 18. The districts around Cheapside, Bucklersbury, Walbrook and the Barge are described by Barron (2004), pp.52, 57, 254, 260, 287; Stow in *STC* 23341 and Stow (1956). Thomas More's description is from Rogers, *SL*, no.2. Information on the Hospital of St Thomas of Acre is from Watney (1906). All details of the layout of the rooms and contents of the Barge are from the handwritten witness statements in the Chancery case of *Clement v. Hill* (1555): NA, C 1/1337/18–19; C 24/42 (unsorted bundle). Notes on selected documents were printed by Reed (1926b), but are incomplete and often inaccurate. In particular, Reed's valuations are often not (as is claimed) taken from the witnesses' depositions, but from the plaintiff's bill and *ex parte* interrogatories which are less reliable, if easier to read. The terms of More's lease are recited in NA, SC 6/Hen VIII/2396; the tax assessments listing the neighbours are from NA, E 179/251/15B. His enjoyment of the garden in summer is from Roper (1935), pp.48–9; Harpsfield (1932), pp.65–6. The view of the house and garden as recorded by a later street map is from Prockter and Taylor (1979), map 23, p.24. Thomas More's verses for family revels and *Merry Jest* are taken from *CW* 1, pp.3–7, 15–29; discussed by Reed (1926a) and Fox (1982). His letter mentioning the 'additions' to the comedy of Solomon is Rogers, *SL*, no.1. His later comments about comedy are from *CW* 13, p.227; *CW* 12, p.83. His own description of his attitude to writing is from Rogers, *SL*, no.4 (p.60). Hall's remarks on More's mocking humour are from Whibley (1904), II, pp.158, 265. Information on Thomas Giggs is taken from C 24/42 (deposition of Ottwell Wyld); C 1/655/25; E 179/144/120, m.8; Roper (1935), p.128. An identification of Thomas Giggs with a Lincoln's Inn lawyer of the same name by Schoeck (1949) is mistaken. Margaret's date of birth is from the age nineteen given on the title page of her treatise on the Pater Noster (*STC* 10477) first published in 1524, supported by '*anno aetatis* 22' (meaning she was in her twenty-second year and therefore still twenty-one) on the Holbein family-group drawing at Basel (see chapter 18). Joanna More's age is settled by the evidence of Simon Elryngton, her maternal uncle, in a Chancery lawsuit: NA, C 1/125/58–62, C 1/126/57–8. Simon testified that, at the time of this case in 1488, Joanna's mother was twenty-three and had lived with John Colt for two years. Married at sixteen, her father considered her too young to leave home at first. Joanna was the eldest of twelve children, born in 1487. Joanna's donation to St Stephen's is from the churchwardens' accounts: Milbourn (1881), pp.352–4. The description of Margaret's baptism follows the rubrics of the Sarum Missal in use at St Stephen's, and clerical handbooks: *Manuale* (1975), appendix 1; *STC* 791, 4115, 12472, 16208. Further information on baptisms is from Cressy (1997), pp.149–66. St Margaret's legend is from *STC* 24873, fo.214ᵛ–15ᵛ. Information on St Stephen's is from Stow (1956), pp.203–4; Milbourn (1881), pp.352, 357–9, 388–90. Thomas More's recollection of 'Mother Maud' and the quotation are from *CW* 12, pp.114–19. His favourite Aesop's *Fables* are from *CW* 1, pp.33, 159–60; *CW* 2, p.93; *CW* 3, Pt2, nos.42, 71, 134–5, 180, 198, 222; *CW* 6, pp.296, 313, 369; *CW* 9, pp.3, 83; *CW* 12, pp.110–11, 180–1, 189, 285–6, 338. Margaret's recollection of the fables in the Tower is from Rogers, *Corr.*, nos.205, 206. Caxton's popular edition and translation of the fables is *STC* 175. The story of the monkey and the rabbits is from Thompson (1965), p.524.

Chapter 2

Milk Street is described by Stow in *STC* 23341 and Stow (1956). Situated in the administrative district known as Cripplegate Ward, the street straddled parish boundaries. Houses furthest from the river were in St Lawrence Jewry's parish; those nearest to it belonged to St Mary Magdalen's. According to tax records, John More's mansion, purchased shortly after his first marriage to Agnes Graunger, stood at the far end, close to Aldermanbury Well at the intersection of Milk Street and Catte or Catton Street (now Gresham Street). St Lawrence's Church abutted the gateway to Guildhall in Catte Street. New information on John More, Joan Marshall and John Rastell, enabling dates and family relationships to be established, is from NA, C 1/35/9, C 1/337/27, C 4/20/81, C 4/46/11, C 1/537/42, STAC 2/35/17, C 1/902/35–7. The wills, and wealth, of John Marshall and John More are from NA, PROB 11/11; PROB 11/23. A tax assessment pinpointing John More's house to St Lawrence's parish and therefore the upper end of Milk Street is from NA, E 179/251/15B. The Mercers' Company connection is from Lyell and Watney (1936); Watney (1906). John Rastell's clash with

Joan Marshall, which also clarifies the conditions of Elizabeth Rastell's marriage settlement and the year of the wedding, is described in NA, C 4/20/81, C 4/46/11, adding greatly to information from Reed (1926a). Thomas More's comments on his ancestry and the quotations about and from his father are from *EW*, pp.165, 233, 1421; *CW* 6, Pt1, pp.158, 313; *CW* 12, p.211. For John More's ancestry, see Hastings in Sylvester and Marc'hadour (1977), pp.92–5. Agnes Graunger's ancestry was identified correctly by Ramsay (1982); see also lawsuits in NA, C 1/11/390, C 1/44/169, C 1/46/272, C 1/48/2, C 1/67/37, and related wills in NA, PROB 11/8, PROB 11/16, PROB 11/20. Documents about John More's acquisitions at Gobions are NA, C 1/149/9, STAC 2/28/68 (a later suit, but which confirms the creation of a deer park). The journey from Milk Street to Gobions was seventeen miles and, if the women rode in a cart, took a day and a half. The family followed the road to Islington, Highgate and Whetstone, lodged overnight at the Lion Inn in Barnet, then took a right fork in the road beside a windmill, half a mile or so north of Barnet Church, heading for Potters Bar and Bell Bar, making the left turn to Gobions as they approached Bell Bar. After heavy rain, when the track was a sea of mud, they were forced to follow a roundabout route via St Albans, adding seven miles to the journey. John More grumbled about this diversion, and bequeathed a substantial sum for 'making and amending of the highway leading from Barnet to Hatfield between Potters Bar and the Bell Bar'. The route is from Walter Smyth's account in *STC* 22869.7 and *STC* 22870. John More's bequest to mend the highway is from his will: NA, PROB 11/23. One of John More's suits for debts owed to Joan Marshall is from C 1/337/27–8. A suit in which he and his friend and fellow lawyer, Thomas Frowicke, were sued as co-trustees is C 1/35/9. His role as the Duke of Buckingham's lawyer is from NA, SP 1/22, fo.79, where he was handsomely retained in the dispute arising from Anne Stafford's marriage settlement. Information on Thomas Bowes's will, Joan Bowes, Joan Marshall's tomb, and John More's lawsuits after his marriage to Joan Bowes is from NA, PROB 11/11, fos.224–5; PROB 11/14, fo.338; C 1/140/19; C1/429/34. Geoffrey Boleyn's benefaction is from his will in NA, PROB 11/5. More's visit to Coventry is from *CW* 15, pp.284–9. His love of music and the family instruments are from *CWE* 7, no.999; *STC* 18066. His description of his visit to Paris and Louvain is from *CW* 15, p.23. Rastell's windfall and the benefaction to young Joan are from Reed (1926a), p.4; PROB 11/26 (Rastell's will). His return to London is worked out from NA, C 4/46/11; Reed (1926a). Margaret's dislike of 'being decked out in another's finery' is from Rogers, *SL*, no.35. The family tradition about More's income is from Roper (1935), pp.8–9; fuller and more accurate information about lawyers' fees and annual earnings is from Ives (1983), pp.285–329. Information on the Colts of Netherhall is from NA, C 140/52/34; E 150/307, no.14. Dowry comparisons are from CLRO, MS Repertory 3, fo.156^v; NA, C 4/46/11. John More's role as legal counsel for the

City of London and Westminster Abbey is from CLRO, MS Repertory 1, fos.148–75; NA, SC 6/Hen.VII/398. The role of serjeants-at-law is explained by Ives (1983); Baker (2003). Thomas More's election as an honorary mercer is from Lyell and Watney (1936), p.320.

Chapter 3

The circumstances of Henry VIII's accession are well explained by Cooper (1959); Gunn (1991); Guy (1988a). The coronation procession, the mercers' preparations and More's eulogy are from Lyell and Watney (1936), pp.323–5; BL, Cotton MS, Tiberius B.8, fos.100ᵛ–10; Hardyng's Chronicle, in STC 12766.7, fos.145ᵛ–6ᵛ; Hall's Chronicle, in Whibley (1904), I, pp.5–7; CW 3, Pt2, nos.19–23; Trapp (1990), pp.42–3; Carley (2000), p.lv. The description of Henry is from LP II.i, no.395; CSPV II, nos.63, 559, 624, 918, 920. The relationship between Erasmus, Lord Mountjoy, Sir William Say, and John and Thomas More is worked out from CWE 1, nos.103–27; Rogers, SL, no.2; CPR, Henry VII, Pt1, pp.283, 307, 399, 439, 488, 488–9; CPR, Henry VII, Pt2, pp.357, 546, 642–3; also relevant on their Hertfordshire connections are: NA, PROB 11/15, PROB 11/18 (wills of Thomas and Elizabeth Frowicke); PROB 11/24 (Sir William Say's will); PROB 11/25 (Mountjoy's will). Erasmus's visit with More and Edward Arnold to see Prince Henry at Eltham is described by Scarisbrick (1968), p.14; CWE 1, no.104. His first surviving letter to More is CWE 1, no.114. Erasmus's first visit to Bucklersbury and character sketch of More are from CWE 2, nos.181, 185, 187, 188, 191, 193–6. His second visit and the writing of the *Praise of Folly* are from CWE 2, pp.146–64; CWE 27, pp.xi–xxx, 78–85; the London court calendar is from Barron (2004), pp.128–96. The visit of Jacob de Wocht, city clerk of Antwerp, is fully described in Lyell and Watney (1936), pp.328–35; Sylvester and Marc'hadour (1977), pp.157–8; Ramsay (1982). Thomas More's role in Parliament, appointment as undersheriff, oath of office and duties in the civic courts are worked out from NA, C 244/166–73; CLRO, MS Journal 11, fo.93; CLRO, MS Repertory 2, fo.98ᵛ; LP I.i, no.132(26); Riley (1861), pp.155–9, 274–5; Guy (1980), pp.4–6; Ramsay (1982); Barron (2004), pp.167–70. The dedication to the *Praise of Folly* is from CWE 27, pp.83–5. Staverton's preferment by Cardinal Morton as an attorney in the civic courts is from CLRO, MS Repertory 1, fo.41. The first of the two references in Harpsfield (1932), p.313, refers not to this Staverton, but to his son, also confusingly named Richard, and relates to the year 1519. Examples of More's willingness to intervene in patronage are from Rogers, SL, no.30; CLRO, MS Repertory 8, fo.39. Staverton's engagement by St Stephen's is from Milbourn (1881), p.354. Information about the Lee family comes from their wills: NA, PROB 11/6 (Sir Richard); PROB 11/11 (Richard jun.); PROB 11/15 (Joyce, wife of Richard jun., mother of Edward and Joyce); ODNB confuses two different Edward Lees, as does Daniel Kinney in his note to CW 15, pp.xxxi–xxxii. Kinney, in any case, is contradicted by A. S. G. Edwards in *CW* 1, pp.xxxix–xl. All doubts are resolved by reading the wills, where the relationships are clearly set out. The information on the advowson at St Stephen's is from Milbourn (1881), pp.385, 388–90. It then passed to the Grocers' Company. More's translation of Pico's writings is edited by C.H. Miller in *CW* 1, pp.51–123; Rastell's edition is *STC* 19897.7; I follow Miller on the date (p.xxxix), rather than Hyatt King (1971), p.202. More's appointment as Marshall of Lincoln's Inn and the description of his duties at the Christmas and New Year revels are from Sylvester and Marc'hadour (1977), p.164; Dugdale (1671), pp.246–8. Ammonio's letter about Joanna More's health is from *CWE* 2, no.221.

Chapter 4

The letters about Erasmus's illness, the family crisis at Bucklersbury and Ammonio's plight, somewhat lost in translation in *CWE* 2, pp.168–200, are best sought in the Latin versions in *OE* 1, nos.225, 226, 228, 232, 236, 243. The sweat and its incidence in relation to epidemic diseases are reinvestigated by Dyer (1997); Thwaites, Taviner and Gant (1997); *idem* (1998); Flood (2003). Contemporary descriptions are found in *STC* 783, 4343, 12766.7; Kingsford (1905), p.193. When the sweat hit Thomas More's household in 1517 and he commented on the effects of the virus, he made no reference to an earlier attack or to his first wife's death: *CWE* 5, no.623. Joanna's funeral is described from the rubrics in *Sarum Missal* (1913), II, pp.174–202. John Middleton's will is from NA, PROB 11/16; his family background is worked out from NA, C 1/28/230, 234; C 1/70/147 (not to be confused with his namesake from the parish of St Lawrence Jewry). The networks connecting the Mores, Says of Essendon, Frowickes of Hertfordshire, Colts, Middletons and Harpers are tracked from ERO, D/DCe/T20, D/DJg/T12/92; NA, C 1/357/94–101, E 150/307/14, C 140/52/32, E 40/644, C 1/27/37–37E; *CPR*, Henry VII, Pt1, p.44; *LP* I.i, no.604 (36); Norrington (1983), pp.12–17. Alice Harper's background is from Norrington (1983), with extra information from her father's will: NA, PROB 11/9. The new facts on Edmund Shaa's inheritance are from NA, SC 6/Hen VIII/6878; C 1/574/34–6; C 1/447/59; C 4/41/71, 116; NA, PROB 11/8; PROB 11/10; PROB 11/14; C 54/420; *LP* II.i, no.73; ERO, D/DSq/T1/12–13. Norrington's study is not free of error, but is useful for its positive reassessment of Alice. John Bouge's testimony is from NA, SP 1/239, fos.223–4ᵛ; Gairdner (1892). The family traditions on More's asceticism are described and examined in Roper (1935), pp.25–9, 48–9; Harpsfield (1932), pp.64–6, 93–4; Stapleton (1928), pp.65–75; Guy (2000b), pp.34–6. More's view of pain is from *CW* 12, p.292. Erasmus's and Ammonio's depictions of Alice are from *CWE* 2, no.236; *CWE* 7, no.999; Harpsfield (1932), pp.93–9. More's wordplay on Alice (*nec bella, nec puella*) relates to St Augustine's *Contra Faustum*, bk22, par.74, p.671, line 24 (*nec bella, nec deus*), in *CSEL*, vol. 25. Quotations from More's semi-autobiographical reflections describing Alice are from *CW* 8, Pt2, pp.604–5; *CW* 12, pp.80–1, 168–9, 219–20, 277. His description of Alice as 'penny wise and pound foolish' is from Cresacre More: *STC* 18066 (p.127). More's renewal of his lease at the Barge is from NA, SC 6/Hen VIII/2396. More and Erasmus's translations from Lucian are from *CW* 3, Pt1; further valuable discussion is by Trapp (1990). Thomas More's remark about 'merry tales', his prelude to the story of the poor man, is from *CW* 6, Pt1, p.69. Bonvisi is described from *CW* 15, pp.50–1, 514; Rogers, *Corr.*, nos.34, 217; Harpsfield (1932), pp.138–9; Sicca (2002); *ODNB*. More's remark about 'the most pleasant sleep' is from his letter to Cranevelt dated 8 Nov. 1528; Miller (1994), pp.13–15. His comment on wives and women is to the same recipient dated 10 Aug. 1524; Miller (1994), p.37. His epigrams on wives are from *CW* 3, Pt2, nos.85–6. The claim that More avoided sexual intercourse with Alice, derived from Harpsfield, is most fully developed by Marius (1984). The early version of his epitaph for himself and his two wives, written before 1518 and probably in 1512 or 1513, is taken from *CW* 3, Pt2, no.258 and pp.410–11.

Chapter 5

More's earliest nominations to represent the City of London at Westminster and the Court are from CLRO, MS Repertory 2, fos.131–51; *LJ* (1767–1846), I, pp.14, 30. The account of Henry VIII's slide into war is from Hall's Chronicle, in Whibley (1904), I, pp.30–57; Scarisbrick (1968), pp.28–34. Wolsey's character is from Sylvester and Harding (1962), pp.12–14, 62; Brown (1854), II, pp.313–15; Guy (1998). The account of the French campaign of 1513 relies on Whibley (1904), I, pp.61–95, 113–18; Nichols (1846), pp.12–15; Scarisbrick (1968), pp.34–7. More's ode on the capture of Tournai is from *CW* 3, Pt1, no.244 and p.404. Rastell's role is worked out from NA, E 101/61/22; SP 1/230, fo.315; *LP* I.i, nos.2301, 3539, 3555; Reed (1926a), pp.7–8. Gianpietro Carafa's mission to London is worked out from *CSPV* II, nos.262, 362, 372, 382, 385; *CSPV* III, no.1485; *LP* I.ii, nos.2448, 2884, 3009, 3018, 3298. His character and his uncle's, and their opinions on the Church and papacy, are sketched from Maio (1969); Oakley (1969); Fenlon (1972); Gogan (1982); Mayer (2000); Oakley (2003). Erasmus's praise of Carafa is from *CWE* 2, no.287; *CWE* 3, no.335 (p.107). The newly discovered documents relating to More's (and Batmanson's) role in the case of the pope's ship are CLRO, MS Repertory 2, fos.206ᵛ; CLRO, MS Repertory 3, fos.16ʳ⁻ᵛ. The civic and mercantile issues illuminating the incident are pieced together from NA, C 1/227/55; C 1/331/8; C 1/334/14; C 1/357/58; C 1/475/18; C 1/477/21; C 1/514/21; C 1/565/55. Other information is from *LP* I.i, nos.1662(48) and (53), 1804(35); *LP* I.ii, nos.2867, 2916, 3107(11), 3205, 3241, 3490; *LP* II.i, nos.211, 571, 849; *LP* II.ii, no.4561, and p.1464; Roper (1935), pp.9–10. Invaluable background on the alum trade and Florentine syndicates is from Singer (1948); Sicca (2002), pp.163–201; Barron (2004), pp.15–16, 93–4; Sicca (2006), pp.6–15. Suffolk's role is briefly discussed by Gunn (1988), p.21. Batmanson's credentials are from Knowles (1959), p.469; Leader (1989), p.273. The events around the accession of Francis I are from *LP* II.i, no.395; Whibley (1904), I, p.200; Knecht (1994), pp.62–87, 105–33. More's mission to Bruges is from *LP* II.i, nos.422, 473, 474, 480, 540, 678, 679, 723, 732, 733, 782, 977, 986; Rogers, *Corr.*, nos.10–14; *CW* 4, appendix A. His letters, describing his mission in his own words, are from *CWE* 3, no.388; *CW* 4, pp.38–45. Gillis's career and the information about the diptych are from *CWE* 5, no.685; Trapp (1990), pp.64–73; Jardine (1993), pp.27–39. Further explanation is from *CW* 4, appendix A. The doodles of Gillis and his colleagues in the Antwerp City Archives were photographed and transcribed by Goddard (1988). The economy and trade of Antwerp are exhaustively investigated by Van der Wee (1963); Ramsay (1965). The rendezvous of More, Gillis and Hythloday is from More (1995), pp.40–9; *CW* 4, pp.46–51. I am indebted to Hexter's interpretation of the two stages of *Utopia*'s composition as set forth in *CW* 4, pp.xv–xxiii, except that I follow Logan in More (1995), p.49 and n.15 as to the placing of the seam. Like Logan, I believe the section of the Introduction written in Antwerp stops at the bottom of More (1995), p.49, which is at the top of *CW* 4, p.54. I agree with Hexter's summary of the sequence of composition, apart from the fact that I include *CW* 4, pp.54–8 with the rest of the material added subsequent to More's return to London. With this minor disagreement, I follow with gratitude Hexter's chronology on p.xxi. More's return to England is described from *CWE* 3, no.388; *CW* 4, appendix A; *LP* II.i, no.1067. Henry's offer of an annuity is from *CWE* 3, no.388 (pp.234–5). Ammonio's comment is from *CWE* 3, no.390 (p.239). Neville's elevation is from Bindoff (1982), III, pp.10–11; Guy (2000b), pp.52–3. Warham's dismissal and Wolsey's oath of office are taken from NA, C 54/383; *LP* II.i, no.1335(1)–(2); Kelly (1963), p.146. More's opinion of Wolsey is from his letter to Erasmus in Rogers, *SL*, no.5 (pp.68–9); *CWE* 3, no.388 (p.233). His intention of dedicating *Utopia* to Wolsey is from Rogers, *SL*, no. 14, where it is misdated. More's illness is from *CWE* 3, p.293. Wolsey's Star Chamber speech on law reform, also establishing John More's membership of the King's Council, is from HEH, Ellesmere MS 2654, fos.9^v–10; Ellesmere MS 2655, fo.10; Guy (1977a), pp.30–1.

Chapter 6

The date of More's entry into the King's Council at Reading is firmly established by *LP* II.ii, no.4025. His oath as a king's councillor is from NA, C 193/1, fo.87^v. The significance of the warrant authorizing his salary of £100 a year, signed by Henry VIII and on the file of warrants for the great seal with the reference NA, C 82/463, is reinterpreted in detail by Guy (2000b), pp.50–2. The background to the events at Reading is established by *LP* II.ii, nos.4023–4, 4034–5, 4044–6, 4053–5; Guy (2000b), pp.52–4, 56–8. More's reluctance to go to Court is from Rogers, *SL*, no.18; Guy (2000b), p.58. The death of Ammonio is from *CWE* 5, nos.623–4; *LP* II.ii, nos.3372, 3638, 3655, 3788, 3807, 4009, 4057, 4125, 4320, 4331; *CSPV* II, nos.944–5. My account of Pace gratefully relies on an exemplary study by Curtis (1996). His role in 1518 is further described by Brown (1854), II, pp.142–5, 162, 210–12. More's early links to John Roper as an arbitrator and in the court for 'poor men's causes' are traced from NA, C 244/163, no.101B; NA, SP 1/19, fo.143 (stamped fo.142); HEH, Ellesmere MS 2655, fo.12. John Roper's biography is from Spelman (1976–7), II, intro., pp.54–7, 363–4; Roper (1935), pp.xxix–xxxi; Hogrefe (1932), pp.523–33. More's reflections to Cromwell on Henry's words at his admission to the Council are from Rogers, *Corr.*, no.199 (p.495). More's and Henry's relationship is from Roper (1935), pp.11–12; Guy (1980), pp.15–16. More's copy of Euclid is from Rose (1977), p.51 n.22. Still bearing More's ownership signature, the book is now in Columbia University Library. The cache of letters between Thomas More, Gonnell and the children is from Rogers, *SL*, nos.17, 20, 22, 23, 29, 31, 32, 33, 35; *CW* 3, Pt2, no.264. See also Stapleton (1928), pp.98–111. Almost all were preserved by Thomas Stapleton, a Catholic exile during Elizabeth's reign. He'd fled to Louvain and Malines, where he knew Margaret Giggs (John Clement's wife) and the printer John Fowler, who had married Alice, daughter of John Harris (More's secretary) and Dorothy Colley (Margaret Roper's maid). Many of the letters were still extant in 1588, when Colley loaned them to Stapleton for his biography of More: *CW* 2, pp.xlviii–l. They may have been in a decayed condition by then, but their accuracy is underscored by the fact that those Stapleton used from More to Frans van Cranevelt collate almost perfectly with More's holographs, subsequently rediscovered in an attic. The dates are often uncertain and I do not always follow those suggested by Rogers if the context dictates otherwise. Erasmus's discussion of the classical theory of 'letter'-writing is from *CWE* 25 (especially pp.20–1), where the translation of *De Conscribendis Epistolis* is based on the 1522 edition. Further information, including the quotation from an earlier, pirate edition of the book issued in Cambridge, is from Jardine (1993), pp.149–53. Information about More's vision of education and choice of set texts is from *CWE* 8, no.1233; Rogers, *SL*, nos.19, 20. Plato's and Pico della Mirandola's views of women's education are from Plato (2000), pp.147, 152–3, 250; Allen (1985–2002), II, Pt2, pp.663, 909–17. The contribution of the Church Fathers is explored by White (1992). Modern accounts of women's education with particular reference to Erasmus, who learned from More, are by Sowards (1982); Sowards (1989). Maybe John Clement was born in or around 1499, the son of a London gold-smith, also John; or maybe one Hugh Clement from Kingston-upon-Thames in Surrey is the father. If so, he and his wife and four other children were alive as late as 1527, but as we hear nothing else about them, it's far more likely we're looking at the goldsmith's son, who was orphaned: NA, PROB 2/158; NA, C 1/82/103; NA, PROB 11/22 (will of Hugh Clement); CWE 3, nos.388, 424; CWE 4, no.468; CWE 5, no.820; CWE 6, nos.907; Rogers, SL, nos.8, 24; More (1995), pp.33–5; Woolfson (1998), pp.222–3. Clement's teaching compendium, including Utopia, is from Jardine (1993), pp.175–80. That Margaret Giggs was taught Greek, and taught it later to her own children, is from Aikin (1780), pp.92–3. Possible additional or alternative pieces of the jigsaw are NA C 1/11/129, C 1/64/1084, C 1/70/160, C 1/76/102, C 1/263/51, C 1/297/97, C 1/546/14. Gonnell's role is from Rogers, SL, no.20; CWE 2, nos.274, 275, 279, 287, 289, 292; CWE 8, nos.1138, 1229. Erasmus's view of the need for 'imitation' of the finest authors is from CWE 25, pp.22–8, 259–60. No evidence exists that CWE 5, no.601 (p.18) refers to Gonnell. Alice Middleton's betrothal, dowry and marriage are from CLRO, MS Repertory 3, fos.69, 156ᵛ; information on the Elryngton estate is from NA C 1/406/9–10, C 1/546/52; NA, PROB 11/21 (will of Thomas Elryngton). The complicated affairs of Edmund Shaa are pieced together from the information in his and his widow's lawsuits: NA, C 1/574/34–6, C 1/447/59, C 1/1317/26. Edmund came of age and obtained livery of his lands on 29 Jan. 1515: LP, II.i, no.73. Margaret's letter mentioning Shaa is from Rogers, SL, no.22. 'Silence is a woman's glory' is from Sophocles, as quoted by Aristotle (1996), p.29. The issues relating to penmanship and handwriting are explored with the help of STC 3363.8. Margaret's handwriting is described from BUW, MS R.254, fos.153–4ᵛ.

Chapter 7

The date of John More's remarriage is from Erasmus's emendations to his vignette of the family after Joan Bowes's death: CWE 7, pp.355–6. More's joke about his new stepmother is from CWE 7, no.999. The ancestry and previous marriages of Alice Clerk are pieced together from Bindoff (1982), II, pp.616–17; NA, C 1/57/303 (lawsuit of John Clerk, grocer, and Alice his wife, late the wife of John Garstang); NA, PROB 11/6 (will of John Garstang); PROB 11/20 (will of Robert Clerk, brother-in-law of John Clerk); C 146/121, 125. A daughter of a quite unrelated John More, once a leading light in the Fishmongers' Company, Alice was the widow of John Clerk, a grocer, whose younger brother, Robert, was a fishmonger. John Clerk, grocer, husband of Alice, is not to be confused with the 'John Clerk, grocer', husband of Katherine, who died in 1484: NA, PROB 11/7. Christopher More, of Loseley in Surrey, mentioned in John More's will (PROB 11/23) and one of his executors, may have been Alice's half-brother, rather than brother as is usually supposed. His will is from NA, PROB 11/33. Information on the Colts and John Colt's marriage to Marie Lisle comes from NA, E 150/307, C 1/686/5, C 1/934/78–81, C 1/1035/31, C 1/1096/46,

C 1/1224/9, REQ 2/3/39; *LP* III.ii, appendix no.31. The trust arising from Joanna's marriage settlement was established in 1506 and dissolved in 1514 after the marriage of George Colt to Elizabeth Makwilliam in 1514: NA, E 150/307, no.14. John Colt's will is from NA, PROB 11/20. William Rastell at More's school is from Sylvester and Marc'hadour (1977), p.439; Frances Staverton is from the preface to *STC* 10477 and *STC* 10477.5; Gee (1937), p.262. The younger John Rastell's apprenticeship to Rowland Hill is from NA, C 1/708/23, C 1/1012/34. Hill's address and role as churchwarden at St Stephen's is from his will at NA, PROB 11/44; Milbourn (1881), p.360. More hired Roger Drew as an additional tutor. Information about him is from NA, C 1/906/1–6; Rogers, *SL*, no.29; *LP* III.ii, no.2807 (15); *LP* IV.i, no.390 (10) [p.169]. An Oxford graduate, Drew lived for two years at the Barge, teaching the younger children before securing a permanent appointment in the Church. Kratzer is from *CWE* 4, no.515; *CWE* 5, no.702; *ODNB* (*s.v.* Nicholas Kratzer). His teaching is from Rogers, *SL*, nos.29, 31. The mathematical problems reappearing in Tunstall's textbook are from *STC* 24319; Smith (1917), pp.64–71. More's discussions with Erasmus about women's education are from *CWE* 8, no.1233. His letters to Margaret and the children from which all quotations in this chapter derive are from Rogers, *SL*, nos.29, 31, 32, 33, 35. Letter no.35 in this edition, as also noted by Reynolds (1960), pp.27–8, is in fact extracts from two separate letters spliced together. The first has to be dated at or around Feb. 1521, when Pole left for Italy. The second refers to Margaret's confinement, awaiting the birth of her first child in 1523. However, although now composite, the two extracts, individually, are genuine, taken from Stapleton (1928), pp.46, 114–15. The issues of decorum and More's changing attitude to his daughter's talents are discussed by McCutcheon (1987), pp.459–61; Jardine (1985), pp.816–17; Jardine (1987), pp.4–6. Margaret's reading of medical texts is from Rogers, *SL*, no.31 (p.149). She is shown reading from Seneca in the Nostell Priory version of Holbein's family-group portrait. Erasmus's advice on Seneca is from *CWE* 25, p.260. I used the 1515 edition of Seneca's *Lucubrationes Omnes*, as edited by Erasmus, from the Fellows' Library, Clare College, Cambridge, especially pp.452–643. Erasmus's comments on his edition, showing he regarded it as a rhetorical work, are from *CW* 9, pp.310–11. Quintilian refers to the case of Hortensia in *Institutio Oratoria*, I.i.6: Quintilian (1996), I, p.23. Buckingham's trial and execution are from NA, KB 9/53; KB 8/5; BL, Harleian MS 283, fo.72; *LP* III.i, nos.1284 (1–5), 1285 (pp.495–505), 1356; *CSPV* III, no.213; Brigden (1989), pp.153–5. More's visits to the Mayor and Aldermen are from CLRO, MS Repertory 5, fos.199ᵛ, 204ʳ⁻ᵛ. My description of More's treatise on the Four Last Things is from *CW* 1, pp.128–82 (esp. pp.153–61); Fox (1982), pp.101–7. Information on Margaret's mock speech, her own treatise on the Last Things and its reception as reported by Margaret Giggs and More's own descendants is from Stapleton (1928), pp.112–13; *STC* 18066, p.184.

Thomas More's advice limiting the extent of Margaret's audience for her written work is from Rogers, *SL*, no.35 (p.155).

Chapter 8

The sermons and homilies of the preaching friars are from *STC* 791–2, 5758–9, 17964, 17973.5, 21429. Information on preaching and late-medieval theology is from Owst (1926), Duffy (1992), Wabuda (2002). My account of the canon law of marriage is from *STC* 4115, 12472; Farmer (1986); Biller (1982). More's view of the cult of the macabre is from *CW* 1, pp.139–40. Agnes Graunger's death and epitaph are investigated by Marc'hadour (1979), who attributes the inscription to Thomas More. Information on Grocyn is from *ODNB* and his will: NA, PROB 11/19. The poem on stepmothers is from *CW* 3, Pt2, p.254. Thomas More's letter to his old schoolmaster, John Holt, is from Rogers, *SL*, no.1. For his education and position in Morton's household, we must rely on Roper (1935); Reed (1926a); Stow in *STC* 23341 and Stow (1956); and the historical notes to Harpsfield (1932). The circle around Grocyn, Linacre and Colet is from Plimpton (1933); Tilley (1938); Nelson (1956); Maddison, Pelling and Webster (1977); Trapp (1990); Carlson (1991); Woolfson (1998); Hellinga and Trapp (1999); supplemented by *ODNB* and the wills of Grocyn, Linacre and Colet: NA, PROB 11/19; PROB 11/21; PROB 11/14. Erasmus's letter in praise of his new friends is from *CWE* 1, no.118. His letter on his return to Paris is from *OE* 1 (also *CWE* 1), no.124, discussed and quoted by Tilley (1938). His remarks on John More are from *CWE* 7, no.999 (p.19). The Rastells' departure from John More's house after the feud with Joan Marshall in 1501 is from NA, C 4/20/81, C 4/46/11.

Chapter 9

My account of the London Charterhouse is from Wines (1998), with archaeological data from Barber and Thomas (2002). The plan of the site and its water supply is in the possession of Sutton's Hospital in Charterhouse (photocopy at NPG). Books copied by the Carthusians are from Wines (1998); Hellinga and Trapp (1999); printed editions (some of a later date and provenance) include *STC* 4602 (especially Pt2, sig.Aiii–Bii); *STC* 5758–9, 14043, 23964. Thomas More later recommended Carthusian-linked devotional books to his own readers: *CW* 8, Pt1, p.37. Modern commentary is by Owst (1926); Rhodes (1974); Hughes (1988); Duffy (1992); Baker (1999); Clark (1995–6). The visitors' house, founded by Bishop Russell, is from Wines (1998). The grant of the rectory and advowson of North Mimms to the Charterhouse is from NA, E 326/8794; a subsequent lawsuit about the rectory is from NA, C1/1297/26–8. Erasmus's account is from *CWE* 7, no.999 (pp.19, 21), where he suggests that More left the monks to marry. The *City of God* is from Dyson (1998); our sole glimpse of

More's lectures is from Stapleton (1928), pp.8–9. I have drawn on a handwritten exposition of St Augustine's theory of law and equity by More's close friend Cuthbert Tunstall for an impression of shared values: NA, SP 6/13, fos.2ᵛ–4. More's own ideas of justice and the contemporary lawyers' debates are described from *CSPV* II, no.1010; Roper (1935), pp.44–5; Guy (1977b); Guy (1985); Doe (1991); Cromartie (2006). Although the writs for the election to the Parliament of 1504 are lost, they were always issued six weeks ahead of the opening ceremony. The opinion that Thomas More sat as MP for Gatton is highly tenuous, a conjecture derived from a prior assumption that he already knew John Colt and had the gift of the seat. Henry VII's punitive treatment of London and John More's role as an adviser to the city are from CLRO, MS Repertory 1, fos.148–75; *Mercers' Ordinances* (1881); Lyell and Watney (1936), p.266. The Act reviewing the statutes of the livery companies is 19 Hen.VII, *c*.7. The extortions of Henry VII's later years are discussed by Cooper (1959); Chrimes (1972); Condon (1979); Guy (1988a); Horowitz (2006). Thomas More's opposition in the 1504 Parliament and his father's imprisonment and fine are from Roper (1935), pp.7–8. Information on the levies and receipts of taxation is from Schofield (1963), pp.179–98; Given-Wilson (2005), vol.16; Wedgwood and Holt (1936); Kingsford (1905), p.260. The privilege of free speech in Parliament was limited. Members might raise issues otherwise *sub judice* in the courts of law, and perhaps contradict royal councillors (if not the Speaker, invariably a crown nominee), but it wasn't acceptable to criticize the king or debate the royal prerogative: Fryde and Miller (1970), II, pp.147–76. Thomas More's remark about a time to marry is from *CW* 3, Pt2, no.143. His letter to Colet is from Rogers, *SL*, no.2. The *terminus ad quem* for the marriage has to be nine months before Margaret Roper's birth. The canonical dates permitting weddings are listed in the rubric in *Sarum Missal* (1913), II, pp.143–4. Some further (often inaccurate) details are given in the historical notes to Roper (1935). The ages of the Colt sisters are worked out from the linked Chancery litigation concerning the stepmother of Jane Elryngton, their mother, which records the dates of legal process from which calendar-year dates and ages can be calculated: NA, C 1/125/58–62, C 1/126/57–8. Joanna's age is settled by the evidence of Simon Elryngton, her maternal uncle. John Elryngton's will is at NA, PROB 11/7, establishing the date of his daughter's wedding. The monumental brass for John Colt still in the chancel of the Church of St Peter-ad-Vincula, Roydon, wrongly gives Joanna's mother's name as Elizabeth, instead of Jane. Her brother Simon's legal testimony proves her name was Jane. Information on the Colts and Jane Trusbet is from Wedgwood and Holt (1936); *ODNB* (*s.v.* Sir William Parr); NA, C 140/52/34; E 150/307. The Colt family trust arising from Thomas More's marriage settlement was established in 1506 and dissolved in 1514 after the marriage of George Colt to Elizabeth Makwilliam: NA, E 150/307, no.14. John Colt's dispute with Buckingham over

Little Parndon is from NA, C 1/357/94–101. His admission to the Middle Temple is from Baker (2003–4), I, p.76. The story of More's 'resort' to Netherhall is from Roper (1935), p.6. The legal age of consent is from Swinburne (1686), pp.47–8. Floyer (1913) gives useful background on Netherhall and its architecture. Erasmus's description of Joanna More is from *CWE* 7, no.999 (p.21); his colloquy of the unhappy wife is edited by Thompson (1965), pp.120–1; see also Guy (2000b). More's Latin poem is from *CW* 3, Pt2, no.143.

Chapter 10

More's fears of enjoying himself too much are from *CW* 13, p.227; *CW* 12, p.83. Hunne's case is reconstructed from Foxe (1843–9), IV, pp.125, 173, 183–205, 662–3, 724–5; Whibley (1904), I, pp.129–42; Davis (1915); Pollard (1929); Ogle (1949); Milsom (1961); Fines (1963); Brigden (1989); Palmer (2002). More's opinion of Hunne is from *CW* 6, pp.317–30; *CW* 7, pp.132–6; *CW* 9, pp.126–7. The speeches of Winchcombe and Standish are from *CW* 9, appendix B; Caryll (1999–2000), II, pp.683–92; Pollard (1929), pp.26–58; Ogle (1949), pp.132–61; Hughes (1950–4), I, pp.149–55. Bishop Fitzjames's speech is from Whibley (1904), I, p.141. My account of the first draft of *Utopia* follows the translations in More (1995) and the 4th edition of *CW* 4 (themselves closely aligned). Greek names and allusions to classical or travel literature in *Utopia* are discussed by Logan (1983); the notes to More (1995); the lengthy commentary to *CW* 4; Crossett (1957); Cave (1991). Other accounts of the meaning of *Utopia*, all of which I have drawn on to a greater or lesser degree, are by Chambers (1935); Ames (1949); Hexter (1952); Surtz (1957); Skinner (1967); Davis (1970); Fenlon (1975); Skinner (1978), vol.1, pp.255–62; Bradshaw (1981); Davis (1981), pp.41–61; Fenlon (1981); Baker-Smith (1983); Skinner (1987); Fox (1989); Baker-Smith (1991); Parrish (1997); Guy (2000b), pp.84–105; Nelson (2001). The exchanges between Dorp and Erasmus are from *CWE* 3, nos.304, 337, 347. More's letter to Dorp is from *CW* 15, pp.2–127; Rogers, *SL*, no.4. The background to the quarrel and its relevance to *Utopia* are explored by Jardine (1993), pp.111–22.

Chapter 11

Information on the *Graunde Abridgement* and its genesis is taken from *STC* 10954; Baker (2003), pp.499–500. John Rastell's career in Coventry and social networking are from the wills of Richard Cook and Thomas Bond, both in NA, PROB 11/15; with further connections to St German and others from NA C 1/159/34; C 1/270/22; *CPR* Henry VII, Pt1, p.604; *CPR* Henry VII, Pt2, p.419; *LP* I.i, no.1662 (24); Guy (1985), pp.6–7. Background on the economic depression in Coventry and the 'mystery' plays is from Block (1922); Phythian-Adams (1979), pp.44, 89–90, 101, 111–12, 145, 173. Cook's donation of English Bibles to Trinity Church, Coventry, and Walsall is from fo.229^v of his will. The accusation of Lollardy against him (and his wife) is from McSheffrey and Tanner (2003), pp.29, 188–9, 315–17, 327. Rastell's taste in theatricals is from NA, E 36/227, fos.2, 31ᵛ–5, 48ᵛ. His pre-Utopian call for reform is from the 'Prologus' to *STC* 9599, embellished in prologues to *STC* 9515.5, 20701. Information on the Coventry Lollards and charges against Alice Rowley is from McSheffrey and Tanner (2003), pp.1–7, 14–23, 123–4, 159–61. Thomas More's views on the English Bible are from *CW* 6, pp.331–42. His tussle with the Coventry friar, described by himself, is from *CW* 15, pp.284–9. Rastell's property moves in London are traced by Reed (1926a), pp.12–14. My account of his buildings, gardens and other improvements at Monken Hadley relies on the litigation in the Court of Requests, the result of a challenge to Rastell's lease in 1532–3 by the heir of the original lessor: NA, REQ 1/5, fo.216 (stamped numbering); REQ 2/6/202. The invitation to Rastell's lawyer friends, including Thomas Cromwell, to join him is from the testimony of Anthony Lowe of London among the bundle of documents at REQ 2/6/202. The complicated, but quite extraordinary story of Rastell's voyage to the New World, with a description of his cargo and intention of annexing Newfoundland, is based on the voluminous litigation: NA, REQ 2/3/192, C 1/562/13, C 1/883/8, C 1/1512/32, C 4/20/81, C 4/46/11; KB 27/1042, m.60. Some (but far from all) of these documents are abstracted by Reed (1926a), appendix 1; Baker (2003), p.214. The *Frances Rastell* may originally have been named the *Nicholas* of Dartmouth before refitting (NA, C 4/46/11 and schedule); the tackle may have been purchased separately. Reed's account of Rastell's dispute with Staverton is flawed, since Reed did not have the benefit of the newly released documents in NA, C 4/20/81, C 4/46/11, and thus was not aware that the disputed debts refer to the Rastells' feud with Joan Marshall. The description of the 'strange men' from North America paraded in Cheapside is from Kingsford (1905), p.258. Bercula's recruitment is from his signed deposition in NA, REQ 2/3/192. More's and Rastell's use of sources and maps is from Nugent (1942), pp.74–88; Axton (1979); Laubenberger (1982), pp.91–113; Cave (1991), pp.212–19; Allen (1992), pp.500–21; Helgerson (1998), pp.1–14; Lakowski (1999), pp.1–19. Connections between Hythloday's descriptions and Vespucci's *New World* and *Four Voyages* are from *CW* 4, pp.281, 282, 301, 302–3, 305, 378, 427, 428, 442, 475, 519, 549–50. For accounts of the Vespucci documents, I have relied chiefly on Herbermann (1907); Formisano (1992); Magnaghi (1924); Cave (1991). The best modern edition of the *Cosmographiae Introductio*, with facsimile, is by von Wieser (1907); another edition is from CUL, Microfiche 719. The passages referring to America are from sigs.Cii and Ciiiᵛ. Schöner's description of 'America' is from Schöner (1515), fos.60–2. A recently discovered copy of Waldseemüller's globe-map, one of only four known to have survived intact, was on view in June 2005 at Christie's, London, Sale no.7137, lot 17. By 1516, Waldseemüller had dropped his advocacy of Vespucci's claim, calling the new fourth continent 'Terra Incognita' or 'Unknown Land' instead. The wall-map was sold as twelve sheets each 23 x 17 inches, and the purchaser had to employ a paper-moulder to integrate them into three overlapping rows of four sheets, 90 x 52 inches overall. The wall-map was seriously expensive, far beyond the means of More or Rastell: only a single copy survives today at the Library of Congress, Washington DC. Rastell's *Four Elements* is from *STC* 20722; Milson (1997), pp.235–93. Hyatt King gives a date for printing as early as 1519 on Rastell's return from Ireland: Hyatt King (1971), pp.197–214. Rastell follows Ringmann, who after describing Europe, Asia and Africa says: 'But now these continents have been widely explored and a fourth discovered by Amerigo Vespucci, as will be seen from my appendix. I do not see what reason anyone would have to object to calling this continent after Amerigo, who first discovered it.' Rastell's own *mappa mundi* is from Roberts (1979), p.37, item 3. His dealings with John More and Staverton are from NA, C 1/883/8, C 1/1512/32, C 4/20/81, C 4/46/11 (which also contains a schedule of the ship's tackle); Reed (1926a), p.14. For the mutual relationships of Staverton, Puncheon and Smyth: NA, PROB 11/26 and PROB 51/35 (will of Puncheon); PROB 11/26 (will of Walter Smyth). For the links of the Mores and Elryngtons to Stephen Puncheon: NA, PROB 11/21 (will of Thomas Elryngton). Thomas More's mission to Calais is from *LP* II.ii, no.3634; Ramsay (1982), p.286. John More's promotion to the Court of Common Pleas is from Spelman (1976–7), II, intro., p.372. The networks involving Cromwell's Lutheran clients in his law practice are from NA, PROB 11/17 (will of Alexander Perpoynt); PROB 11/25 (will of John Purser); C 1/869/1, C 1/571/17, C 1/571/18, C 1/482/21, C 1/1177/45, C 1/567/59, C 1/677/34; SP 46/186 (fos.38–40); *LP* IV.i, nos.437, 1751; *LP* IV.iii, no.5330; Brigden (1988), pp.31–50. Thomas More's later discovery of the 'night school' is from *CW* 6, Pt1, pp.328–9. Rastell's exchange over the character of Richard Hunne is from NA, C 1/560/48–9.

Chapter 12

More's awkwardness in a Court milieu is from Stapleton (1928), pp.76–7; his letter to Fisher is from Rogers, *SL*, no.18; *CW* 12, pp.206–45. His sartorial preferences are from *CWE* 7, no.999 (p.18); Ascham in *STC* 832, fo.61. Wolsey's reform policy is worked out from HEH, Ellesmere MS 2654, fos.22^v–3; HEH Ellesmere MS 2655, fos.10, 16; Lodge (1791), I, pp.13–27; NA, STAC 2/15/188–90, STAC 2/16/365–72, STAC 2/18/161, STAC 2/26/103, STAC 2/32/bundle of unlisted fragments (Roger Barbor's case); NA, KB 29/148, mm.6–8, 17, 43–4; *TRP* (1964–9), I, nos.75, 80, 81, 94, 110, 114, 118, 119, 121, 123, 125, 127; Leadam (1897); Scarisbrick (1977), pp.256–9; Scarisbrick (1978), pp.45–67; Guy (1977a), pp.23–50. More's remark about 'the little gnats and flies' comes from *CW* 12, p.225. Pace and More's role as Henry's secretaries without differentiation relies on Rogers, *Corr.*, nos.77–9; Elton (1974b–92), I, pp.142–3; Guy (1980), pp.15–19. Wolsey and Henry's aims in foreign policy and my description of the 1518 negotiations are from *LP* II.ii, nos.4357–62, 4467–80, 4483, 4504, 4550, 4564; *CSPV* II, nos.1014–95; Brown (1854), II, pp.146–322; Whibley (1904), I, pp.165–77; Knecht (1994), pp.62–87; Scarisbrick (1968), pp.67–96. Campeggio's arrival is from Whibley (1904), I, pp.166–7. The big ideas about peace, including Pace's sermon, are from *CWE* 27, pp.290–322; Curtis (1996), pp.162–83. The Turkish threat to Europe is from *LP* II.i, pp.cclii–lv, and nos.1709, 1874, 2017; *LP* III.i, pp.cccxc–ccccxii. Wolsey's *de facto* role as chief plenipotentiary legate, despite the seeming equality of his commission with Campeggio, is settled by his designation and placing as 'chief legate' in the seating arrangements for the conference: RSL, MS 61, fos.56ᵛ–7; *LP* II.ii, p.1345 (a later, incomplete copy). My accounts of the commissioning of Wolsey to organize the Field of Cloth of Gold, reception of Charles V at Canterbury, description of the English palace at Guisnes, and second interview with Charles at Calais are from *LP* III.i, nos.700–7, 718–50, 803–9, 851–2, 855, 869–71, 906–8, 919; *CSPV* III, nos.43–111; Whibley (1904), I, pp.177–221; Scarisbrick (1968), pp.80–8; Anglo (1969), pp.124–69. The detailing of More as an 'esquire' and his entitlements are from Jerdan (1842), pp.28–33; Nichols (1846), pp.19–26. The movements of More and Erasmus are traced from *CWE* 7, nos.1083, 1087, 1090, 1093, 1096, 1097, 1106, 1107; *CWE* 8, nos.1138, 1145, 1173. More's negotiations with the German Hanseatic merchants are from Ramsay (1982), pp.286–7; Lloyd (1991), pp.65–6. Erasmus's account of the letters he received from More's children is from *CWE* 8, no.1233 (p.296). The quarrel between More and de Brie is from *CW* 3, Pt2, pp.469–659 (quotations from p.649); *CWE* 7, nos.1087 (especially pp.245, 253–4), 1093, 1096 (especially pp.275–7); *CWE* 8, nos.1131, 1133, 1184. More's joke that he is not yet numbered among the saints is from *CW* 3, Pt 2, p.552 n.1. His claim that someone should 'fart' in de Brie's face and 'piss' into his open mouth is from *CWE* 7, pp.253–4. Erasmus's remark that he was not so blindly devoted to More is from *CWE* 8, no.1131. More's quarrels with Lee and Batmanson are from *CW* 15, pp.xxxi–xlv, 152–95, 198–311 (especially 153, 165–9, 199–205, 215–37, 259–71, 301–11); *CWE* 7, nos.1030, 1053, 1061, 1083, 1089, 1090, 1097, 1099, 1100, 1113; *CWE* 8, nos.1139, 1127A. Erasmus's view is from *CWE* 8, no.1126. More's defence of Erasmus's New Testament project on the eve of the revision of *Utopia* is from his open letter to Dorp: *CW* 15, pp.2–127; Rogers, *SL*, no.4. Erasmus's view of Luther is from *CWE* 6, no.980; *CWE* 7, nos.1033, 1041, 1102, 1113; *CWE* 8, no.1127A. 'The pot matches the lid' is from *CW* 15, p.263. Leo X's excommunication of Luther and its English aftermath is from *LP* III.i, pp.ccccxii–xxviii, ccccxxxviii–xxxix, and nos.1193, 1197, 1210, 1218, 1220, 1233, 1234, 1273, 1274, 1275, 1279; Rex (1989), pp.85–106; Rex (1991), pp.78–92; Guy (2000b), pp.114–17. The ceremony at St Paul's is from *CSPV* III, nos.210, 213; Fisher's sermon is from

STC 10894. More's appointment as Under-Treasurer and his knighthood are from NA, E 407/67/3; Elton (1974b–92), I, p.134; Guy (1980), p.24. The Under-Treasurer's salary was £173 6s. 8d. 'Erasmus is an eel' is from Bietenholz and Deutscher (1985–7), II, p.363. Erasmus's candid acknowledgement of his own weakness is from *CWE* 8, no.1218. His comparison with St Peter refers to Matt. 26:69–75, Mark 14:66–72, Luke 22:56–62, John 18:25–7. Erasmus, writing to Budé, first drew attention to More's talent for controversy: *CWE* 8, no.1184.

Chapter 13
Erasmus's decision to leave Louvain for Basel is from *CWE* 8, nos.1174, 1175, 1203, 1219, 1236. The quotation is from *CWE* 8, no.1203 (p.212). The proceedings at Blackfriars and Baynard's Castle are reconstructed from Caryll (1999–2000), II, pp.683–92; Pollard (1929), pp.26–58; Ogle (1949), pp.132–61. More's own account of what he heard at Baynard's Castle is from *CW* 6, Pt1, pp.318–25. The authentic version of Henry's verdict is from HEH, Ellesmere MS 6109 (in vol. 34/C/49). The bishop's chancellor's discharge is from NA, KB 27/1019, m.4 (rex). Wolsey afterwards fined him £600, banishing him to obscurity in Exeter. Then, when Henry rewarded Friar Standish with a bishopric, Wolsey prosecuted him for neglecting to pay homage for his temporal lands before he was consecrated, which by statute was *praemunire*, so taking his revenge. He also punished Sir Robert Sheffield, who was fined 8,000 marks (£5,333) for defaming the clergy, then sent to the Tower for aiding and abetting a murderer in his home county of Lincolnshire. With inexhaustible thoroughness, Wolsey unearthed the skeletons in the cupboards of anyone who'd caused him hassle: Pollard (1929), p.51; Guy (1977a), pp.76–8. His approach to rectifying abuses of 'benefit of clergy' is from Spelman (1976–7), II, intro., pp.326–46; Caryll (1999–2000), II, pp.712–13; Dyer (1993–4), I, pp.173–4. More's report of Standish's conspiracy against Erasmus is from Rogers, *SL*, no.9 (p.79); *CWE* 4, no.481. Erasmus's view is from *CWE* 8, no.1126. Thomas More's remark about 'wicked factions' opposing Greek learning is from Rogers, *SL*, no.19 (p.101). His description of Cardinal Morton is from *CW* 2, pp.90–3; see also Fox (1982), pp.76, 94–5. The dedication of *Utopia* to Gillis with information about the time spent on the revisions and the arrangements for printing is from More (1995), pp.30–9; *CW* 4, pp.38–45. Information on the 'History of King Richard III' is from *CW* 2, esp. pp.lix–civ, 3–93; Logan (2005), pp.xv–li. Seneca's maxim on tyranny (from Erasmus's 1515 edition of Seneca's works) is from Seneca (1515), pp.113, 643, and 'index locorum'. Similar sentiments can be found in More's Latin poems: *CW* 3, Pt2, nos. 80, 109, 111, 112, 114, 115, 120, 121, 162, 198. More's invented speech by Morton to the old Duke of Buckingham with the fable of the Lion King is from *CW* 2, pp.92–3. The fresh material inserted into Book I of *Utopia* comprises More (1995), pp.49–107; *CW* 4, pp.54–109. My interpretation of Book I relies on

More (1995), pp.49–53, 55–7, 63–77, 81–7, 89, 91–3, 95–8, 101, and closely follows Davis (1970), pp.27–49. Further background on *Utopia* (including printing, reprinting and reception) is from *LP* II.i, nos.2492, 2540, 2558, 2614, 2726; *LP* II.ii, nos.2748, 2842, 2974, 2996, 3413, 3543, 3626, 3627, 3659, 3665, 3684, 3831, 3991. Testimony to *Utopia*'s wisdom is from Jerome de Busleyden, in More (1995), pp.250–5. Examples illustrating its realism are from More (1995), pp.31–9, 259, 261–3, 267–9; *CW* 4, p.292; Guy (2000b), p.92. More may have had second thoughts about publishing *Utopia*, since while thanking his dinner companion, Antonio Bonvisi the merchant banker, for his high opinion of the book, he warned him that this 'issues from affection rather than judgement'. 'Love,' says Thomas, 'when it settles deep in men, spreads darkness over their thinking, which I see has happened to you, especially since my *Utopia* has pleased you so much, a book which I think clearly deserves to hide itself away for ever in its own island': Rogers, *SL*, no.15.

Chapter 14

Jane Roper's character is from Wood (1846), III, pp.1–2, and from her will: NA, PROB 11/30. The Roper family members are from John Roper's will printed in *Statutes of the Realm* (1810–28), III, pp.310–15; Collins (1768), VI, pp.622–3; Hogrefe (1932), pp.523–33; Roper (1935), pp.xxix–xxxii; Bindoff (1982), III, pp.213–17. William's correct age is from his own sworn testimony to the Court of Chancery as Steward of the Manor of Stepney: NA, C 2/Eliz/B9/60; C 2/Eliz/C23/47; C 24/57–60; Roper (1935), p.xxxi; his description is from the Holbein miniature: MMA, Rogers Fund, 1950 (50.69.1). John's landholdings in Kent and London, and investment in the office of Chief Clerk in the Court of King's Bench, are worked out from his will, and from Spelman (1976–7), II, intro., pp. 54–5. The family quarrel is from the sworn depositions in *LP* IV.i, no.1518, read in conjunction with John Roper's will to which this testimony refers. The grant to Thomas More of the keepership of the foreign exchanges is from NA, C 66/635, m.4 (*LP* III.i, no.1073). How the monopoly worked with payments in cash to the grantees is from a later lawsuit brought by Ardeson against Vivaldi's factor: NA, C 1/714/44–8. The grant to More of South manor and its valuation if leased at rack rents is from *LP* III.ii, no.2239; NA, SC 6/Hen.VII/1076; SC 6/Hen.VIII/5795; SC 6/Hen.VIII/5842. John Roper's view of the appropriate rate for a dowry is from the provisions he made for his own daughters in his will. His appointment as Attorney-General is from *LP* III.ii, no.1389. The warrant is in the form of a signed bill, drafted by the grantee, then presented to Henry by his secretary for signature, then forwarded on to Chancery for enrolment, where it was received on 3 July: NA, C 82/506. The marriage licence is from Chester and Armytage (1887), p.2. William Roper himself confirms that satisfaction for Margaret's jointure was delayed until

March 1534, when the freehold of Butts Close was conveyed to them: Roper (1935), p.79. Contrary to what is often stated, this particular conveyance was not later reversed by Parliament. The description of St Stephen's Walbrook and the names of its clergy are from the churchwardens' accounts: Milbourn (1881), pp.352–9. See also the inventories of church goods: NA, E 117/4/56. The canonical dates permitting weddings are listed in the rubric in *Sarum Missal* (1913), II, pp.143–4. Liturgical rubrics (including the blessing of the bedchamber) are taken from the same source, pp.144–61. Pre-marital courting etiquette is from Fantazzi (2000), pp.155–72. More's letter to Margaret with its tease about his son-in-law is from Rogers, *Corr.*, pp.254–5. His letters to Cranevelt about the embassy to Calais and Bruges are from Miller (1994), pp.7–11, 17–21. My account of the threat of war and European politics relies on Whibley (1904), I, pp.226–36; Anglo (1969), pp.170–206; Knecht (1994), pp.175–82; Wilkie (1974), pp.114–25; Gwyn (1980), pp.755–72. More's account of his editorial advice on the manuscript of Henry's *Assertio* is from his letter to Cromwell: Rogers, *SL*, no.53, p.212. For the context and presentation of the king's book, I have relied on *CW* 5, pp.718–22. The *Assertio* is from *STC* 13070; the presentation is from *STC* 13083. Pace's mission, Wolsey's diplomacy at Rome, and Adrian VI's election as pope are from Wilkie (1974), pp.120–36. Wolsey's accusations against Pace are from *LP* III.ii, no.1713. More's visit to Bruges and the aftermath are from his letters, written from 'the country' on his return: Miller (1994), pp.23–33. The location must be Gobions, not Chelsea as suggested by the editor, since More had not yet purchased or leased any property in Chelsea. The account of More's tertian fever is from Miller (1994), p.25; *CW* 12, pp.88–90, 368–9. The traditional English diagnosis, with symptoms as critiqued by More and Margaret Giggs, is from *STC* 1537, fos.98ᵛ–9. The events after More's return to Court, illustrating the gradual deterioration of his relationship with Wolsey, follow Guy (1980), pp.16–23. Diplomacy with Charles and his visit to England are from Whibley (1904), I, pp.245–57; Anglo (1969), pp.170–206; Knecht (1994), pp.182–4, 200. Greeted by More on behalf of the Mayor and Aldermen, the two sovereigns, magnificently attired in identical surcoats of finest cloth of gold, processed in state from Southwark across London Bridge towards St Paul's. Approaching the Stocks Market, round the corner from Bucklersbury, they were treated to a spectacular, staged entertainment choreographed by John Rastell, culminating in a golden image of 'the Father of Heaven', which descended from the clouds to the singing of a heavenly choir, a placard in his hands bearing the words: 'Blessed are the peacemakers, for they shall be called the Sons of God.' More's unsolicited opinion on foreign policy is taken from Rogers, *Corr.*, no.110. Wolsey's 'loans' and handling of taxation and Parliament are from NA, E 179/ 251/15B; *LP* III.ii, nos.2483, 2485–6; Goring (1971), pp.681–705; Bernard (1986a), pp.110–30; Guy (1988b), pp.1–18. More's petition for free speech in the Commons is from Roper (1935), pp.14–16; Tunstall's speech, possibly written in collaboration with More, is from NA, SP 6/13, fos.2–10; Bridgeman's case is from Rowe (1977), p.xiii. Henry and Wolsey's campaign strategy is from *State Papers* (1830–52), I, p.143; Scarisbrick (1968), pp.128–34; Gunn (1986), pp.596–634. Wolsey's reminder to Henry about the Speaker's fees is from *State Papers* (1830–52), I, p.124. More's letter about Margaret's pregnancy is from Rogers, *SL*, no.35 (p.155). The dedication in the edition of Prudentius is from *CWE* 9, no.1341A (p.310); Roper (1935), p.xxxii; Harpsfield (1932), pp.331–2.

Chapter 15
Margaret's devotions and mealtime readings are from Stapleton (1928), pp.67–8, 97. Her Book of Hours is illustrated in the Holbein miniature of her: MMA, Rogers Fund, 1950 (50.69.2). Thomas More's efforts to secure patronage for Vives are from *CWE* 8, no.1222. Vives's career and writings are from Fantazzi (2000), pp.3–35. His praise of Margaret, her sisters and Margaret Giggs is from his book on women's education: Fantazzi (2000), pp.70–1. More's absence from Bucklersbury during the months of Vives's visit is from Rogers, *Corr.*, nos.115–26; NA, C 82/535–6. His *Answer to Luther* is from *CW* 5, Pts1–2, esp. Pt1, pp.100–298, 300–5, 412–17, 626–9. More revised the book in response to advice from Thomas Murner, the German translator of Henry's *Assertio*: Rogers, *Corr.*, no.115 (pp.276–7); *CWE* 5, Pt2, pp.760–74, 786–8. Margaret's correction of the error in the misattributed letter, with quotations, is from Stapleton (1928), p.113; *STC* 18066, p.184; Harpsfield (1932), pp.81, 332–3. Erasmus's edition of St Cyprian was prepared in 1519 at Louvain and first published in 1521 at Basel. His error can be seen on p.65 of the CUL copies: shelfmarks 3.15.32, F152.a.3.1, Tb.53.3 (all copies dated 1521), and CUL 3.15.34 (dated 1525). In modern editions, the letter is no.30, as in Cyprian (1844), pp.62–8. Novatian is from von Mosheim (1854), II, pp.59–73; Eusebius (1965), pp.280–92. The More family's interest in Eusebius is from BL, Harleian MS 1860; *STC* 18066, p.189 (which associates Margaret with translating the *History* out of Greek, besides her daughter, Mary Basset). Erasmus's colloquy in Margaret's honour is from Thompson (1965), pp.217–23; Furey (2006), pp.14–15. Thomas Elryngton's death and testamentary dispositions (including his funeral arrangements) are from his will: NA, PROB 11/21. Young Alice's pregnancy is from the will, where provision was made for her child. Elryngton's lawsuits, inherited by Thomas More as executor, are from NA, C 1/406/9–10, C 1/546/52; *LP* IV.i, no.366 (p.155). John More's role as Sir Giles Alington's executor and principal land trustee are from Sir Giles's will: NA, PROB 11/22. His death and the infection at Cambridge Castle are from Whibley (1904), I, p.240. His debts and wish to sell his son's marriage are from his will. Alington's composition, Alice's jointure and Thomas More's role are worked out from NA, CP 40/1045, m.137; C 1/546/52; *LP* IV.i,

no.366 (p.155). Conveyancing by Thomas More with Roper's participation is from CP 40/1059, m.151; C 54/397, m.20. The value of Elryngton's estates during the minority of his sons is estimated from the claims made for income and losses during his own minority: NA, C 1/546/52. The attack on the estate and deer at Gobions is from STAC 2/28/68. The affair of Staverton's promotion is from CLRO, MS Repertory 4, fos.63^v–4, 170; MS Repertory 5, fo.360. Staverton's attempts to secure his niece's lands near Bray, Berkshire, and related actions and cross-suits, are from NA, STAC 2/35/17; C 1/537/42; CP 40/1040, m.575; CP 40/1041, mm.16, 215; CP 40/1043, m.537; CP 40/1044, mm.97,140; CP 40/1045, m.665; KB 27/1056, m.67; *LP* IV.i, no.413. For an *ex parte* view of the case from the viewpoint of Staverton's son: NA, C 1/902/35–7. When Isabel (Staverton's niece) died, her younger sister, Eleanor, inherited her claim. Robert Logan, Eleanor's husband, made the counter-claim against Staverton on his wife's behalf, as well as inheriting, and fighting off, legal liability for the alleged breach of covenant by Staverton's niece when she had married. Heron's wardship, his time spent at university, his age, character and easygoing attitude to borrowing to fund his lifestyle, are worked out from NA, C 1/478/33, C 1/645/9–11, C 54/394, STAC 2/16/235, LC 4/5; *LP* III.ii.2900; *LP* IV.i.1533(18); Roper (1935), pp.117–22. His inheritance is from his father's will: NA, PROB 11/21. Anne Cresacre's story is from NA, C 1/491/43–6, C 1/563/15, STAC 2/29/44, SP 1/34, fos.5–8; HEH, Ellesmere MS 2652, fo.13; BL Lansdowne MS 639, fos.56^v–7; *LP* IV.i.1136 (22); Guy (1980), pp.25–6. Henry VIII's intervention denying Constable the right to marry Anne is stated in Wolsey's interim decree from SP 1/34, fos.5–8, where Anne's age is also said to be less than the age of consent for a women to marry, namely twelve; the date of the decree is given in HEH Ellesmere MS 2652, fo.13. The significance of Anne's disavowal in the context of under-age marriages and 'espousals' is explained by Swinburne (1686), pp.40–1, 47–8, 237. Anne's teasing of More for his hair-shirt is from Roper (1935), pp.48–9; Harpsfield (1932), pp.65–6. Her taste in clothes is from Holbein's drawing of her (see illustration). Her lifelong friendship with Lady Alice More is from Muir Wood (2001). More's lease and subsequent resale of Crosby Place are from the Bonvisi deed (private collection), photocopy at NPG; Stow (1956), pp.155–6; Clapham and Godfrey (1912), pp.119–38; Sicca (2002), pp.179–82. Further information on the house is from NA, C 142/121/117. More's lease of the manor of Sutton in Chiswick is from NA, C 1/851/39; Lysons (1795), pp.186–93. More's property deals in Chelsea are worked out from NA, CP 25/2/27/179/16HenVIIITrin, nos.51, 53; C 1/540/78; C 66/715, m.6; PROB 11/21 (will of Meautis). The identity of Keyle, the seller of Butts Close and the wharf, is from Watney (1906), pp.102, 107. Biographical information on Meautis, also steward of Kensington, is from NA, STAC 2/29/154, C 1/415/77, C 1/383/84, C 1/472/36. The land agent Grenville's role is from NA, C 1/533/18; *LP* VII, no.384; his character is from

C 1/803/16–21, C 1/1225/25; *Lisle Letters*, I, p.655; *Lisle Letters*, II, p.195. More hired as his lawyer Robert Norwich, an expert in specific performance: NA, C 1/540/78. My account of landownership in Chelsea and the location of the More estate has been greatly assisted and refined by reference to Croot (2004), pp.14–26, 107–45 (esp. pp.115–18). Other information is from Lysons (1795), pp.79–114, 148. Dr Croot clears up numerous factual errors as to the site and buildings, not least the dire confusion in almost every previous study between More's 'mansion' and the mid-century Winchester Place or 'Great House', later Beaufort House. Scholars previously misled include Clapham and Godfrey (1912), pp.79–103; Norrington (1983), pp.55–65; Guy (2000b), pp.78–9. The plans of the Chelsea estate, made *c.*1595 and now at Hatfield House, refer to Winchester Place, constructed by William Paulet, 1st Marquis of Winchester, who was granted More's estate on his attainder and started building in the garden in mid-century. Although Winchester Place almost certainly incorporated elements of More's newly built garden annexe or 'New Building' containing his gallery and library, this was never the same building as More's 'mansion', which was by the riverside. It is, however, possible that some of the old riverside buildings shown on the plans may equate with remnants of More's 'mansion' and the almshouses beside the gatehouse. Beyond this, the plans offer no guide to the site in the 1520s and 1530s. A catalogue and description of the Hatfield plans is from Skelton and Summerson (1971), nos.160–5. The originals (which I have examined by kind permission of the Librarian and Archivist to the Marquis of Salisbury) are among the Cecil Papers. Butts Close and the house there, later known as the Morehouse, still belonged in 1595 to Antony Roper, who bequeathed them to his son, Henry (NA, PROB 11/90). The location of the site is still evident from the map of 1717 by James Hamilton, Local Studies Map Collection, Royal Borough of Kensington and Chelsea Public Libraries. More's 'mansion' or 'place' is so described from NA, SC 6/HenVIII/7247. His barge and watermen are from Roper (1935), p.52. The garden vista is described by Heywood (1556), pp.13–14; Deakins (1972), pp.4–5. That the move was completed by 1 Oct. is suggested by Richard Hyrde's preface to Margaret's *Devout Treatise*: *STC* 10477, sig.biii^v; DeMolen (1971), p.104. More's appointment by Wolsey and the Council on 6 Nov. 1524 to coordinate the privy searches for Chelsea, Kensington, Knightsbridge and Hammersmith is further confirmation: NA, SP 1/234, fos.118–19 (*LP Addenda*, I, no.430).

Chapter 16

Margaret's book is from *STC* 10477, 10477.5. Khanna (2001) has a facsimile of BL, C.37e.6. An edition in original spelling but with some modernized orthography is by DeMolen (1971), pp.97–124. An argument exists as to whether the first edition is lost. The only known copies are likely to be from the second and

third editions, printed by Thomas Berthelet, undated, but probably issued in
c.1525 and 1531. A 1524 edition is known to have existed from Hyrde's preface,
which speaks of 'the labour I have had with it about the printing', and gives Oct.
in that year as the date of first publication. My description of Margaret's amplifi-
cation of Erasmus and use of vocatives relies on McCutcheon (1987), pp.460–2.
Other textual and literary information is from Gee (1937), pp.257–71; DeMolen
(1971), pp.93–6. Margaret's principles of translation are those she later taught
to her daughter, Mary Basset, taken from BL, Harleian MS 1860, fos.5–7. Her
prior association with Mary Basset's project is from STC 18066, p.189. Quotations from Margaret's book are from DeMolen's edition, pp.104, 105, 106, 108,
109, 111, 112, 113, 114, 115, 116, 117, 118, 122, 123. The collect is from ibid.,
p.117. Hyrde's eulogy of Margaret is from his preface, ibid., pp.97–104, which
also records the circumstances of publication and the date. Biographical
information on Hyrde is from Gee (1937), pp.262–3; Trapp (1990), p.47. The
almshouses are from Stapleton (1928), pp.72–3; Bridgett (1924), p.143. The
grain survey of Chelsea listing foodstocks and the numbers of people fed at
More's house is from NA, E 36/257, fo.55. John Watson as More's steward is from
NA, C 24/52 (Phyllis Parker's deposition). Roper's description of the New
Building is from Roper (1935), pp.25–6. More's work in the court for 'poor men's
causes' with Abbot Islip is from NA, SP 1/19, fo.143 (stamped fo.142). His
retainer from Westminster Abbey is from WAM, MSS 23021, 23023; another
from King's College, Cambridge, is from KCAR MS 3/3/1/1/1, fo.270. John
More's dinner menu is from WAM, MS 33324, fo.36ᵛ. All information relating
to the building works is from examples out of WAM, MS 63509. The recom-
mendations of Vitruvius are from Vitruvius (1511), copy from the Fellows'
Library, Clare College, Cambridge; see also Vitruvius (1692), pp.66–8, 142–3.
More's arrangement of rooms on the Greek model is from Stapleton (1928),
pp.95–6. His prayers with his family and on Good Friday are from Roper (1935),
pp.25–6; Stapleton (1928), p.96. Information on long galleries is from Coope
(1984), pp.446–7; Coope (1986), pp.47–8. Information on the More Chapel is
from Lysons (1795), pp.103–4; NA, E 315/498/1. More's nominee for the post of
rector of Chelsea was John Larke: Lysons (1795), p.114; Brigden (1989), p.354
and n.157. The special licence is from Chester and Armytage (1887), p.2; the
proviso is from Roper (1935), pp.115–16. Heron's coming of age, with the
conditions for the repossession of his lands, is from NA, C 54/394 (indenture
dated 2 July 1525); his grant of livery is from LP IV.i.1533 (18). His trail of debts
is from NA, LC 4/5. More's connection with Sir John Daunce in conveyances of
crown lands is from NA, E 41/528. Their role with John Rastell and John Roper
on legal committees is from NA, C 193/3, fo.95; STAC 10/4, Pt2; KB 9/501–4.
Biographical background on the Daunces is from Bindoff (1982), II, pp.22–4.
The marriage articles and indenture are from NA, C 66/666, m.24 (LP VIII,

no.962 [10]), which also illuminates the timing and the difficulties. The fact that Sir John was determined to recover his bond ten years later after More's execution, and got letters patent to do so, shows how hefty the potential damages must have been. Sir John's mistress is from his will: NA, PROB 11/31. The financial circumstances of his future wife are from the will of her deceased husband, Sir John Skeffington: NA, PROB 11/21. More's request to Wolsey about the Battersea house, with the conditions and William Daunce's promise, is from the transcript of Wolsey's own account: Ellis (1824–46), 2nd series, II, pp.30–2. The 'disputation' before Henry VIII is from Rogers, *Corr.*, no.168 (p.405), where the letter is misdated by the editor. A letter like this, by John Palsgrave, could only have been written while he was Fitzroy's tutor, which is in the narrow frame of late June 1525 to Feb. 1526: Murphy (2003), pp.66–73. Henry's movements are from NA, OBS 1419. Fitzroy's ennoblement is from *LP* IV.i, no.1431 (1–8). The subjects of the More sisters' disputations are from Reynolds (1960), pp.25–6; *STC* 18066, pp.188–9; Stapleton (1928), pp.116–17. Quintilian's versions can be found in Quintilian (1686), pp.1–24, 321–46. The real-life case on bees is *Tutton and Others v. A. D. Walter Ltd.*, Queen's Bench Division, Lewes (1982 T. No.76; 1986 QB 61), hearing dates 8–12 Oct. 1984. Foxford's action against Berthelet is from Reed (1926a), pp.165–6, 169–73. The woodcut of Wolsey's coat of arms is from *STC* 10477, sig.aj^v. Hyrde's friendship with Gardiner is from *LP* IV.ii, no.4090 (p.1809); *LP* IV.ii, no.4103. An earlier translation of the Pater Noster by John Colet is from *STC* 15992, sigs.xiij^v–xx^v. Tyndale's translation of the *Manual* may possibly be identified with *STC* 10479, but the matter is uncertain. A version by him was made while he was with Sir John Walsh at Little Sodbury (*c.*1522). Manuscript copies were in circulation. Tyndale's patron, the merchant Humphrey Monmouth, claimed to have burnt them all, but added that two copies had been given away, one to Fisher. Perhaps seized by Cromwell on Fisher's attainder, this copy could have been the one passed to Cromwell's tame printer, John Byddell, in 1533. More research is needed, but a version by him once existed. Tyndale's early career is from Daniell (1994), pp.64–151. On 25 Oct. 1526 Tunstall sent again for the booksellers, organizing another bonfire at St Paul's, burning 2,000 copies of Tyndale's New Testament and preaching a sermon in which he claimed Tyndale had made 3,000 gross errors of translation: Brigden (1989), pp.158–9; Rex (1989), pp.101–4.

Chapter 17
Suffolk's march on Paris is from Gunn (1986), pp.596–634. Bourbon's revolt is from Knecht (1994), pp.200–15. Giulio de Medici's election is from Wilkie (1974), pp.137–41. The gradual shift in England's diplomacy is worked out from *State Papers* (1830–52), VI, pp.218–488. Wolsey's alliance with France is from *LP* IV.i, nos.1525, 1526, 1531, 1570, 1571, 1573, 1578, 1579, 1595, 1600–4, 1609;

Scarisbrick (1968), pp.135–62; Gwyn (1990), pp.380–410. The tax debacle is from Whibley (1904), II, pp.35–7; Guy (1988a), pp.102–4. Wolsey's retort to the King's Council is from *CW* 12, pp.217–18. A similar story is from Stapleton (1928), pp.136–7; Margaret's account in her letter to her stepsister is from Rogers, *Corr.*, no.206 (p.518). Wolsey's reshuffle is NA, SP 1/37, fos.33–103; Bodleian, MS Laud, Misc. 597; BL, Cotton MS, Vespasian C.14, fos.287–94^v; Guy (1980), pp.26–8. The relevance of the sinecure to More's loss of income is from Guy (1980), p.27. More's final assessment of Wolsey is from *CW* 12, p.213. Francis I's ransom is from Knecht (1994), pp.246–53. More's role as Chancellor of the Duchy and continued presence at Court as a royal secretary are from Guy (1980), pp.19, 28–9. The administration of the Duchy of Lancaster is from Baker (2003), pp.223–4. The Duchy office at Blackfriars is from NA, DL 5/5, fo.258. William Roper's role as an arbitrator in the Court of the Duchy Chamber is from NA, DL 5/5, fo.341^v. His call to the bar at Lincoln's Inn and subsequent inactivity in his career from 1525 to 1534 are from Hogrefe (1932), p.524, n.8. John Roper's death is from NA, E 356/25, m.43. William's 'sinister means' in his probate case and the clash between Warham and Wolsey are from Warham's letters in Galt (1846), appendix, pp.417–19. Warham's imprisonment, ostensibly for debt, is from NA, C 244/168/38B. Roper's lapse into heresy is described by Harpsfield (1932), pp.85–7; Brigden (1989), pp.110, 158–9. Harpsfield, More's first official biographer writing in the 1550s, is the source of the quotation about Thomas More being the man Roper then 'did most abhor' (p.87). Stapleton's account is a whitewash, wrongly suggesting that Roper's apostasy lasted no more than a few days: Stapleton (1928), p.70. As Roper had donated funds to Stapleton's group of Catholic exiles, he would naturally have expected his reputation to be protected. The *Image of Love* is from *STC* 21471.5; *CW* 6, Pt2, appendix A, pp.729–59; Aston (1988), pp.174–81. Its proscription by Tunstall's vicar-general is from Reed (1926a), pp.166–9. More's raids on the German Steelyard are from *CW* 6, Pt2, p.456, n.2; *CW* 7, pp.xxxi–xxxii; *LP* IV.i, no.1962; Elton (1974b–92), I, p.148; Guy (2000b), pp.118–19. Roper's citation before Wolsey's commissaries and his release are from Harpsfield (1932), pp.86–7. More's talk in the garden at Chelsea is from ibid., pp.87–8. Biographical information on Walter Smyth including his love of Chaucer and Boccaccio is from his will: NA, PROB 11/26. His service with More since 1520 is from CLRO, MS Repertory 8, fo.39. Rastell's theatre at Finsbury Fields is from Reed (1926a), pp.16–17 and appendix 8. The *Widow Edyth* is from the first edition: *STC* 22869.7 (deposited at Magdalene College, Cambridge), which also fixes the date. A more readily accessible edition is that of 1573 (*STC* 22870), but there are differences. Many of the topical allusions are explained in depth by Reed (1918), pp.186–99, a fine piece of detective work marred only by its reluctance to discuss (or even mention) the bawdier passages. A later version of the article was incorporated into Reed

(1926a), pp.148–59. More's continued relationship with Sir Thomas Neville is from HEH, Ellesmere MS 2655, fo.18; Guy (1980), p.14. The identification of the house at Foots Cray with John Heron the younger is from his father's will: NA, PROB 11/21. That 'bonus deus, bonus deus' was one of Lady Alice's favourite oaths is from STC 18066, p.307.

Chapter 18

Roper's own account confirms that Thomas More did not give him the money for Margaret's dowry so that a jointure could be purchased for her according to the marriage articles until 1534: Roper (1935), p.79. The marriage of Margaret Giggs and John Clement is from the churchwardens' accounts: Milbourn (1881), p.360. The date must have avoided days prohibited by the Church according to the Sarum rite. It therefore has to have fallen between the week after Epiphany (13 Jan.) and Septuagesima (28 Jan.), since reference to it in the churchwardens' accounts follows their purchase of frankincense for the Three Wise Men and is the final entry preceding the end of the financial year for 1525–6 on the eve of Lady Day (25 March). The Church forbade marriages by banns between the first Sunday in Advent (3 Dec.) and the week after Epiphany, and between Septuagesima and the week after Easter. Easter Day fell on 1 April in 1526. Other information on the Clements is from CW 12, pp.368–9; Reed (1926b), p.330; Reed (1926a), p.48; Woolfson (1998), pp.222–3. Kratzer's cryptic (and admittedly ungrammatical) note is an annotation on Holbein's Basel drawing of the More family group: Müller and Kemperdick (2006), pp.370–1. The arrangements for the Clements at the Barge are from NA, C 1/1337/18–19, C 1/1418/23–6. Joan Staverton's bequest to her goddaughter, Mary Roper, is from Guildhall MS 9171/11, fo.80. Hyrde's departure is from Carley in ODNB (s.v. John Leland). The life of Henry Patenson and his connections are worked out from his will: Guildhall MS 9171/11, fo.93. More's description of 'Master Harry' and his mission to Bruges is from CW 8, Pt2, pp.900–1. Possibly 'Harry' was related to John Patenson of Chelsea: NA, E 312/12/57; Nichols (1867), p.134. Patenson's likeness and description as 'morus' or 'fool' are from Kratzer's notes on Holbein's drawing of the More family group. The fool's close resemblance to Henry VIII c.1525–6 can be seen from a miniature by Lucas Horenbout of the bearded king in the Royal Collection at Windsor Castle, and c.1540 from a chalk drawing in the Staatliche Graphische Sammlung, Munich. The evidence for Rastell's stage and Wolsey's gift of the red buckram is from NA, REQ 2/8/14. Described in the documents as 'an old remnant of red buckram that went about my Lord Cardinal's great chamber, 30 yards', the entry has been incorrectly transcribed in all previous studies of theatre history. Rastell's Four Elements and the printing of his cheeky song are from STC 20722; Milsom (1997), pp.242–3, 254–60, where the wrong STC number is cited on p.256, n.24. Anne Cresacre and John More's betrothal must have been before the spring of 1527, since Anne is by then described as 'sponsa' to John in Holbein's drawing of the family group. Fourteen and sixteen were the commonest ages, even though legally it was possible to consent to marriage at fourteen (for a man) and twelve (for a woman). Information on betrothals *de futuro* and *de praesenti* and on the age of consent is from Swinburne (1686), pp.40–1, 46–7, 56–7. Since the ages given on the drawing of the More family group are '*anno aetatis*' ('in the year of his or her age') they mean 'in his nineteenth year' (i.e. he was eighteen), 'in her fifteenth year' (i.e. she was fourteen), and so on, when the drawing was made. Erasmus's dispatch of Holbein is from *CWE* 12, no.1740. More's reply to Erasmus about the 'painter' is *CWE* 12, no.1770 (pp.417–18). The financial accounts for Holbein's commission and those of Rastell and his associate Clement Armstrong for the Greenwich revels are from NA, E 36/227, fos.11–57ᵛ; SP 2/C, fos.328ᵛ–48. The summary of the revels is from *CSPV* IV, no.105; Whibley (1904), II, pp.84–8; Anglo (1969), pp.211–24; Foister (2004), pp.121–8. Holbein's family-group portrait is described from Ganz (1950), pp.276–84; Foister (2004), pp.9, 24, 46, 54–5, 123, 233, 247–51; Müller and Kemperdick (2006), pp.370–4; Rowlands (1985), pp.69–72, 222–3. I am extremely grateful to Dr Susan Foister of the National Gallery, London, for allowing me to discuss my ideas about the lost wall-hanging and its relationship to the Basel sketch and various Lockey reinterpretations over dinner. I am greatly in her debt, and she is in no way responsible for any mistakes or misunderstandings I may have made. A valuable general introduction to the meaning of the various portraits is by Martz (1990). A useful basic guide to the relationship of the lost wall-hanging to the various copies is Lewis (1998). Holbein's preparatory sketch is Kunstmuseum Basel, Kupferstichkabinett, Inv.1662.31. I am most grateful to the curators of Tate Britain and to the BBC for inviting me to the press preview of the Holbein Exhibition at the Tate in Sept. 2006, when I was able to examine the sketch at the closest possible quarters. Recognition of Kratzer's role in annotation begins with Pacht (1944). My discussion of the positioning of the diagonals relies on Müller and Kemperdick (2006), p.373. The oil painting of More in the Frick Collection in New York is from Rowlands (1985), pp.132–3; Foister (2004), pp.11, 59, 75, 77, 117, 232, 252. I gladly acknowledge the kindness of the curators of the Frick Collection for allowing me to observe the painting at close quarters for over an hour in 2005, and of the late Professor J. B. Trapp and the National Gallery, London, for showing me copies of the X-radiographs. An official report is from *Frick Collection* (1968–2003), I, p.231. The chalk drawings at Windsor are from Parker (1983), nos.1–8. I am most grateful for the opportunity to examine most of them at close quarters at Tate Britain. The later history of the lost wall-hanging is from Cust (1912), pp.43–4; Grossmann (1944); Benesch (1944); Sutton (1947). Other information on the Lockey reproductions is from Kurz (1957), pp.12–16;

Lewis (1998), pp.20–46. I am very grateful to the curators of the National Portrait Gallery, London, for allowing me to read the packet-file on their Lockey reinterpretation as well as examine the ektachromes of the painting before and after restoration. I did a great deal of archival research on the commissioning of the Lockey copies, but as this yielded little bearing on the debate about the contents of the original Holbein version, I will postpone discussion until a later date. I am most grateful to Dr A. J. Timothy Jull of the NSF Arizona AMS Laboratory in the Department of Physics and Atmospheric Sciences, University of Arizona, for kindly supplying information relating to the attempted radio-carbon dating of the Nostell Priory painting by Professor Paul Damon in 1983, and for further advice about the validity of the results of that test which was based on counting, not accelerator mass spectrometry, and required a dilution of the sample. 'The painting speaks' and More's appreciation of classical art theory are from CWE 5, nos.683, 684; Jardine (1993), pp.30–9. The advice of Isocrates is from Elyot (1962), p.37. Information about collars of 'Ss' is from Trapp and Herbrüggen (1977), p.31. A soft fur hat like that worn by Margaret Giggs in the chalk drawing can be seen in the oil portrait of Anne Lovell in the National Gallery, London, also painted by Holbein c.1527 (The Lady with a Squirrel and a Starling): Müller and Kemperdick (2006), pp.378–80. The Aldine edition of Seneca's tragedies is from CUL, Norton.d.188. The dedication is dated 9 Oct. 1517, and the consecutive pages reproduced in the Nostell Priory copy are from fo.94$^{r–v}$. The layout is astonishingly exact. Halfway down fo.94 begins the passage starting 'Fata si liceat mihi' with which the left-facing page in the picture corresponds. Fo.94^v begins: 'Alta dum demens petit', which is the top line of text of the right-facing page in the picture and the line to which Margaret's finger points. 'Alta' is a sixteenth-century variant of 'astra', which has since become the accepted reading. The modern numeration of the legible lines of the Chorus is 882–99 in the Loeb edition: Fitch (2004), p.98. The quotation is from Miller (1917), p.509. The significance of the passage as a statement of the unambitious life is discussed, among many others, by Boyle (1997). The use of the Lutheran hymnal in The Ambassadors is from Foister, Roy and Wyld (1997), pp.40–1. Erasmus's own account of his role in the Aldine edition and of his 'fresh recension' after arriving in England is from CWE 9, no.1341A (p.310). Erasmus's classic reference to 'we must obey fate' is from his letter to Barbier: CWE, 5, p.343. His fascination with Seneca's Oedipus is clear from CWE 1, pp.76, 101, 102, 189, 366; CWE 2, pp.12, 108, 220; CWE 4, pp.58, 328; CWE 5, p.45; CWE 8, pp.362, 496; CWE 12, pp.523, 740. My identification of the other books is based on a viewing of the Nostell Priory painting. I am most grateful to the National Trust and its curators at Nostell Priory, West Yorkshire, for allowing me to examine the picture at close quarters. The exchange of letters between Erasmus and Margaret Roper about the gift to him of the preliminary sketch of the family group is from *OE* 8, nos.2212, 2233, brilliantly discussed by Jardine (1993), pp.30–1. Margaret's letter is catalogued by Enthoven (1906), p.108, and the original is from BUW, MS R.254, fos.153–4ᵛ. More's defiant insistence on the reality of a non-political life was discussed in a review of the 2006 Holbein Exhibition at Tate Britain by Jonathan Jones in the *Guardian*, 26 Sept. 2006. The inversion of More's collar of 'Ss' was first observed by Leslau (1978), *idem* (1981), *idem* (1990–1). In Lockey's copies at Nostell Priory and the National Portrait Gallery, London, inversion is on one side of the collar only, maybe indicating a further alteration in the composition. In Holbein's preparatory sketch, the reversal is complete and clearly visible.

Chapter 19

The events of Wolsey's fall and More's appointment to the Chancellorship are summarized from NA, C 54/398, m.19; Whibley (1904), II, pp.150–65; Harpsfield (1932), pp.38–9; Roper (1935), pp.39–40; Guy (1980), pp.30–3, 97–8; Ives (1991), pp.286–315. More's letter to Erasmus is from Rogers, *SL*, no.43. The divorce and its origins are from Scarisbrick (1968), pp.163–240; Ives (2004), pp.84–126; Starkey (2003), pp.257–367. The Venetian ambassador's description of Anne Boleyn is from *CSPV* IV, no.824 (p.365). More's description of his interview with Henry at Hampton Court is from Rogers, *Corr.*, no.199 (pp.493–5). The date is worked out from Henry's itinerary: NA, OBS 1419. The various 'King's books' or dossiers, iteratively compiled by Foxe and his team, are described by Surtz and Murphy (1988), pp.i–xxxvi. European diplomacy from the League of Cognac to Clement VII's captivity is from Knecht (1994), pp.253–60; Scarisbrick (1968), pp.147–62, 198–202. Wakefield's contribution to the divorce campaign is from Surtz and Murphy (1988), pp.xii–xiii; Rex (1991), pp.165–70. Pace's role as a friend of Wakefield and the use of his library for its pro-conciliar, anti-papal volumes are from Curtis (1996), pp.249–59. The link between Henry's argument on incest and his definition of 'private law' and 'conscience' was discovered by Murphy on whose account I have relied: Surtz and Murphy (1988), pp.xxviii–xxxvi, 167–85, 267–9. The Blackfriars court is from Whibley (1904), II, pp.150–4; Scarisbrick (1968), pp.224–8. Henry's second interview with More on the divorce after his appointment as Lord Chancellor is from More's own account: Rogers, *Corr.*, no.199 (pp.495–7). More's references to 'concealed prophecies' are from Rogers, *SL*, no.4 (pp.34–5); *CW* 6, Pt1, p.146. His views of Antichrist and of Luther and his confederates as his harbingers are from *CW* 6, Pt1, pp.146, 434–5. The 'tokens' of Antichrist are from *STC* 670 and 793.3. For a calculation of the 'number of the Beast' in expectation of the Second Coming by St German, see *CW* 10, p.xx, n.4, and appendix B, pp.384–7. The return of the sweating sickness is from *LP* IV.ii, nos.4332–3, 4360, 4383, 4398, 4403, 4408–9, 4417–18, 4422, 4428–9, 4439–40, 4450, 4452–3; *STC* 4343;

310 A DAUGHTER'S LOVE

Floud (2003), pp.147–76. Margaret's illness is from Roper (1935), pp.28–9; Stapleton (1928), pp.70–1. The prescription is from *STC* 13434 (*s.v.* 'glyster'); *STC* 24721, fo.ccxvi. Henry's progress in Oxfordshire and More's role are from *LP* IV.iii, nos.5911, 5965; Whibley (1904), II, p.154. Information on the fire at Chelsea is from More's letter to Lady Alice: Rogers, *SL*, no.170. Henry's obsession with obedience emerges with his growing frustration with Wolsey in the 1520s and the divorce campaign. The quotation is from *State Papers* (1830–52), I, p.79. Henry's habit of beginning sentences with 'Well' at the beginning of a decisive comment is from *Lisle Letters* (1981), III, p.412. He could speak through his teeth to ambassadors: *CSPSp* IV.i, no.224 (p.350). More's dress at the mass for the opening of Parliament is from *Complete Peerage* (1987), IX, appendix B, p.21.

Chapter 20
The events of the 1529 session of Parliament are from Guy (1980), pp.113–25; Lehmberg (1970), pp.76–104. More's opening speech to Parliament is from NA, C 65/138, m.1; Whibley (1904), II, pp.163–4; *CSPSp* IV.i, no.211 (pp.323–5). Wolsey's submission and partial remission are from Guy (1980), pp.31–3, 126–7. As it turned out, the parliamentary planning that counted wasn't so much Henry's, but arose in the Mercers' Company, where a cell of Lutherans had met to prepare draft laws: Brigden (1989), pp.174–8, 182. George Robinson and Robert Packington led the secret cell: NA, C 1/772/57, C 1/565/74–81, C 1/669/4–5, C 1/673/50, C 1/880/51–2, C 1/830/23, C 1/1153/42–3; PROB 11/27 (will of Packington). The work of the select committees is from Guy (1980), pp.118–20; Lehmberg (1970), pp.81–9, 91–4. Hall's account of the proceedings is from Whibley (1904), II, pp.165–71. The rise of Cromwell is from Guy (1980), pp.130–1, 133–52; Guy (1988a), pp.154–6. Roper's riverside conversation is from Roper (1935), pp.24–5. His election to Parliament is from Bindoff (1982), III, pp.215–17. Henry's dinner party is from *CSPSp* IV.i, no.224 (pp.349–50). The *Dialogue Concerning Heresies* is from *CW* 6, Pt1, pp.3–435. Information on variant editions is from *CW* 6, Pt2, pp.548–87. Topical allusions to More's family at Chelsea are from *CW* 6, Pt2, pp.487–94. The link to William Roper's apostasy is from Anderegg (1976), pp.225–6. More's opinion of the English Bible is from *CW* 6, Pt1, pp.331–42. His scatology against Luther is from *CW* 6, Pt1, p.346; *CW* 8, Pt1, p.262. Other quotations on heresy and heretics are from *CW* 6, Pt1, pp.152, 346, 374–6, 405–10; *CW* 8, Pt1, pp.226–7, 262–3; *CW* 8, Pt2, pp.766–7; *CW* 10, p.23. The 'pissing she-mule' is from *CW* 5, Pt1, pp.180–1. More's lumping together of infidels, Turks, Saracens and heretics is from *CW* 6, Pt1, pp.200, 236, 243, 407; *CW* 8, Pt1, pp.94, 111, 147, 245, 252–3. His defence of violence is from *CW* 6, Pt1, pp.32–3, 405–10. His Star Chamber decree is from BL, Lansdowne MS 160, fo.312. The proclamation is from *TRP* (1964–9), I, pp.193–7, where the appendix of prohibited books from Tunstall's register is

omitted. There were possibly two versions: Guy (1980), pp.171–3; *CW* 6, Pt2, p.883. The trial and public penance of Purser, Somer and John Tyndale are from HEH, Ellesmere MS 2652, fo.15; *CSPV* IV, no.642; *CSPSp* IV.i, no.509; Brigden (1988), pp.33–5; Brigden (1989), pp.183–4. Purser's life is from NA, C 1/691/7, C 1/874/55, C 1/869/1; PROB 11/25 (his will); *LP* V, no.1176; Brigden (1989), pp.190–1, 197, 220, 381–2, 420. Scribbled on the back of a letter to Cromwell in 1529 is the message, 'here hath been Purser two times to speak with you, desiring you that in any ways he may speak with you this night.' The boarding of Dick Purser is from NA, C 1/874/55. His admission to, and expulsion from, More's household follow Brigden (1988), p.35. His appointment as Cromwell's leopard-keeper is from NA, E 36/256, fos.147ᵛ, 155, 161. Somer's life and friendship with Cromwell follow NA, C 1/571/17, C 1/571/18, C 1/571/19, C 1/571/20, C 1/571/21; PROB 11/24 (his will); SP 46/186, fos.38–40; STAC 2/8/1–3; *LP Addenda*, I, no.429; Brigden (1988), p.35; Brigden (1989), pp.183–4, 196, 206, 220, 381–2. He was described to Cromwell as 'your own assured [in] both heart and body', and was known to be honest and wealthy, losing money in some overseas ventures but making a second fortune after marrying the widow of a shipowner trading in Crete. John Tyndale is from NA, C 1/909/54; BL, Harleian MS 425, fo.15; Brigden (1989), pp.111, 171, 183–4, 191, 206, 408. A variant of the same case is from HEH, Ellesmere MS 436. John Petyt's story is from NA, PROB 11/24 (his will); *Narratives of the Reformation* (1859), pp.25–8 (including Lucy Petyt's own account); Bindoff (1982), III, pp.98–9; Brigden (1988), pp.44–5; Brigden (1989), pp.113, 122, 162, 176, 178, 184–5, 188, 196, 205, 220, 229, 381–2. The marriage of Lucy Petyt and John Parnell is from NA, C 1/875/8–10; CLRO, MS Repertory 8, fo.241. The hiring of John Rastell is from NA, C 1/875/8. Some confusion exists as to which wharf was owned by whom. *Narratives of the Reformation* is emphatic that More came to Petyt's house at Lyon's Quay, but the Chancery documents prove that his lease from the Mayor and Aldermen was for Somer's Quay. He most likely had rights to both, as the quays were adjacent beside Billingsgate. Parnell's supply of timber on credit for Rastell's theatre at Finsbury Fields in the parish of St Giles Cripplegate Without is from his will: NA, PROB 11/27. Parnell is from NA, C 1/640/27, C 1/679/33, C 1/553/35, C 1/677/5, C 1/685/39, C 1/869/1, C 1/875/8–10; Brigden (1989), pp.121–2, 158, 197, 229–30, 418, 420. Less conclusive evidence exists for other Londoners allegedly hauled by More into the Star Chamber. Thomas Patmore, a draper, was accused of being John Tyndale's accessory. He was sent on remand to the Poultry, awaiting trial for heresy in the Church courts. Left by the vicar-general to rot in gaol, he was freed three years later. His servant, John Stanton, tried to petition the House of Lords on his behalf. John Field, a fishmonger, was also imprisoned, whether justifiably or not is impossible to judge. He accused More of holding him at Chelsea against his will for eighteen days. He was released, but bound over to appear in the Star Chamber and sent to prison on remand. When he fell sick, he was allowed home, then returned to gaol on the Duke of Norfolk's orders, and finally freed on bail. John Cook was allegedly imprisoned for possessing Tyndale's New Testament, but the facts are hazy. Patmore's case is from NA, LC 4/5 (his loan of £40); PROB 11/20 (his father's will); BL, Harleian MS 425, fo.15; NA, SP 1/70, fos.2–3; *LP* V, no.982; Brigden (1988), p.36; Brigden (1989), pp.121–2, 125, 190, 197, 205–7, 222. Field's case is from NA, SP 1/78, fos.246–7; *LP* VI, no.1059. Cook's case is from HEH, Ellesmere MS 2652, fo.15. Information on Henry and Katherine's separation is from *LP* V, no.340. Barnes is from Foxe (1843–9), V, pp.414–42; *CW* 8, Pt3, pp.1367–414; Brigden (1989), pp.184–5. Grynaeus is from *LP* V, nos.145, 287, 382; Stapleton (1928), pp.62–4. Barnes's stay is from *LP* V, no.593; *CSPSp* IV.i, no.865; *CW* 8, Pt3, pp.1390–5; Brigden (1989), p.185. The close friendship of Barnes and Parnell is from Foxe and from Parnell's will: Foxe (1843–9), V, p.416; NA, PROB 11/27. The best short summary of the heresy law is from *STC* 9518, fos.cxxxvi–cxxxvii. The significa-tion by Warham of Hitton's conviction for heresy leading to the writ *de heretico comburendo* is from NA, C 85/25/23. More's description of Hitton is from *CW* 8, Pt1, pp.14–17; *CW* 8, Pt3, pp.1207–9. Other quotations are from *CW* 7, pp.233–4; *CW* 8, Pt1, pp.16–17, 28, 222, 979; *CW* 10, p.70. Margaret's suggestive idioms in her *Devout Treatise* are from *STC* 10477; DeMolen (1971), pp.94, 106, 107, 111, 113, 115–16, 118, 119, 120. Constantine's case is from *LP* V, 574; *CW* 8, Pt1, pp.10, 18–20; *CW* 8, Pt3, pp.1248, 1470–1, 1247–8; *CW* 9, pp.118–19; Guy (1980), pp.166–7. Bayfield's case is from *LP* V, 583; *CW* 8, Pt1, pp.10, 17–18; *CW* 8, Pt3, pp.1183–4, 1247–8, 1385, 1468–71; *CW* 9, p.113; *ODNB* (*s.v.* Richard Bayfield). Tewkesbury's case is from *LP* V, no.589; *CW* 8, Pt1, pp.21–2, 518; *CW* 8, Pt3, pp.1247–9, 1251, 1471; *CW* 9, pp.29, 94, 322, 363, 368; *STC* 11225, II, p.1026 (col.2, transcript from Bishop Stokesley's register). Although Foxe's opinions in his *Acts and Monuments* are heavily biased towards the Protestants, his transcripts of documents are reliable: Foxe (1843–9), IV, pp.643–52, 664, 670–1, 688–94, 697–707; V, pp.3–11, 18–26, 29, 99–100, 181. Further heresy cases are those of James Bainham and Thomas Bilney. Bainham, like John Rastell a former pupil of St German, had been overheard calling St Thomas Becket 'a damnable traitor'. He was arrested by More and sent to the Tower. Nicknaming him 'Bainham the jangler' (i.e. chatterer or idle talker), Thomas handed him over to the Church court, which found that he'd denied the doctrines of purgatory and the mass. Initially recanting, Bainham afterwards reaffirmed his Protestant beliefs and was burnt: *LP* V, no.583; *CW* 8, Pt1, pp.518; *CW* 8, Pt2, pp.590, 710; *CW* 8, Pt3, pp.1251, 1645; *CW* 9, pp.29, 88, 94, 322, 438; Corrie (1845), pp.221–4. More ordered a judicial review of Bilney's burning in the Lollards' Pit at Norwich after hearing that the city's Mayor had threatened to petition Parliament. Summoning eyewitnesses into the Star Chamber and forcing them to answer his interrogatories on oath, More concluded that Bilney, when faced by 'the fire of hell', had recanted his heresies. But to reach that conclusion, he was forced to rule much of the evidence he'd collected inadmissible: NA, SP 1/66, fos.296–317; SP 1/68, fos.45–52, 80–5, 86–9; *LP* V, nos.372, 522, 560, 569; *CW* 8, Pt1, pp.23–6, 518; *CW* 8, Pt3, pp.1140, 1143, 1151, 1157, 1163, 1170–1, 1183, 1198, 1247, 1249, 1251, 1344–5, 1370, 1377, 1471, 1642; *CW* 9, pp.93, 229, 245, 304, 311, 356, 364, 369, 373; Guy (1980), pp.167–73. The Protestant reaction to More's policy is from *CW* 6, pp.30–3. Erasmus's claims that no heretic had been burnt by More are from *OE* 10, nos.2750, 2780. More's letter putting him right and enclosing the epitaph by which he wished to be remembered is from *OE* 10, no.2831; Rogers, *SL*, no.46. The words of the epitaph, afterwards etched in stone on the More family vault at Chelsea, could still be read in 1631. By 1795, however, they'd been sanitized, the stone slab replaced by another declaring that More had been 'grievous' only to 'thieves and murderers': *STC* 25223 (pp.522–3); Lysons (1795), pp.83–4.

Chapter 21

Useful background to More's career as Lord Chancellor is from Guy (1977b), pp.275–92; Guy (1980), pp.37–93. Information on the More family's seats in Parliament is from Bindoff (1982), I, pp.307–8; II, pp.23–4, 350–1; III, pp.176–9; Lehmberg (1970), pp.29–31. Since Rastell lacked Cornish connections, the Duke of Norfolk may have intervened there too, or perhaps More's friend, Bishop Vesey, who had so admired Margaret's work when Thomas had 'accidentally' discovered it, in whose diocese Dunheved lay, was the intermediary. The private Act for Roper's will is from *Statutes of the Realm* (1810–28), III, pp.309–15; NA, C 54/398, m.6; Hogrefe (1932), pp.529–33. The legal view of primogeniture in Parliament is from Spelman (1976–7), II, intro., pp.208–9. The lands finally given to Christopher Roper descended to his son, John, and can be worked out from NA, C 54/917; C 1/1353/10–11; C 1/1468/43. William's share is described in NA, C 142/181/122; WARD 7/20/72. Daunce's complaint as reported by Roper is from Roper (1935), pp.40–2; Guy (1980), pp.80–1. His eviction of the caretaker's family is from Wolsey's letter to Cromwell, demanding redress: Ellis (1824–46), 2nd series, II, pp.30–2. Heron's suits in Chancery are from NA, C 1/643/32–3, C 1/626/20–3, C 1/645/9–11. More's decree and later proceedings against Heron are from NA, C 1/626/20–3 (endorsements), and his order for contempt with threat of imprisonment in the Tower is from NA, C 54/400 (entry for 18 Dec.1531). Roper's comments are from Roper (1935), pp.42–3. Heron's true inheritances from his father are listed in the latter's will: NA, PROB 11/21. His borrowing is from NA, LC 4/5. The case against Staverton is from NA, C 1/612/42. John Rastell's suit with the injunction endorsed on the bill is from NA, C 1/671/27. Antonio Bonvisi was also rebuffed by More. His business interests were so extensive, litigation involving him carried on more or less continuously, and the petition he delivered to his old friend was relatively trivial, concerning a small supply of fine claret. More left the case in the pile: NA, C 1/605/25. The case of the disgruntled suitor is from NA, C 1/706/34. The dinner and meeting about injunctions are from Roper (1935), pp.44–5; Guy (1980), pp.81, 87–90. John More's final salary instalment is from NA, E 356/26, m.38ᵛ. His bequests are from NA, PROB 11/23. Among them were silver plate and a set of twelve silver spoons for Elizabeth Rastell, and £5 for Margaret Roper. The Gresham suit and cup are from NA, C 1/636/50–2; Roper (1935), pp.60–3; Guy (1980), pp.82–3. In 1980 I suggested the donor might be John Gresham, also a mercer, but I had not then spotted the documents in C 1/636/50–2. Gresham's biography and links to the Mores are from *ODNB* (*s.v.* Sir Richard Gresham). The case of the Vaughans against Parnell is from NA, C 1/685/39–41, C 1/553/35, C 1/587/15, 41; Roper (1935), pp.61–3; Guy (1980), pp.75–7. Cross-suits by Parnell are from NA, KB 27/1082, m.37; CP 40/1063, m.17. The information about Kite is from Parnell's will: NA, PROB 11/27. Other litigation involving Parnell that might have shaped More's opinion of him is from NA, C 1/640/27, C 1/679/33, C 1/677/5. Parnell as a vintner to the Boleyns is from the creditors listed in his will: NA, PROB 11/27.

Chapter 22

The parliamentary manoeuvres of 1531 are from Scarisbrick (1956), pp.22–39; Guy (1982), pp.481–503; Lehmberg (1970), pp.105–30; Guy (1980), pp.136–8, 148–51. Foxe and Cranmer's updated dossier (the so-called 'Collectanea satis copiosa') is from BL, Cotton MS, Cleopatra E.6, fos.16–135; Nicholson (1977), pp.74–214; Guy (1980), pp.131–6, 138–9, 141, 143, 145, 150, 156–7; Fox and Guy (1986), pp.151–69; Nicholson (1988), pp.19–30. More's advice to Cromwell on awakening sleeping giants is from Roper (1935), pp.56–7. The proclamation against bulls from Rome is from *TRP* (1964–9), I, no.130; *CSPSp* IV.i, nos.433 (p.727), 539; *CSPV* IV, no.621; Brigden (1989), p.184. William Tracy's case is from *Concilia* (1737), III, pp.725, 746–7; Lehmberg (1970), p.117; Bindoff (1982), III, pp.471–2. The Coventry connections of Rastell and St German are from NA C 1/159/34; C 1/270/22; *CPR* Henry VII, Pt1, p.604; *CPR* Henry VII, Pt2, p.419; *LP* I.i, no.1662 (24); Guy (1985), pp.6–7. St German's call is from St German (1974), pp.176–7. Biographical information on him is from Guy (1985), pp.3–94; *CW* 10, pp.xxix–xlvi. The Coventry heresy trials are from McSheffrey and Tanner (2003), pp.3–47, 322–42. St German's critical analysis of the heresy law is from *CW* 10, pp.xlvii–xcii. An example of a forced abjuration for 'vehement suspicion' is from the first trial of Thomas Bilney: Guildhall MS 9531/10, fo.120. St German's proposals for legislation on heresy and the English Bible are from NA, SP 6/7, fos.28–38 (formerly pp.55–74); Guy (1980), pp.151–6; Guy (1985), pp.25–8, 127–35. Rastell's heresy bill in the Commons, written in his own inimitable handwriting throughout, is from NA, SP 2/N, fos.20–2. It proposes that trials in the Church courts should no longer be allowed without at least two witnesses. Heresy suspects should be told the exact nature of the allegations against them, and in writing, together with the names of their accusers; and should be granted bail and legal counsel for their defence. Most sensationally and devastatingly, the bishops were to be restricted to the pre-trial investigation of heresy, stripped by Parliament of their right to sit in judgement. All suspects would have to be tried in the royal courts by 'due process of law' and with a jury. Only then could the penalty of a burning be sought. I provisionally dated this document to 1529 in my introduction to *CW* 10, pp.lviii–lix, at which time I was not in possession of genuine examples of Rastell's handwriting. It is now clear the writing is Rastell's, and the date cannot be before 1530, when he still held traditional Catholic opinions, as is made plain by *STC* 20719. As there was no session of Parliament in 1530, the bill cannot have been submitted before 1531. It might, conceivably, have been submitted in 1532 rather than 1531, but as Rastell was working hand-in-glove with St German, as is also argued by Bindoff (1982), III, p.178, an attribution to 1531 is most likely. Bindoff's co-editors were not, it seems, aware of Rastell's independent bill, but discuss the link between the two men over St German's draft. Bibliographical information on William Rastell's edition of More's *Dialogue Concerning Heresies* is from *CW* 6, Pt2, pp.556–75. William's new fount of type can be clearly seen in *STC* 18085, which also establishes the date; see also Reed (1926a), pp.76–8. William's edition of the *Dialogue* is stated to have been begun in '1530' (i.e. before 25 March 1531), and finished in 'May 1531': *CW* 6, Pt1, p.3, 435. More's statement in Parliament before the House of Lords is from *LP* V, no.171; *CSPV* IV, no.664; his speech in the Commons is from Whibley (1904), II, p.185; Lehmberg (1970), pp.128–30; Guy (1980), pp.156–8. The opinions of the universities are from Whibley (1904), II, pp.185–95; Surtz and Murphy (1988), pp.5–27. Foxe and Cranmer's research was afterwards published on 7 November 1531: Surtz and Murphy (1988), pp.31–273. Roper's account of More's self-doubt and inclination to resign is from Roper (1935), pp.50–1. Chapuys' favourable opinion of More is from *LP* V, no.120; *CSPSp* IV.ii, no.646. Charles V's letter to More is from Schulte Herbrüggen (1966), no.183A (p.97); *LP* V, no.148; Guy (1980), pp.159–60. Chapuys' attempt to deliver the letter is from *LP* V, no.171. The ruling of the Faculty of Law at Paris is from *LP* V, no.424; the ceremony at Chelsea is from NA, E 30/1017. Audley's draft bill is from NA, SP 2/N, fos.155–62. Cromwell's first draft bill is from NA, SP 2/N, fos.163–4. Lee's oath as Archbishop of York is from NA, E 30/1019. A paper by Foxe and Cranmer underpinning Cromwell's bill on annates is from BL, Cotton MS, Cleopatra E.6, fos.274–5; Nicholson (1977), pp.139–44. The bill on annates is itself not extant, but its likely contents can be

worked out from the version of the Act brought into effect by Henry's letters
patent in 1532: 23 Hen.VIII, *c.*20. Cromwell's observation on the progress of the
bill is from Merriman (1902), I, p.343. Henry's appearances and calls for votes
in both Houses of Parliament are from *LP* V, nos.879, 898. The Commons'
'Supplication' is from NA, SP 6/7, fos.105–14, 114ᵛ–19; SP 2/L, fos.193–292;
SP 6/1, fos.90–103. The 'Answer' of the prelates is from NA, SP 6/7, fos.120–42;
Concilia (1737), III, pp.750–2. The draft of a second 'Answer' that may not have
been presented is from BL, Cotton MS, Cleopatra F.1, fos.101–3; *Concilia* (1737),
III, pp.752–3 (citing the older foliation of the Cotton MS). The debate of the
'Supplication' in Parliament is from Whibley (1904), II, pp.202–5, 210–12.
Modern accounts of the parliamentary manoeuvres are by Elton (1974b–92),
II, pp.107–36; Cooper (1957), pp.616–41; Kelly (1965), pp.97–119; Lehmberg
(1970), pp.138–42, 145–53; Scarisbrick (1968), pp.297–300; Guy (1980),
pp.186–200. Peyto's sermon and its aftermath are from *LP* V, nos.941, 989;
CSPSp IV.ii, nos.934, 948. Henry's articles imposing conditions on Convocation
are from *Concilia* (1737), III, p.749; Kelly (1965), pp.112–13. The Commons'
delegation with Audley as Speaker to Henry at Whitehall Palace is from Whibley
(1904), II, pp.210–12. The title of Cromwell's bill for the resumption of the
liberties of the prelates is known from NA, SP 1/74, fos. 146–7. The bill itself
would seem to be NA, SP 2/L, fos.78–80 (draft corrected by Cromwell); SP 2/P,
fos.17–19 (fair copy incorporating the changes of the draft). More's opposition
with Gardiner as reported by Chapuys is from *LP* V, no.1013; *CSPSp* IV.ii, no.951
(where the original French of the crucial passage is on p.446). The events leading
to Convocation's submission are described from *Concilia* (1737), III, pp.753–5;
Kelly (1965), pp.114–17; Lehmberg (1970), pp.151–3; Guy (1980), pp.199–201.
Henry's ultimatum is from NA, SP 1/70, fo.38. The official description of More's
resignation is from NA, C 54/401, m.24 (*LP* V, no.1075). More's own account is
from his later letter to Henry VIII: Rogers, *SL*, no.52 (p.202). Chapuys' account to
Charles V is from *LP* V, no.1046. Roper's account is from Roper (1935), pp.51–2.
Audley's release of the Protestants is from *OE* 10, no.2780; Brigden (1989), p.197.
More's letters explaining away the circumstances of his resignation are from
OE 10, nos.2659, 2831; Rogers, *SL*, nos.45, 46.

Chapter 23

The family conference is from Roper (1935), pp.52–5. As after the fire three years
earlier, Thomas More found new jobs for all those he made redundant, in the
case of his oarsmen by donating his barge to Audley. The Mayor of London hired
Walter Smyth as his ceremonial sword-bearer and gave 'Master Harry' Patenson
a civic pension: CLRO, MS Repertory 8, fo.39; Repertory 9, fo.113ᵛ; Repertory 10,
fo.27ᵛ. Patenson ended his days in the service of Sir Richard Gresham, where he
got into further scrapes: CLRO, MS Repertory 10, fo.59. More's chest pains are

from Rogers, *Corr.*, no.197 (p.488). His jests about diets and begging are from Roper (1935), pp.53–4. His prank in the pews is from Roper (1935), p.55. Information on the Clements is from Reed (1926b), pp.329–39. The special licence for Anne Cresacre and John More to inherit Anne's lands after their marriage is from *LP* V, no.318 (24). Joan Alleyn and Dorothy Colley are from Rogers, *Corr.*, no.218 (p.564). 'Sir Edmond' is from NA, C 24/52 (Phyllis Parker's deposition). Rastell's conversion to Protestantism is from Reed (1926a), pp.220–2. His fervent Protestant beliefs are from his will: NA, PROB 11/26. He was converted by John Frith, a young disciple of Tyndale, who was supposed to be on remand in the Tower, whereas a sympathetic gaoler was letting him make clandestine visits into London at night. More wrote a 10,000-word denunciation of Frith: Brigden (1989), p.188; Rogers, *Corr.*, no.190; *CW* 7, pp.cxviii–clix, 231–58. Other information is from Whibley (1904), II, pp.261–3. Rastell's suits against the Mores, Richard Staverton and Puncheon, and Widow Alice's defence are from NA, C 4/46/11, C 4/20/81, C 1/883/8. A related (later) suit is NA, C 1/880/9. The NA catalogue entry stating that C 4/20/81 in reply to Rastell should be dated post-1548 is wrong: dead men cannot file lawsuits in their own name! At issue was money allegedly recouped fraudulently from Rastell: some cash, and the cash equivalent of a silver-gilt cup, both given when the Rastells had left Milk Street for Coventry. Puncheon, Judge John's factor after Rastell had sailed for the New World, had later sold Rastell's surplus ship's tackle, then handed the proceeds to Judge John (see chapter 11). Thomas Shaa's inheritance of Markhall is from NA, C 1/1317/26. His marriage to Puncheon's daughter, making him Puncheon's son-in-law, is from Puncheon's will: NA, PROB 11/26. Rastell's mining project, with Cromwell's share in the syndicate, is from *LP* VII, no.923 (pp.345, 354); NA, E 41/219. His letters to Cromwell are from *LP* VII, nos.1071–3; Reed (1926a), pp.23–4. Payments of More's annuity are from NA, E 405/102–4. His income is from Roper (1935), p.55. The meeting at Calais is from *CSPV* IV, no.824; Knecht (1994), pp.297–302. Henry and Anne's secret marriage is from Whibley (1904), II, pp.221–3. Their plighting of troths, the date and its relationship to the secret marriage are worked out by MacCulloch (1996), pp.637–8. Cromwell's role in the Act of Appeals is from Lehmberg (1970), pp.161–81; Fox and Guy (1986), pp.151–78. The opposition of More's friends and family to the Act is from NA, SP 1/99, fo.234 (stamped fo.202); *LP* IX, no.1077. Cranmer's annulment of Henry's marriage to Katherine is from *LP* VI, nos.528, 529. More's remark on oaths is from Roper (1935), p.57. Christopher Roper's career as Cromwell's servant is from Robertson (1975), p.552; *LP* XIII.ii, no.857 (possibly misdated). His wood purchases from Cranmer are from his will: NA, PROB 11/42B. Rastell's service is from *LP* V, nos.955, 1151. Giles Alington's role at the coronation banquet is from Bindoff (1982), I, p.307. More's fable is from Tacitus's *Annals of Imperial Rome*: Roper (1935), pp.58–9; Chambers (1935), pp.292–3. Parnell's complaint about the Vaughan cup is from Roper (1935), pp.61–3. The Gresham cup is from Roper (1935), pp.63–4. Protestant accusations against More appear in *CW* 9, pp.84–172, and are fully developed in Foxe's *Acts and Monuments* (or *Book of Martyrs*): Foxe (1843–9), IV, pp.643–52, 664, 670–1, 688–94, 697–707; V, pp.3–11, 18–26, 29, 99–100, 181. More's exoneration by the King's Council is from *CW* 9, p.127. The fact that Cromwell was central to the investigation is made clear by his own remarks on the examination of heretics to More in Tower: Rogers, *SL*, no.64 (pp.251–2). Foxe's retraction of the worst accusations comes, with other retractions, in the second edition of the *Book of Martyrs* in 1570: Guy (2000b), p.108. More confessed to flogging Dick Purser and the mentally deranged man in *CW* 9, pp.117–18. His denial of violent abuse is from *CW* 9, p.118. His hatred of the 'vice' of the heretics is from *CW* 9, p.167. Princess Elizabeth's birth is from *State Papers* (1830–52), I, p.407. Elizabeth Barton's case is from Rogers, *SL*, nos.47, 50, 51, 53 (p.206), 54 (p.222); *LP* VI, nos.1419, 1464, 1465, 1466, 1519, 1546; *LP* VII, no.522; Bernard (2005), pp.87–101. Henry's excommunication by the pope is from *LP* VI, no.953. Hales's letter to Cromwell is from *LP* VI, no.1148. The law of treason is from Elton (1972), pp.263–92. The inclusion of More and Fisher in the bill of attainder is from Rogers, *SL*, nos.50, 51, 52, 53; *LP* VII, nos.48, 52, 107, 238, 239, 240. The police raid on William Rastell's shop is from *CW* 10, pp.xvii–xxvii. More's letter to Cromwell dated 1 Feb. is from Rogers, *SL*, no.49. The chronology of More's publications in late 1533 is verified from *CW* 11, pp.xvii, lxxxvi–lxxxvii. The *Articles* are from Pocock (1870), II, pp.524–31; Elton (1972), pp.180–3, 206–9. More's *Apology* is from *CW* 9, pp.3–172; reinforced by his *Debellation of Salem and Bizance*: *CW* 10, especially pp.7, 76–83, 133–6. More's exhortation to maintain the 'old faith' and not the 'new' is from *CW* 9, pp.168–9. His letter to Cromwell about the bill of attainder is from Rogers, *SL*, no.50. His petition against the bill and the proceedings of the commissioners are from Roper (1935), pp.64–71; Lehmberg (1970), pp.194–6. The Act of Attainder is 25 Hen.VIII, *c*.12. Roper's message to Margaret is from Roper (1935), p.71. More's quotation from Salimbene de Adam is from his *Chronicle*, p.453, line 2 (MS Cronica, fo.339, col.c) in Brepolis Library of Latin Texts (CLCLT) at http://clt.brepolis.net. Salimbene's biography is from Schulman (2002), pp.388–90; background is from Barraclough (1966), pp.231–3. The Act of Succession is from NA, SP 2/P, fos.33–127; 25 Hen.VIII, *c*.22. More's conversation with Norfolk is from Roper (1935), pp.71–2. Walter Marsh is from Lyell and Watney (1936), pp.433, 480, 487, 512, 524, 528, 559, 680, 683, 696, 710, 752, 754, 761–2. More's first conveyance of his property to trustees is from Bodleian, MS Ch.Middlesex.a.2, fo.35 (formerly numbered 96). The legality is discussed by Derrett (1965), pp.19–26, but as Derrett writes following Roper, without seeing More's deed now in the Bodleian Library, my account differs in some respects. The second conveyance to William Roper is not extant, but is described by Roper (1935), pp.79–80. The property conveyed is from *CPR*, Edward VI, I, pp.67–8. Dorothy Colley and John Harris, later her husband, were able to tell the story of More's macabre dinner during their exile at Louvain: Stapleton (1928), p.159. More's speech to his family asking for their support is from Roper (1935), pp.55–6. The pursuivant's visit to find More at Clement's house is from Stapleton (1928), p.160; *CW* 12, p.368. Stapleton erroneously states this was Palm Sunday.

Chapter 24
More's long letter to Margaret describing the events at Lambeth is from *EW*, pp.1428–30 (Rogers, *SL*, no.54). Henry's choice of commissioners is from *LP* VII, no.392. More's note on perjury, made in the Tower, is from *CW* 6, Pt2, appendix B (p.765). The swearing of members of Parliament on 30 March with the form of the oath annexed is from *LJ* (1767–1846), I, p.82; *LP* VII, no.391; Whibley (1904), II, p.260; Lehmberg (1970), p.199. Stapleton's defence of William Roper, Giles Heron, and 'John' [*recte* William] Daunce as conscientious objectors is factually incorrect: Stapleton (1928), p.215. The topography of Lambeth Palace is from *Survey of London* (1951), pp.81–103. Cranmer's letter to Cromwell is from Cox (1846), no.107. Cromwell's letter to Cranmer is from Merriman (1902), I, no.71. Fisher gave his reasons for refusing the oath: Van Ortroy (1893), pp.136–7. More's journey to the Tower and reception are from Roper (1935), pp.74–7. Fisher's incarceration is from Van Ortroy (1891), p.166; Van Ortroy (1893), pp.137–43. The topography of the Bell Tower and description of More's cell are from Bayley (1821), pp.133–4; Bell (1877), pp.66–91; Keay (2001), pp.27–39, and plan 1. More's riposte to Walsingham is from Roper (1935), p.77. Walsingham's career is from *ODNB* (*s.v.* Sir Edmund Walsingham). He was the brother of William Walsingham, neighbour and friend of the children of Joan Bowes, Judge John More's third wife, who successfully beat Richard Rich to the post of common serjeant of London while More was Henry's secretary. The costs of More's board and lodging are from BL, Cotton MS, Titus B.1, fo.155 (*LP* XII.ii, no.181). Wood is from NA, SP 1/93, fos.47, 49; Roper (1935), p.75. Information on the 'picture in parchment' and algorism stone is from Rogers, *SL*, no.66. More's second, shorter letter to Margaret from the Tower is from *EW*, pp.1430–1 (Rogers, *SL*, no.55). William Roper's sudden interest in his career at Lincoln's Inn in and after 1534 is from Roper (1935), p.xxxiv; Hogrefe (1932), p.524, n.8. The miniatures are from MMA, Rogers Fund, 1950 (50.69.1) and (50.69.2). I have followed the standard authorities in preferring to attribute dating on the basis of Margaret's age as recorded by Holbein, except that 'anno aetatis' means 'in the year of her age' and thus she is still twenty-nine, and not thirty. William Roper was several times misleading about his age, and I believe Holbein's date of 'anno aetatis 42' (meaning William was forty-one) is

mistaken by four or five years. Roper's true age in 1534 was thirty-six, relying on his own sworn testimony: NA, C 2/Eliz/B9/60; C 2/Eliz/C23/47; C 24/57–60; Roper (1935), p.xxxi. Margaret's wish to be in John Wood's stead is from Rogers, *Corr.*, no.203. More's thoughts about death and the dangers of seeking martyrdom are from Rogers, *SL*, no.64 (p.253); Rogers, *Corr.*, no.206 (pp.529–30). Margaret's ruse to gain access to her father in the Tower is from Stapleton (1928), p.114. Her reservation in taking the oath is from *EW*, p.1441 (marginal note). The concession to the Carthusians is from Marshall (2006), p.217. That Margaret alone had a licence to see her father is confirmed by More himself: Rogers, *SL*, no.57. Stapleton was aware of More's deeply ambiguous reaction to it: Stapleton (1928), pp.162–8. More's rebuke of Margaret is from Rogers, *SL*, no.56. His fears and thoughts in the Tower are from Rogers, *Corr.*, nos.202, 206, 208; *CW* 13, pp.clxxvi–clxxvii. In particular, his fears of 'eager' martyrdom relate to the division of opinion in the Catholic Church between the views of St Ignatius of Antioch, who strongly recommended willing martyrdom, and his critics. Others discussing the topic, including St Ambrose, Origen and St Augustine, agree that martyrs should show confidence, fortitude and constancy. The greatest danger is fear or despair, and anyone dying in despair cannot be a martyr. St Thomas Becket is among those criticized by some authorities for seeking martyrdom out of spiritual pride. Margaret's intercepted letter is lost, but its contents can be worked out from her father's reply: Rogers, *SL*, no.56; Rogers, *Corr.*, no.202. The building works at the Tower are from *LP* VII, no.1011. Bonvisi's gifts are from NA, SP 1/93, stamped fo.46ᵛ (I was allowed to transcribe this extremely difficult and damaged document under ultra-violet light by courtesy of the NA). The gifts and tokens from Lady Conyers and Margaret Giggs are from Rogers, *SL*, no.66. The subornation of George Gold to carry messages, with the advice of More and Fisher regarding what he should say if he was caught, is from NA, SP 1/93, stamped fo.46. Corroboration is from SP 1/93, stamped fo.42ᵛ. Other arrangements in the Tower are from the depositions in SP 1/93, stamped fos.41–50. Clement's prescriptions and Bonvisi's help are from SP 1/93, stamped fo.48. More's own illnesses are from Rogers, *Corr.*, no.206 (pp.514–15). Margaret's arrival, her prayers with her father and the topics of their conversation are from Rogers, *Corr.*, no.206 (p.515). More's *Dialogue of Comfort* is from *CW* 12, pp.3–320; Miles (1966a), pp.7–33; Miles (1996b), pp.556–60; Elton (1978), pp.399–404. The suggestion that Margaret is the model for 'Vincent' is from Miles (1966a), pp.18–19. The fable of the ass, the wolf and the fox is from *CW* 12, pp.114–18. Alice Alington's letter to Margaret is from Rogers, *Corr.*, no.205. Aesop's fable of the Lion King (from Caxton's translation) is from *STC* 175, fos.lxvᵛ–lxvi. Annoyed by an ape, the Lion King finds a false pretext to put him to death. He wants all his subjects to say that, 'because ye be king, all is at your commandment'. The moral (according to Caxton's translation) is, 'It is perilous and harmful to be in the fellowship of a tyrant . . . and well happy is he that may escape from his bloody hands.' That was More's situation exactly, and nobody could have failed to see it. Although the character of the Lion King is skirted by More and Margaret, we can be sure it dominated their thoughts as they made up their stories. The long 'letter' of Margaret Roper to Alice Alington is from *EW*, pp.1434–43; Rogers, *Corr.*, no.206.

Chapter 25

The vile weather is from *LP* VII, nos.1257, 1457, 1516, 1529. Complaints against Henry and Anne include Ellis (1824–46), 3rd series, II, pp.332–4; *LP* VII, nos.454, 630, 953, 1090, 1609; Lehmberg (1970), p.200. The attacks on the friars and the monasteries are from *LP* VII, nos.590, 650, 807, 841, 856, 939, 953, 977, 1020, 1057, 1090, 1095, 1307, 1488, 1607; Knowles (1959), pp.202–11; Youings (1971), pp.145–7. Cromwell's warning to Margaret is from Rogers, *Corr.*, no.206 (p.529). The Act of Supremacy is 26 Hen.VIII, *c.*1 and the Act of Treason is 26 Hen.VIII, *c.*13 (*STC* 9386). The original MS of More's attainder is HLRO, MS HL/PO/PU/1/1534/26H8n22; the printed version (wrongly numbered) is 26 Hen.VIII, *c.*23; Elton (1972), pp.402–3. The eyewitness report is from NA, SP 1/93, stamped fo.40. Cromwell's list of the committee's membership is from NA, SP 1/87, fo.106ᵛ; Bindoff (1982), I, pp.12, 732. More's encounter with Lady Alice in the Tower is from Roper (1935), pp.82–3; Harpsfield (1932), pp. 95–6. Her view of her husband's scruple of conscience is from Rogers, *Corr.*, no.212. Vives's letter to Erasmus is from *OE* 10, no.2932. More's solitary confinement after his attainder is from Rogers, *Corr.*, nos.209 (p.539), 210 (p.540). The search at Chelsea is from Rogers, *Corr.*, no.210 (p.540). A copy of the valuation of the properties is incorporated into NA, SC 6/HenVIII/7247; SC 6/HenVIII/7249. Sir John Daunce's petition for the return of his daughter-in-law's marriage articles is from NA, C 66/666, m.24. Lady Alice's petition is from Rogers, *Corr.*, no.212. Her income, and in particular the value of the rents in Hitchin, is worked out from NA, E 179/141/127, E 179/141/131, covering the period 1540–2, by which time her annual income was £50, including an annuity of £20 from Henry granted in 1537, so making the annual value of her rents £30. More's gifts to Fisher are from NA, SP 1/93, stamped fo.42ᵛ, and arrangements for Fisher's meals are from stamped fo.46. There is a scribal error in the manuscript, which appears to suggest that the value of the gold coins was £2,000 sterling. This is impossible. The sheer weight of such a hoard alone would rule this out, as at the prevailing exchange rate, so many gold coins would have weighed 30 kilos. The confiscation of Fisher's property is from NA, SP 1/93, stamped fos.106–11. Margaret's conversation with Audley is from Van Ortroy (1893), pp.153–4. Cromwell and Audley's deception is from Van Ortroy (1893), pp.152–3. More's letter to Leder is from Rogers, *SL*, no.62. 'Master' Leder is identified as one of the Six Clerks in

Chancery from NA, C 1/537/30, C 1/1028/16–19, C 1/1452/62–3; STAC 4/6/77. His role as Lady Alice's unpaid legal adviser is from NA, C 24/52. More's letter to Nicholas Wilson is from Rogers, *SL*, no.58. Letters between More and Margaret between 16 Jan. and 2/3 May 1535 are from Rogers, *Corr.*, nos.209, 210, 211, 214. More's opening letter to Margaret in this phase is lost, as is her second reply to him, but the gist of the missing documents is evident from the replies. I believe More's letter of 2/3 May (no.214) to have followed on almost immediately from his previous letter (no.211), so that no reply is missing at that point. An invaluable guide to the events underlying the differing phases of these clandestine letters is from the later confessions of Gold and Wood: NA, SP 1/93, stamped fos.46, 49. Robert Fisher's visit to the Tower on 2 Feb. (Candlemas) with the message carried by Gold to More about the Acts is from SP 1/93, stamped fos.40–43ᵛ. More's annotations in his psalter and Book of Hours are from Beinecke Rare Book and Manuscript Library, Yale University, MSS Vault More; Trapp and Herbrüggen (1977), pp.116–17. Margaret's devout prayer is from Rogers, *Corr.*, no.211 (pp.544–5); *CW* 13, pp.clvi–clvii. More's extended meditation on the same theme is from *CW* 13, pp.228–31. His Latin commentary on Christ's agony in the Garden of Gethsemane, known as *De Tristitia Christi*, is from *CW* 14, Pt1, pp.3–681. My interpretation and More's quotation rely on *CW* 14, Pt2, pp.774–6. The arrests and interrogations of the Carthusian priors and Reynolds are from *LP* VIII, nos.565, 566. Rastell's failed efforts to convert the Carthusians are from *LP* VIII, no.600. Whalley is from *LP* VIII, nos.600–2; Robertson (1975), p.586. Feron and Hale are from *LP* VIII, nos.565, 567. Their trials are from NA, KB 8/7, Pt1 (incorrectly calendared in *LP* VIII, no.609); Harpsfield (1932), pp.229–30. Roper's nomination to the jury is from KB 8/7, Pt1, fo.6. There can be no mistake, as William Roper is listed as 'armiger' or Esquire, which clinches the identification. For Roper's status as Esquire, see also NA, C 24/52 (interrogatories and depositions *ex parte* 'William Roper armiger'), and Roper (1935), p.xl. William had lately acquired the right to call himself 'Esquire' as a newly promoted bencher and officer-holder at Lincoln's Inn: Roper (1935), pp.xxxiv, xl. A check of the tax records for Middlesex confirms that he was the only 'William Roper, Esquire' in the county. The affair of the London civic election is from *LP* IV.ii, no.2639. Richard Rich's connections to Bucklersbury and St Stephen's are from the will of George Gowsell, grocer and churchwarden: NA, PROB 11/21. More himself said he'd known Rich for many years and they'd lived in the same parish. His doubts about Rich's character are from Roper (1935), pp.87–8. Cromwell's interrogation of More on 30 April is from Rogers, *SL*, no.63. Margaret's visit to the Tower on 4 May is from Roper (1935), pp.80–1. The execution of the Carthusians, Reynolds and Hale is from *LP* VIII, nos.661, 666; *CSPSp* V.i, no.156; *CSPM* I, no.965; Guildhall MS 1231; Wines (1998). Margaret's pregnancy is from *State Papers* (1830–52), I, pp.434–5. Antony's benediction from the *Dialogue of Comfort* is from *CW* 12, p.34. The two silver bowls are from Antony Roper's will: NA, PROB 11/90. Lady Alice's petition to Cromwell, also mentioning that the plague had touched Chelsea, is from Rogers, *Corr.*, no.215. Henry's six-week deadline is from *CSPSp* V.i, no.156.

Chapter 26

Fisher's appointment as a cardinal is from *LP* VIII, no.742; Van Ortroy (1893), pp.162–3. Margaret Roper's message to Fisher and Bonvisi's sources of information are from NA, SP 1/93, stamped fos.45, 46, 46^v, 47^v, 48^v, 50. The official minutes of More's interrogation by Cromwell and others on 3 June 1535 are from NA, SP 2/R, fo.20 (formerly fo.24). More's own account of the scene is from Rogers, *SL*, no.64. The circumstances under which he wrote this letter are from NA, SP 1/93, stamped fo.49, which quotes from it. Fisher's use of the metaphor of a 'two-edged sword' on 3 June is from Harpsfield (1932), p.273. Cromwell's interrogation of the Tower servants, who briefly quote from the clandestine correspondence and messages between More and Fisher and describe how the letters were burnt, is from NA, SP 1/93, stamped fos.42^v, 43^v, 44^v, 45, 45^v, 46, 47, 49–50. Their evidence about the letters from More to Margaret is from SP 1/93, stamped fos.46, 49. The Council's irritation with Walsingham for his laxity is from SP 1/93, stamped fo.44. Rich's own handwritten description of his visit to the Tower to confiscate More's books with his transcript of their conversation is from NA, SP 2/R, fos.20–1 (formerly fos.24–5). The document is damaged by damp and vermin, and I am most grateful to the staff of the NA for allowing me to transcribe it under ultra-violet light. Roper's retrospective account of the visit is from Roper (1935), pp.84–6, but this is tainted by what Rich, according to Roper's informants, gave in evidence at More's trial. For what happened on 12 June alone, Rich's own memo is to be preferred, not just because it was written at the time and sent to Cromwell, but because it makes it clear that More had said little, if anything, that was new. The memo also tallies closely with More's indictment: Harpsfield (1932), appendix 3, pp.269–76. Any change in the evidence was thus made on the day of the trial after the indictment had been read out in court. Rich's visit to Fisher, in which he tricked him into denying the king's title by inviting him to send Henry a confidential message by way of spiritual counsel, is from Van Ortroy (1893), p.161; Harpsfield (1932), pp.232–4, 238–9. More's swipe against Rich for claiming it was all the same to deny the Act or keep silent is from *State Papers* (1830–52), I, p.434. The official minutes of More's interrogation of 14 June are from *State Papers* (1830–52), I, pp.433–6. Fisher's trial is from NA, KB 8/7, Pt2; Van Ortroy (1893), pp.170–88; Harpsfield (1932), appendix 1, pp.236–41 (where William Rastell is the author). Henry's expenditure on physic for Fisher and the use of the barge are from Van Ortroy (1893), pp.166, 170. Cromwell's notes or 'remembrances' for his interview with Henry after Fisher's trial are from BL, Cotton MS, Titus B.1, fo.475 (new foliation). The official record of More's trial is from NA, KB 8/7, Pt3. Roper's retrospective, second-hand account is from Roper (1935), pp.86–96. Roper is valuable, but must be used with caution as he was writing in Mary Tudor's reign when the key issue of principle for which More was said to have died was the papal supremacy, not the subordination of Parliament to the 'general faith' and unity of Christendom as a whole. The all-important jury list in More's trial is from NA, KB 8/7, Pt3, fo.5. Palmer, Spert, Lovell and Chamber are identified from *LP* VIII, nos.12, 816, 1148; *LP* XII.ii, nos.490, 783, 835, 852, 857, 1060 (p.373); Bindoff (1982), III, pp.54–6; *ODNB*, (*s.v.* Sir Thomas Spert). There is proof that Cromwell was rigging juries: his 'remembrances' in connection with Fisher's trial include the note, 'Item, to remember Sir Wa[l]ter Hungerford in his well doings': BL, Cotton MS, Titus B.1, fo.475 (new foliation). The official trial records show that this same Hungerford was a juror for Fisher's trial: NA, KB 8/7, Pt2. He had also been on the jury for the trial of the Carthusian priors: NA, KB, 8/7, Pt1. This cannot be a mere coincidence. More's appearance as he walked into court is from *LP* X, no.975. My reconstruction of the court proceedings is based on the following sources: KB 8/7, Pt3; Roper (1935), pp.86–96; the so-called 'Paris Newsletter'; and the Latin reports circulating in Europe shortly after the trial, of which the best and fullest is the so-called 'R'. The 'Paris Newsletter' is from BNF, MS FF 1701 (fos.185–90), 2832 (fos.191–3), 2960 (fos.64–70), 2981 (fos.44–5), 3969 (fos.63–7), 12795 (fos.29–32), 16539 (fos.30–3). The edited text of MS FF 2981 is from Harpsfield (1932), appendix 2, pp.258–66. The edited text of 'R' is from Derrett (1960), pp.214–23. The circulation of news of More's death was extremely fast as is documented by the multiple copies of the 'Newsletter' around in Paris and Rome. A copy supplied to the Vatican in Italian is from ASV, Archivum Arcis, Arm I–XVIII, MS 3265 (I am most grateful to Dr Jessica Sharkey of Clare College, Cambridge, for this information and for a transcript of fo.108). The best modern account of the trial is by Derrett (1964a), pp.449–77. I have followed Derrett's exemplary reconstruction with very few exceptions, as considered in Guy (2000b), pp.186–205. The events of More's return journey to the Tower and his reunion with Margaret on Tower Wharf are reconstructed from Roper (1935), pp.97–9; 'Paris Newsletter', in Harpsfield (1932), appendix 2, p.265; *LP* X, no.975. The Old Swan is from Stow (1956), pp.206, 214, 217. The narrow, seldom-used drawbridge enabling prisoners to enter the Tower from Tower Wharf is from Stow (1956), p.46. The procedure for executions at the Tower is taken from Van Ortroy (1893), pp.187–96. Although this describes Fisher's execution, it reflects the system then in operation. More's farewell letter to Margaret is from Rogers, *SL*, no.66. His delivery of his hair-shirt is from Roper (1935), p.99. Morton's list of special festivals at Oxford is from Amici (2004), p.179. Becket as the patron saint of the Mercers' Company is from Watney (1906), pp.3, 119, 142, 159–60.

Chapter 27

The attack on Henry from abroad is from *LP* X, no.975. Cromwell's prepared speech for the ambassador in Rome is from *State Papers* (1830–52), VII, pp.633–6; *LP* IX, no.240. More's execution is from Roper (1935), pp.100–3; Harpsfield (1932), appendix 2, p.266. The sycophantic Edward Hall's retrospective account is full of hoary legends at More's expense: Whibley (1904), II, pp.265–6. An analysis of the scaffold speech, based on the notes of the representatives from the French embassy and published as the so-called 'Paris Newsletter', is from Guy (2000b), pp.209–11. More's burial is from Roper (1935), p.101; Stapleton (1928), pp.213–14. Margaret's intention of printing her father's collected works is from Cresacre More: *STC* 18066, p.364; Reed (1923), p.38. Erasmus's theory linking 'letters', biography and reputation is from Jardine (1993), pp.171–89. The copies of More's early drafts of letters to Henry VIII and Cromwell are from Rogers, *Corr.*, nos.198, 199. Margaret Giggs's charity to the Carthusians is from Knowles (1959), pp.235–6; Durrant (1925), pp.184–6. The interrogation of Geoffrey Pole and his servants is from *LP* XIII.ii, nos.695 (pp.264, 266–7), 828 (pp.334–5), 830 (p.342). Margaret's examination by Cromwell is from *STC* 18066, p.364. Cresacre More merges this with her examination about recovering More's head from its pole in Stapleton (1928), pp.213, 215, but the incidents are more likely to be separate. Henry's act of Parliament reversing More's deed of trust is from HLRO, MS HL/PO/PU/1/1535/27H8n54; the printed version (wrongly numbered) is 27 Hen.VIII, *c*.58. Of the two leases slipping through Cromwell and Henry's net, one relates to the Battersea farm, the other to the manor of Sutton near Chiswick. More's lease of Battersea, the valuation (showing a rent of £5 6s. 8d. and profits in excess of £20 per annum), with accounts and acquittances, are from WAM, MSS 22905, 30647, 30698, 30722, 30758, 30792, 30795, 30824, 30846, 30910, 30947, 30956, 30973, 30991, 31026, 31038, 31045, 31067, 31073, 31237, 31259, 31943, 32094, 33609. Information relating to Sutton is from NA, C 1/851/38–40. The feud between Roper and Lady Alice is from NA, C 3/1531/1–3, C 24/52. Roper's lease is from E 315/213, fo.48; *LP* XVI, no.1500 (p.727). The depositions of Phyllis Parker and Margery Hillary are from NA, C 24/52. Roper's position in the manorial court is from NA, SC 2/188/42. Henry's grant of the Chelsea estate to the courtier, Sir William Paulet, is from NA, C 66/668, m.15 (*LP* X, no.777 [5]). That Lady Alice had, however, obtained a licence to stay for up to ten years notwithstanding Paulet's grant is from NA, SC 6/HenVIII/7247. Henry's grant to her of the lease for twenty-one years of a nearby smaller property, once part of the More estate, to encourage her to leave is from NA, C 66/715, m.6 (*LP* XVII, no.714 [2]). Lady Alice's backdated pension of £20 is from NA, C 66/671, m.23 (*LP* XII.i, no.795 [28]). Heron's case is from *LP* XIV.i, nos.358, 1219; *LP* XIV.ii, nos.359, 424, 494 (p.176), 554; Lehmberg (1977), p.102. His family's petitions are from NA, SC 12/11/21; *LP* XV, no.450. His debts and the valuation of his lands are from NA, SC 12/11/21. Margaret's invitation to Ascham is from Vos (1989), pp.248–51. Ascham mentions Henry Cole and John Christopherson as tutors to Mary, but Christopherson was appointed by William Roper after his wife's death. Cole's links to the Ropers are from Ballard (1775), p.37; Guildhall MS 9171/11, fo.80 (will of Joan Staverton); NA, PROB 11/45 (will of Richard Alington of Lincoln's Inn); *ODNB* (*s.v.* Henry Cole). Mary remembered Harris with tangible affection in her will: NA, PROB 11/54. Harris and Colley had drafts and copies of other letters and papers from More, which they took into exile at Louvain. Their daughter, Alice, married John Fowler, a printer. See the notes to chapter 6. William Rastell's career and his marriage to Winifred Clement are from Reed (1923), pp.39–45. His folios include a book printed from Judge John More's collected notebooks: *STC* 20836. The plot against Cranmer is from *LP* XVIII.ii, no.546 (esp. pp.297–9); *LP* XIX.i, no.444 (5–6, 11); Stapleton (1928), p.216; Graves (1913), pp.4–9; Zell (1976), pp.241–54. Roper's pardon is from *LP* XVII, no.267 (p.147). Margery Hillary's account of Margaret's death is from NA, C 24/52. A plague epidemic was raging in London and Westminster: *LP* XIX.ii, no.246. William Roper's brief note about her burial is from his will: NA, PROB 11/60. Margaret Roper's bequests are from Durrant (1925), 184–6; *CW* 14, Pt2, p.717; will of Mary Basset from NA, PROB 11/54; will of William Roper from NA, PROB 11/60. Leland's accolade is from Ballard (1775), pp.34–5; Ascham's is from Vos (1989), pp.249–50. Tax records show that Roper had moved his household out of Butts Close before May 1545: NA, E 179/141/138, 146, 160, 167, 173, 180. Roper's lawsuit with Bonvisi, in which they were represented by William Rastell, is from NA, C 1/1259/30–4. The affair of Cakehill Lane in the manorial court was recounted by the elderly deponents in a later Chancery case: NA, E 133/10/1523 (7th interrogatory and depositions). Stevenson may be the same man mentioned as an Eltham freeholder and juror in the case of Cakehill Lane. Stephen Clerke, his father Walter, and uncle John, all of Hadleigh in Suffolk, are from *LP* XX.ii, no.1068 (44); PROB 11/37 (will of Walter Clerke, with bequests to Mary Clerke née Roper); Craig (1999), pp.17–19. The marriage of Roper's nephew is from Bindoff (1982), I, p.325. Mary Clerke's translation of Eusebius is from BL, Harleian MS 1860, fos.1–379. It must have been made in the late 1540s, because it is dedicated to the 'Lady Mary', her title under Henry VIII after the Boleyn marriage. The translation of *De Tristitia* is from *CW* 14, Pt2, appendix C, pp.1077–165. The flight of the Clements, Rastells and Antonio Bonvisi to Louvain is from NA, C 1/1337/18, C 1/1337/20, C 1/1418/23–6; NA,

C 142/94/24, C 142/121/117; Reed (1923), pp.41–3; Reed (1926a), pp.87–9; Reed
(1926b), pp.329–39; Graves (1913), pp.9–12. Cranmer's role in Edward VI's reign
is from MacCulloch (1996), pp.351–553; the iconoclasm is from Brigden (1989),
pp.423–33. A semi-official context for Ralph Robinson's 1551 translation of
Utopia is from Gywn (1984), pp.18–24, and from my own work in progress.
A good idea of the work undertaken towards the 1557 folio at Louvain is
from *EW*, sig.Cii–Cii^v; *CW* 12, pp.xxviii–xlix. The 1553 *Dialogue of Comfort*
is from *STC* 18082; *CW* 12, pp.xlix–lvii. A second folio, this time containing
More's Latin works, appeared at Louvain in 1565, published by Jean Bogard.
Rastell may have contributed to it, although he was dead by the time it was
printed. More likely, Harris furnished Bogard with materials: *CW* 2, pp.xlviii–l.
The editors speak only of 'the works which have come into our hands': *Opera
Omnia* (1565), title page. Since William Roper sat as a member for Rochester in
the first Parliament of Edward's reign, and as a magistrate in Kent and Middlesex, he must have sworn the obligatory oaths of supremacy and allegiance: *CPR*,
Edward VI, I, pp.85–6; Bindoff (1982), III, pp.215–17. Winifred Rastell's death
is from Reed (1923), p.43. Further information on Mary Clerke is from her
father-in-law's will: NA, PROB 11/37. Her father-in-law, despite his grumpiness,
was a zealous Catholic and had been one of Queen Mary's most loyal gentry
backers in the first fortnight of her reign, when Edward's councillors had plotted
to exclude her from the succession. Mary Clerke sat in a place of honour at the
coronation, becoming a gentlewoman of the privy chamber and a personal
friend of the queen. Her husband, Stephen, must have been dead before his
father's will was made in March 1552, since she is already described there as
'widow, late the wife of my son Stephen Clerke'. Her place of honour at Queen
Mary's coronation is from *Revised CSPD, Mary* (1998), no.20. She had married
James Basset by June 1556: Bindoff (1982), I, pp.392–4. His political significance
is from Beer and Jack (1974), pp.117, 119, 139, 141; *Revised CSPD, Mary* (1998),
nos.163–4, 171, 177, 181, 188, 207–8, 218, 237, 252, 257, 266, 269, 275, 285, 289,
252. Further information is from their wills: NA, PROB 11/54 (Mary Basset);
PROB 11/42A (James Basset). Pole's income and expenditure accounts for 1556–7
are from *Revised CSPD, Mary* (1998), nos.659, 662, 665. The gifts and rewards
for 'divers of his kin and others' are from ibid., no.662. Rastell's preface is from
EW, sig.Cii–Cii^v. The exiles under Elizabeth are from Graves (1913), pp.10–20;
Reed (1923), pp.45–7; *CW* 2, pp.xlviii–l. Roper was appointed to royal commissions until 1568, when he was arrested again on suspicion, but released, when
nothing could be proved against him: *CSPD* (1856–72), I, pp.311, 347; Bindoff
(1982), I, pp.215–17. His purchase of the lordship and manor of Farningham is
from NA, C 54/531. His possessions at his death are from NA, C 142/181/122;
NA, WARD 7/20/72. Roper's *Life* is from *STC* 21316; Roper (1935), pp.3–104.
The ways in which More's stance on the papacy was doctored to fit the priorities

of the 1550s is from Guy (2000b), pp.7–9, 186–205. The *Life* began as 'notes' for the use of Nicholas Harpsfield, whom Roper commissioned to write the official Catholic biography of More. Some ambiguity exists over the chronology. Roper evidently wrote the 'notes' after Harpsfield showed him a first draft of his commission. Harpsfield refers halfway through to Rastell's 1557 folio as still in preparation (Harpsfield [1932], pp.xlv, 100), saying that it will 'shortly' be printed, and yet he also quotes from Roper's notes, which cite Rastell's printed folio as if it had already appeared. Harpsfield had finished his biography by 1557 or 1558, but when Elizabeth turned the country Protestant, he was sent to the Fleet prison. His biography circulated in manuscript, but wasn't printed until 1932: Harpsfield (1932), pp.xxi–ccxiv. William Rastell also began a biography, perhaps intended as a sequel to the 1557 folio (and possibly as a rival to Harpsfield's), but all trace had disappeared by the eighteenth century, a few fragments apart. All that is known is that it ran to three books, one of which had fifty-eight chapters: Harpsfield (1932), pp.ccxv–ccxix, 237–8. That William Roper lacked copies of More's Tower letters is proved by the fact that, when writing his own memoir, he had to send for the copies that William Rastell printed in *EW*: Roper (1935), pp.73, 84. Roper's will is from NA, PROB 11/60. Information about the removal of Margaret Roper and her father's head to the vault beneath the Roper Chapel, about the inscription and the arrangement of the vault is from Canterbury Cathedral Archives, MS Dcb/E/F/Canterbury, St Dunstan/37; Albin (1979–80), pp.29–35.

BIBLIOGRAPHY

Early English Books, 1460–1640

STC 175 (1484). Aesop, *Here begynneth the book of the subtyl historyes and fables of Esope whiche were translated out of Frensshe in to Englysshe by wylham Caxton at westmynstre in the yere of oure Lorde M.CCCC.[l]xxxii[i]j*, London

STC 670 (1525). Anon., *Here begynneth the byrthe and lyfe of the moost false and deceytfull Antechryst*, London

STC 783 (1525). Arnold, Richard, [Chronicle] *In this booke is conteined ye names of the baylyfs custose mayers and sherefs of ye cyte of london from the tyme of kynge Richard the fyrst*, London

STC 791 (1503). Anon., *The book intytuled The art of good lywyng [and] good deyng*, Paris

STC 792 (1505). Anon., *[The crafte to lyue well and to dye well]*, Westminster

STC 793.3 (1505). Doesborch, Jan van, *Here beginneth a lytel treatyse the whiche speketh of the xv. tokens the whiche shullen bee shewed afore ye drefull daye of judgement. And who that our lorde shalt after chenyng of euery body of his wordis, workis and thoughtes. And who oure lorde wyll shewe us other in tokens of his pasion, to theym that been deyeth in dedely synne*, Antwerp

STC 832 (1570). Ascham, Roger, *The scholemaster or plaine and perfite way of teachyng children, to vnderstand, write, and speake, the Latin tong but specially purposed for the priuate bryngyng vp of youth in ientlemen and noble mens houses, and commodious also for all such, as haue forgot the Latin tonge*, London

STC 1537 (1537). Anglicus, Bartholomeus, *Anno. M.D.XXXV. Bertholomeus De proprietatibus rerum*, 2nd edn, London

STC 3363.8 (1620). Billingsley, Martin, *A Newe booke of copies containing divers sortes of sundry hands, as the English and French secretarie, and bastard secretarie, Italian, Roman, chancery, and court hands / set forth by the most excellent writers of the sayd hands for the instruction of the vnskilfull*, London

STC 4115 (1510). [Borough, John], *Pupilla oculi o[mn]ibus presbyteris precipue Anglicanis summe necessaria: per sapientissimu[m] diuini cultus moderatore[m] Iohannem de burgo quonda[m] alme vniuersitatis Cantabrigien. cancellariu[m]: et sacre pagine professore[m] necno[n] ecclesie de Colingam rectore[m]*, London [printed Paris]

STC 4343 (1552). Caius, John, *A boke, or counseill against the disease commonly called the sweate, or sweatyng sicknesse*, London

STC 4602 (1516). Hilton, Walter, *Here begynneth the kalendre of the newe legende of Englande*, London

STC 5317.5 (1535). Cicero, Marcus Tullius, *Florentii Voluzeni scholia seu com[m]entariorum epitome in Scipionis somnium ad egregium Gregorium Crumvveluum*, London

STC 5758 (1479). [Denys the Carthusian], *Thus endeth the prologue of this book named Cordyal. Whiche treteth of the four last and final thinges that ben to come*, Westminster

STC 5759 (1496). [Denys the Carthusian], *Here after foloweth the prologue of the foure last thynges. [Cordiale quattuor novissimorum]*, Westminster

STC 7677 (1511). Anon., *Of the newe la[n]des and of ye people founde by the messengers of the kynge of porty[n]gale named Emanuel Of the. x. dyuers nacyons crystened. Of pope Iohn and his landes, and of the costely keyes and wonders molodyes that in that lande is*, Antwerp

STC 9386 (1534). [Parliament], *Anno XXVI. Henrici VIII. Actes made in the session of this present parlyament holden upon prorogation at Westm[inster], the .III. day of Noue[m]bre, in the. XXVI. yere of the reygne of our moste drad soueraigne lorde kynge Henry the VIII*, London

STC 9515.5 (1519). Rastell, John, *The statutes prohemium Ioha[n]nis Rastell: i[m]pri[n]tid by ye same Iohn[n] ye xxv day of october in ye xi yere of ye reyn of our souereyn lord kyng he[n]ry the viii wyth ye pryuylege of our seyd souerei[n] lord grau[n]tyd to ye seyd Iohn[n]*, London

STC 9518 (1527). Rastell, John, *The statutes prohemium Iohannis Rastell*, 2nd edn, London

STC 9599 (1514). Rastell, John, *Tabula libri assisaru[m] [et] pl[ac]itorum corone*, [London]

STC 9991 (1480). [Caxton, William], *In the yere of thyncarnacion of our lord Ih[es]u crist M.CCCC.lxxx. and in the xx. yere of the regne of kyng Edward the fourthe, atte requeste of dyuerce gentilmen I haue endeauourd me to enprinte the cronicles of Englond as in this booke shall by the suffraunce of god folowe*, London

STC 10477 (*c.*1525). Roper, Margaret, *A deuoute treatise vpon the Pater noster, made fyrst in latyn by the moost famous doctour mayster Erasmus Roterodamus, and tourned in to englisshe by a yong vertuous and well lerned gentylwoman of. xix. yere of age*, 2nd edn, London

STC 10477.5 (1531). Roper, Margaret, *A deuoute treatise vpon the Pater noster made first in latyn by the moost famous doctour mayster Erasmus Roterodamus, and turned into englishe by a yo[n]ge vertuous and well lerned gentylwoman of xix yere of age*, 3rd edn, London

STC 10479 (1533). [Tyndale, William], *A booke called in latyn Enchiridion militis christiani, and in englysshe the manuell of the christen knyght replenysshed with moste holsome preceptes, made by the famous clerke Erasmus of Roterdame, to the whiche is added a newe and meruaylous profytable preface*, London

STC 10894 (1521). Fisher, John, *The sermon of Ioh[a]n the bysshop of Rochester made agayn the p[er]nicious doctryn of Martin luther w[i]t[h]in the octaues of the asce[n]syon by the assigneme[n]t of the most reuerend fader i[n] god the lord Thomas Cardinal of Yorke [and] legate ex latere from our holy father the pope*, London

STC 10954 (1514–17). Fitzherbert, Anthony et al., *[La graunde abbregement de le ley]*, 3 vols, London

STC 11225 (1583). Foxe, John, *Actes and monuments of matters most speciall and memorable, happenyng in the Church with an vniuersall history of the same, wherein is set forth at large the whole race and course of the Church, from the primitiue age to these latter tymes of ours*, 2 vols, London

STC 12472 (1502). Anon., *Manipulus curatorum*, London

STC 12510.5 (c.1531). Anon., *Disputatio inter clericum et militem super potestate prelatis ecclesiae atq[us] principibus terrarum commissa sub forma dialogi*, London

STC 12766.7 (1543). Hardyng, John, *The chronicle of Ihon Hardyng in metre, fro[m] the first begynnyng of Engla[n]de, vnto ye reigne of Edwarde ye fourth where he made an end of his chronicle. And from yt time is added with a co[n]tinuacion of the storie in prose to this our tyme*, London

STC 13079 (1521). *Assertio septem sacramentorum aduersus Martin. Lutheru[m], aedita ab inuictissimo Angliae et Franciae rege, et do. Hyberniae Henrico eius nominis octauo*, London

STC 13083 (1521). *Libello huic regio haec insunt Oratio Ioannis Clerk apud Ro.pon.in exhibitione operis regij. Responsio roman.pont.ad. eandem ex tempore facta. Bulla ro.pon.ad regiam maiestatem, pro eius operis confirmatione*, London

STC 13434 (1525). Brunschwig, Hieronymus, *The noble experyence of the vertuous handy warke of surgeri, practysyd [and] compyled by the moost experte mayster Iherome of Bruynswyke, borne in Straesborowe in Almayne . . . Item there after he hath authorysed and done it to vnderstande thrugh the trewe sentences of the olde doctours and maysters very experte in the scyence of surgery*, London

STC 14043 (1507). Hilton, Walter, *Scala perfectionis*, London

STC 14286 (c.1531). [Cranmer, Thomas and Foxe, Edward], *Grauissimae, atq[ue] exactissimae illustrissimaru[m] totius Italiae, et Galliae academiaru[m] censurae efficacissimis etiam quorundam doctissimorum uiroru[m] argumentationibus explicatae, de ueritate illius propositionis,* London

STC 14287 (c.1531). [Cranmer, Thomas and Foxe, Edward], *The determinations of the moste famous and mooste excellent vniuersities of Italy and Fraunce, that it is so vnlefull [sic] for a man to marie his brothers wyfe, that the pope hath no power to dispence therewith,* London

STC 15609.3 (c.1516). Lily, William, *Guilielmi Lilii Angli Rudimenta Paruuloru[m] Lilii nuper Impressa [et] correcta,* [York]

STC 15635 (c.1512). Linacre, Thomas, *Linacri progymnasmata grammatices vulgaria,* [London]

STC 15992 (n.d.). Anon, *The prymer of Salysbery use, bothe in Englyshe and in Laten,* Antwerp

STC 16208 (1527). Anon., *Missale ad vsum insignis ac preclare ecclesie Sarum vna cu[m] dicte ecclesie institutis, co[n]suetudinibusq[ue] nuper elimatissime impressum. Adiectis plurib[us] que i[n] ceteris desiderantur,* Paris

STC 17964 (1495). [Mirk, John], *Incipit liber qui vocatur festiualis de nouo correctus et impressus,* Paris

STC 17973.5 (1519). Mirk, John, *Here begynneth the festyuall,* London

STC 18066 (c.1631). More, Cresacre, *The life and death of Sir Thomas Moore Lord high Chancellour of England. Written by M. T.M. and dedicated to the Queens most gracious Maiestie,* Douai

STC 18076 (1557). [More, Thomas], *The workes of Sir Thomas More Knyght, sometyme Lorde Chauncellour of England, wrytten by him in the Englysh tonge,* London

STC 18082 (1553). More, Thomas, *A dialoge of comfort against tribulacion, made by Syr Thomas More Knyght, and set foorth by the name of an Hu[n]garie[n], not before this time imprinted,* London

STC 18085 (1531). More, Thomas, *A dyaloge of syr Thomas More knyghte: one of the counsayll of our souerayne lorde the kyng and chauncelloure of hys duchy of Lancaster Wheryn be treatyd dyuers maters, as of the veneracyon [and] worshyp of ymagys [and] relyques, prayng to sayntis, [and] goynge on pylgrymage. Wyth many other thyngys touchyng the pestylent secte of Luther [and] Tyndale, by the tone bygone in Saxony, [and] by the tother laboryd to be brought in to England. Newly ouersene by the sayd syr Thomas More chauncellour of England,* 2nd edn, London

STC 19897.7 (c.1510). Pico della Mirandola, Giovanni, *Here is co[n]teyned the lyfe of Johan Picus erle of Myra[n]dula a grete lord of Italy an excellent co[n]ning man in all scie[n]ces [And] vertuous of lyuing. with dyuerse epistles [and] other warkis of the seyd Johan Picus full of grete science vertew and wysedome,* [London]

STC 20701 (1523). Rastell, John, *The exposicions of [the] termys of [the] law of england [and] the nature of the writts with diuers rulys [and] principalles of the law as well out of the bokis of Mayster Littelton as of other bokis of the law gaderyd and breuely compyled for yong men very necessarye,* [London]

STC 20719 (1530). Rastell, John, *A new boke of purgatory whiche is a dyaloge [and] dysputacyon betwene one Comyngo an Almayne a Christen man, [and] one Gyngemyn a turke of Machoinett law, dysputynge by naturall reason and good philosophye, whether there be a purgatorye. which boke is deuyded into thre dyalogys*, London

STC 20722 (c.1525). Rastell, John, *A new iuterlude [sic] and a mery of the nature of the .iiii. element declarynge many proper poynt of phylosophy naturall, and of dyuers straunge landys and of dyuers straunge effects [and] causis, whiche interlude yf ye hole matter be playd wyl conteyne the space of an hour and a halfe, but yf le lyst ye may leue out muche of the sad mater as the messengers p[ar]te, and some of experyens p[ar]te [and] yet the matter wyl depend conuenyently, and than it wyll not be paste thre quarters of an hour of length*, London

STC 20836 (1531). Rastell, William, *Registrum omniu[m] breuium tam originaliu[m] q[uam] iudicialium*, London

STC 21316 (1626). Roper, William, *The mirrour of vertue in worldly greatnes. Or The life of Syr Thomas More Knight, sometime Lo. Chancellour of England*, St Omer

STC 21429 (1485). Anon., *This book was compyled [and] made atte requeste of kyng Phelyp of Fraunce . . . whyche book is callyd in frensshe. le liure Royal, that is to say the ryal book, or a book for a kyng*, Westminster

STC 21471.5 (1525). Ryckes, John, *The ymage of loue Here foloweth a goostly pamphlete or mater co[m]pendyously extract of holy scrypture, and doctours of ye chyrche, called ye ymage of loue, very necessary for all vertuous persones to loke vpon*, London

STC 22869.7 (1526). Smyth Walter, *The wydow Edyth .xii. Mery gestys of one callyd Edyth*, London

STC 22870 (1573). Smyth, Walter, *XII. mery iests, of the wyddow Edyth this lying widow, false and craftie, late i[n] Engla[n]d, hath deceiued many . . . Now newly printed, this present yeare, for such as delite, mery iests for to here*, London

STC 23341 (1598). Stow, John, *A suruay of London. Contayning the originall, antiquity, increase, moderne estate, and description of that citie*, London

STC 23964 (1531). Kempis, Thomas à, *A boke n[ew]ly translated out of Latyn [in] to Englisshe, called The folowing of Christe with the Golden epistel of saynt Barnard*, tr. Richard Whitford, London

STC 24319 (1522). Tunstall, Cuthbert, *De arte supputandi libri quattuor Cutheberti Tonstalli*, London

STC 24721 (1550). Vigo, Giovanni da, *The most excelent worckes of chirurgery, made and set forth by maister Iohn Vigon, head chirurgien of oure tyme in Italy, traunslated into Englishe. Wherunto is added an exposition of straunge termes and vnknowen symples, belongynge vnto the arte*, London

STC 24873 (1483). Voragine, Jacobus de, *Legenda aurea sanctorum, sive, Lombardica historia*, London

STC 25223 (1631). Weever, John, *Ancient funerall monuments within the vnited monarchie of Great Britaine, Ireland, and the islands adiacent with the dissolued monasteries therein contained: their founders, and what eminent persons haue beene in the same interred*, London

STC 25569.7 (1520). Whittinton, Robert, *Vulgaria Roberti Whitintoni Lichfeldiensis et de institutione grammaticulor[um] opusculu[m]: libello suo de concinnitate grammatices accommodatum: et i[n] quatuor partes digestu[m]. Eiusdem distichon*, London

STC 25576 (1525). Whittinton, Robert, *Vulgaria Roberti Whitintoni Lichfeldiensis & de institutione gra[m]maticulor[um] opusculum: libello suo de concinnitate grammatices accommodatum: & in quattuor partes digestum. Eiusdem distichon*, 2nd edn, London

Printed Primary Sources

Ames, J. (1785–6). *Typographical Antiquities or An Historical Account of the Origin and Progress of Printing in Great Britain and Ireland*, 3 vols, London

Annals of the Reformation (1725–7). *Annals of the Reformation and Establishment of Religion*, ed. J. Strype, 3 vols, London

APC (1890–1964). *Acts of the Privy Council of England*, New Series, ed. J. R. Dasent et al., 46 vols, London

Aristotle (1926). *The Art of Rhetoric*, ed. and tr. J. H. Freese, London

Aristotle (1996). *The Politics and the Constitution of Athens*, ed. S. Everson, Cambridge

Axton, Richard (1979). *Three Rastell Plays*, Cambridge

Baildon, W. P. (1897–2001). *The Records of the Honourable Society of Lincoln's Inn: The Black Books*, 6 vols, London

Baker, J. H. (2003–4). *Reports of Cases from the Time of King Henry VIII*, 2 vols, Selden Society, London

Ba[rker], Ro[bert] (1950). *The lyfe of Syr Thomas More, sometymes Lord Chancellor of England*, ed. E. V. Hitchcock and P. E. Hallett, Early English Text Society, Original Series, 222, London

Bayne, C. G.; Dunham, W. H. (1958). *Select Cases in the Council of Henry VII*, Selden Society, London

Beer B. L.; Jack, S. M. (1974). 'The Letters of William, Lord Paget of Beaudesert, 1547–1563', *Camden Miscellany*, 25, Camden Society, 4th Series, 13, London

Block, K. S. (1922). *Ludus Coventriae; Or the Plaie called Corpus Christi, Cotton MS. Vespasian C.VIII*, Early English Text Society, Extra Series, 120, London

Brown, Rawdon (1854). *Four Years at the Court of Henry VIII. Selection of Despatches Written by the Venetian Ambassador, Sebastian Giustinian, and Addressed to the Signory of Venice, January 12th 1515 to July 26th 1519*, 2 vols, London

Bruce, John (1838). 'Inedited Documents Relating to the Imprisonment and Condemnation of Sir Thomas More', *Archaeologia*, 27, pp.361–74

Burnet, Gilbert (1679–1715). *History of the Reformation of the Church of England*, 3 vols, London

Caryll, J. (1999–2000). *Reports of Cases by John Caryll*, ed. J. H. Baker, 2 vols, Selden Society, London

CCR (1949–53). *Calendar of Close Rolls, 1461–1476*, 2 vols, London

CCR (1954). *Calendar of Close Rolls, 1476–1485*, London

CCR (1955–63). *Calendar of Close Rolls, 1485–1509*, 2 vols, London

CFR (1949). *Calendar of Fine Rolls, 1461–1471*, London

CFR (1961). *Calendar of Fine Rolls, 1471–1485*, London

CFR (1963). *Calendar of Fine Rolls, 1485–1509*, London

Chester, J. L.; Armytage, G. J. (1887). *Allegations for Marriage Licenses issued by the Bishop of London, 1520–1610*, Harleian Society, London

Cicero, M. T. (1999). *On the Commonwealth and the Laws*, ed. J. E. G. Zetzel, Cambridge

CJ (1742–1803). *Journals of the House of Commons*, 28 vols, London

Clark, J. P. H. (1989). *The Latin Versions of 'The Cloud of Unknowing': Nubes Ignorandi, MS. Bodley 856; The English Text of 'The Cloud of Unknowing' in MS. British Library Harley 959*, 2 vols, Salzburg

Clark, J. P. H. (1995–6). *'The Cloud of Unknowing: An Introduction'; Notes on 'The Cloud of Unknowing'; Notes on 'The Book of Privy Counselling'*, 3 vols, Salzburg

Collins, A. (1768). *The Peerage of England: Containing a Genealogical and Historical Account of All the Peers*, 4th edn, 7 vols, London

Complete Peerage (1987). *The Complete Peerage of England, Scotland, Ireland, Great Britain and the United Kingdom by G.E.C[okayne]*, 13 vols in 6, Gloucester

Concilia (1737). *Concilia Magnae Britanniae et Hiberniae*, ed. D. Wilkins, 4 vols, London

Corrie, G. E. (1845). *Sermons and Remains of Hugh Latimer*, Parker Society, Cambridge

Cox, J. E. (1846). *Miscellaneous Writings and Letters of Thomas Cranmer*, Parker Society, Cambridge

CPR (1897). *Calendar of Patent Rolls, 1461–1467*, London

CPR (1900). *Calendar of Patent Rolls, 1467–1477*, London

CPR (1901). *Calendar of Patent Rolls, 1476–1485*, London

CPR (1914–16). *Calendar of Patent Rolls, 1485–1509*, 2 vols, London

CPR (1924–9). *Calendar of Patent Rolls, 1547–1553*, 6 vols, London

CPR (1937–9). *Calendar of Patent Rolls, 1553–1558*, 4 vols, London

CPR (1939–73). *Calendar of Patent Rolls, 1558–1575*, 6 vols, London

CSPD (1856–72). *Calendar of State Papers, Domestic, of the Reigns of Edward VI, Mary, Elizabeth, and James I*, 12 vols, London

CSPM (1912). *Calendar of State Papers and Manuscripts Existing in the Archives Collection of Milan, 1359–1618*, 1 vol. [series not completed], London

CSPS, Series 1 (1862–1954). *Calendar of Letters, Despatches, and State Papers Relating to the Negotiations between England and Spain*, 13 vols, London

CSPS, Series 2 (1892–99). *Letters and State Papers Relating to English Affairs Preserved Principally in the Archives of Simancas*, 4 vols, London

CSPS Supplement (1940). *Further Supplement to Letters, Despatches and State Papers Relating to the Negotiations between England and Spain*, ed. G. Mattingly, London

CSPV (1864–1947). *Calendar of State Papers and Manuscripts Relating to English Affairs, Existing in the Archives and Collections of Venice and in Other Libraries of Northern Italy*, 38 vols, London

Cyprian, St [Bp of Carthage] (1521). *Opera Diui Caecilij Cypriani . . . ab innumeris mendis repurgata*, ed. D. Erasmus, Basel

Cyprian, St [Bp of Carthage] (1844). *The Epistles of St Cyprian, Bishop of Carthage and Martyr, with the Council of Carthage on the Baptism of Heretics*, Oxford

Deakins, R. L. (1972). *Il More. Ellis Heywood's Dialogue in Memory of Thomas More*, Cambridge, Mass.

Dudley, E. (1948). *The Tree of Commonwealth*, ed. D. M. Brodie, Cambridge

Dugdale, William (1671). *Origines Juridiciales, or Historical Memorials of the English Laws, Courts of Justice, Forms of Trial, Punishment in Cases Criminal, Law-Writers, Law-Books, Grants and Settlements of Estates, Degrees of Serjeant, Inns of Court and Chancery*, 2nd edn, London

Dyer, J. (1993–4). *Reports from the Lost Notebooks of Sir James Dyer*, ed. J. H. Baker, 2 vols, Selden Society, London

Dyson, R. W. (1998). *Augustine: The City of God against the Pagans*, Cambridge

Ellis, H. (1824–46). *Original Letters, Illustrative of British History*, 1st–3rd Series, 11 vols, London

Elyot, Sir Thomas (1946). *Of the Knowledge which Maketh a Wise Man*, ed. E. J. Howard, Oxford, Ohio

Elyot, Sir Thomas (1962). *The Book Named the Governor*, ed. S. E. Lehmberg, London

Elyot, Sir Thomas (1967). *Four Political Treatises by Sir Thomas Elyot*, ed. Lillian Gottesman, Gainesville, Florida

Enthoven, L. K. (1906). *Briefe an Desiderius Erasmus von Rotterdam*, Strasbourg

Erasmus, D. (1523). *Precatio dominica in septem portiones distributa*, Basel

Erasmus, D. (1974–). *The Collected Works of Erasmus*, ed. R. A. B. Mynors et al., 76 vols, Toronto

Eusebius [Bp of Caesarea] (1965). *The History of the Church from Christ to Constantine*, London

Fantazzi, C. (2000). *Juan Luis Vives: The Education of a Christian Woman, A Sixteenth-Century Manual*, Chicago

Fiddes, R. (1724). *The Life of Cardinal Wolsey*, London

Fitch, J. G. (2003). *Seneca: Oedipus, Agamemnon, Thyestes, Hercules, Octavia*, Cambridge, Mass.

Formisano, L. (1992). *Letters from a New World: Amerigo Vespucci's Discovery of America*, tr. D. Jacobson, New York

Fortescue, Sir John (1885). *The Governance of England: Otherwise Called the Difference between an Absolute and a Limited Monarchy*, ed. C. Plummer, Oxford

Fortescue, Sir John (1949). *De laudibus legum anglie*, ed. S. B. Chrimes, Cambridge

Foxe, John (1843–9). *The Acts and Monuments of John Foxe*, ed. G. Townsend, 8 vols, London

Gairdner, James (1892). 'A Letter concerning Bishop Fisher and Sir Thomas More', *English Historical Review*, 7, pp. 712–15

Gardiner, Stephen (1930). *Obedience in Church and State*, ed. P. Janelle, Cambridge

Gee, H.; Hardy, W. J., eds (1910). *Documents Illustrative of English Church History*, London

Given-Wilson, C. (2005). *The Parliament Rolls of Medieval England, 1275–1504*, 16 vols, London

Harpsfield, Nicholas (1932). *The life and death of Sir Thomas Moore, knight, some-tymes Lord high Chancellor of England, written in the tyme of Queene Marie*, ed. E. V. Hitchcock, Early English Text Society, Original Series, 186, London

HC 1509–1558 (1982). *The House of Commons, 1509–1558*, ed. S. T. Bindoff, 3 vols, London

HC 1558–1603 (1981). *The House of Commons, 1558–1603*, ed. P. Hasler, 3 vols, London

Heywood, E. (1556). *Il Moro d'Heliseo Heivodo Inglese*, Florence

HMC Salisbury MSS. (1883–1976). *Historical Manuscripts Commission, Calendar of the Manuscripts of the Most Honourable the Marquis of Salisbury*, 24 vols, London

Household Ordinances (1790). *A Collection of Ordinances and Regulations for the Government of the Royal Household*, Society of Antiquaries, London

Jerdan, W. (1842). *Rutland Papers. Original Documents illustrative of the Courts and Times of Henry VII and Henry VIII*, Camden Society, 1st Series, 21, London

Khanna, L. C. (2001). *Early Tudor Translators: Margaret Beaufort, Margaret More Roper and Mary Basset*, Early Modern Englishwoman: Facsimile Library of Essential Works, 1st Series, 4, Aldershot

Kingsford, C. L. (1905). *Chronicles of London*, ed. with an introduction and notes, Oxford

Leadam, I. S. (1897). *The Domesday of Enclosures, 1517–1518*, 2 vols, London

Letters and Papers (1862–1932). *Letters and Papers, Foreign and Domestic, of the Reign of Henry VIII*, ed. J. S. Brewer, J. Gairdner and R. H. Brodie, 21 vols in 32 parts, and Addenda, London

Lisle Letters (1981). *The Lisle Letters*, ed. M. St Clare Byrne, 6 vols, Chicago and London

LJ (1767–1846). *Journals of the House of Lords*, 61 vols, London

Lodge, E. (1791). *Illustrations of British History, Biography and Manners in the Reigns of Henry VIII, Edward VI, Mary, Elizabeth, and James I*, 3 vols, London

Logan, G. M. (2005). *Thomas More: The History of King Richard III*, Bloomington, Indiana

LP Richard III and Henry VII (1861–3). *Letters and Papers, Richard III and Henry VII*, ed. J. Gairdner, 2 vols, London

Lyell, L.; Watney, F. D. (1936). *Acts of Court of the Mercers' Company, 1453–1527*, Cambridge

Lyndwood, W. (1679). *Provinciale seu Constitutiones Angliae*, Oxford

Lysons, D. (1795). *The Environs of London: being an Historical Account of the Towns, Villages and Hamlets within Twelve Miles of that Capital: II, County of Middlesex*, London

Machiavelli, N. (1950). *The Prince and the Discourses*, ed. M. Lerner, New York

Manuale (1875). *Manuale et Processionale ad Usum Insignis Ecclesiae Eboracensis* [with appendix 1: *Manuale ad Usum Insignis Ecclesiae Sarum*], Surtees Society, York

Martin, D. (1997). *Carthusian Spirituality: The Writings of Hugh of Balma and Guigo de Ponte*, New York

Materials, Henry VII (1873–7). *Materials for a History of the Reign of Henry VII from Original Documents Preserved in the Public Record Office*, ed. W. Campbell, 2 vols, London

McSheffrey, S; Tanner, N. (2003). *Lollards of Coventry, 1486–1522*, Camden Society, 5th Series, 23, Cambridge

Memorials, Henry VII (1858). *Memorials of Henry the Seventh, Bernardi Andreae Tholosatis vita Regis Henrici Septimi; necnon alia quaedam ad eundem Regem Spectantia*, ed. J. Gairdner, London

Mercers' Ordinances (1881). *The Charter, Ordinances and Bye-Laws of the Mercers' Company*, London

Merriman, R. B. (1902). *Life and Letters of Thomas Cromwell*, 2 vols, Oxford

Miller, C. H. (1994). 'Thomas More's Letters to Frans van Cranevelt', *Moreana*, 31, pp.3–66

Miller, F. J. (1917). *Seneca's Tragedies with an English Translation*, Cambridge, Mass.

More, Cresacre (1828). *The Life of Sir Thomas More*, ed. J. Hunter, London

More, Thomas (1973–97). *The Yale Edition of the Complete Works of St Thomas More*, ed. R. S. Sylvester, Clarence Miller et al., 15 vols in 21 parts, New Haven, Conn.

More, Thomas (1995). *Utopia. Latin Text and English Translation*, ed. G. M. Logan, R. M. Adams and Clarence H. Miller, Cambridge

More, Thomas (2000). *The Last Letters of Thomas More*, ed. A. de Silva, Grand Rapids, Michigan

More, Thomas (2001). *Utopia*, ed. Clarence H. Miller, New Haven and London

Mosheim, J. L. von (1854). *Historical Commentaries on the State of Christianity during the first Three Hundred and Twenty-five Years*, 2 vols, New York

Narratives of the Reformation (1859). *Narratives of the Days of the Reformation*, ed. J. G. Nicholls, Camden Society, 1st Series, 77, London

Nelson, William (1956). *A Fifteenth-Century Schoolbook from a Manuscript in the British Museum*, London

Newcourt, R. (1710). *Repertorium Ecclesiasticum Parochiale Londinense: An Ecclesiastical Parochial History of the Diocese of London*, 2 vols, London

Nichols, J. G. (1846). *The Chronicle of Calais in the Reigns of Henry VII and Henry VIII to the Year 1540*, Camden Society, 1st Series, 35, London

Opera Omnia (1565). *Thomae Mori . . . Omnia quae hucusque ad manas nostras prevenerunt, Latina Opera:quorum aliqua nunc primum in lucem prodeunt*, Louvain

Plato (2000). *The Republic*, ed. G. R. F. Ferrari and T. Griffith, Cambridge

Pocock, N. (1870). *Records of the Reformation: the Divorce, 1527–1533*, 2 vols, Oxford

Proceedings and Ordinances (1834–7). *Proceedings and Ordinances of the Privy Council of England*, ed. N. H. Nicolas, 7 vols, London

Prockter and Taylor (1979). *The A to Z of Elizabethan London*, London Topographical Society, vol.122, London

Quintilian, M. F. (1686). *The Declamations of Quintilian*, London

Quintilian, M. F. (1996). *Quintilian: Institutio Oratoria, Books I–III*, ed. H. E. Butler, Boston, Mass.

Revised CSPD, Edward VI (1992). *Calendar of State Papers, Domestic Series, of the Reign of Edward VI, 1547–1553*, revised edn, ed. C. S. Knighton, London

Revised CSPD, Mary (1998). *Calendar of State Papers, Domestic Series, of the Reign of Mary I, 1553–1558*, revised edn, ed. C. S. Knighton, London

Riley, H. T. (1861). *Liber Albus: The White Book of the City of London*, London

Rogers, E. F. (1947). *The Correspondence of Sir Thomas More*, Princeton, N.J.

Rogers, E. F. (1961). *St Thomas More: Selected Letters*, New Haven, Conn.

Roper, William (1935). *The Lyfe of Sir Thomas Moore knighte, written by William Roper, Esquire, whiche married Margaret, daughter of the sayed Thomas Moore*, ed. E. V. Hitchcock, Early English Text Society, Original Series, 197, London

Rowe, M. M. (1977). *Tudor Exeter: Tax Assessments 1489–1595 including the Military Survey 1522*, Devon and Cornwall Record Society, New Series, 22, Torquay

Sarum Missal (1913). *The Sarum Missal in English*, ed. and tr. F. E. Warren, 2 vols, Alcuin Club, Oxford

Schöner, J. (1515). *Luculentissima quaeda[m] terrae totius descriptio, cu[m] multis utilissimis cosmographiae iniciis: nouaq[ue] & [quam] ante fuit verior Europae*, Nuremberg

Schulte Herbrüggen, H. (1966). *Sir Thomas More: Neue Briefe*, Münster

Scriveners' Company (1968). *Scriveners' Company Common Paper, 1357–1628. With a Continuation to 1678*, ed. F. W. Steer, London Record Society, London

Seneca, L. A. (1515). *Lucubrationes Omnes*, ed. D. Erasmus, Basel

Seneca, L. A. (1517). *Senecae Tragoediae*, Venice

Spelman, Sir John (1976–7). *The Reports of Sir John Spelman*, ed. J. H. Baker, 2 vols, Selden Society, London

St German, Christopher (1974). *St German's Doctor and Student*, ed. T. F. T. Plucknett and J. L. Barton, Selden Society, London

Stapleton, Thomas (1588). *Tres Thomae, seu de S. Thomae Apostoli rebus gestis, de S. Thoma Archiepiscopo Cantuariensi et Martyre, D. Thomae Mori Angliae quondam Cancellarii Vita*, Douai

Stapleton, Thomas (1928). *The Life and Illustrious Martyrdom of Sir Thomas More*, ed. P. E. Hallett, London

Starkey, D. R.; Ward, P.; Hawkyard, A. (1998). *The Inventory of King Henry VIII. Vol. I: The Transcript*, Society of Antiquaries, London

Starkey, Thomas (1948). *A Dialogue between Reginald Pole and Thomas Lupset*, ed. K. Burton, Cambridge

Starkey, Thomas (1989). *A Dialogue between Pole and Lupset*, ed. T. F. Mayer, Camden Society, 4th Series, 37, London

State Papers (1830–52). *State Papers during the Reign of Henry VIII*, 11 vols, Record Commission, London

Statutes of the Realm (1810–28). *Statutes of the Realm*, ed. A. Luders, T. E. Tomlins, J. Raithby et al., 11 vols, London

STC (1976–91). *A Short-Title Catalogue of Books Printed in England, Scotland and Ireland, and of English Books Printed Abroad*, ed. W. A. Jackson, F. S. Ferguson and K. F. Pantzer, 2nd edn, 3 vols, London

Stow, John (1956). *Stow's Survey of London*, ed. H. B. Wheatley, London

Strype, J. (1840). *Memorials of Thomas Cranmer*, 2 vols, Oxford

Surtz, E.; Murphy, V. M. (1988). *The Divorce Tracts of Henry VIII*, Angers

Swinburne, H. (1686). *A Treatise of Spousals or Matrimonial Contracts wherein all the Questions relating to that Subject are Ingeniously Debated and Resolved*, London

Sylvester, R. S.; Harding, D. P. (1962). *Two Early Tudor Lives: the Life and Death of Cardinal Wolsey by George Cavendish; The Life of Sir Thomas More by William Roper*, ed. R. S. Sylvester and D. P. Harding, New Haven, Conn.

Synodalia (1842). *Synodalia. A Collection of Articles of Religion, Canons, and Proceedings of Convocations*, comp. E. Cardwell, 2 vols, Oxford

Thompson, C. R. (1965). *The Colloquies of Erasmus*, Chicago

TRP (1964–9). *Tudor Royal Proclamations*, ed. P. L. Hughes and J. F. Larkin, 3 vols, New Haven, Conn.

Tudor Economic Documents (1924). *Tudor Economic Documents*, ed. R. H. Tawney and E. Power, 3 vols, London

Tudor Tracts (1903). *Tudor Tracts, 1532–1588*, ed. A. F. Pollard, London

Tyndale, William (1848). *Doctrinal Treatises and Introductions to Different Portions of the Holy Scriptures by William Tyndale*, ed. H. Walter, Parker Society, Cambridge

Van Ortroy, F. (1891). 'Vie du Bienheureux Martyr Jean Fisher, Cardinal', *Analecta Bollandiana*, 10, pp.121–365

Van Ortroy, F. (1893). 'Vie du Bienheureux Martyr Jean Fisher, Cardinal', *Analecta Bollandiana*, 12, pp.97–287

Vergil, P. (1950). *The Anglica Historia of Polydore Vergil*, ed. D. Hay, Camden Society, 3rd Series, 74, London

Vitruvius, M. (1511). *M. Vitruvius per Iocandum solito castigatior factus*, Venice

Vitruvius, M. (1522). *De architectura libri decem*, Florence

Vitruvius, M. (1692). *An Abridgment of the Architecture of Vitrivius*, London

Vocht, H. de (1947). *Acta Thomae Mori. History of the Reports of his Trial and Death with an Unedited Contemporary Narrative*, Louvain

Vos, A. (1989). *Letters of Roger Ascham*, tr. M. Hatch and A. Vos, New York and Paris

Watney, John (1906). *Some Account of the Hospital of St Thomas of Acon in the Cheap, London and the Plate of the Mercers' Company*, 2nd edn, London

Whibley, C. (1904). *Henry VIII* [an edition of Hall's Chronicle], 2 vols, London

Wieser, F. R. von (1907). *Die Cosmographiae Introductio des Martin Waldseemüller (Ilacomilus) in Faksimiledruck*, Strasbourg

Wood, M. A. E. (1846). *Letters of Royal and Illustrious Ladies of Great Britain*, 3 vols, London

Young, S. (1890). *The Annals of the Barber-Surgeons of London, Compiled from their Records and Other Sources by Sydney Young, One of the Court of Assistants*, London

Secondary Sources

Ackroyd, P. (1998). *The Life of Thomas More*, London

Agrarian History, 1500–1640 (1967). *The Agrarian History of England and Wales, IV, 1500–1640*, ed. Joan Thirsk, Cambridge

Aikin, J. (1780). *Biographical Memoirs of Medicine in Great Britain from the Revival of Literature to the time of Harvey*, London

Albin, H. O. (1979–80). 'Opening of the Roper Vault in St Dunstan's, Canterbury', *Moreana*, 16, pp.29–35

Allen, J. L. (1992). 'From Cabot to Cartier: the Early Exploration of Eastern North America, 1497–1543', *Annals of the Association of American Geographers*, 82, pp.500–21

Allen, P. (1985–2002). *The Concept of Woman*, 2 vols in 3 parts, Grand Rapids, MI, and Cambridge

Alsop, J. D. (1982). 'The Theory and Practice of Tudor Taxation', *English Historical Review 97*, pp.1–30

Alsop, J. D. (1984). 'Innovation in Tudor Taxation', *English Historical Review*, 99, pp.83–93

Alsop, J. D. (1986). 'The Structure of Early Tudor Finance, *c.*1509–1558', in *Revolution Reassessed: Revisions in the History of Tudor Government and Administration*, ed. C. Coleman and D. R. Starkey, Oxford, pp.135–62

Ames, R. (1949). *Citizen Thomas More and his Utopia*, Oxford

Amici, B. A. L. (2004). 'Music in the Chapel of All Souls College, Oxford', *Renaissance Studies*, 18, pp.171–207

Anderegg, M. A. (1976). 'Nicholas Harpsfield, Thomas More and William Roper's Lapse into Heresy', *Notes and Queries, New Series*, 23, pp.225–6

Anglo, S. (1969). *Spectacle, Pageantry, and Early Tudor Policy*, Oxford

Anglo, S. (1992). *Images of Tudor Kingship*, London

Appleby, A. B. (1978). *Famine in Tudor and Stuart England*, Liverpool

Archer, I. W. (2001). 'The Burden of Taxation in Sixteenth-Century London', *Historical Journal*, 44, pp.599–627

Aston, M. (1960). 'Lollardy and Sedition, 1381–1431', *Past and Present*, no. 17, pp.1–44

Aston, M. (1964). 'Lollardy and the Reformation: Survival or Revival?', *History*, 49, pp.149–70

Aston, M. (1988). *England's Iconoclasts, Vol. I, Laws against Images*, Oxford

Aston, M. (1993). *The King's Bedpost: Reformation and Iconography in a Tudor Group Portrait*, Cambridge

Baker, D. N. (1999). 'The active and the contemplative lives in Rolle, the Cloud-Author and Hilton', in *The Medieval Mystical Tradition: England, Ireland and Wales*, ed. M. Glasscoe, Exeter Symposium, Cambridge, pp.85–102

Baker, J. H. (1985). *The Legal Profession and the Common Law: Historical Essays*, London

Baker, J. H. (2000). *Readers and Readings in the Inns of Court and Chancery*, Selden Society, Supplementary Series, London

Baker, J. H. (2003). *The Oxford History of the Laws of England: Vol. VI, 1483–1558*, Oxford

Baker-Smith, D. (1983). ' "A Fool Among Knaves": the Humanist Dilemma of Counsel', *Bulletin of the Society for Renaissance Studies*, 1:1, pp.1–9

Baker-Smith, D. (1991). *More's Utopia*, London

Ballard, G. (1775). *Memoirs of British Ladies who have been Celebrated for their Writings or Skill in the Learned Languages, Arts and Sciences*, London

Barber, B.; Thomas, C. (2002). *The London Charterhouse*, Museum of London Archaeological Monograph, London

Barraclough, G. (1966). *The Origins of Modern Germany*, Oxford

Barron, C. M. (2004). *London in the Later Middle Ages: Government and People, 1200–1500*, Oxford

Bätschmann, O.; Griener, P. (1997). *Hans Holbein*, London

Bayley, J. (1821). *The History and Antiquities of the Tower of London with Memoirs of Royal and Distinguished Personages*, 2 vols, London

Bell, D. C. (1877). *Notices of the Historic Persons buried in the Chapel of St Peter ad Vincula in the Tower of London*, London

Benesch, O. (1944). 'Holbein and Others in a Seventeenth Century Collection', *Burlington Magazine*, 84, pp.129–30

Bennett, J. W. (1968). 'John Morer's Will: Thomas Linacre and Prior Sellyng's Greek Teaching', *Studies in the Renaissance*, 15, pp.70–91

Bernard, G. W. (1985). *The Power of the Early Tudor Nobility: a Study of the Fourth and Fifth Earls of Shrewsbury*, Brighton

Bernard, G. W. (1986a). *War, Taxation and Rebellion in Early Tudor England: Henry VIII, Wolsey and the Amicable Grant of 1525*, Brighton

Bernard, G. W. (1986b). 'The Pardon of the Clergy Reconsidered', *Journal of Ecclesiastical History*, 37, pp.258–82

Bernard, G. W. (1996). 'The Fall of Wolsey Reconsidered', *Journal of British Studies*, 35, pp.277–310

Bernard, G. W. (1998). 'The Making of Religious Policy: Henry VIII and the Search for the Middle Way', *Historical Journal*, 41, pp.321–49

Bernard, G. W. (1999). 'The Piety of Henry VIII', in *The Education of a Christian Society: Humanism and the Reformation in Britain and the Netherlands*, ed. N. Scott Amos, A. D. M. Pettegree and H. van Nierop, Aldershot, pp.62–88

Bernard, G. W. (2005). *The King's Reformation: Henry VIII and the Remaking of the English Church*, London

Bevan, A. S. (1985). 'The Role of the Judiciary in Tudor Government, 1509–1547', unpublished Cambridge Ph.D. dissertation

Bietenholz, P. G.; Deutscher, T. B. (1985–7). *Contemporaries of Erasmus: A Biographical Register of the Renaissance and Reformation*, 3 vols, Toronto

Biller, P. P. A. (1982). 'Birth-Control in the West in the Thirteenth and Fourteenth Centuries', *Past and Present*, 94, pp.3–26

Bindoff, S. T. (1982). *The House of Commons, 1509–1558*, 3 vols, History of Parliament, London

Blatcher, M. (1978). *The Court of King's Bench, 1450–1550*, London

Blayney, P. W. M. (1972). 'The Booke of Sir Thomas Moore Re-examined', *Studies in Philology*, 69, pp.167–91

Bowker, M. (1968). *The Secular Clergy in the Diocese of Lincoln*, Cambridge

Bowker, M. (1981). *The Henrician Reformation: the Diocese of Lincoln under John Longland, 1521–1547*, Cambridge

Boyle, A. J. (1997). *Tragic Seneca: An Essay in the Theatrical Tradition*, London

Bradshaw, B. (1981). 'More on Utopia', *Historical Journal*, 24, pp.1–27

Bradshaw, B. (1985). 'The Controversial Sir Thomas More', *Journal of Ecclesiastical History*, 36, pp.535–69

Bradshaw, B. (1991). 'Transalpine Humanism', in *The Cambridge History of Political Thought, 1450–1700*, ed. J. H. Burns and M. Goldie, Cambridge, pp.95–131

Bridgett, T. E. (1924). *Life and Writings of Blessed Thomas More*, London

Brigden, S. (1979). 'The Early Reformation in London, 1520–1547: the Conflict in the Parishes', unpublished Cambridge Ph.D. dissertation

Brigden, S. (1984). 'Religion and Social Obligation in Early Sixteenth-Century London', *Past and Present*, no. 103, pp.67–112

Brigden, S. (1988). 'Thomas Cromwell and the Brethren', in *Law and Government under the Tudors*, ed. Claire Cross, D. M. Loades and J. J. Scarisbrick, Cambridge, pp.31–50

Brigden, S. (1989). *London and the Reformation*, Oxford

Brigden, S. (2000). *New Worlds, Lost Worlds: the Rule of the Tudors, 1485–1603*, London

Burgess, C.; Kümin, B. (1993). 'Penitential Bequests and Parish Regimes in Late Medieval England', *Journal of Ecclesiastical History*, 44, pp.610–30

Byron, B. (1972). *Loyalty in the Spirituality of St Thomas More*, Bibliotheca Humanistica et Reformatorica, no. 4, Nieuwkoop

Campbell, T. P. (2007). *The Art of Majesty: Henry VIII's Tapestry Collection*, New Haven and London

Carley, J. P. (1989). 'John Leland and the Foundations of the Royal Library: the Westminster Inventory of 1542', *Bulletin of the Society for Renaissance Studies*, 7, pp.13–22

Carley, J. P. (1998). ' "Her moost lovying and fryndely brother sendeth gretyng": Anne Boleyn's Manuscripts and their Sources', in *Illuminating the Book: Makers and Interpreters*, ed. Michelle P. Brown and Scot McKendrick, London and Toronto, pp.261–80

Carley, J. P. (2000). *The Libraries of King Henry VIII*, London

Carlson, D. R. (1991). 'Royal Tutors in the Reign of Henry VII', *Sixteenth Century Journal*, 22, pp.253–79

Carpenter, C. (1992). *Locality and Polity: a Study of Warwickshire Landed Society, 1401–1499*, Cambridge

Carpenter, C. (1997). *The Wars of the Roses: Politics and the Constitution in England, c.1437–1509*, Cambridge

Cave, A. A. (1991). 'Thomas More and the New World', *Albion*, 23, pp.209–29

Chambers, D. S. (1965). 'Cardinal Wolsey and the Papal Tiara', *Bulletin of the Institute of Historical Research*, 38, pp.20–30

Chambers, R. W. (1935). *Thomas More*, London

Chibi, A. A. (1997). *Henry VIII's Conservative Scholar: Bishop John Stokesley and the Divorce, Royal Supremacy and Doctrinal Reform*, Bern

Chrimes, S. B. (1936). *English Constitutional Ideas in the Fifteenth Century*, Cambridge

Chrimes, S. B. (1972). *Henry VII*, London

Clapham, A. W.; Godfrey, W. H. (*c.*1912). *Some Famous Buildings and their Story*, Westminster

Clark, P.; Slack, P. (1976). *English Towns in Transition, 1500–1700*, Oxford

Clebsch, W. A. (1964). *England's Earliest Protestants, 1520–1535*, New Haven, Conn.

Colvin, H. M. (1982). *The History of the King's Works, IV, 1485–1625 (Part 2)*, London

Condon, M. M. (1979). 'Ruling Elites in the Reign of Henry VII', in *Patronage, Pedigree and Power*, ed. Charles Ross, Gloucester, pp.109–42

Conrad, F. W. (1992). 'The Problem of Counsel Reconsidered: the Case of Sir Thomas Elyot', in *Political Thought and the Tudor Commonwealth*, ed. P. A. Fideler and T. F. Mayer, London, pp.75–107

Conrad, F. W. (1995). 'Manipulating Reputations: Sir Thomas More, Sir Thomas Elyot, and the Conclusion of William Roper's *Lyfe of Sir Thomas Moore, Knighte*', in *The Rhetorics of Life-Writing in Early Modern Europe. Forms of Biography from Cassandra Fedele to Louis XIV*, ed. T. F. Mayer and D. R. Woolf, Ann Arbor, MI, pp.133–61

Coope, R. (1984). 'The Gallery in England: Names and Meanings', *Architectural History*, 27, pp.446–55

Coope, R. (1986). 'The "Long Gallery": its Origins, Development, Use and Decoration', *Architectural History*, 29, pp.43–72, 74–84

Cooper, J. P. (1957). 'The Supplication Against the Ordinaries Reconsidered', *English Historical Review*, 72, pp.616–41

Cooper, J. P. (1959). 'Henry VII's Last Years Reconsidered', *Historical Journal*, 2, pp.103–29

Cox, V. (1992). *The Renaissance Dialogue: Literary Dialogue in its Social and Political Context, Castiglione to Galileo*, Cambridge

Craig, J. (1999). 'Reformers, Conflict and Revisionism: the Reformation in Sixteenth-Century Hadleigh', *Historical Journal*, 42, pp.1–23

Crawford, P. (1993). *Women and Religion in England, 1500–1720*, London

Cressy, D. (1997). *Birth, Marriage and Death: Ritual, Religion and the Life-Cycle in Tudor and Stuart England*, Oxford

Cromartie, A. (2006). *The Constitutionalist Revolution: An Essay on the History of England, 1450–1642*, Cambridge

Croot, P. E. C. (2004). *A History of the County of Middlesex, XII: Chelsea*, Victoria County History, London

Crossett, J. (1957). 'More and Lucian', *Modern Language Notes*, 72, pp.169–70

Curtis, C. (1996). 'Richard Pace on Pedagogy, Counsel and Satire', unpublished Cambridge Ph.D. dissertation

Cust, L. (1912). 'The Family of Sir Thomas More', *Burlington Magazine*, 22, pp.43–4

Daniell, D. (1994). *William Tyndale: A Biography*, London

Davies, C. S. L. (1987). 'Bishop John Morton, the Holy See, and the Accession of Henry VII', *English Historical Review*, 102, pp.2–30

Davies, C. S. L. (1998). 'Tournai and the English Crown, 1513–1519', *Historical Journal*, 41, pp.1–26

Davies, G. S. (1903). *Hans Holbein the Younger*, London

Davis, E. Jeffries (1915). 'The Authorities for the Case of Richard Hunne, 1514–1515', *English Historical Review*, 30, pp.477–88

Davis, J. C. (1970). 'More, Morton and the Politics of Accommodation', *Journal of British Studies*, 9, pp.27–49

Davis, J. C. (1981). *Utopia and the Ideal Society: A Study of English Utopian Writing, 1516–1700*, Cambridge

Davis, J. F. (1983). *Heresy and Reformation in the South-East of England, 1520–1559*, London

DeMolen, R. L. (1971). *Erasmus of Rotterdam: A Quincentennial Symposium*, New York

Derrett, J. D. M. (1960). 'Neglected Versions of the Contemporary Account of the Trial of Sir Thomas More', *Bulletin of the Institute of Historical Research*, 33, pp.202–23

Derrett, J. D. M. (1964a). 'The Trial of Sir Thomas More', *English Historical Review*, 79, pp.449–77

Derrett, J. D. M. (1964b). 'The "New" Document on Thomas More's Trial', *Moreana*, 3, pp.5–19

Derrett, J. D. M. (1965). 'More's Conveyance of his Lands and the Law of "Fraud"', *Moreana*, 5, pp.19–26

Derrett, J. D. M. (1983). 'Sir Thomas More as a Martyr', *Downside Review*, 101, pp.187–93

Devereux, E. J. (1999). *A Bibliography of John Rastell*, Montreal and London

Dickens, A. G. (1959a). *Lollards and Protestants in the Diocese of York, 1509–1558*, Oxford

Dickens, A. G. (1959b). *Thomas Cromwell and the English Reformation*, London

Dickens, A. G. (1987). 'The Early Expansion of Protestantism in England, 1520–1558', *Archiv für Reformationsgeschichte*, 78, pp.187–222

Dickens, A. G. (1989). *The English Reformation*, 2nd edn, London

Dietz, F. C. (1964). *English Public Finance, 1485–1641*, 2 vols, 2nd edn, London

Doe, N. (1990). *Fundamental Authority in Late Medieval English Law*, Cambridge

Dolson, G. B. (1922). 'Imprisoned English Authors and the Consolation of Philosophy of Boethius', *American Journal of Philology*, 43, pp.168–9

Dowling, M. (1984). 'Anne Boleyn and Reform', *Journal of Ecclesiastical History*, 35, pp.30–46

Duffy, E. (1992). *The Stripping of the Altars: Traditional Religion in England, 1400–1580*, New Haven, Conn. and London

Duggan, A. (2004). *Thomas Becket*, London and New York

Durrant, C. S. (1925). *A Link Between Flemish Mystics and English Martyrs*, London

Dyer, A. (1997). 'The English Sweating Sickness of 1551: An Epidemic Anatomized', *Medical History*, 41, pp.362–84

Edmunds, J. (1980). *A History of Latton*, [Latton]

Eliav-Feldon, M. (1982). *Realistic Utopias: the Ideal Imaginary Societies of the Renaissance 1516–1630*, Oxford

Elton, G. R. (1953). *The Tudor Revolution in Government*, Cambridge

Elton, G. R. (1972). *Policy and Police: the Enforcement of the Reformation in the Age of Thomas Cromwell*, Cambridge

Elton, G. R. (1973). *Reform and Renewal: Thomas Cromwell and the Common Weal*, Cambridge

Elton, G. R. (1974a). *England under the Tudors*, 2nd edn, London

Elton, G. R. (1974b–92). *Studies in Tudor and Stuart Politics and Government*, 4 vols, Cambridge

Elton, G. R. (1977). *Reform and Reformation: England, 1509–1558*, London

Elton, G. R. (1978). Review of *The Complete Works of St Thomas More, vols 12, 13, 14* [untitled], *English Historical Review*, 93, pp.399–404

Elton, G. R. (1982). *The Tudor Constitution*, 2nd edn, Cambridge

Elton, G. R. (1988). 'Tudor Government', *Historical Journal*, 31, pp.425–35

Emery, A. (2000). *Greater Medieval Houses of England and Wales, 1300–1500. Vol. II: East Anglia, Central England, and Wales*, Cambridge

English, M. (2003). 'Lost Autographs of John Skelton, David Lyndsay and Thomas More?', *Notes and Queries, New Series*, 50, p.385

Farmer, Sharon (1986). 'Persuasive Voices: Clerical Images of Medieval Wives', *Speculum*, 61, pp.517–43

Fenlon, D. (1972). *Heresy and Obedience in Tridentine Italy. Cardinal Pole and the Counter Reformation*, Cambridge

Fenlon, D. (1981). 'Thomas More and Tyranny', *Journal of Ecclesiastical History*, 32, pp.453–76

Fenlon, D. B. (1975). 'England and Europe: Utopia and its Aftermath', *Transactions of the Royal Historical Society, 5th Series*, 25, pp.115–36

Ferguson, A. B. (1963). 'The Tudor Commonweal and the Sense of Change', *Journal of British Studies*, 3, pp.11–35

Ferguson, A. B. (1979). *Clio Unbound: Perceptions of the Social and Cultural Past in Renaissance England*, Durham, N.C.

Fideler, P. A. (1992). 'Poverty, Policy and Providence: the Tudors and the Poor', in *Political Thought and the Tudor Commonwealth*, ed. P. A. Fideler and T. F. Mayer, London, pp.194–222

Fildes, Valerie (1988). *Wet Nursing: A History from Antiquity to the Present*, Oxford

Fines, J. (1963). 'The Post-Mortem Condemnation for Heresy of Richard Hunne', *English Historical Review*, 78, pp.528–31

Fines, John (1963). 'Heresy Trials in the Diocese of Coventry and Lichfield, 1511–12', *Journal of Ecclesiastical History*, 14, pp.160–74

Fisher, F. J. (1965). 'Influenza and Inflation in Tudor England', *Economic History Review, 2nd Series*, 18, pp.120

Fleisher, M. (1973). *Radical Reform and Political Persuasion in the Life and Writings of Thomas More*, Geneva

Fletcher, A.; MacCulloch, D. (1997). *Tudor Rebellions*, 4th edn, London

Flood, J. L. (2003). ' "Safer on the Battlefield than in the City": England, the "Sweating Sickness", and the Continent', *Renaissance Studies*, 17, pp.147–76

Floyer, J. K. (1913). 'English Brick Buildings of the Fifteenth Century', *Archaeological Journal*, 70, pp.121–32

Foister, S. (1981). 'Holbein and his English Patrons', unpublished London Ph.D. thesis

Foister, S. (2004). *Holbein and England*, New Haven and London

Foister, S. (2006). *Holbein in England*, with contributions by Tim Batchelor, London

Foister, S.; Roy, A.; Wyld, M. (1997). *Making and Meaning: Holbein's Ambassadors*, London

Fox, Alistair (1982). *Thomas More: History and Providence*, Oxford

Fox, Alistair (1989). *Early Tudor Literature: Politics and the Literary Imagination*, Oxford

Fox, Alistair (1997). *The English Renaissance. Identity and Representation in Elizabethan England*, Oxford

Fox, Alistair; Guy, John (1986). *Reassessing the Henrician Age: Humanism, Politics, and Reform*, Oxford

Freeman, T. S. (1997). 'The Importance of Dying Earnestly: the Metamorphosis of the Account of James Bainham in "Foxe's Book of Martyrs"', in *The Church*

Retrospective, Studies in Church History, 33, ed. R. N. Swanson, Woodbridge, pp.267–88

Frick Collection (1968–2003). *The Frick Collection: An Illustrated Catalogue*, 9 vols, New York

Froide, A. M. (2001). 'Female Relationships in Early Modern England', *Journal of British Studies*, 40, pp.279–89

Fryde, E. B. (2000). *The Early Palaeologan Renaissance, 1261–c.1360*, Leiden

Fryde, E. B.; Miller, E. (1970). *Historical Studies of the English Parliament*, 2 vols, Cambridge

Furey, C. M. (2006). *Erasmus, Contarini and the Religious Republic of Letters*, Cambridge

Galt, J. (1846). *Life of Cardinal Wolsey with Additional Illustrations from Cavendish's 'Life of Wolsey' and Other Sources*, London

Ganz, P. (1950). *The Paintings of Hans Holbein*, London

Gee, J. A. (1937). 'Margaret Roper's English Version of Erasmus's *Precatio Dominica* and the Apprenticeship behind Early Tudor Translation', *Review of English Studies*, 13, pp.257–71

Gibson, R. W.; Patrick, J. M. (1961). *St Thomas More: A Preliminary Bibliography of His Works and of Moreana to the Year 1750*, New Haven, Conn.

Ginsberg, D. (1988). 'Ploughboys versus Prelates: Tyndale and More and the Politics of Biblical Translation', *Sixteenth Century Journal*, 19, pp.45–61

Goddard, S. H. (1988). '*Probationes Pennae*: Some Sixteenth-Century Doodles on the Theme of Folly Attributed to the Antwerp Humanist Pieter Gillis and his Colleagues', *Renaissance Quarterly*, 41, pp.242–67

Gogan, Brian (1982). *The Common Corps of Christendom: Ecclesiological Themes in the Writings of Sir Thomas More*, Leiden

Goring, J. J. (1971). 'The General Proscription of 1522', *English Historical Review*, 86, pp.681–705

Gowing, Laura (1996). *Domestic Dangers. Women, Words, and Sex in Early Modern London*, Oxford

Grace, F. R. (1961). 'The Life and Career of Thomas Howard, Third Duke of Norfolk', unpublished Nottingham M.A. dissertation

Graves, T. S. (1913). 'The Heywood Circle and the Reformation', *Modern Philology*, 10, pp.553–72

Griffiths, R. A.; Thomas, R. S. (1985). *The Making of the Tudor Dynasty*, Gloucester

Gross, A. (1996). *The Dissolution of the Lancastrian Kingship. Sir John Fortescue and the Crisis of Monarchy in Fifteenth-Century England*, Stamford

Grossmann, F. (1944). 'Notes on the Arundel and Imstenraedt Collections', *Burlington Magazine*, 84, pp.145, 151–4; 85, pp.172–6

Grummitt, D. (1999). 'Henry VII, Chamber Finance and the "New Monarchy": Some New Evidence', *Historical Research*, 72, pp.229–43

Gunn, S. J. (1986). 'The Duke of Suffolk's March on Paris in 1523', *English Historical Review*, 101, pp.596–634

Gunn, S. J. (1988). *Charles Brandon, Duke of Suffolk, 1484–1545*, Oxford

Gunn, S. J. (1991). 'The Accession of Henry VIII', *Historical Research*, 64, pp. 278–88

Gunn, S. J. (1993). 'The Courtiers of Henry VII', *English Historical Review*, 108, pp.23–49

Gunn, S. J. (1994). 'Off with their Heads: the Tudor Nobility, 1485–1603', in *The House of Lords: A Thousand Years of British Tradition*, ed. Robert Smith and John S. Moore, London, pp.52–65

Gunn, S. J. (1995a). *Early Tudor Government, 1485–1558*, London

Gunn, S. J. (1995b). 'The Structures of Power in Early Tudor England', *Transactions of the Royal Historical Society, 6th Series*, 5, pp.59–90

Gunn, S. J. (1995c). 'State Development in England and the Burgundian Dominions, *c.*1460–*c.*1560', *Publications du Centre Européen d'Études Bourguignonnes*, no. 35, pp.133–49

Gunn, S. J. (1996). 'Henry VIII's Foreign Policy and the Tudor Cult of Chivalry', in *François Ier et Henry VIII, Deux Princes de la Renaissance, 1515–1547*, ed. C. Giry-Deloison, Centre d'Histoire de la Région du Nord et de l'Europe du Nord-Ouest, Collection 'Histoire et Littérature Régionales', 13, Lille and London, pp.25–36

Guy, John (1977a). *The Cardinal's Court: the Impact of Thomas Wolsey in Star Chamber*, Hassocks

Guy, John (1977b). 'Thomas More as Successor to Wolsey', *Thought: Fordham University Quarterly*, 52, pp.275–92

Guy, John (1980). *The Public Career of Sir Thomas More*, Brighton

Guy, John (1982). 'Henry VIII and the *Praemunire* Manoeuvres of 1530–1531', *English Historical Review*, 97, pp.481–503

Guy, John (1985). *Christopher St German on Chancery and Statute*, Selden Society, London

Guy, John (1988a). *Tudor England*, Oxford

Guy, John (1988b). 'Wolsey and the Parliament of 1523', in *Law and Government under the Tudors*, ed. Claire Cross, D. M. Loades and J. J. Scarisbrick, Cambridge, pp.1–18

Guy, John (1991). 'Wolsey and the Tudor Polity', in *Cardinal Wolsey: Church, State and Art*, ed. S. J. Gunn and P. Lindley, Cambridge, pp.54–75

Guy, John (1998). *Cardinal Wolsey*, Oxford

Guy, John (2000a). 'The Search for the Historical Thomas More', *History Review*, 36, pp.15–20

Guy, John (2000b). *Thomas More*, London

Gwyn, David (1984). 'Richard Eden, Cosmographer and Alchemist', *Sixteenth Century Journal*, 15, pp.13–34

Gwyn, Peter (1980). 'Wolsey's Foreign Policy: the Conferences at Calais and Bruges Reconsidered', *Historical Journal*, 23, pp.755–72

Gwyn, Peter (1990). *The King's Cardinal: the Rise and Fall of Thomas Wolsey*, London

Haigh, C. A. (1975). *Reformation and Resistance in Tudor Lancashire*, Cambridge

Haigh, C. A. (1983). 'Anticlericalism and the English Reformation', *History*, 68, pp.391–407

Haigh, C. A. (1993). *English Reformations: Religion, Politics, and Society under the Tudors*, Oxford

Harris, Barbara J. (1986). *Edward Stafford, Third Duke of Buckingham, 1478–1521*, Stanford, Ca.

Harrison, C. J. (1972). 'The Petition of Edmund Dudley', *English Historical Review*, 87, pp.82–99

Hatcher, John (1977). *Plague, Population and the English Economy, 1348–1530*, London

Hay, Denys (1967). 'A Note on More and the General Council', *Moreana*, 15, pp.249–51

Headley, J. M. (1967). 'More against Luther: On Laws and the Magistrate', *Moreana*, 15, pp.211–23

Heath, Peter (1969). *The English Parish Clergy on the Eve of the Reformation*, London

Heinze, R. W. (1976). *The Proclamations of the Tudor Kings*, Cambridge

Helgerson, R. (1998). 'Introduction', *Early Modern Literary Studies*, 4, pp.1–14

Hellinga L.; Trapp, J. B. (1999). *The Cambridge History of the Book in Britain. Vol. III: 1400–1557*, Cambridge

Hepburb, F. (1997). 'Arthur, Prince of Wales and his Training for Kingship', *Historian*, 55, pp.4–9

Hexter, J. H. (1952). *More's 'Utopia': the Biography of an Idea*, Princeton, N.J.

Hoak, D. E. (1995). 'The Iconography of the Crown Imperial', in *Tudor Political Culture*, ed. D. E. Hoak, Cambridge, pp.54–103

Hogrefe, P. (1932). 'Sir Thomas More's Connection with the Roper family', *Proceedings of the Modern Language Association*, 47, pp.523–33

Horowitz, M. R. (1982). 'Richard Empson, Minister of Henry VII', *Bulletin of the Institute of Historical Research*, 55, pp.35–49

Horowitz, Mark (2006). ' "Agree with the King": Henry VII, Edmund Dudley and the Strange Case of Thomas Sunnyff', *Historical Research*, 79, pp.325–66

Hoskins, W. G. (1964). 'Harvest Fluctuations and English Economic History, 1480–1619', *Agricultural History Review*, 12, pp.28–46

Hoskins, W. G. (1976). *The Age of Plunder: the England of Henry VIII, 1500–1547*, London

Houlbrooke, R. A. (1979). *Church Courts and the People during the English Reformation, 1520–1570*, Oxford

House, S. B. (1987). 'Sir Thomas More and Holy Orders: More's Views of the English Clergy, both Secular and Regular', unpublished St Andrews Ph.D. dissertation

House, S. B. (1989). 'Sir Thomas More as Church Patron', *Journal of Ecclesiastical History*, 40, pp.208–18

House, S. B. (1995). 'Literature, Drama and Politics', in *The Reign of Henry VIII: Politics, Policy and Piety*, ed. D. MacCulloch, London, pp.181–202

Howard, M.; Wilson, E. (2003). *The Vyne: A Tudor House Revealed*, London

Hoyle, R. W. (1994). 'Crown, Parliament and Taxation in Sixteenth Century England', *English Historical Review*, 109, pp.1174–96

Hoyle, R. W. (1995a). 'War and Public Finance', in *The Reign of Henry VIII: Politics, Policy and Piety*, ed. D. MacCulloch, London, pp.75–100

Hoyle, R. W. (1995b). 'The Origins of the Dissolution of the Monasteries', *Historical Journal*, 38, pp.275–305

Hughes, D. W. (1987). 'The History of Halley's Comet', *Philosophical Transactions of the Royal Society of London, Series A*, 323, pp.349–67

Hughes, J. (1988). *Pastors and Visionaries: Religion and Secular Life in Late Medieval Yorkshire*, Woodbridge

Hughes, P. (1950–4). *The Reformation in England*, 3 vols, London

Hyatt King, A. (1971). 'The Significance of John Rastell in Early Music Printing', *Library, 5th Series*, 26, pp.197–214

Ives, E. W. (1972). 'Faction at the Court of Henry VIII: the Fall of Anne Boleyn', *History*, 57, pp.169–88

Ives, E. W. (1981). 'Crime, Sanctuary, and Royal Authority under Henry VIII: the Exemplary Sufferings of the Savage Family', in *Of the Laws and Customs of England*, ed. M. S. Arnold, T. A. Green, S. A. Scully and S. D. White, Chapel Hill, N.C.

Ives, E. W. (1983). *The Common Lawyers of Pre-Reformation England*, Cambridge

Ives, E. W. (1991). 'The Fall of Wolsey', in *Cardinal Wolsey: Church, State and Art*, ed. S. J. Gunn and P. Lindley, Cambridge, pp.286–315

Ives, E. W. (1995). 'Henry VIII: the Political Perspective', in *The Reign of Henry VIII: Politics, Policy and Piety*, ed. D. MacCulloch, London, pp.13–34

Ives, E. W. (2004). *The Life and Death of Anne Boleyn*, 2nd edn, Oxford

James, M. E. (1986). *Society, Politics and Culture: Studies in Early Modern England*, Cambridge

Jardine, L. (1985). ' "O Decus Italiae Virgo", or The Myth of the Learned Lady in the Renaissance', *Historical Journal*, 28, pp.799–819

Jardine, L. (1987). 'Cultural Confusion and Shakespeare's Learned Heroines: "These are Old Paradoxes"', *Shakespeare Quarterly*, 38, pp.1–18

Jardine, L. (1993). *Erasmus, Man of Letters: The Construction of Charisma in Print*, Princeton, N.J.

Jones, A. R.; Stallybrass, P. (2000). *Renaissance Clothing and the Materials of Memory*, Cambridge

Jones, M. D. W. (2000). *Clash of Empires, Europe, 1498–1560*, Cambridge

Kantorowicz, E. H. (1955). 'Mysteries of State: an Absolutist Concept and its Late Medieval Origins', *Harvard Theological Review*, 48, pp.65–91

Kantorowicz, E. H. (1957). *The King's Two Bodies: a Study in Medieval Political Theology*, Princeton, N.J.

Kautsky, K. (1927). *Thomas More and his Utopia with a Historical Introduction*, tr. H.J. Stenning, London

Keay, A. (2001). *The Elizabethan Tower of London: The Haiward and Gascoyne Plan of 1597*, London Topographical Society, London

Kelly, H. A. (1976). *The Matrimonial Trials of Henry VIII*, Stanford, Ca.

Kelly, M. (1963). 'Canterbury Jurisdiction and Influence during the Episcopate of William Warham, 1503–1532', unpublished Cambridge Ph.D. dissertation

Kelly, M. (1965). 'The Submission of the Clergy', *Transactions of the Royal Historical Society, 5th Series*, 15, pp.97–119

Kempshall, M. S. (1999). *The Common Good in Late Medieval Political Thought*, Oxford

Kenny, Anthony (1983). *Thomas More*, Oxford

Kerridge, Eric (1969). *Agrarian Problems in the Sixteenth Century and After*, London

King, J. N. (1994). 'Henry VIII as David: the King's Image and Reformation Politics', in *Rethinking the Henrician Era: Essays on Early Tudor Texts and Contexts*, ed. P. C. Herman, Urbana, Il., pp.78–92

King, J. N. (1995). 'The Royal Image, 1535–1603', in *Tudor Political Culture*, ed. D. E. Hoak, Cambridge, pp.104–32

Kisby, Fiona (1999). 'Kingship and the Royal Itinerary: A Study of the Peripatetic Household of the Early Tudor Kings 1485–1547', *Court Historian*, 4, pp.29–39

Kisby, Fiona (2000). 'Officers and Office-holding at the English Royal Court. A Study of the Chapel Royal, 1485–1547', *Royal Musical Association Research Chronicle*, 32, pp.1–61

Kisby, Fiona (2001). ' "When the King Goeth a Procession": Chapel Ceremonies and Services, the Ritual Year, and Religious Reforms at the Early Tudor Court, 1485–1547', *Journal of British Studies*, 40, pp.44–75

Knecht, R. J. (1984). *French Renaissance Monarchy: Francis I and Henry II*, London

Knecht, R. J. (1994). *Renaissance Warrior and Patron: the Reign of Francis I*, Cambridge

Knowles, David (1959). *The Religious Orders in England, III, The Tudor Age*, Cambridge

Kolata, Gina (1987). 'Wet-Nursing Boom in England Explored', *Science, New Series*, 235, pp.745–7

Kümin, Beat (1996). *The Shaping of a Community. The Rise and Reformation of the English Parish c.1400–1560*, Aldershot

Kurz, O. (1957). 'Rowland Lock[e]y', *Burlington Magazine*, 99, pp.12–16

Lakowski, R. I. (1999). 'Utopia and the "Pacific Rim": the Cartographical Evidence', *Early Modern Literary Studies*, 5, pp.1–19

Lander, J. R. (1980). *Government and Community: England, 1450–1509*, London

Langbein, J. H. (1974). *Prosecuting Crime in the Renaissance*, Cambridge, Mass.

Langbein, J. H. (1977). *Torture and the Law of Proof*, Chicago, Il.

Laubenberger, F. (1982). 'The Naming of America', *Sixteenth Century Journal*, 13, pp.91–113

Laurence, A. (1994). *Women in England, 1500–1760: a Social History*, London

Leader, D. R. (1989). *A History of the University of Cambridge, Vol. I: The University to 1546*, Cambridge

Lehmberg, S. E. (1970). *The Reformation Parliament, 1529–1536*, Cambridge

Lehmberg, S. E. (1977). *The Later Parliaments of Henry VIII, 1536–1547*, Cambridge

Leslau, J. (1978). 'Holbein and the Discreet Rebus', *The Ricardian*, Sept. issue, pp.2–14

Leslau, J. (1981). 'Further to the Holbein Rebus', *The Ricardian*, June issue, pp.11–19

Leslau, J. (1990–1). 'Holbein and the Discreet Rebus', *Issues in Architecture, Art and Design*, 1, pp.43–72

Levine, M. (1973). *Tudor Dynastic Problems, 1460–1571*, London

Levy, F. J. (1967). *Tudor Historical Thought*, San Marino, Ca.

Lewis, Lesley (1998). *The Thomas More Family Group Portraits after Holbein*, Leominster

Litzenberger, C. (1997). *The English Reformation and the Laity: Gloucestershire, 1540–1580*, Cambridge

Lloyd, C.; Thurley, S. (1990). *Henry VIII. Images of a Tudor King*, London

Lloyd, T. H. (1991). *England and the German Hanse, 1157–1611: A Study of their Trade and Commercial Diplomacy*, Cambridge

Loades, D. M. (1986). *The Tudor Court*, London

Loades, D. M. (1998). 'Books and the English Reformation prior to 1558', in *The Reformation and the Book*, ed. J.-F. Gilmont and K. Maag, Aldershot, pp.264–91

Logan, F. D. (1988). 'Thomas Cromwell and the Vicegerency in Spirituals: a Revisitation', *English Historical Review*, 103, pp.658–67

Logan, G. M. (1983). *The Meaning of More's 'Utopia'*, Princeton, N.J.

MacCulloch, D. (1986). *Suffolk and the Tudors: Politics and Religion in an English County, 1500–1600*, Oxford

MacCulloch, D. (1991). 'The Myth of the English Reformation', *Journal of British Studies*, 30, pp.1–19

MacCulloch, D. (1995). 'Henry VIII and the Reform of the Church', in *The Reign of Henry VIII: Politics, Policy and Piety*, ed. D. MacCulloch, London, pp.159–80

MacCulloch, D. (1996). *Thomas Cranmer: a Life*, New Haven, Conn. and London

Mack, Peter (2005). 'Rhetoric, Ethics and Reading in the Renaissance', *Renaissance Studies*, 19, pp.1–21

Maddison, F.; Pelling, M.; Webster, C. (1977). *Essays on the Life and Work of Thomas Linacre c. 1460–1524*, Oxford

Magnaghi, A. (1924). *Amerigo Vespucci: Studio Critico, con speciale riguardo ad una nuova valutazione delle fonte e con documenti inediti dal Codice Vaglienti*, 2 vols, Rome

Maio, Romeo de (1969). *Savonarola e la Curia Romana*, Rome

Mansfield, H. C. (2000). 'Bruni and Machiavelli on Civic Humanism', in *Renaissance Civic Humanism: Reappraisals and Reflections*, Cambridge, pp.223–46

Marc'hadour, Germain (1963). *L'Univers de Thomas More*, Paris

Marc'hadour, Germain (1969). *Thomas More et la Bible. La place des livres saints dans son apologétique et sa spiritualité*, Paris

Marc'hadour, Germain (1969–71). *The Bible in the Works of St Thomas More*, 5 vols, Nieuwkoop

Marc'hadour, Germain (1979). 'The Death-Year of Thomas More's Mother', *Moreana*, 1, pp.13–16

Marius, R. (1984). *Thomas More*, New York

Marius, Richard (1962). 'Thomas More and the Heretics', unpublished Yale Ph.D. dissertation

Marius, Richard (1968). 'Thomas More and the Early Church Fathers', *Traditio*, 24, pp.379–407

Marius, Richard (1978). 'Henry VIII, Thomas More, and the Bishop of Rome', in *Quincentennial Essays on St Thomas More*, ed. M. J. Moore, Boone, N.C., pp.89–107

Marshall, P. (1996). 'The Debate over "Unwritten Verities" in Early Reformation England', in *Protestant History and Identity in Sixteenth-Century Europe*, ed. Bruce Gordon, 2 vols, Aldershot, I, pp.60–77

Marshall, P. (2006). *Religious Identities in Henry VIII's England*, Aldershot

Martz, L. L. (1977). 'Thomas More: the Sacramental Life', *Thought*, 52, pp.300–18

Martz, L. L. (1990). *Thomas More: the Search for the Inner Man*, New Haven, Conn.

Mayer, T. F. (1988). 'Thomas Starkey: an Unknown Conciliarist at the Court of Henry VIII', *Journal of the History of Ideas*, 49, pp.207–27

Mayer, T. F. (1989). *Thomas Starkey and the Commonweal: Humanist Politics and Religion in the Reign of Henry VIII*, Cambridge

Mayer, T. F. (1992). 'Nursery of Resistance: Reginald Pole and his Friends', in *Political Thought and the Tudor Commonwealth*, ed. P. A. Fideler and T. F. Mayer, London, pp.50–74

Mayer, T. F. (1995). 'On the Road to 1534: the Occupation of Tournai and Henry VIII's Theory of Sovereignty', in *Tudor Political Culture*, ed. D. E. Hoak, Cambridge, pp.11–30

Mayer, T. F. (2000). *Reginald Pole: Prince and Prophet*, Cambridge

McConica, J. K. (1965). *English Humanists and Reformation Politics*, Oxford

McConica, J. K. (1986). *The History of the University of Oxford, III, The Collegiate University*, ed. J. K. McConica, Oxford

McCready, W. D. (1996). 'Isidore, the Antipodeans, and the Shape of the Earth', *Isis*, 87, pp.108–27

McCutcheon, E. (1987). 'Margaret More Roper: The Learned Woman in Tudor England', in *Women Writers of the Renaissance and Reformation*, ed. K. M. Wilson, Athens, GA, pp.449–80

McGlynn, M. (1997). 'The King and the Law: *Praerogativa Regis* in Early Tudor England', unpublished Toronto Ph.D. dissertation

Mendelson, S.; Crawford, P. (1998). *Women in Early Modern England, 1550–1720*, Oxford

Metzger, F. (1976). 'Das Englische Kanzleigericht Unter Kardinal Wolsey 1515–1529', unpublished Erlangen Ph.D. dissertation

Milbourn, T. (1881). 'The Church of St Stephen Walbrook', *Transactions of the London and Middlesex Archaeological Society*, 5, pp.327–402

Miles, L. (1966a). 'The Literary Artistry of Thomas More: the *Dialogue of Comfort*', *Studies in English Literature, 1500–1900*, 6, pp.7–33

Miles, L. (1966b). 'The *Dialogue of Comfort* and More's Execution: Some Comments on Literary Purpose', *Modern Language Review*, 61, pp.556–60

Miller, C. H. (1978). 'The Heart of the Final Struggle: More's Commentary on the Agony in the Garden', in *Quincentennial Essays on St Thomas More*, ed. M. J. Moore, Boone. N. C., pp.108–23

Miller, H. (1962). 'London and Parliament in the Reign of Henry VIII', *Bulletin of the Institute of Historical Research*, 35, pp.128–49

Miller, H. (1986). *Henry VIII and the English Nobility*, Oxford

Milsom, J. (1997). 'Songs and Society in Early Tudor London', *Early Music History*, 16, pp.235–93

Milsom, S. F. C. (1961). 'Richard Hunne's "Praemunire"', *English Historical Review*, 76, pp.80–2

Moran, J. A. H. (1985). *The Growth of English Schooling, 1340–1548: Learning, Literacy and Laicization in Pre-Reformation York Diocese*, Princeton, N.J.

Morison, S. (1963). *The Likeness of Thomas More: an Iconographical Survey of Three Centuries* supplemented by N. Barker, London

Muir Wood, W. (2001). 'Anne Cresacre', paper to University of Bristol, Women's Studies Group, read 24 Nov. 2001

Müller, C.; Kemperdick, S. (2006). *Hans Holbein the Younger: The Basel Years, 1515–1532*, Munich and New York

Murphy, B. A. (2003). *Bastard Prince: Henry VIII's Lost Son*, Stroud

Murphy, V. M. (1984). 'The Debate over Henry VIII's First Divorce: an Analysis of the Contemporary Treatises', unpublished Cambridge Ph.D. dissertation

Murphy, V. M. (1995). 'The Literature and Propaganda of Henry VIII's First Divorce', in *The Reign of Henry VIII: Politics, Policy and Piety*, ed. D. MacCulloch, London, pp.135–58

Nelson, E. (2001). 'Greek Nonsense in More's *Utopia*', *Historical Journal*, 44, pp.889–917

Nichols, J. G. (1867). 'Henry Patenson', *Notes and Queries, 3rd Series*, 11, p.134

Nicholson, G. D. (1977). 'The Nature and Function of Historical Argument in the Henrician Reformation', unpublished Cambridge Ph.D. dissertation

Nicholson, G. D. (1988). 'The Act of Appeals and the English Reformation', in *Law and Government under the Tudors*, ed. Claire Cross, D. M. Loades and J. J. Scarisbrick, Cambridge, pp.19–30

Norrington, Ruth (1983). *In the Shadow of a Saint: Lady Alice More*, Waddesdon

Nugent, E. M. (1942). 'Sources of John Rastell's "The Nature of the Four Elements"', *Proceedings of the Modern Language Association*, 57, pp.74–88

Oakley, F. (1969). *Council over Pope? Towards a Provisional Ecclesiology*, New York

Oakley, F. (1980). 'Headley, Marius and Conciliarism', *Moreana*, 64, pp.82–8

Oakley, F. (2003). *The Conciliarist Tradition: Constitutionalism in the Catholic Church, 1300–1870*, Oxford

Ogle, A. (1949). *The Tragedy of the Lollards' Tower*, Oxford

Olson, R. J. M. (1984). 'And They Saw Stars: Renaissance Representations of Comets and Pretelescopic Astronomy', *Art Journal*, 44, pp.216–24

Owst, G. R. (1926). *Preaching in Medieval England: An Introduction to Sermon Manuscripts of the Period, c.1350–1450*, Cambridge

Pacht, O. (1944). 'Holbein and Kratzer as Collectors', *Burlington Magazine*, 84, pp.132, 134–9

Palmer, R. C. (2002). *Selling the Church: The English Parish in Law, Commerce and Religion, 1350–1550*, Chapel Hill and London

Parker, K. T. (1983). *The Drawings of Hans Holbein in the Collection of Her Majesty the Queen at Windsor Castle*, with an appendix by Susan Foister, London and New York

Parr, J. (1945). 'More Sources of John Rastell's "Interlude of the Four Elements"', *Proceedings of the Modern Language Association*, 60, pp.48–58

Parrish, J. M. (1997). 'A New Source for More's *Utopia*', *Historical Journal*, 40, pp.493–8

Phelps Brown, E. H.; Hopkins, S. V. (1956). 'Seven Centuries of the Prices of Consumables, Compared with Builders' Wage Rates', *Economica, New Series*, 23, pp.296–314

Phythian-Adams, C. (1979). *Desolation of a City: Coventry and the Urban Crisis of the Late Middle Ages*, Cambridge

Pineas, R. (1968). *Thomas More and Tudor Polemics*, Bloomington, In.

Plimpton, G. A. (1933). 'Grammatical Manuscripts and Early Printed Grammars in the Plimpton Library', *Transactions and Proceedings of the American Philosophical Association*, 64, pp.150–78

Pollard, A. F. (1902). *Henry VIII*, London

Pollard, A. F. (1929). *Wolsey*, London

Potter, D. (1995a). *A History of France, 1460–1560. The Emergence of a Nation State*, London

Potter, D. (1995b). 'Foreign Policy', in *The Reign of Henry VIII: Politics, Policy and Piety*, ed. D. MacCulloch, London, pp.101–34

Power, E.; Poston, M. M. (1933). *Studies in English Trade in the Fifteenth Century*, London

Quinn, D. B. (1974). *England and the Discovery of America, 1481–1620*, New York

Ramsay, G. D. (1957). *English Overseas Trade during the Centuries of Emergence*, London

Ramsay, G. D. (1965). 'The Growth of the Antwerp Market and the European Economy', *English Historical Review*, 80, pp.795–800

Ramsay, G. D. (1982). 'A Saint in the City: Thomas More at Mercers' Hall, London', *English Historical Review*, 97, pp.269–88

Rawcliffe, Carole (1978). *The Staffords, Earls of Stafford and Dukes of Buckingham, 1394–1521*, Cambridge

Rawcliffe, Carole (1979). 'Baronial Councils in the Later Middle Ages', in *Patronage, Pedigree and Power in Later Medieval England*, ed. Charles Ross, Gloucester, pp.87–108

Redworth, G. (1987). 'Whatever happened to the English Reformation?', *History Today*, 37 (Oct.), pp.29–36

Redworth, G. (1990). *In Defence of the Church Catholic: the Life of Stephen Gardiner*, Oxford

Reed, A. W. (1918). 'The Widow Edyth', *The Library, 3rd Series*, 9, pp.186–99

Reed, A. W. (1919). 'John Rastell's Plays', *The Library, 3rd Series*, 10, pp.1–17

Reed, A. W. (1923). 'The Editor of Sir Thomas More's English Works: William Rastell', *The Library, 4th Series*, 4, pp.25–49

Reed, A. W. (1926a). *Early Tudor Drama: Medwall, The Rastells, Heywood and the More Circle*, London

Reed, A. W. (1926b). 'John Clement and his Books', *The Library, 4th Series*, 6, pp.329–39

Rex, R. (1989). 'The English Campaign against Luther in the 1520s', *Transactions of the Royal Historical Society, 5th Series*, 39, pp.85–106

Rex, R. (1991). *The Theology of John Fisher*, Cambridge

Rex, R. (1993). *Henry VIII and the English Reformation*, London

Rex, R. (1996). 'The Crisis of Obedience: God's Word and Henry's Reformation', *Historical Journal*, 39, pp.863–94

Rex, R. (1999). 'The Role of English Humanists in the Reformation up to 1559', in *The Education of a Christian Society: Humanism and the Reformation in Britain and the Netherlands*, ed. N. Scott Amos, A. D. M. Pettegree and H. van Nierop, Aldershot, pp.19–40

Reynolds, E. E. (1953). *Saint Thomas More*, London

Reynolds, E. E. (1954). *Thomas More and Erasmus*, London

Reynolds, E. E. (1960). *Margaret Roper, Eldest Daughter of St Thomas More*, London

Reynolds, E. E. (1964). *The Trial of St Thomas More*, London

Reynolds, E. E. (1968). *The Field is Won: the Life and Death of St Thomas More*, London

Rhodes, J. (1974). 'Private Devotion in England on the Eve of the Reformation', unpublished Durham Ph.D. dissertation

Richardson, G. (1995). 'Entertainments for the French Ambassadors at the Court of Henry VIII', *Renaissance Studies*, 9, pp.404–15

Richardson, G. (1999). 'The Privy Chamber of Henry VIII and Anglo-French Relations, 1515–1520', *Court Historian*, 4, pp.119–40

Ridley, J. (1982). *The Statesman and the Fanatic: Thomas Wolsey and Thomas More*, London

Roberts, R. J. (1979). 'John Rastell's Inventory of 1538', *The Library, 6th Series*, 1, pp.34–42

Robertson, M. L. (1975). 'Thomas Cromwell's Servants: the Ministerial Household in Early Tudor Government and Society', unpublished U.C.L.A. Ph.D. dissertation

Rose, P. L. (1977). 'Erasmians and Mathematicians at Cambridge in the Early Sixteenth Century', *Sixteenth Century Journal*, 8, pp.46–59

Ross, C. D. (1974). *Edward IV*, London

Ross, C. D. (1981). *Richard III*, London

Routh, E. M. G. (1934). *Sir Thomas More and His Friends 1477–1535*, London

Rowe, C. (2000). 'Aristotelian Constitutions', in *The Cambridge History of Greek and Roman Political Thought*, ed. C. Rowe and M. Schofield, Cambridge, pp.366–95

Rowlands, J. (1985). *Holbein: The Paintings of Hans Holbein the Younger*, Oxford

Royal Collection (1978). *Holbein and the Court of Henry VIII*, London

Ruggeri, R. (2000). *Polidoro Virgili: Un Umanista Europeo*, Bergamo

Rupp, E. G. (1947). *Studies in the Making of the English Protestant Tradition*, London

Scarisbrick, J. J. (1956). 'The Pardon of the Clergy, 1531', *Cambridge Historical Journal*, 12, pp.22–39

Scarisbrick, J. J. (1960). 'Clerical Taxation in England, 1485 to 1547', *Journal of Ecclesiastical History*, 11, pp.41–54

Scarisbrick, J. J. (1968). *Henry VIII*, London

Scarisbrick, J. J. (1977). 'Thomas More: the King's Good Servant', *Thought*, 52, pp.249–68

Scarisbrick, J. J. (1978). 'Cardinal Wolsey and the Common Weal', in *Wealth and Power in Tudor England*, ed. E. W. Ives, R. J. Knecht and J. J. Scarisbrick, London, pp.45–67

Scarisbrick, J. J. (1984). *The Reformation and the English People*, Oxford

Schilling, E. (1937). *Drawings of the Holbein Family*, London

Schoeck, R. J. (1949). 'Two Notes on Margaret Gigs Clement, Foster Daughter of Sir Thomas More', *Notes and Queries, Old Series*, 194, pp.532–3

Schoeck, R. J. (1976). 'The Place of Sir Thomas More in Legal History and Tradition', *Moreana*, 51, pp.83–94

Schofield, R. S. (1963). 'Parliamentary Lay Taxation, 1485–1547', unpublished Cambridge Ph.D. dissertation

Schofield, R. S. (1968). 'The Measurement of Literacy in Pre-Industrial England', in *Literacy in Traditional Societies*, ed. J. Goody, Cambridge, pp.311–25

Schofield, R. S. (1986). 'Did the Mothers Really Die? Three Centuries of Maternal Mortality in "The World We Have Lost"', in *The World We Have Gained: Histories of Population and Social Structure. Essays presented to Peter Laslett on his Seventieth Birthday*, ed. L. Bonfield et al., Oxford, pp.231–60

Schofield, R. S. (1988). 'Taxation and the Political Limits of the Tudor State', in *Law and Government under the Tudors*, ed. Claire Cross, D. M. Loades and J. J. Scarisbrick, Cambridge, pp.227–56

Schofield, R. S. (2005). ' "Monday's Child is Fair of Face": Favoured Days for Baptism, Marriage and Burial in Pre-Industrial England', *Continuity and Change*, 20, pp.93–109

Schulman, J. K. (2002). *The Rise of the Medieval World, 500–1300*, Westport, Conn., and London

Sharpe, Kevin (1999). 'Representations and Negotiations: Texts, Images, and Authority in Early Modern England', *Historical Journal*, 42, pp.853–81

Sheldrake, P. (1979). 'Authority and Consensus in Thomas More's Doctrine of the Church', *Heythrop Journal*, 20, pp.146–72

Sicca, C. M. (2002). 'Consumption and Trade of Art between Italy and England in the first half of the Sixteenth Century: the London House of the Bardi and Cavalcanti Company', *Renaissance Studies*, 16, pp.163–201

Sicca, C. M. (2006). 'Pawns of International Finance and Politics: Florentine Sculptors at the Court of Henry VIII', *Renaissance Studies*, 20, pp.1–34

Simon, Joan (1966). *Education and Society in Tudor England*, Cambridge

Singer, C. (1948). *The Earliest Chemical Industry. An Essay in the Historical Relations of Economics and Technology Illustrated from the Alum Trade*, London

Skeeters, M. C. (1993). *Community and Clergy: Bristol and the Reformation, c.1530–c.1570*, Oxford

Skelton, R. A.; Summerson, J. (1971). *A Description of Maps and Architectural Drawings in the Collection made by William Cecil, First Baron Burghley, now at Hatfield House*, Roxburghe Club, Oxford

Skinner, Quentin (1967). 'More's *Utopia*', *Past and Present*, 38, pp.153–68

Skinner, Quentin (1978). *The Foundations of Modern Political Thought*, 2 vols, Cambridge

Skinner, Quentin (1987). 'Sir Thomas More's *Utopia* and the Language of Renaissance Humanism', in *The Languages of Political Theory in Early Modern Europe*, ed. A. Pagden, Cambridge, pp.123–57

Skinner, Quentin (1996). *Reason and Rhetoric in the Philosophy of Hobbes*, Cambridge

Slack, P. (1979). 'Mortality Crises and Epidemic Disease in England, 1485–1610', in *Health, Medicine and Mortality in the Sixteenth Century*, ed. C. Webster, Cambridge, pp.9–59

Slack, P. (1985). *The Impact of Plague in Tudor and Stuart England*, London

Smith, C. (1981). 'An Updating of R.W. Gibson's *St Thomas More: A Preliminary Bibliography*', *Sixteenth Century Bibliography*, 20, pp.i–iii, 1–46

Smith, D. E. (1917). 'On the Origin of Certain Typical Problems', *American Mathematical Monthly*, 24, pp.64–71

Smith, L. B. (1971). *Henry VIII: the Mask of Royalty*, London

Smith, R. B. (1970). *Land and Politics in the England of Henry VIII: the West Riding of Yorkshire, 1530–46*, Oxford

Somerville, Robert (1939). 'Henry VII's "Council Learned in the Law"', *English Historical Review*, 54, pp.427–42

Sowards, J. K. (1982). 'Erasmus and the Education of Women', *Sixteenth Century Journal*, 13, pp.77–89

Sowards, J. K. (1989). 'On Education: More's Debt to Erasmus', *Moreana*, 26, no.100, pp.103–23

Stahl, W. H. (1959). 'Dominant Traditions in Early Medieval Latin Science', *Isis*, 50, pp.95–124

Starkey, D. R. (1973). 'The King's Privy Chamber, 1485–1547', unpublished Cambridge Ph.D. dissertation

Starkey, D. R. (1977). 'Representation through Intimacy: a Study in the Symbolism of Monarchy and Court Office in Early-Modern England', in *Symbols and Sentiments: Cross-cultural Studies in Symbolism*, ed. I. Lewis, London, pp.187–224

Starkey, D. R. (1987a). 'Court History in Perspective', in *The English Court from the Wars of the Roses to the Civil War*, ed. D. R. Starkey et al., London, pp.1–24

Starkey, D. R. (1987b). 'Intimacy and Innovation: the Rise of the Privy Chamber', in *The English Court from the Wars of the Roses to the Civil War*, ed. D. R. Starkey et al., London, pp.71–118

Starkey, D. R. (1988). 'A Reply. Tudor Government: the Facts?', *Historical Journal*, 31, pp.921–31

Starkey, D. R. (1991). 'Court, Council and Nobility in Tudor England', in *Princes, Patronage and the Nobility: the Court at the Beginning of the Modern Age c.1450–1650*, ed. R. G. Asch and A. M. Birke, Oxford, pp.175–203

Starkey, D. R. (2003). *Six Wives: The Queens of Henry VIII*, London

Stevens, W. M. (1980). 'The Figure of the Earth in Isidore's "De natura rerum"', *Isis*, 71, pp.268–77

Stone, L. (1966). 'Social Mobility in England, 1500–1700', *Past and Present*, no. 33, pp.16–55

Strong, R. (1983). *Artists of the Tudor Court: the Portrait Miniature Rediscovered, 1520–1620*, London

Surtz, E. (1957). *The Praise of Wisdom: A Commentary of the Religious and Moral Problems and Backgrounds of St Thomas More's 'Utopia'*, Chicago, Il.

Survey of London (1951), 'Lambeth Palace', *Survey of London*, 23, English Heritage, London, pp.81–103

Sutton, D. (1947), 'Thomas Howard, Earl of Arundel and Surrey, as a Collector of Drawings', *Burlington Magazine*, 89, pp.32–4, 37

Sylvester, R. S. (1966). 'Thomas More: Humanist in Action', in *Medieval and Renaissance Studies*, ed. O. B. Hardison Jr., Chapel Hill, N.C., pp.125–37

Sylvester, R. S. (1972). *St Thomas More: Action and Contemplation. Proceedings of the Symposium held at St John's University, October 9–10, 1970*, New Haven, Conn.

Sylvester, R. S.; Marc'hadour, Germain (1977). *Essential Articles for the Study of Thomas More*, Hamden, Conn.

Thomson, J. A. F. (1965). *The Later Lollards, 1414–1520*, Oxford

Thornley, I. D. (1924). 'The Destruction of Sanctuary', in *Tudor Studies Presented to A. F. Pollard*, ed. R. W. Seton-Watson, London, pp.182–207

Thurley, S. (1993). *The Royal Palaces of Tudor England. Architecture and Court Life, 1460–1547*, New Haven, Conn. and London

Thurley, S. (1999). *Whitehall Palace. An Architectural History of the Royal Apartments, 1240–1698*, New Haven, Conn. and London

Thwaites, G.; Taviner, M.; Gant, V. (1997). 'The English Sweating Sickness, 1485–1551', *New England Journal of Medicine*, 336, pp.580–2

Thwaites, G; Taviner, M.; Gant, V. (1998). 'The English Sweating Sickness, 1485–1551: A Viral Pulmonary Disease?', *Medical History*, 42, pp.96–8

Tilley, Arthur (1938). 'Greek Studies in England in the Early Sixteenth Century', *English Historical Review*, 53, pp.221–39, 438–56

Trapp, J. B. (1979). 'Supplementa Iconographica Moreana: Portraits of Thomas More in Italy and in Spain', *Moreana*, 16:62, pp.73–82

Trapp, J. B. (1990). *Erasmus, Colet and More: The Early Tudor Humanists and their Books*, London

Trapp, J. B.; Schulte Herbrüggen, H. (1977). *'The King's Good Servant': Sir Thomas More 1477/8–1535*, London

Trevor-Roper, Hugh (1978–9). 'The Intellectual World of Sir Thomas More', *American Scholar*, 48, pp.19–32

Tudor-Craig, Pamela (1989). 'Henry VIII and King David', in *Early Tudor England: Proceedings of the 1987 Harlaxton Symposium*, ed. D. Williams, Woodbridge, pp.183–205

Ullmann, W. (1965). *A History of Political Thought: the Middle Ages*, London

Ullmann, W. (1966). *Principles of Government and Politics in the Middle Ages*, 2nd edn, London

Ullmann, W. (1979). ' "This Realm of England is an Empire"', *Journal of Ecclesiastical History*, 30, pp.175–203

Van der Wee, H. (1963). *The Growth of the Antwerp Market and the European Economy*, 3 vols, The Hague

Viroli, M. (1992). *From Politics to Reason of State: the Acquisition and Transformation of the Language of Politics, 1250–1600*, Cambridge

Wabuda, Susan (2002). *Preaching during the English Reformation*, Cambridge

Walker, G. (1988). *John Skelton and the Politics of the 1520s*, Cambridge

Walker, G. (1991). *Plays of Persuasion: Drama and Politics at the Court of Henry VIII*, Cambridge

Walker, G. (1999). 'Dialogue, Resistance and Accommodation: Conservative Literary Responses to the Henrician Reformation', in *The Education of a Christian Society: Humanism and the Reformation in Britain and the Netherlands*, ed. N. Scott Amos, A. D. M. Pettegree and H. van Nierop, Aldershot, pp.89–111

Wall, A. (2000). *Power and Protest in England, 1525–1640*, London

Warner, J. C. (1998). *Henry VIII's Divorce: Literature and the Politics of the Printing Press*, Woodbridge

Warnicke, R. M. (1985). 'The Harpy in More's Household: Was It Lady Alice?', *Moreana*, 22, pp.5–13

Watts, J. L. (1996). *Henry VI and the Politics of Kingship*, Cambridge

Wedgwood, J. C; Holt, A. D. (1936). *Biographies of the Members of the Commons House, 1439–1509*, History of Parliament, London

Weiss, R. (1957). *Humanism in England during the Fifteenth Century*, 2nd edn, Oxford

Wells, K. (1981). 'The Iconography of Saint Thomas More', *Studies (Ireland)*, 70, pp.55–71

Wentworth, M. D. (1995). *The Essential Sir Thomas More: An Annotated Bibliography of Major Modern Studies*, New York

Wernham, R. B. (1966). *Before the Armada: the Emergence of the English Nation, 1485–1588*, New York

White, C. (1992). *Christian Friendship in the Fourth Century*, Cambridge

Whiting, R. (1989). *The Blind Devotion of the People: Popular Religion and the English Reformation*, Cambridge

Wilkie, W. E. (1974). *The Cardinal Protectors of England: Rome and the Tudors before the Reformation*, Cambridge

Williams, P. (1979). *The Tudor Regime*, Oxford

Wines, A. R. (1998). 'The London Charterhouse in the Later Middle Ages: An Institutional History', unpublished Cambridge Ph.D. dissertation

Woolf, D. R. (2000). *Reading History in Early Modern England*, Cambridge

Woolfson, J. (1998). *Padua and the Tudors. English Students in Italy, 1485–1603*, Cambridge

Wrigley, E. A. (1997). 'How Reliable is Our Knowledge of the Demographic Characteristics of the English Population in the Early Modern Period?', *Historical Journal*, 40, pp.571–95

Wrigley, E. A.; Schofield, R. S. (1981). *The Population History of England, 1541–1871: a Reconstruction*, London

Youings, J. (1971). *The Dissolution of the Monasteries*, London

Zeeveld, W. G. (1948). *Foundations of Tudor Policy*, Cambridge, Mass.

Zell, M. (1976). 'The Prebendaries' Plot of 1543: A Reconsideration', *Journal of Ecclesiastical History*, 27, pp.241–54

INDEX